BUSTED

MUG SHOTS AND ARREST RECORDS OF THE FAMOUS AND INFAMOUS

Thomas J. Craughwell

Black Dog
& Leventhal
Publishers

Front cover, clockwise from top left: Bill Gates, Jane Fonda, Jeffrey
Dahmer, Al Capone, Zacarias Moussaoui, Mel Gibson, Roman Polanski,
Rush Limbaugh, Bridgette Bardot, Vladimir Lenin

Back cover, clockwise from top left: Ted Kaczynski, Heather Locklear,
Dennis Hopper, Jay-Z, Lucky Luciano, Bernie Madoff, Rosa Parks

Published by
Black Dog & Leventhal Publishers, Inc.
151 West 19th Street
New York, NY 10011

Distributed by
Workman Publishing Company
225 Varick Street
New York, NY 10014

Manufactured in the United States

Cover and interior design by Andy Taray / Ohioboy Art & Design

ISBN-13: 978-1-57912-865-4

h g f e d c b a

Library of Congress Cataloging-in-Publication Data available upon
request

TABLE OF CONTENTS

INTRO

Lots of people have run-ins with the law, and this book chronicles hundreds of them, ranging from the notorious to the famous to the hilarious. You'll find the truly terrifying Jeffrey Dahmer, the rapist, torturer, killer, and cannibal, but also the hapless Levi Detweiler, an Amish teenager who tried to outrun the cops in his horse and buggy. In between are serial killers, burglars, war criminals, chiselers, spies, assassins, and, of course, the stars of Hollywood, few of whom, it seems, can resist the temptation to get behind the wheel of car when they've had a snoot-full.

Flipping through this book is a lot like snooping through police files—you never know who you're going to find. That Lizzie Borden, O. J. Simpson, and Mel Gibson appear here will surprise no one, but what about Offer "Vince" Shlomi, from the ShamWow television commercials: He was arrested for punching a prostitute in the face. But he had his reasons—the woman bit his tongue and wouldn't let go.

Then there's the short story writer, O. Henry. Before he began writing, he embezzled more than $800 from the bank where he worked as teller. His three-year stint in jail introduced to him to lots of colorful inmates and prison guards who would become the inspiration for characters in his stories.

The crime of tax evasion attracts an interesting cross-section of society: There's the gangster Al Capone, the action-adventure movie star Wesley Snipes, and the immortal Henry David Thoreau. Capone and Snipes received lengthy prison sentences, but Thoreau spent only one night in jail—his aunt paid his back taxes for him.

Anyone who has watched an episode of MTV's reality series *Jersey Shore* knew it was only a matter of time before Nicole "Snooki" Polizzi would get picked up on a disorderly conduct charge, but who would have believed that at age 21 Al Pacino was arrested for carrying a concealed weapon? He told the arresting officer the gun was a stage prop he was taking to an audition—which is a great alibi. As it turns out, Pacino was telling the truth.

There are plenty of cringe-worthy moments here, including Congressman Larry Craig getting booked after cruising for sex in an airport men's room; Ozzy Osbourne being arrested for relieving himself on the Alamo; and the little-known case of Sada Abe, a Japanese Lorena Bobbitt.

A surprising number of cases are still being debated. Did Bruno Hauptmann kill the Lindbergh baby? Were Sacco and Vanzetti executed because they were killers or because they were anarchists? Was Henry Wirz, the commandant of the Andersonville prisoner of war camp, a heartless sadist? Did the cops who beat Rodney King get off easy?

Of course, not everyone who gets busted is a lowlife. Think of Nelson Mandela, Mahatma Gandhi, and Rosa Parks. For social and political reformers, jail time is almost a badge of honor.

Here then is an arresting, informative, entertaining selection of some of the most notable jailbirds of the last 150 years.

FRANK WILLIAM ABAGNALE

(1948–)

NATIONALITY
American

WHO IS HE?
With an IQ of 140 and looks that made him appear older than his actual age, Frank Abagnale began life as a con man at age 16.

WHAT DID HE DO?
Abagnale passed $2.5 million in bad checks in every state in the Union and in 26 foreign countries. Between the ages of 16 and 21, he successfully passed himself off as an airline pilot, an attorney, a college professor, and a pediatrician.

DATE OF ARREST
1969

CIRCUMSTANCES OF THE ARREST
While living in France, Abagnale was spotted by an ex-girlfriend who notified the French police. They arrested Abagnale while he was grocery shopping near his apartment in Montpellier.

THE CHARGES
Fraud and forgery

THE SENTENCE
Abagnale was sentenced to a year in prison in France, but after serving six months he was extradited to Sweden, where he was tried and sentenced to a year in prison. Then the Swedish government sent him to the United States where he was sentenced to 12 years. After serving 5 years, he was paroled. Abagnale was 26 years old.

AFTERWARD
Abagnale found a new career working for the FBI as a teacher and consultant to the Bureau's Fraud Prevention program.

THE MOVIE
Steven Spielberg's 2002 film, *Catch Me If You Can*, is based on Abagnale's autobiography of the same name. Leonardo Di Caprio played Frank Abagnale.

UMAR FAROUK ABDULMUTALLAB, "THE CHRISTMAS DAY BOMBER"

(1986–)

NATIONALITY
Nigerian

WHO IS HE?
Umar Farouk Abdulmutallab is the son of a wealthy Nigerian banker. After high school he studied Arabic in Sana'a, Yemen, and then enrolled at University College in London, where he studied mechanical engineering and became head of the university's Islamic Society. At some point he was recruited by Al Qaeda, and in November 2009 he disappeared. Abdulmutallab's father, Alhaji Umaru Mutallab, went to the U.S. embassy in Abuja to report that, given Umar's association with Islamic extremists, he feared that his son had become a security threat. Embassy officials and a CIA officer sent a report of the meeting to Washington, but did not revoke Abdulmutallab's visa to the United States.

WHAT DID HE DO?
On Christmas Eve 2009, Abdulmutallab used cash to purchase a ticket from Lagos, Nigeria, to Detroit, via Amsterdam. He had no luggage. Several hours later, as the plane carrying 278 passengers approached Detroit, Abdulmutallab returned from the bathroom, threw a blanket over his lap, and tried to activate explosives made of PETN, or pentaerythritol, which he had concealed in his underpants. The bomb misfired, giving off a loud pop, and then setting fire to Abdulmutallab's pants. Many of the passengers panicked, but Jasper Schuringa, a Dutch filmmaker, leapt on top of Abdulmutallab and tried to put out the fire. It was doused by members of the cabin crew with fire extinguishers.

DATE OF ARREST
December 25, 2009

CIRCUMSTANCES OF THE ARREST
Abdulmutallab was taken into custody at the Detroit airport and transported for treatment to the University of Michigan Burn Center in Ann Arbor. He was arraigned the next day, handcuffed to a wheelchair.

THE CHARGES
Attempted murder and attempted use of a weapon of mass destruction

AFTERWARD
At the time of his arrest, Abdulmutallab was interrogated by agents of the FBI. At some point it was determined that he should be read the Miranda rights and given access to a lawyer, at which point Abdulmutallab stopped cooperating with his interrogators. The mirandizing of Abdulmutallab set off a firestorm of debate about whether he should be treated as an enemy combatant or as a criminal. Weeks later the United States brought two members of Abdulmutallab's family to visit him; after this visit, he began to cooperate with his interrogators once again. As of 2010, he was being held at the Federal Correctional Institution in Milan, Michigan.

OMAR ABDEL-RAHMAN, "THE BLIND SHEIKH"

(1938–)

NATIONALITY
Egyptian

WHO IS HE?
Omar Abdel-Rahman is a leader of the Islamic Group, a militant Islamist organization founded in Egypt and regarded by the governments of Egypt and the United States as a terrorist organization. The Islamic Group is suspected of having carried out the 1997 Luxor Massacre, a terrorist attack on tourists at the Temple of Hatshepsut, in which 63 foreigners and Egyptians were killed and 26 were wounded. In 1990, Abdel-Rahman entered the United States on a tourist visa. As a leader of MAK, a forerunner of Al-Qaeda, he traveled throughout the United States and Canada recruiting mujahideen, or holy warriors, to fight the Soviets in Afghanistan. He also preached in mosques in the United States, urging Muslims to make war on the West: "Cut the transportation of their countries, tear it apart, destroy their economy, burn their companies, eliminate their interests, sink their ships, shoot down their planes, kill them on the sea, air, or land."

WHAT DID HE DO?
Abdel-Rahman led a cell that planned the 1993 World Trade Center bombing. On February 26, 1993, a member of the cell, Eyad Ismoil, drove a rented van, packed with explosives, into an underground parking garage of the North Tower of the World Trade Center in Lower Manhattan. Adbel-Rahman and his fellow conspirators hoped the explosion would bring the North Tower toppling down onto the South Tower, killing thousands. The explosion did not bring down the towers, but it did kill six and wounded over 1,000.

DATE OF ARREST
July 2, 1993

CIRCUMSTANCES OF THE ARREST
When federal agents came to arrest him, Abdel-Rahman was holed up inside a mosque in the Midwood section of Brooklyn. He remained inside with a large congregation of supporters until shortly after 6:00 p.m. when he emerged from the mosque and surrendered.

THE CHARGES
Seditious conspiracy, conspiracy to murder, among other charges

THE SENTENCE
Life in prison

AFTERWARD
In 2005, one of Abdel-Rahman's defense attorneys, Lynne Stewart, was convicted of passing messages from the sheikh to members of the Islamic Group in Egypt.

THE MONEY MAN
It is believed that funding for the 1993 World Trade Center bombing came from Khalid Sheikh Mohammed, who is also alleged to have planned the murder of *Wall Street Journal* reporter Daniel Pearl, the Bali nightclub bombings, and the September 11 attacks.

SADA ABE
(1905–1970?)

NATIONALITY
Japanese

WHO WAS SHE?
Sada Abe was in born in Tokyo to a family of prosperous tatami mat makers. At age 15, Abe was raped; in reaction to the trauma she became an especially difficult, rebellious teenager. In 1922, her father sold her to a geisha house. As she had no training as a geisha, she was assigned to providing sexual favors for male visitors. After five years she left the geisha house for a brothel where she hoped to make more money. In 1935, Abe gave up the life of a prostitute to open a small restaurant. She apprenticed under a 42-year-old restaurateur, Kichizo Ishida, with whom she began a passionate love affair.

WHAT DID SHE DO?
In May 1936, Abe and Ishida met for a tryst at an inn in Ogu. They experimented with rough sex, including erotic asphyxiation. After Ishida fell asleep, Abe wrapped her sash around his neck and strangled him. Then she cut off his genitals with a kitchen knife.

DATE OF ARREST
May 20, 1936

CIRCUMSTANCES OF THE ARREST
Abe had checked into an inn in Shinagawa where she planned to commit suicide. When the police came to the door she said, "Don't be so formal. You are looking for Sada Abe, right? Well, that's me. I am Sada Abe." Her demeanor confused the police, who doubted that she was telling the truth. She convinced them by producing Ishida's penis.

THE CHARGES
Murder and mutilation of a corpse

THE SENTENCE
Abe was found guilty and sentenced to six years in prison.

AFTERWARD
Along with many other convicts, Abe's sentence was commuted as part of the nationwide celebration of the 2,600th anniversary of the founding of Japan. She took a lover, wrote her memoirs, and became a minor celebrity. Her life was the subject of several books and at least four movies.

UNUSUAL FACT
No one knows what became of Sada Abe. In 1970, she simply disappeared.

MEHMET ALI AGCA

(1958–)

NATIONALITY
Turkish

WHO IS HE?
As a boy, Mehmet Ali Agca was a petty criminal and gang member. As a young adult, he joined the Grey Wolves, a Turkish ultranationalist organization. In 1979, he murdered Abdi Ipekci, a prominent newspaper editor, and was sentenced to life imprisonment. Agca escaped from prison, and in 1981 he traveled to Rome.

WHAT DID HE DO?
On May 13, 1981, Pope John Paul II was driven through a large crowd of pilgrims who had assembled in St. Peter's Square for his weekly public audience. As John Paul's popemobile drew close, Agca pulled out a pistol and began firing. He struck the pope four times, and wounded two bystanders.

DATE OF ARREST
May 13, 1981

CIRCUMSTANCES OF THE ARREST
Before Agca could escape from St. Peter's Square, he was seized by several pilgrims and the Vatican's chief of security, Camillo Cibin.

THE CHARGE
Attempted assassination

THE SENTENCE
In July 1981, an Italian court sentenced Agca to life in prison. Shortly thereafter, Pope John Paul II asked a crowd of pilgrims to "pray for my brother whom I have sincerely forgiven."

AFTERWARD
Although his four wounds were serious, John Paul II survived. In 1983, he visited Agca in prison, and over the years he made contact with Agca's family, receiving his mother and his brother in private audiences at the Vatican. In 2000, the president of Italy, Carlo Azeglio Ciampi pardoned Agca and had him deported to Turkey, where he was imprisoned once again for the Ipekci murder. He was paroled in 2006. Since then, Agca has behaved erratically. He claimed to have converted to Christianity, then proclaimed that he was Christianity's true Messiah. He has asked to return to Rome to visit the tomb of John Paul II; he has requested permission to spend the rest of his life living in Poland, John Paul's homeland; he has offered to collaborate on a book with Dan Brown, author of *The Da Vinci Code*. All these requests have been declined or ignored.

MARV ALBERT

(1941–)

NATIONALITY
American

WHO IS HE?
Marv Albert was a sportscaster for NBC, often called "the voice of the New York Knicks," famous for his trademark exclamation, "Yesss!"

WHAT DID HE DO?
On February 12, 1997, Albert and Vanessa Perhach went to a hotel in Pentagon City, Virginia. The couple had had a relationship for ten years. Perhach alleged that during a sexual encounter, Albert bit her back a dozen times, then forced her to perform oral sex.

DATE OF ARREST
May 27, 1997

THE CHARGE
Forcible sodomy

THE SENTENCE
After Albert apologized on the witness stand, the judge sentenced him to a year of unsupervised probation and ordered him to see a mental health counselor.

ALBERT'S TESTIMONY
During his apology, Albert explained to the court, "Ms. Perhach and I had a ten-year relationship. In the past, there was consensual biting."

AFTERWARD
NBC Sports fired Marv Albert, but rehired him two years later.

FELIX ALDERISIO

(1912–1971)

WHAT DID HE DO?

During his criminal career, Alderisio was arrested at least 36 times on a variety of charges that ranged from bootlegging and counterfeiting to bombing and murder for hire. But lack of witnesses and evidence prevented prosecutors from indicting him for any of these crimes. Ultimately, he was arrested for bank fraud and illegal possession of a firearm.

DATE OF ARREST

July 27, 1969

THE CHARGES

Bank fraud and illegal gun possession

THE SENTENCE

Alderisio was sentenced to five years in prison.

AFTERWARD

Felix Alderisio died in prison of natural causes on September 25, 1971.

NATIONALITY

American

WHO WAS HE?

In the 1950s and 1960s, Felix Alderisio was renowned in the Outfit (as the Chicago Mob was known) as an enforcer, or hit man, and a bagman, who delivered cash payoffs to police and political officials in Chicago. He operated a burglary ring that targeted the homes of wealthy Chicagoans in the ritzy Gold Coast neighborhood. Alderisio also owned bordellos, striptease joints, and nightclubs, as well as restaurants and meatpacking plants.

MUHAMMAD ALI
(1942–)

NATIONALITY
American

WHO IS HE?
One the greatest boxers in U.S. history, Muhammad Ali was born Cassius Marcellus Clay, Jr. He began taking boxing lessons at age 12, and won the 1956 Golden Gloves Championship for novices in the light heavyweight class at age 14. Four years later, Clay was a member of the U.S. Olympic Boxing Team. At the Games in Rome, he won the gold medal. After the Olympics, Clay turned professional, and in 1964 he knocked out Sonny Liston, becoming the heavyweight boxing champion of the world. That year, he joined the Nation of Islam and took the name Muhammad Ali.

WHAT DID HE DO?
In 1966 the U.S. armed forces declared Ali eligible to be drafted into the army. Ali declared publicly that he would not serve in the military because he was a conscientious objector. He went on to tell journalists, "I ain't got no quarrel with the Vietcong. No Vietcong ever called me Nigger."

DATE OF ARREST
April 28, 1967

CIRCUMSTANCES OF THE ARREST
Ali went to the induction center in Houston. Three times his name was called, but he refused to step forward. The officer in charge warned him that draft evasion was a felony punishable with five years in prison and $10,000 fine. When Ali still refused, he was arrested. Later that day, the New York State Athletic Commission stripped him of his title and suspended his boxing license.

THE CHARGE
Draft evasion

THE SENTENCE
Ali was found guilty, banned from professional boxing, sentenced to five years in prison, and fined $10,000. He appealed his sentence all the way to the Supreme Court, where the justices threw out his conviction.

AFTERWARD
Ali lost his heavyweight title to Joe Frazier in 1971, and Frazier lost it to George Foreman. In 1974, Ali defeated Foreman in one of the most heavily publicized fights in history—"the Rumble in the Jungle," in Kinshasha, Zaire. In 1979, Ali retired from boxing. In 1984, he was diagnosed with Parkinson's disease.

DENNIS "MR. DEATH" ALLEN

(1951–1987)

NATIONALITY
Australian

WHO WAS HE?
Dennis Allen was the eldest son of Kath Pettingill, the matriarch of one of Australia's most notorious crime families. He was a convicted rapist and is alleged to have been one of the leading heroin dealers in Melbourne. Melbourne police believe that between 1982 and 1987, Allen murdered approximately 12 people.

WHAT DID HE DO?
In 1984, Allen spent the afternoon and evening with a friend, Wayne Stanhope, watching television, drinking, and injecting themselves with amphetamines. At 11:00 p.m., Stanhope got up to change a record on the stereo. For unknown reasons, Allen drew two guns and emptied the clips into Stanhope.

DATE OF ARREST
March 11, 1987

CIRCUMSTANCES OF THE ARREST
At the time of the murder, Allen and Stanhope were not alone: Allen's girlfriend, his nephew, and two friends were in the house. The friends went to the police, who sent two homicide detectives to arrest Allen. They picked him up as he left a hospital where he had been treated for heart trouble.

THE CHARGE
Murder

AFTERWARD
The case never went to trial. Allen's health was so poor, he was taken from jail to St. Vincent's Hospital in Melbourne where he was kept under police guard until his death in April 1987.

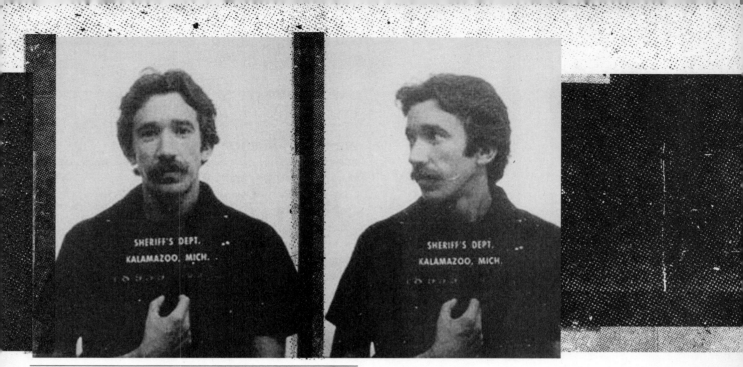

TIM ALLEN

(1953–)

NATIONALITY
American

WHO IS HE?
Tim Allen is a popular actor and comedian, the star of the television sitcom *Home Improvement* and such films as *Galaxy Quest*. He is the voice of Buzz Lightyear in the *Toy Story* movies.

WHAT DID HE DO?
Allen was caught at the Kalamazoo/Battle Creek International Airport carrying 1.4 pounds of cocaine.

DATE OF ARREST
October 2,1978

THE CHARGE
Possession of cocaine

THE SENTENCE
Under the laws at the time, Allen could have been sentenced to life imprisonment. Instead, he pled guilty and turned state's evidence, giving the police the names of other cocaine dealers. For his cooperation, Allen received a reduced sentence of five years. He served 28 months and was released.

AFTERWARD
In 1997, Allen struck Henry Armstrong with his car, injuring the 73-year-old man. In an interview with a reporter for the *National Enquirer*, Armstrong said that at the time of the accident, Allen appeared "drunk or high." Allen sued Armstrong for $8 million, alleging that he had made false statements. Allen dropped the lawsuit in 1999 "out of humanitarian reasons" after learning that Armstrong was suffering from brain cancer.

ALDRICH AMES

(1941–)

DATE OF ARREST
February 24, 1994

CIRCUMSTANCES OF THE ARREST
FBI agents arrested Ames with his wife, Rosario Ames, who was charged with aiding and abetting.

THE CHARGE
Espionage

THE SENTENCE
Aldrich and Rosario Ames both pled guilty. He told the court that during the nine years he spied for the Soviets, he had revealed the names of "virtually all Soviet agents of the CIA and other American and foreign services known to me." Aldrich Ames was sentenced to life imprisonment with no possibility of parole. Rosario Ames was sentenced to 63 months in prison.

AMES'S VICTIMS
According to *Time* magazine, through the information Ames provided the KGB, at least three dozen agents in Russia were lost, ten of whom were executed, including Adolf Tolkachev, who passed along information about Soviet advances in stealth aircraft technology; Valeri Martinov, a lieutenant colonel in the KGB; and Dmitri Polyakov, a general in Soviet military intelligence.

NATIONALITY
American

WHO IS HE?
For 31 years, Aldrich Ames worked for the Central Intelligence Agency (CIA) as a specialist in the intelligence services of the Soviet Union. He was fluent in Russian and used his language skills and expertise to recruit Soviet agents to spy for the United States.

WHAT DID HE DO?
In 1985, Ames contacted KGB agents assigned to the Soviet embassy in Washington and offered to provide them with classified documents that revealed how the United States collected information about the Soviet Union. During the first four years that he worked for the Russians, Ames received payments totaling $1.88 million. It is believed that the intelligence Ames provided to the Russians led to the arrest and execution of Russian double agents who worked secretly for the United States.

YIGAL AMIR
(1970–)

WHAT DID HE DO?

On November 4, 1995, Prime Minister Rabin attended a rally in support of the Oslo Accords at Kings of Israel Square in Tel Aviv. Amir waited for him in a parking lot near the prime minister's limousine. As Rabin walked toward the car, Amir fired, hitting Rabin in the arm and back and wounding one of Rabin's bodyguards, Yoram Rubin.

DATE OF ARREST

November 4, 1995

CIRCUMSTANCES OF THE ARREST

Amir was seized immediately at the scene of the crime by Rabin's bodyguards. At police headquarters, Amir learned that Rabin had died. "I'm satisfied," he said, adding that he had "no regrets" about assassinating the prime minister.

THE CHARGES

Murder, conspiracy to murder, and aggravated injury

THE SENTENCE

Amir pled guilty and was sentenced to life in prison, plus an additional six years for wounding Yoram Rubin. Prime Minister Benyamin Netanyahu has stated publicly that there will be no pardon, parole, or reduction of the sentence for Yigal Amir.

AFTERWARD

In 2004, Amir married; in 2007, he and his wife had a son. The boy was circumcised at the prison so Amir could be present at the ceremony.

NATIONALITY

Israeli

WHO IS HE?

Yigal Amir was an Orthodox Jewish law and computer student who became involved in radical right-wing politics. He was a vocal opponent of the Mideast peace process. Amir organized demonstrations to protest Israeli Prime Minister Yitzhak Rabin's signing of the Oslo Accords, which provided Palestinians with self-government through a Palestinian National Authority.

ALLEN ANDRADE

(1976–)

NATIONALITY
American

WHO IS HE?
Allen Andrade is a habitual criminal who had pled guilty to three separate felonies between 2000 and 2004: possession of contraband, theft, and providing false information to a pawnbroker. For these crimes, he was sentenced to five years and two months in prison.

WHAT DID HE DO?
On July 15, 2008, Andrade met 18-year-old Angie Zapata for a sexual encounter. They spent two days together in Zapata's apartment in Greeley, Colorado. On July 16, Andrade discovered photographs that led him to conclude that Zapata was born male (since age 16, Zapata had been living as a woman). Andrade confronted Zapata, grabbed her crotch, and when he felt male genitals he became enraged. He grabbed a fire extinguisher and bludgeoned Zapata to death.

DATE OF ARREST
July 29, 2008

CIRCUMSTANCES OF THE ARREST
Neighbors called police at approximately 1:45 a.m., complaining of noise coming from a parked car. Initially, the police arrested Andrade for several unpaid parking tickets; then they realized that the car in which they had found him might have belonged to Angie Zapata. They also found on his person Zapata's credit card, which Andrade had used several times to buy gas.

THE CHARGES
Murder, commission of a hate crime, automobile theft, and identity theft

THE SENTENCE
The jury took only two hours to find Andrade guilty of all four charges. The judge sentenced Andrade to life in prison without parole.

SIGNIFICANCE OF THE CASE
The Angie Zapata case was the first time someone was convicted of murdering a transgender person under a state hate crimes statute.

LOWELL LEE ANDREWS

(1939–1962)

NATIONALITY
American

WHO WAS HE?
Lowell Lee Andrews was a sophomore at the University of Kansas, where he majored in zoology and played the bassoon in the university band. A neighbor described him as "the nicest boy in Wolcott"— the Andrews family's hometown.

WHAT DID HE DO?
On November 28, 1958, Andrews took a .22-caliber rifle and a German Luger pistol and shot and killed his father, his mother, and his older sister. He shot each family member multiple times—his father 17 times, his mother 4 times, and his sister 3 times. He tried to make the scene appear like a burglary that had gone wrong, then he drove to his boardinghouse near the university in Lawrence, Kansas, to es-tablish his alibi—that he had gone back to pick up his typewriter. He dismantled the rifle and the Luger and threw the parts into the Kansas River, then returned home to summon the police.

DATE OF ARREST
November 28, 1958

CIRCUMSTANCES OF THE ARREST
When police arrived at the Andrews home, they found the burglary scenario unconvincing and were surprised by Andrews's demeanor—although his entire family had been murdered, he showed no emotion. In fact, when the police pulled up to the house, they found Andrews outside playing with his dog.

THE CHARGE
Murder

THE SENTENCE
Andrews was found guilty and sentenced to death by hanging.

AFTERWARD
On Death Row at the prison in Lansing, Kansas, Andrews shared a cell with Richard Hickock and Perry Smith, whose murder of the Clutter family Truman Capote chronicled in *In Cold Blood*. Lowell Lee Andrews was hanged on November 30, 1962. He never expressed any remorse for murdering his family. An *Associated Press* story reported that Andrews declined to say any last words, and went to his death smiling slightly.

SUSAN B. ANTHONY

(1820–1906)

NATIONALITY
American

WHO WAS SHE?
Susan B. Anthony was one of the leaders of the Women's Rights Movement in 19th-century America. With Elizabeth Cady Stanton, she founded the National Woman's Suffrage Association to secure for women the right to vote.

WHAT DID SHE DO?
On Election Day 1872, Anthony and seven or eight other women went to their local polling stations in Rochester, New York, and voted. It was illegal for women to vote at that time, yet the election officials at the polling place voted two to one to accept the women's ballots. (Anthony voted Republican.)

DATE OF ARREST
November 5, 1872

CIRCUMSTANCES OF THE ARREST
U.S. Commissioner William C. Storrs, who issued the warrant for Anthony's arrest, sent her a message requesting that she call upon him at his office. She sent back a reply, saying "that I had no social acquaintance with him and didn't wish to call on him." So a deputy marshal came to Anthony's home to arrest her. Fourteen other women who had voted were also arrested, as were the election officials who had accepted their ballots.

THE CHARGE
Illegal voting

THE SENTENCE
Anthony was found guilty and ordered to pay a fine of $100 plus court costs.

AFTERWARD
Anthony refused to pay the fine and costs, and the court made no serious effort to collect. She had 3,000 copies of the transcript of her trial printed and distributed them to fellow suffragists, politicians, and public libraries.

ROSCOE "FATTY" ARBUCKLE

(1887–1933)

NATIONALITY
American

WHO WAS HE?
A famously chubby comic actor, Fatty Arbuckle was the first Hollywood star to be paid $1 million a year. He was a regular in the Keystone Cops short features, and had his own series, *Fatty and Mabel*, with Mabel Normand as his costar. It is believed that Fatty Arbuckle was on the receiving end of the first pie-in-the-face gag, in the 1913 short, *A Noise from the Deep*.

WHAT DID HE DO?
Over Labor Day weekend, 1921, Arbuckle hosted a lavish party at the St. Francis Hotel in San Francisco. He reserved three suites, hired a caterer and a jazz band, and brought in a great deal of bootleg liquor (in 1921, Prohibition was still in effect). On the afternoon of September 6, Arbuckle found his friend, Virginia Rappe in his bathroom, violently ill. He helped her to his bed, called the hotel's manager, and asked for a doctor. Several days later, Rappe died of a ruptured bladder. One of the guests at the party, Maude Delmont, went to the police, charging that Arbuckle had been responsible for Rappe's death.

DATE OF ARREST
September 11, 1921

THE CHARGE
Manslaughter

THE TRIALS
Arbuckle was tried three times. In the first two cases, the juries could not agree on a verdict. In the meantime, some newspapers, including William Randolph Hearst's *San Francisco Examiner*, were printing tabloid tales of Arbuckle forcing himself on Rappe, his weight fatally crushing her. The third jury deliberated for six minutes before returning a verdict of not guilty. They also delivered to the court a statement, signed by every juror, in which they said, "Acquittal is not enough for Roscoe Arbuckle. We feel that a great injustice has been done him. We feel also that it was only our plain duty to give him this exoneration, under the evidence, for there was not the slightest proof adduced to connect him in any way with the commission of a crime."

AFTERWARD
In spite of the acquittal, Arbuckle's reputation was ruined. He could get no work as an actor, so he became a director, using an alias, William B. Goodrich, in the credits. In the 1930s, Jack Warner was prepared to help Arbuckle return to the screen, but before any of their film projects were completed, Arbuckle died of a heart attack.

KEEPING THE WEIGHT ON
Fatty Arbuckle was contractually obligated to keep his weight above 250 pounds. Furthermore, if he managed to gain 50 or 100 pounds, he would receive an annual bonus. For his entire film career, he kept his weight at 300 pounds or more.

AMY ARCHER-GILLIGAN

(1873–1962)

NATIONALITY
American

WHO WAS SHE?
In 1907, Amy Archer and her husband, James Archer, opened a nursing home for the elderly and convalescents in Windsor, Connecticut. In 1910, James died. In 1913, Amy married again—Michael Gilligan, who died three months later. And Amy's husbands were not the only deaths—between 1907 and 1911, at least 60 of the residents of the nursing home died.

WHAT DID SHE DO?
Nellie Pierce, a sister of one of the boarders who died unexpectedly, launched an investigation that led to her brother's body being exhumed. The coroner found a very high level of arsenic present in the corpse, enough to kill several men. The body of Michael Gilligan was exhumed, as were the corpses of four of the boarders, and all were found to have died of arsenic or strychnine poisoning. Windsor storekeepers reported that for years Amy had purchased large quantities of arsenic—"To kill rats," she had explained.

DATE OF ARREST
May 8, 1916

THE CHARGE
Murder

THE TRIALS
In her first trial, the jury took only four hours to find Amy guilty of murder. Citing an error in the proceedings, her attorneys arranged for Amy to be tried again. They mounted an insanity defense, bringing in psychiatrists who testified that Amy was mad; Amy's daughter, Mary Archer, swore that her mother had lost possession of her senses after becoming addicted to morphine.

THE SENTENCE
In the first trial Amy had been sentenced to hang. In the second, she was sentenced to life in prison. After seven years, she was declared insane and sent to a mental asylum where she spent the last 38 years of her life.

INSPIRED BY A SERIAL KILLER
Playwright Joseph Kesselring took Amy Archer-Gilligan's story as his inspiration for the 1941 Broadway hit comedy, *Arsenic and Old Lace*. In 1944, Frank Capra directed the movie version, starring Cary Grant.

LOUIS ARMSTRONG

(1901–1971)

NATIONALITY
American

WHO WAS HE?
Louis Armstrong is regarded as one of the greatest jazz musicians of all time. He learned to play the cornet during the two years he spent in a reformatory, the Colored Waif's Home, in New Orleans. (Armstrong was given a two-year sentence for firing a pistol into the air on New Year's Eve; he was 12 years old at the time.) At age 16, he began playing with jazz bands in bars in the Storyville district of New Orleans. In the 1920s, Armstrong began smoking marijuana, a habit he would never give up.

WHAT DID HE DO?
Between sets at the Cotton Club in Culver City, California, Armstrong and Vic Berton, a drummer, went out to the parking lot to smoke a joint.

DATE OF ARREST
November 18, 1930

CIRCUMSTANCES OF THE ARREST
Almost immediately, two narcotics detectives appeared and arrested Armstrong and Berton. During the ride to jail, one of the detectives admitted that a rival bandleader at another club had tipped off the police about Armstrong's marijuana habit.

THE CHARGE
Possession of marijuana

THE SENTENCE
Armstrong was found guilty, but the judge suspended the sentence of six months in prison and a $1,000 fine.

AFTERWARD
Louis Armstrong started several jazz bands, but arguably the most influential was Louis Armstrong and His Orchestra. Their style epitomized the Swing era and the band was one of the most popular in the 1930s and 1940s. He also had a film career: Between 1936 and 1969, Armstrong appeared in 14 movies, the last being *Hello Dolly!* In which he sang a duet with Barbra Streisand.

ON BROADWAY
In 1929, Louis Armstrong was cast in the Broadway musical, *Hot Chocolates*; he brought the house down with his rendition of Fats Waller's "Ain't Misbehavin'."

RAYMOND AUBRAC

(1914–)

NATIONALITY
French

WHO WAS HE?
Raymond Aubrac (his real surname was Samuel) was a French Jew, an engineer, and a veteran of the French army. His wife, Lucie Aubrac, was a French Catholic and a secondary school teacher. After the Nazi invasion and occupation of France, the Aubracs joined the Resistance. By 1943, the Aubracs' cell was part of a larger organization directed by Jean Moulin.

WHAT DID HE DO?
The Aubracs published an underground newspaper, *Liberation*, and participated in acts of sabotage against the Germans. The Nazis regarded all members of the Resistance as criminals.

DATE OF ARREST
June 21, 1943

CIRCUMSTANCES OF THE ARREST
Jean Moulin had arranged to meet Aubrac and several other members of the Resistance at the office of Dr. Frédéric Dugoujon in Caliure, a suburb of Lyon. The housekeeper had just shown the men into the doctor's waiting room when the Gestapo burst in and arrested everyone—Moulin and his companions, Dr. Dugoujon, and the patients in the waiting room.

THE SENTENCE
In Montluc prison, Gestapo agents tortured Aubrac and planned to execute him.

AN UNEXPECTED DEVELOPMENT
Lucie Aubrac was five months pregnant with her second child when Raymond was arrested. She went to Gestapo headquarters where she presented herself as Aubrac's lover and pleaded to be married to him before he was executed. Incredibly, the German officer who heard Lucie's appeal granted her request. On the appointed day, Lucie and Raymond were "married" in a brief civil ceremony at Gestapo headquarters. Then Lucie went outside where a car with two members of the Resistance was waiting at the curb. As the prison truck carrying Raymond pulled out into the boulevard, the Resistance men followed. The driver pulled the car alongside the truck, and the man in the passenger seat fired, killing the German driver. The truck came to a halt and Lucie and her companions leapt out of the car, spraying the truck with bullets. They killed all the German guards, but Raymond was unharmed. As he climbed down from the truck, a second car sped onto the scene. Raymond dove into the back seat as Lucie and her friends drove off in their car.

AFTERWARD
The Resistance arranged for a plane to fly Lucie, Raymond, and their two-year-old son to England, where Lucie gave birth to a daughter. The family remained in England for the duration of the war. Then the Aubracs returned to France where they were active in the French Communist Party. Lucie Aubrac died in 2007, at age 94. As of 2010, Raymond Aubrac was still alive.

STONE COLD STEVE AUSTIN

(1964–)

NATIONALITY
American

WHO IS HE?
Stone Cold Steve Austin wrestled for World Championship Wrestling, Extreme Championship, and the World Wrestling Federation (now World Wrestling Entertainment, or WWE). During his professional wrestling career (1989–2003), Austin won 19 wrestling championships.

WHAT DID HE DO?
On June 15, 2002, Austin argued with his wife, Debra Williams. During the argument he struck her, raising a welt on Williams's face and bruising her back. Then he left the house. Williams called 911 and the police brought a "uniformed evidence technician" to make a record of Williams's injuries.

DATE OF ARREST
August 14, 2002

CIRCUMSTANCES OF THE ARREST
In July 2002, Williams filed for divorce from Austin. In August, she decided to press charges against Austin.

THE CHARGE
Domestic abuse

THE SENTENCE
Austin pled guilty to a misdemeanor charge of assault and was sentenced to one year's probation. The judge ordered him to enroll in a domestic violence course and pay a $1,000 fine.

JOHNSON AZIGA

(1957–)

NATIONALITY
Ugandan-born Canadian citizen

WHO IS HE?
Johnson Aziga worked as a research analyst at the Ontario Ministry of the Attorney General. At the time of his arrest he was married, although estranged from his wife.

WHAT DID HE DO?
Aziga, who had known since 1996 that he was infected with the AIDS virus, had unprotected sex with 13 women and never disclosed his HIV status to any of them. Two of these women became infected and died of AIDS-related diseases.

DATE OF ARREST
August 30, 2003

THE CHARGE
Murder

AZIGA AND HIS LAWYERS
Three times Aziga fired his defense attorneys, usually just as the trial was about to begin. Each time the judge declared a mistrial because Aziga was not represented by legal counsel. The case finally came to trial in 2008.

THE SENTENCE
On April 4, 2009, Aziga was found guilty of two counts of first-degree murder and sentenced to life imprisonment. He must serve 25 years before becoming eligible for parole.

SIGNIFICANCE
Johnson Aziga was the first person in Canada to be convicted of first-degree murder for knowingly spreading the HIV virus.

LENA BAKER

(1901–1945)

NATIONALITY
American

WHO WAS SHE?
Lena Baker was the daughter of black sharecroppers in Cuthbert, Georgia. To support herself and her three children, she worked in the cotton fields and took menial jobs. In the early 1940s, Ernest Knight, a white man and the owner of a local textile mill, broke his hip; he hired Baker as his private nurse. At some point their business relationship developed into a love affair.

WHAT DID SHE DO?
On April 30, 1944, Baker and Knight spent the day drinking and arguing. At one point he locked her inside a room in his mill. When he returned several hours later, Knight demanded that Baker have sex with him. She refused. He grabbed a metal pipe and came toward her; they wrestled and the pistol Knight was carrying went off. The bullet pierced his skull; he died instantly.

DATE OF ARREST
April 30, 1944

CIRCUMSTANCES OF THE ARREST
Baker reported the shooting to the town coroner, who urged her to surrender to the sheriff. Instead, she went home, where she was arrested later that night.

THE CHARGE
Murder

THE SENTENCE
A jury composed entirely of white men found Baker guilty of murder. The judge sentenced her to death by electrocution. The governor of Georgia granted a reprieve so the case could be reviewed by the Board of Pardons and Parole. In January 1945, the board denied Baker's petition for clemency.

AFTERWARD
As she entered the execution chamber, Baker said, "What I done, I did in self-defense. I have nothing against anyone. I'm ready to meet my God." In 2001, Baker's family petitioned the Georgia Board of Pardons and Parole to revisit her case. In 2005, the board granted her a full pardon, stating that she should have been convicted of manslaughter, which would have reduced her sentence to 15 years in prison.

JIM BAKKER

(1940–)

DATE OF INDICTMENT
December 5, 1988

THE CHARGES
Mail fraud, wire fraud, and conspiracy

THE SENTENCE
Bakker was sentenced to 45 years in prison. He appealed the sentence, and it was reduced to 8 years. After serving 5 years, Bakker was paroled, but the IRS insists that he is still liable for approximately $6 million in back taxes.

AFTERWARD
In 1992, his wife, Tammy Faye, divorced him. In 1998, Bakker married Lori Graham, a Christian inspirational speaker. They host *The Jim Bakker Show*, which is broadcast from Branson, Missouri.

NATIONALITY
American

WHO IS HE?
Jim Bakker was an Assembly of God minister who, with his then-wife, Tammy Faye Bakker, founded the PTL Club, an international television network. In the 1980s, the Bakkers were among the most prominent televangelists in the world. In Fort Mills, South Carolina, they built a Christian theme park, Heritage USA, which in the 1980s was the third most popular theme park in America, after Disney World in Florida and Disneyland in California.

WHAT DID HE DO?
The U.S. government alleged that Bakker and several associates had skimmed about $4 million for themselves from the PTL bank accounts. They also oversold Lifetime Partnerships to the Heritage USA theme park in Fort Mills, South Carolina. Approximately 9,700 partners were promised luxurious rooms at the park, but, as *Time* magazine reported, the accommodations "turned out to be a single bunkhouse with 48 beds."

DANIEL BALDWIN
(1960–)

THE CHARGE
Grand theft auto

THE FUGITIVE
Baldwin failed to appear at his arraignment hearing. The judge issued a bench warrant for Baldwin's arrest, and the police put out an All Points Bulletin for him.

THE TRIAL
When Baldwin did finally come to court, the owner of the vehicle, who initially had reported it stolen, came forward and stated that he had loaned the SUV to Baldwin for two days, and that the theft was a misunderstanding. Consequently, Baldwin was cleared of all charges.

NATIONALITY
American

WHO IS HE?
Daniel Baldwin is the second oldest of the Baldwin brothers, a family of actors that includes Alec Baldwin, William Baldwin, and Stephen Baldwin.

WHAT DID HE DO?
Police had reason to believe that Baldwin stole a white 2003 GMC Yukon SUV.

DATE OF ARREST
November 8, 2006

CIRCUMSTANCES OF THE ARREST
The vehicle had been reported stolen. When police in Santa Monica, California, spotted the SUV, they pulled Baldwin over. He was arrested, then released on $20,000 bail.

THE BALI NINE

Andrew Chan (1984–), Si Yi Chen (1985–), Michael Czugaj (1986–), Renae Lawrence (1977–), Tan Duc Thanh Nguyen (1983–), Matthew Norman (1986–), Scott Rush (1985–), Martin Stephens (1976–), Myuran Sukumaran (1981–)

NATIONALITY
Australian

WHO ARE THEY?
In 2005, the Bali Nine were a group of friends and acquaintances in Sydney and Brisbane, Australia. Several of them worked together for the same catering company.

WHAT DID THEY DO?
The Bali Nine plotted to smuggle heroin from Indonesia into Australia for distribution.

DATE OF ARREST
April 17, 2005

CIRCUMSTANCES OF THE ARREST
Indonesian police arrested Chan, Czugaj, Lawrence, Rush, and Stephens at Bali's Ngurah Rai International Airport; the latter four were wearing beneath their clothes plastic bags filled with heroin taped or strapped to their bodies. Among them, the four carried 18 pounds of heroin. The police arrested Chen, Nguyen, Norman, and Sukumaran at their hotel near Kuta Beach; they found 12 ounces of heroin in the room.

THE CHARGE
Drug smuggling

THE SENTENCE
All of the Bali Nine were found guilty of drug smuggling. Chan and Sukumaran, the ringleaders of the smuggling plot, were sentenced to death by firing squad. The other seven were sentenced to life in prison.

AFTERWARD
All nine appealed their sentences. In the first round of appeals, Chen, Czugaj, Lawrence, Nguyen, and Norman had their life sentences reduced to 20 years. But the process was not over. In March 2008, the justices of Indonesia's Supreme Court reviewed the sentences and imposed life in prison on Chen, Czugaj, Nguyen, and Norman. The Supreme Court sentenced Scott Rush to death. As of August 2010, Chan, Rush, and Sukumaran were launching one final appeal to have their death sentences commuted.

THE TIP-OFF
The Bali Nine were arrested after Australian federal police received a tip about the smuggling operation and alerted the police in Indonesia.

KLAUS BARBIE, "THE BUTCHER OF LYON"

(1913–1991)

NATIONALITY
German

WHO WAS HE?
Klaus Barbie's mother and father were schoolteachers. In 1935, he joined the intelligence branch of the Nazi Party. After serving in the Netherlands, Barbie was appointed head of the Gestapo in Lyon, France, 1942–1944.

WHAT DID HE DO?
Known as "the Butcher of Lyon," Barbie is said to have been responsible for the deaths of 4,000 Jews and Gentiles. He tortured to death the leader of the Resistance in Lyon, Jean Moulin, and deported 41 Jewish children, aged 3 to 13, from their hiding place at Izieu to Auschwitz, where they were murdered in the gas chambers.

DATE OF ARREST
January 19, 1983

CIRCUMSTANCES OF THE ARREST
Since 1951, Barbie had been living in Bolivia under the alias, Klaus Altmann. By 1971, the renowned Nazi hunters, Beate and Serge Klarsfeld had tracked Barbie to Bolivia, but the Bolivian government had always refused to extradite him for trial. That changed in 1982 when Hernan Siles Zuazo, the newly elected president of Bolivia, agreed to arrest Barbie and send him to France for trial.

THE CHARGE
Crimes against humanity

THE SENTENCE
During his trial, Barbie had declared, "When I stand before the throne of God, I shall be judged innocent." The French court, however, found Barbie guilty of crimes against humanity and sentenced him to life imprisonment.

AFTERWARD
Four years after his conviction, Klaus Barbie died in prison of leukemia.

CAMERAS IN THE COURTROOM
In the 1980s it was rare for trials to be filmed, but the Cour d'assises agreed to permit cameras to record the trial because of the historic nature of the case.

BRIGITTE BARDOT

(1934–)

DATE OF PROSECUTION
April 15, 2008

THE CHARGE
Inciting racial hatred

THE SENTENCE
Bardot was sentenced to two months in prison, although the sentence was suspended, and she was fined 15,000 euros. Since 1997, it was her fifth conviction for "inciting hatred." The public prosecutor told the court that she was "tired of prosecuting Mrs. Bardot."

NATIONALITY
French

WHO IS SHE?
Brigitte Bardot began her career as a fashion model. Early in the 1950s, she was in several landmark French films, including Roger Vadim's *And God Created Woman*, Jean-Luc Godard's Contempt, and Louis Malle's *Viva Maria*! She has become an outspoken advocate for animal rights and an equally outspoken critic of the impact of homosexuals and Muslims on French society.

WHAT DID SHE DO?
In December 2006, Bardot wrote to Nicolas Sarkozy, then France's minister of the interior, to protest the way Muslims slaughtered sheep during the Eid al-Adha festival; Bardot demanded that the Muslims anesthesize the sheep before slitting their throats. She went on to complain about what she regarded as Islam's growing influence in France. She said she was "fed up with being under the thumb of this population which is destroying us, destroying our country, and imposing its habits."

BUST

CHARLES BARKLEY

(1993–)

NATIONALITY
American

WHO IS HE?
Charles "Sir Charles" Barkley is a National Basketball Association (NBA) Hall of Famer. He played 16 seasons for the Philadelphia 76ers, the Phoenix Suns, and the Houston Rockets. At the 1992 and 1996 Olympics, he won two gold medals as a member of the U.S. basketball "Dream Team." Barkley was named league MVP in 1993, and an NBA All-Star 11 times.

WHAT DID HE DO?
At 1:30 in the morning of December 31, 2008, in Scottsdale, Arizona, police pulled Barkley over after he ran a red light then drove up to the curb where a woman was standing. Police arrested Barkley on suspicion that he was driving under the influence.

DATE OF ARREST
December 31, 2008

MAKING MATTERS WORSE
Barkley told the police that he knew the woman he tried to pick up. The week before she had performed oral sex on Barkley. According to the police report, Barkley said "it was the best one he had ever had in his life." The woman was not charged.

THE CHARGE
Suspicion of drunk driving

THE SENTENCE
Barkley was found guilty of drunk driving and sentenced to pay a $2,000 fine and spend ten days at Maricopa County's Tent City jail.

The jail sentence was reduced to five days, but Barkley was required to enroll in an alcohol abuse education program and attend traffic school.

THE JAIL
The Tent City jail houses prisoners in un–air-conditioned tents and requires them to wear pink underwear and black-and-white-striped prison uniforms.

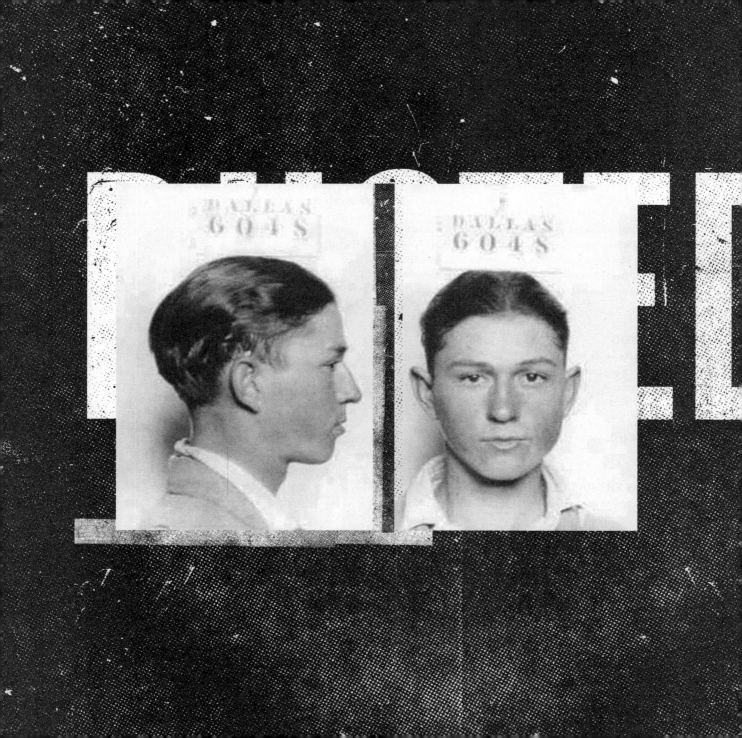

CLYDE BARROW

(1909–1934)

NATIONALITY
American

WHO WAS HE?
Clyde Barrow's family was dirt-poor. After they left their farm for West Dallas, they lived for a time in a tent beneath a viaduct.

WHAT DID HE DO?
With his older brother, Buck, Clyde stole a small flock of turkeys from a farm in East Texas.

DATE OF ARREST
December 1926

CIRCUMSTANCES OF THE ARREST
Police became suspicious when they saw two young men driving a car with a flock of turkeys in the back seat.

THE CHARGE
Possession of stolen property

THE SENTENCE
Buck took full responsibility for the theft and spent several days in jail. Clyde, who was 17 at the time, looked so boyish the police let him go.

A LIFE OF CRIME
After the turkey caper, Clyde became a full-time petty criminal, robbing stores and gas stations, and stealing cars. In spite of repeated arrests and serving short jail terms, Clyde would not go straight. When he was arrested again, in April 1930, for burglary, a judge sentenced him to a year at Eastham Prison Farm. In prison, an inmate made Clyde his sex slave—until Clyde smashed the man's skull with a length of pipe.

BONNIE AND CLYDE
In January 1930, Clyde met Bonnie Parker, a 19-year-old waitress whose husband was serving a life sentence for murder. When Clyde was paroled from Eastham in 1932, he and Bonnie became a couple and began a two-year crime spree that included many robberies, kidnappings, and 13 murders. On January 16, 1934, Clyde masterminded a prison break for five inmates at Eastham. Two prison guards were wounded in the escape.

THE AMBUSH
In May 1934, FBI agents and Texas and Louisiana police set up an ambush, concealing themselves in the bushes along the highway outside Sailes, Louisiana. As Bonnie and Clyde's car drove by, the agents and police emptied their shotguns, automatic rifles, and pistols into the vehicle. Bonnie and Clyde were killed in the hail of bullets.

THE MOVIE AND THE CRITICS
Director Arthur Penn's 1967 film, *Bonnie and Clyde*, starring Faye Dunaway and Warren Beatty, brought an unprecedented level of sex and violence to the screen. Bosley Crowther, film critic for the *New York Times*, hated the movie: "This blending of farce with brutal killings is as pointless as it is lacking in taste, since it makes no valid commentary upon the already travestied truth. And it leaves an astonished critic wondering just what purpose Mr. Penn and Mr. Beatty think they serve with this strangely antique, sentimental claptrap."

KEVIN BARRY

(1902–1920)

WHAT DID HE DO?

On the morning of September 20, 1920, Barry was one of several IRA men sent to intercept a British army truck and disarm the soldiers. The IRA succeeded in stopping the truck and collecting the British soldiers' weapons, but then someone's gun went off. The IRA opened fire, killing one soldier and mortally wounding two others.

DATE OF ARREST

September 20, 1920

CIRCUMSTANCES OF THE ARREST

During the firefight, Barry's gun jammed. He dove under the truck for cover, but as the IRA men retreated, Barry was captured.

THE CHARGE

Murder

THE SENTENCE

Barry was tried before a British military court. He was found guilty of the deaths of the three British privates and sentenced to be hanged.

AFTERWARD

Kevin Barry was hanged in the courtyard of Dublin's Mountjoy Prison and buried there with other Irish rebels. In 2001, after a state funeral, their remains were moved to Glasnevin Cemetery, where many of Ireland's national heroes lie buried.

THE BALLAD

Kevin Barry became the subject of a ballad, which is still sung in Irish pubs.

NATIONALITY

Irish

WHO WAS HE?

Kevin Barry was a medical student at University College Dublin and a section commander of the Irish Republican Army (IRA). Since the age of 15, he had participated in a variety of IRA operations, including seizing a cache of weapons intended for the Royal Irish Constabulary.

MARION BARRY

(1936–)

NATIONALITY
American

WHO IS HE?
In the 1960s and 1970s, Marion Barry was a civil rights activist in Washington, D.C. A defining moment in his career came in 1977 when he was shot and nearly killed by radical Black Muslim terrorists who occupied the Islamic Center, B'nai B'rith offices, and the District Building. From 1978 to 1990, he was mayor of Washington. The first allegations that Barry used cocaine surfaced in 1981.

WHAT DID HE DO?
Barry took a room at Washington's Vista Hotel with his former lover, Hazel Diane "Rasheeda" Moore. There he smoked crack cocaine.

DATE OF ARREST
January 18, 1990

CIRCUMSTANCES OF THE ARREST
FBI agents had planted a surveillance camera in the room, which filmed the mayor smoking crack. It was a sting operation in which Moore cooperated with the FBI. After his arrest, Barry said of Moore, "Bitch set me up ... I shouldn't have come up here ... goddamn bitch."

THE CHARGES
Possession of crack cocaine, possession of cocaine, and perjury

THE SENTENCE
The jury found Barry guilty of one charge of possession of cocaine—a misdemeanor—but after eight days of deliberation the jurors could not reach a verdict on the 13 other charges. One juror said, "I believe [the federal government] was out to get Marion Barry." The judge declared a mistrial on the other charges. For the charge on which he was found guilty, Barry was sentenced to six months in prison.

AFTERWARD
After his release from prison, Barry returned to politics. He was elected to the City Council in 1992 and was elected mayor again in 1996. In 2004, he returned to his old City Council seat.

JEAN-MARIE BASTIEN-THIRY

(1927–1963)

NATIONALITY

French

WHO WAS HE?

Jean-Marie Bastien-Thiry was active in the Organisation de L'armée Secrète (OAS), an organization of mostly military men opposed to de Gaulle's policy of granting independence to France's colony, Algeria.

WHAT DID HE DO?

On August 22, 1962, Bastien-Thiry led a team of 12 assassins in an ambush against General Charles de Gaulle. Using machine guns, they fired 100 rounds at the limousine carrying the general, his wife, and secret service agents. Incredibly, no one was hurt. De Gaulle dismissed his would-be killers, saying, "They shot like pigs."

DATE OF ARREST

September 17, 1962

CIRCUMSTANCES OF THE ARREST

Although leaders of the OAS had been eager to help Bastien-Thiry leave the country, he insisted on remaining in France and standing trial. Police arrested him at his home.

THE CHARGE

Conspiracy to assassinate

THE TRIAL

Bastien-Thiry defended himself in court, stating that the assassination was an act of tyrannicide, comparable to Colonel Claus von Stauffenberg's plot to assassinate Adolf Hitler.

THE SENTENCE

Bastien-Thiry was found guilty and sentenced to death by firing squad. Often de Gaulle had granted reprieves to members of the OAS under sentence of death, but he showed no clemency to Bastien-Thiry.

AFTERWARD

The anti-Gaullists revered Bastien-Thiry as a martyr. The pro-Gaullists saved the bullet-riddled car and later placed it on display in the Musee Charles de Gaulle in Lille. The Trianon Café, which was sprayed with bullets during the assassination attempt, was renamed Le Trianon de la Fusillade. In 1968, Charles de Gaulle died peacefully while watching television.

THE BOOK

Jean-Marie Bastien-Thiry's plot was the inspiration for Frederick Forsyth's 1971 novel, *The Day of the Jackal*.

THE BEATLES:

JOHN LENNON (1940–1980), PAUL MCCARTNEY (1942–), GEORGE HARRISON (1943–2001)

NATIONALITY
English

WHO ARE/WERE THEY?
The Beatles—John Lennon, Paul McCartney, George Harrison, and Ringo Starr—was one of the most influential, most acclaimed, and most successful bands in history. They produced many hit singles and hit albums, but their 1967 album, *Sgt. Pepper's Lonely Hearts Club Band*, is generally considered their masterpiece.

WHAT DID THEY DO?
Lennon and Harrison had marijuana in their homes. McCartney had marijuana in his luggage.

DATES OF ARRESTS
October 19, 1968: John Lennon.
March 12, 1969: George Harrison
January 16, 1980: Paul McCartney

CIRCUMSTANCES OF THE ARRESTS
Lennon was arrested in his home in London with Yoko Ono. Days earlier they had announced that Ono was pregnant, which caused an uproar, since both Lennon and Ono were married to other people at the time. Harrison was arrested with his wife, Patti. McCartney was arrested at Tokyo International Airport when customs officials found more than seven pounds of marijuana in his luggage.

THE CHARGE
Drug possession

THE SENTENCE
Lennon and Ono were fined £150. The Harrisons were fined £250. McCartney spent nine days in a Tokyo jail before being deported. Between his legal fees and the concerts in Japan he was forced to cancel, McCartney's stint in jail cost him $350,000.

THE ARRESTING OFFICER
Lennon, Ono, and the Harrisons were all busted by Officer D. S. Pilcher, who also arrested Mick Jagger and Eric Clapton on drug charges. Pilcher's career ended when he was found guilty of corruption and sentenced to jail.

BYRON DE LA BECKWITH

(1920–2001)

NATIONALITY
American

WHO WAS HE?
Until the American Civil War, Byron De La Beckwith's family had prospered in the South. After the defeat of the Confederacy, the family's fortunes crumbled, and De La Beckwith's family hit hard times. As an adult, he made a living as a manure dealer. He was a member of two racist organizations, the Ku Klux Klan and the White Citizens' Council.

WHAT DID HE DO?
Shortly after midnight on June 12, 1963, De La Beckwith lay in wait for Medgar Evers, the field secretary of the Mississippi chapter of the National Association for the Advancement of Colored People (NAACP). As Evers climbed out of his car, De La Beckwith shot him in the back. Evers's family and neighbors drove him to a hospital in Jackson, Mississippi, where he died.

DATE OF INDICTMENT
July 2, 1963

THE CHARGE
Murder

THE TRIAL
Among witnesses for the defense were three police officers who testified that on the night Evers was murdered in Jackson, De La Beckwith had been in Greenwood, about 96 miles away. On the witness stand, De La Beckwith stated that the murder weapon had belonged to him, but claimed that sometime before the killing it had been stolen.

THE SENTENCE
The trial ended with a hung jury. Prosecutors tried De La Beckwith again, and this ended in a hung jury, too.

AFTERWARD
In 1974, De La Beckwith was back in court, this time in Louisiana where he was accused of plotting to blow up the headquarters of the Anti-Defamation League in New Orleans. The jury found him guilty, and he was sentenced to three years in prison. By 1991, prosecutors were ready to indict De La Beckwith again; they had collected new evidence, including testimony of eyewitnesses over the years who had heard De La Beckwith brag about shooting Evers. In 1994, Byron De La Beckwith was convicted of murder and sentenced to life in prison, where he died in 2001.

MENAHEM MENDEL BEILIS

(1874–1934)

NATIONALITY
Russian

WHO WAS HE?
Menahem Mendel Beilis was a Jew who worked at a brick kiln in Kiev, Ukraine. Although his family was observant, he was not religious.

WHAT DID HE DO?
Beilis was accused of kidnapping a 13-year-old Ukrainian Christian boy, Andrei Yushchinsky, murdering him, mutilating the body, and draining the blood for use in making matzas.

DATE OF ARREST
July 21, 1911

CIRCUMSTANCES OF THE ARREST
After Yushchinsky disappeared in March, an investigation led police to the conclusion that he had been murdered by a gang of criminals operating in the area. In the meantime, several anti-Semitic newspapers and organizations, such as the Black Hundred, had begun a campaign claiming that the boy had been the victim of a ritual murder. In July, a lamplighter told police that he had seen a Jew from the brick kiln drag Yushchinsky away.

THE CHARGE
Ritual murder

THE TRIAL
Beilis was imprisoned for two years before he was brought to trial. Among witnesses testifying for the prosecution was a Catholic priest, Justin Pranaitis, who claimed that the wounds on Yushchinsky's body proved that he had been slaughtered according to rituals specified in the Talmud. The defense called as expert witnesses Rabbi Jacob Mazeh and Alexander Glagolev of the Kiev Theological Seminary, who showed that Pranaitis knew nothing about Judaism and that his claim that human blood was used in Jewish rituals was utterly false.

THE SENTENCE
After deliberating for several hours, the jury rendered a unanimous verdict of not guilty.

AFTERWARD
After the trial, Beilis and his family emigrated to Palestine—now modern-day Israel—then part of the Ottoman Empire. In 1920, the Beilis family emigrated to the United States.

UNUSUAL FACT
In 1966, the American author Bernard Malamud published a novel, *The Fixer*, based on the Beilis case. The book won the Pulitzer Prize for fiction.

NADJA BENAISSA

(1982–)

NATIONALITY
German

WHO IS SHE?
Nadja Benaissa is one of the founding members of the über-successful girl band, No Angels. She also produced her first solo pop album in 2006.

WHAT DID SHE DO?
Between 2004 and 2006, Benaissa had unprotected sex with three men without telling any of them that she was infected with the HIV virus.

DATE OF ARREST
April 11, 2009

CIRCUMSTANCES OF THE ARREST
Benaissa was preparing for a solo concert in Frankfurt when she was arrested by German police. At the time of her arrest, one of her sexual partners had tested positive for HIV.

THE CHARGE
Causing bodily harm

THE SENTENCE
Benaissa admitted in court that she had not told her sexual partners that she was HIV-positive. "I am truly sorry from the heart," she said. The judge found her guilty of causing bodily harm and gave her a two-year suspended sentence. Benaissa was obliged to perform 300 hours of community service with people infected with the HIV virus.

AFTERWARD
After her conviction, Nadja Benaissa left No Angels.

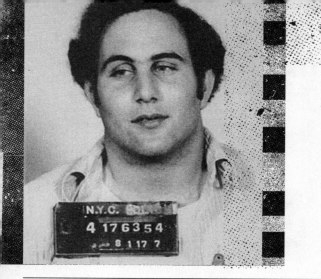

DAVID BERKOWITZ
(1953–)

NATIONALITY
American

WHO IS HE?
David Berkowitz was a U.S. Army veteran who worked for a time as a security guard before becoming a postal clerk. He lived in Yonkers, New York.

WHAT DID HE DO?
Between July 29, 1976, and July 31, 1977, Berkowitz shot and killed six young people and wounded seven, most of them dark-haired young women. A neighbor, named Sam Carr, had a noisy dog, which Berkowitz imagined was "a demon dog" that commanded him to murder young women.

THE LETTERS
Berkowitz sent several letters to *New York Daily News* columnist Jimmy Breslin, which Breslin published in his newspaper; Berkowitz signed the letters "Son of Sam." In one letter Berkowitz wrote, "Sam's a thirsty lad and he won't let me stop killing until he gets his fill of blood." He also wrote to Captain Joseph Borrelli of the New York Police Department. "I am the 'Monster'—'Beelzebub'—the chubby behemouth [sic]," he wrote. "The wemon [sic] of Queens are prettyist [sic] of all. It must be the water they drink."

DATE OF ARREST
August 10, 1977

CIRCUMSTANCES OF THE ARREST
New York City police got their first break the night Berkowitz attacked Stacy Moskowitz and Bobby Violante. He parked his car, a Ford Galaxie, illegally, blocking a fire hydrant. The car's license plate would lead the police to the Son of Sam. When the arresting officers asked Berkowitz, "What's your name?" he replied, "I'm Sam." Then he confessed to all the attacks and killings.

THE CHARGE
Murder

SENTENCE
On May 8, 1978, Berkowitz pleaded guilty to killing Stacy Moskowitz and attempting to kill Bobby Violante. Berkowitz was sentenced to 365 years in prison.

AFTERWARD
David Berkowitz was imprisoned in Attica. In 1979, a fellow inmate attacked him, slashing open his throat. The wound required 56 stitches, but Berkowitz survived.

THE MOVIE
Spike Lee made a film based on the Son of Sam murders: *Summer of Sam*, starring John Leguizamo and Mira Sorvino, which was released in 1999.

THE SELF-HELP TAPES
In prison, Berkowitz became an evangelical Christian. He released two self-help tapes, Son of Sam/Son of Hope and The Choice Is Yours, with David Berkowitz.

PAUL BERNARDO
(1964–)

KARLA HOMOLKA
(1970–)

NATIONALITY
Canadian

WHO ARE THEY?
Paul Bernardo and Karla Homolka both grew up in Ontario. At the time they met, Homolka was working as a veterinarian's assistant; Bernardo had lost his job at the accounting firm Price Waterhouse, and was earning a living smuggling cigarettes. They shared a taste for sado-masochistic sex.

WHAT DID THEY DO?
Bernardo raped at least 12 young women; he and Homolka kidnapped, tortured, and killed three—possibly four—young women. Their first victim was Homolka's 14-year-old sister, Tammy. Fifteen days before their wedding, they raped, killed, and dismembered a 14-year-old girl.

DATE OF ARREST
February 17, 1993

CIRCUMSTANCES OF THE ARREST
In January 1993, Bernardo had beaten Homolka with a flashlight. She walked out on him and went to the police. For 71 days, police searched the couple's home, but they failed to discover, hidden in a bathroom ceiling light fixture, videotapes of Bernardo and Homolka raping and torturing four of their victims. Later, the tapes would be collected by Ken Murray, Bernardo's lawyer; he kept them a secret for 16 months.

THE CHARGES
Bernardo: Kidnapping, aggravated sexual assault, and murder
Homolka: Manslaughter

THE TRIAL
Homolka cut a deal with the prosecution, agreeing to testify against her ex-husband (she divorced Bernardo in 1994, while in custody); in exchange, Homolka agreed to plead guilty to manslaughter and received a 12-year prison term. After the plea bargain had been finalized and Homolka's trial concluded, videotapes of the couple's crimes surfaced, showing that Homolka was more vicious than her husband in the torture and murder of their victims. There was a tremendous public outcry against what was called "the deal with the devil," but ultimately the Canadian judiciary insisted that the terms of the plea bargain must be honored.

THE SENTENCE
Bernardo was found guilty of two counts of first-degree murder and sentenced to life in prison with no chance of parole. Homolka was sentenced to 12 years and was released after 10.

AFTERWARD
In 2005, Karla Homolka was released from prison. She adopted a new name, Leanne Teale, and in 2007 gave birth to a baby boy. Paul Bernardo is still in prison.

CHUCK BERRY

(1926–)

NATIONALITY
American

WHO IS HE?
Hailed as one of the founding fathers of rock 'n' roll, Chuck Berry was an inspired songwriter, a great guitarist, and a mesmerizing performer. His hits include "Maybellene," "Johnny B. Goode," and "Roll Over Beethoven."

WHAT DID HE DO?
In Mexico, Berry met Janice Escalanti, 14 years old at the time, and offered her a job as a hat-check girl at his nightclub outside St. Louis, Missouri. When local authorities discovered that the hat-check girl was also freelancing as a prostitute, they charged Berry with transporting a minor across state lines for immoral purposes.

DATE OF ARREST
December 23, 1959

THE CHARGE.
Violation of the Mann Act

THE TRIAL
At the trial, Escalanti testified that on the trip from Mexico to St. Louis she and Berry shared hotel rooms and had sex many times. Berry admitted to sharing rooms with her, but insisted that he had not had sex with the girl. When asked why he brought Escalanti to St. Louis, Berry said, "She needed a job and I had a job for her in the club."

THE SENTENCE
The jury convicted Berry and he was sentenced to pay a $5,000 fine and serve five years in prison. That conviction was vacated because of racist comments the judge made in court. In his new trial, Berry was found guilty once again and sentenced to two years in prison; he served 20 months before he was paroled.

AFTERWARD
A friend described Berry after his release from prison as "cold, real distant, and bitter." But he was not washed up. British music fans had discovered Berry, so he began touring in the UK. He wrote more hit singles, including "Nadine."

BACK TO PRISON
In 1979, Chuck Berry was in court again—on charges of income tax evasion. He was sentenced to 4 months in jail.

HALLE BERRY

(1966–)

NATIONALITY
American

WHO IS SHE?
Halle Berry is an actress and former beauty queen. For her title performance in *Introducing Dorothy Dandridge* she won an Oscar for Best Actress, as well as an Emmy, a Golden Globe, a SAG Award, and an NAACP Image Award.

WHAT DID SHE DO?
At 2:30 in the morning of February 23, 2000, Berry drove through a red light, smashing her Chevy Blazer into a Pontiac Sunfire driven by Heta Raythatha, a real estate agent and accountant. After totaling Raythatha's car, Berry drove off. Later, while Raythatha waited for treatment for her injuries in the emergency room of Cedars-Sinai Medical Center, she saw Berry walk by, a small bandage on her forehead. At the time, Raythatha did not know that Berry had hit her car.

THE INJURIES
Raythatha's wrist was broken in several places, and her back and neck were injured. Berry gashed her forehead, requiring 22 stitches.

DATE OF INDICTMENT
March 31, 2000

THE CHARGE AND INDICTMENT
Charge: Leaving the scene of an accident
Indictment: Berry was indicted on this misdemeanor charge rather than felony hit-and-run because at the hospital she reported the accident to the police.

THE SENTENCE
Berry pled guilty to leaving the scene of an accident. She was fined $13,500, sentenced to three years' probation, and required to perform 200 hours of community service. Raythatha filed a civil suit against Berry, which was settled out of court; the details of the settlement were not disclosed to the public.

RAINEY BETHEA

(1909/1913–1936)

NATIONALITY
American

WHO WAS HE?
Rainey Bethea was born in Roanoke, Virginia. By 1933, he had moved to Owensboro, Kentucky, where he supported himself as a laborer. Several times between 1933 and 1936 he was arrested for theft.

WHAT DID HE DO?
Early in the morning of June 7, 1936, a drunken Rainey Bethea climbed through 70-year-old Lischia Rarick Edwards's bedroom window. Later he told police that he had intended only to steal Edwards's jewelry, but while he rifled through her things, she woke up. Before the woman could call for help, Bethea wrapped his hands around her throat to silence her. Then he raped and murdered her. He wrapped the jewelry in one of Edwards's dresses and climbed out the window.

DATE OF ARREST
June 10, 1936

CIRCUMSTANCES OF THE ARREST
Bethea had been barefoot when he entered Edwards's room—police found his muddy footprints on the roof outside the victim's window, as well as his fingerprints on Edwards's bed. And there was one more piece of evidence: Before leaving the house, Bethea had tried on one of Mrs. Edwards's rings, leaving behind his black celluloid prison ring.

THE CHARGE
Rape

WHY NOT MURDER?
In Kentucky in 1936, a convicted rapist was hanged in public, but a convicted murderer was executed in private in the electric chair. The prosecutors preferred to see Bethea punished in public, so they indicted him solely on charges of rape.

THE SENTENCE
The jury found Bethea guilty of rape. He was sentenced to be hanged.

THE SHERIFF
At the time of the Bethea case, the local sheriff was a woman, Florence Thompson. For the first time in American history a female sheriff would supervise the execution of a male criminal. Newspapers across the country speculated that Thompson would be required to be Bethea's hangman.

THE EXECUTION
A crowd estimated at between 15,000 and 20,000 crowded into Owensboro on the morning of August 14, 1936, to witness the execution. Florence Thompson still had not revealed to reporters if she would execute Bethea personally. She did take her place on the scaffold with other witnesses, but it was a former policeman, Arthur Hash, who had been designated to spring the trapdoor beneath Bethea's feet. Hash arrived at the scaffold severely drunk. When the moment for the execution arrived, Hash could not operate the lever, so one of Sheriff Thompson's deputies released the trapdoor.

THE SIGNIFICANCE
Rainey Bethea's hanging was the last public execution in the United States.

STEPHEN BIKO

(1946–1977)

NATIONALITY
South African

WHO IS HE?
Stephen Biko was the founder of the South African Students' Organization, which provided legal aid and medical clinics for black South Africans. He was an outspoken critic of South Africa's apartheid system, which led the government to "ban," or confine him to his hometown, King William's Town in the Eastern Cape.

WHAT DID HE DO?
In spite of his confinement, Biko continued to agitate for an end to apartheid. The government believed he was behind many of the strikes and anti-apartheid riots that swept across South Africa in 1976 and 1977.

DATE OF ARREST
August 18, 1977

CIRCUMSTANCES OF THE ARREST
South African police arrested Biko and a fellow activist, Peter Cyril Jones, at a roadblock close to King William's Town, and took him to a jail in Port Elizabeth.

THE CHARGE
Violation of the Terrorism Act

THE INTERROGATION
Stephen Biko was never tried. During his interrogation, he was severely beaten and fell into a coma. Physicians who examined Biko recommended that he be taken to Pretoria for medical treatment; he died at the Pretoria hospital.

AFTERWARD
Initially, the South African government claimed that Biko had died of starvation while on a hunger strike. Eventually, the autopsy report was published, revealing that Biko had died of injuries to the brain caused by "application of force to the head." The officers who had arrested and interrogated Biko were tried, but were acquitted by the court.

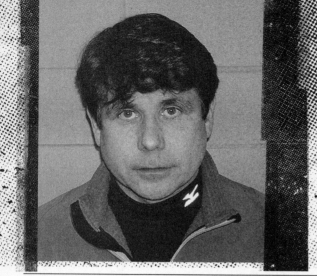

ROD BLAGOJEVICH
(1956–)

NATIONALITY
American

WHO IS HE?
Rod Blagojevich was born in Chicago, the son of immigrants from Serbia. He married Patricia Mell, the daughter of a Chicago alderman, Richard Mell. Through his father-in-law's influence, Blagojevich was introduced to Chicago and Illinois politics. He served as a state representative, then as a member of the House of Representatives. Blagojevich was elected governor of Illinois in 2002 and 2006.

WHAT DID HE DO?
Blagojevich was charged with political corruption, such as awarding state contracts and granting state permits in exchange for campaign contributions. Most famously, Blagojevich was charged with attempting to sell to the highest bidder President-elect Barack Obama's vacated seat in the U.S. Senate. Exactly one month after his arrest, the Illinois House of Representatives voted to impeach Blagojevich and removed him from office.

DATE OF ARREST
December 9, 2008

CIRCUMSTANCES OF THE ARREST
Before dawn, police came to Blagojevich's home to arrest him. The governor was taken in handcuffs before a federal magistrate where he was charged, then released on his own recognizance.

THE CHARGES
Conspiracy to commit wire fraud and solicitation to commit bribery

THE TRIAL
On August 17, 2010, after deliberating for 14 days, the federal jury that heard the Blagojevich case returned a guilty verdict on one count of lying to the FBI. On the 23 other counts of the indictment, the jury was deadlocked.

AFTERMATH
Prosecutors announced that they would seek a new trial on the 23 counts that produced a hung jury.

ROBERT BLAKE

(1933–)

NATIONALITY
American

WHO IS HE?
Robert Blake is an Emmy Award-winning actor best remembered for his TV detective series *Baretta* and his performance as Perry Smith in the 1967 film *In Cold Blood*.

WHAT DID HE DO?
On May 4, 2001, Blake's wife, Bonny Lee Bakley, was shot and killed while sitting in her car outside a Los Angeles restaurant. Almost one year later, police arrested Blake and charged him with murdering his wife.

DATE OF ARREST
April 18, 2002

CIRCUMSTANCES OF THE ARREST
Blake had admitted openly that he and Bakley had been lovers and that when she became pregnant, she coerced him into marrying her. The marriage was not a success, although Blake loved the daughter he and Bakley had together. Police suspected that Blake had tried to hire a hit man to kill Bakley, but when that failed he killed her himself.

THE CHARGE
Murder

THE CRIMINAL TRIAL
After deliberating for nine days, the jury found Blake not guilty. Blake burst into tears and embraced his attorney.

THE CIVIL TRIAL
On April 29, 2002, attorneys representing the children of Bonny Lee Bakley filed a civil law suit that accused Robert Blake of causing the death of their mother. The jury found Blake liable and awarded the children $30 million. Blake appealed the verdict. In 2008, a Los Angeles court upheld the verdict, but cut the monetary award to $15 million.

YASMINE BLEETH

(1968–)

NATIONALITY

American

WHO IS SHE?

Yasmine Bleeth appeared in a baby shampoo commercial when she was ten months old. From 1994 to 1997, she played a lifeguard in the long-running action drama series, *Baywatch*. In 1995, she was included in *People* magazine's list of "The 50 Most Beautiful People."

WHAT DID SHE DO?

Bleeth was driving a rental car on Interstate-94 near Romulus, Michigan, when she lost control of the vehicle and crashed into a highway median.

DATE OF ARREST

September 12, 2001

CIRCUMSTANCES OF THE ARREST

When police arrived on the scene, they gave Bleeth field sobriety tests, which she failed. They found four syringes in her purse, one of which contained traces of cocaine.

THE CHARGES

Cocaine possession and operating a vehicle under the influence of narcotics

THE SENTENCE

Bleeth pled guilty to possessing less than 25 grams of cocaine and driving while impaired. The judge sentenced her to two years' probation, and ordered her to submit to regular drug tests and perform 100 hours of community service.

THE CONFESSION

In April 2003, *Glamour* magazine published an article by Bleeth about her recovery from drug addiction, titled, "Back from My Drugs Hell."

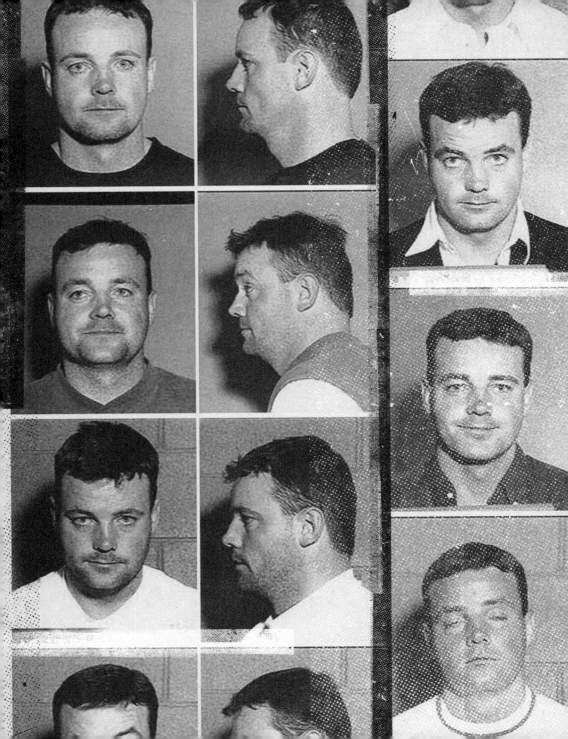

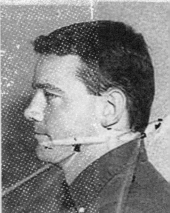

JOHN WAYNE BOBBITT

(1968–)

NATIONALITY

American

WHO IS HE?

John Wayne Bobbit was a former Marine lance corporal whose name became a punch line after his wife, Lorena, sliced off his penis. Shortly after the couple's trials (John was tried and found not guilty of malicious assault against his wife; Lorena was tried and found not guilty of malicious wounding against her husband), John moved to Las Vegas where he became engaged to a stripper named Kristina Elliott.

WHAT DID HE DO?

Elliott accused John of throwing her against a wall.

DATE OF ARREST

May 6, 1994

THE CHARGE

Assault

AWAITING TRIAL

John pled not guilty and was released on bail. He announced to a crowd of reporters that the penis reattachment surgery had been a complete success. "It's like it was before," he said. "There's no problem." In June 1994, John acknowledged that he was the father of a 17-month-old boy and reached a financial settlement with the child's mother, Beatrice L. Williams of Niagara Falls, New York.

THE SENTENCE

John was convicted of misdemeanor assault. The judge sentenced him to 60 days in jail, but suspended 45 days. He ordered John to join Alcoholics Anonymous.

THE FILMS

In 1994, John starred in an adult film, *John Wayne Bobbitt: Uncut*. He made another adult film, *Frankenpenis*, in 1996, the same year he was ordained a minister by the Universal Life Church.

AFTERWARD

John had recurring troubles with the law. In 1999, he was convicted of grand larceny and of harassing an ex-girlfriend; in 2002, his wife accused him of punching her; in 2004, his wife accused him of punching her and her 14-year-old son (John was acquitted of that charge).

LORENA BOBBITT

(1970–)

NATIONALITY
Ecuadorian-born American citizen

WHO IS SHE?
Lorena Bobbitt emigrated to the United States from Ecuador. In 1989, she married John Wayne Bobbitt. They lived in an apartment in Manassas, Virginia. She worked as a manicurist; John as a bouncer at a nightclub.

WHAT DID SHE DO?
Lorena alleged that John returned home from a party at about 3:00 in the morning of June 23, 1993; he was drunk. When they went to bed, he raped her. Lorena climbed out of bed and went into the kitchen, where she saw an eight-inch-long carving knife lying on the counter. She took the knife, went back to the bedroom, and cut off John's penis. Then she left the apartment.

DATE OF ARREST
June 23, 1993

CIRCUMSTANCES OF THE ARREST
When Lorena drove away from the apartment complex, she still had John's penis in her hand. She tossed it out the car window, into a field near a 7-Eleven convenience store. Then she pulled over, called 911, and waited for the police to come.

THE CHARGE
Malicious wounding

THE SURGERY
The Bobbitts had a houseguest, Robert Johnston. John woke up Johnston and asked him to drive him to the emergency room. In the car John said, "They better be able to make me a new penis." At the hospital, a urologist, Dr. James T. Sehn, informed John that unless the penis was found, his only option was to suture the stump. Soon thereafter, the police arrived with John's penis, packed in ice. Dr. Sehn called in Dr. David E. Berman, a microsurgeon, and after nearly ten hours of surgery they succeeded in reattaching John's penis.

THE TRIAL
In court, Lorena claimed that she had been a victim of sexual and physical abuse. Her defense attorney argued that on the night of the incident she suffered a bout of temporary insanity and succumbed to an "irresistible impulse" to punish her husband.

THE SENTENCE
After deliberating for six hours, the jury concluded that Lorena had been temporarily insane when she cut off John's penis. They found her not guilty. The court required her to submit to a psychiatric examination; after several weeks, she was released from the hospital.

AFTERWARD
The Bobbitts divorced in 1994. Lorena became a licensed real estate agent and an advocate against domestic violence.

AMY MAUD BOCK

(1859–1943)

NATIONALITY
New Zealander

WHO WAS SHE?
Amy Maud Bock was born in Tasmania and lived in several locations in Australia before settling in New Zealand in the mid-1880s. She took jobs as a governess, a housekeeper, or a companion, and invariably delighted her employers with her efficiency and charming personality. Only later would they discover that Bock was a con artist and a thief who had a penchant for pawning her employers' belongings—usually small items such as jewelry, but, on at least one occasion, a room full of furniture.

WHAT DID SHE DO?
In 1908, in Port Molyneux, Bock presented herself as a young man, a wealthy sheepfarmer named Percival Leonard Carol Redwood. She courted a young woman named Agnes Ottaway, and married her in a lavish ceremony.

DATE OF ARREST
April 25, 1909

CIRCUMSTANCES OF THE ARREST
Four days after the wedding, the bride revealed to her family that her "husband" was a woman. Police arrested Bock at the Ottaway family home.

THE CHARGES
False pretenses and forgery

THE SENTENCE
Bock was found guilty and sentenced to two years in prison. The Ottaways had the marriage annulled.

AFTERWARD
Amy Maud Bock continued her life as a con artist, making her last appearance in court in 1931. The judge gave the 72-year-old crook a suspended sentence, but ordered her to spend the rest of her life in a Salvation Army home for the elderly.

WHAT DID HE DO?

Relying on insider information about companies that were about to be sold or taken over, he bought or sold large blocks of the endangered companies' stock. From these transactions, Boesky accumulated a personal fortune estimated at about $200 million.

DATE OF ARREST

November 14, 1986

THE CHARGE

Insider trading

THE PLEA DEAL

Boesky's attorneys reached an agreement with the feds: He would serve 22 months in prison, pay a fine of $100 million, and never work in the securities market again.

AFTERWARD

At Boesky's request, the Jewish Theological Seminary removed his name from the school's library building. After his release from prison, Boesky took classes at the seminary. He has remained out of the public eye.

IVAN BOESKY

(1937–)

NATIONALITY

American

WHO IS HE?

Ivan Boesky was one of the wealthiest and most successful stock traders in the United States in the mid-1980s. The offices of Boesky Corp. were located in midtown Manhattan; he had a 200-acre estate outside New York. He and his wife, Seema Silberstein, gave lavishly to charity, including the Jewish Theological Seminary and the Harvard School of Public Health.

DANNY BONADUCE

(1959–)

NATIONALITY
American

WHO IS HE?
At age 11, Danny Bonaduce was cast as Danny Partridge, the wise-cracking, wise-beyond-his-years kid on *The Partridge Family*. From 1970 to 1974, the show was one of the most successful musical sitcoms on television.

WHAT DID HE DO?
On March 31, 1991, Bonaduce, who was under the influence of something, was driving in Phoenix, Arizona, when he pulled over to pick up a hooker. Once he could see "her" in the light, Bonaduce realized that he had just picked up a transvestite. He ordered the transvestite, named Darius Barney, out of the car, but Barney refused to leave until Bonaduce paid him $40 for his time. Bonaduce climbed out, pulled Barney from the car, and attacked him.

BONADUCE'S RATIONALE
Later Bonaduce described the scene this way: "When I [pulled him out of the car], I see he's this huge guy, about 220 pounds. I weighed 150 pounds! I attacked him first, not because I wanted to, I just thought I was going to have to and I'm too small to take the punishment from a 220-pound man. If he had hit first, I would have gone down and stayed down. So I attacked him and it turned into a fight."

DATE OF ARREST
March 31, 1991

THE CHARGES
Assault and battery

THE SENTENCE
The judge placed Bonaduce on probation. But executives at KKFR in Phoenix, where Bonaduce hosted a radio program, fired him.

AFTERWARD
It spite of recurring problems with alcohol and drugs, including steroids, Bonaduce seems always to land on his feet, particularly in reality TV, where he has starred in *Breaking Bonaduce* and *Re-inventing Bonaduce*.

WILLIAM BONIN, "THE FREEWAY KILLER"

(1947–1996)

NATIONALITY
American

WHO IS HE?
William Bonin was a convicted sex offender who had served five years at the Atascadero State Hospital, in Atascadero, California, in the early 1970s. He was released on probation, but was sent back to prison after he kidnapped and raped two teenage boys. In 1978, he was a free man again.

WHAT DID HE DO?
Between 1978 and 1980, Bonin abducted, raped, and murdered 21 teenage boys and young men. Typically, he disposed of the bodies in out-of-the-way-spots, such as construction site dumpsters, or behind gas stations along the highways of southern California. Before Bonin's identity was revealed, this serial murderer was known as "the Freeway Killer."

DATE OF ARREST
June 11, 1980

CIRCUMSTANCES OF THE ARREST
In June 1980, the police got a break: A suspect arrested for auto theft said that he believed that he had met the Freeway Killer. He had been given a ride by a man named William Bonin. Bonin never admitted to being the Freeway Killer, but the glove compartment of his van was stuffed with articles about the murders clipped from newspapers. The police traced Bonin and arrested him in his van as he was raping his latest victim.

THE ACCOMPLICES
Bonin bragged about his exploits to at least four friends: Vernon Butts, Gregory Miley, James,Michael Munro, and Billy Pugh.

THE CHARGES
Attempted abduction, molestation, murder, rape, and sexual assault

THE SENTENCE
Bonin was found guilty and given the death penalty. For 16 years, his attorneys filed appeals on his behalf. When the appeals process was exhausted, William Bonin was executed by lethal injection.

THE FATE OF THE ACCOMPLICES
Vernon Butts hanged himself in jail before his trial began. Gregory Miley was sentenced to 25 years to life in prison. James Michael Munro was sentenced to 15 years to life. Billy Pugh was sentenced to 6 years in prison.

BRIAN BONSALL

(1981–)

THE CHARGE
Assault

OUTSTANDING CHARGES
In 2007, after a domestic dispute with his girlfriend, Bonsall was charged with assault, false imprisonment, and interfering with a phone call that his girlfriend was making to the police. He skipped his court date in Boulder, Colorado, and was regarded as a fugitive.

THE SENTENCE
In the Trujillo case, Bonsall pled guilty to menacing and assault. He also pled guilty to assaulting his girlfriend. He was sentenced to five days in a work-release program and ordered to perform 40 hours of community service.

NATIONALITY
American

WHO IS HE?
Brian Bonsall is an actor who played Andy, the youngest child on the TV sitcom, *Family Ties*, which starred Michael J. Fox.

WHAT DID HE DO?
During a night of heavy drinking in an apartment in Colorado, Bonsall got into an argument with a friend, Michael Trujillo, grabbed a broken wooden barstool, and hit Trujillo in the face.

DATE OF ARREST
December 5, 2009

CIRCUMSTANCES OF THE ARREST
The police report recorded Bonsall's explanation of the incident: "Bonsall then said that he and Trujillo both are bipolar and like drugs. Bonsall said that he takes a lot of drugs and sometimes those drugs make him forget things."

LIZZIE BORDEN

(1860–1927)

NATIONALITY
American

WHO WAS SHE?
Lizzie Borden was the younger of Andrew Borden's two unmarried daughters. Her father was a prominent, well-to-do businessman in Fall River, Massachusetts, yet the family lived in a modest wood-frame house. In 1892, she was 32, unmarried, living in her father's house with her sister, Emma, and their stepmother, Abby. Her entertainments were limited to attending meetings of the Women's Christian Temperance Society and various committees of her Congregational church.

WHAT DID SHE DO?
According to the indictment, on the morning of August 4, 1892, Lizzie Borden took an axe and attacked her stepmother, killing her with 18 or 19 blows to the head. Then she went downstairs to the sitting room where her father was resting on a sofa. She murdered him with ten blows to the head and face.

DATE OF ARREST
August 11, 1892

CIRCUMSTANCES OF THE ARREST
Police officers interviewed the Bordens' friends and neighbors who repeated tales of quarrels and resentments in the family, particularly Lizzie's dislike for her stepmother. On August 7, 1892, Emma and a friend observed Lizzie burning, in the kitchen stove, the dress she was wearing at the time of the murders. Four days later, after a closed inquest, police arrested Lizzie Borden for the murder of her father and stepmother.

THE CHARGE
Double murder

THE SENTENCE
At the trial, the prosecution's evidence was entirely circumstantial; there was no physical evidence that linked Lizzie to the crime. As for Lizzie, she was represented by one of the best attorneys in Fall River, and she had the sympathy of her fellow citizens and the press behind her. It was unthinkable that a woman from such a distinguished family could commit murder. On June 20, 1892, the jury found Lizzie Borden not guilty.

AFTERWARD
In the years after her acquittal, the public came to the conclusion that Lizzie Borden had indeed killed her father and stepmother. Although she and Emma moved into a new house in a fashionable section of Fall River, Lizzie was frozen out of local society. To break up the monotony of life as a recluse, she made occasional trips to Boston and Washington, D.C., and she made new friends among actors and actresses, such as the renowned Nance O'Neill. She died on June 1, 1927. Nine days later Emma died. Both sisters are buried in the Borden family plot, beside their father and stepmother.

UNUSUAL FACT
Contrary to the popular rhyme, Lizzie Borden did not give her mother 40 whacks and her father 41. According to the coroner, the number of whacks Andrew and Abby Borden received totaled 28 or 29.

MOHAMMED BOUYERI

(1978–)

NATIONALITY
Possesses dual Dutch and Moroccan citizenship

WHO IS HE?
Mohammed Bouyeri's parents emigrated from Morocco to the Netherlands; Bouyeri was born in Amsterdam. After his mother's death in 2003, Bouyeri became a fervent Muslim. He associated with Islamic extremists and became prominent in the Islamic terrorist organization, the Hofstad Group.

WHAT DID HE DO?
On November 2, 2004, Bouyeri ambushed Theo van Gogh, a Dutch filmmaker and outspoken critic of fundamentalist Islam. He had recently made a film, *Submission*, which was critical of how women are treated under Islamic law. As van Gogh pedaled his bicycle down an Amsterdam street, Bouyeri attacked him, shooting, stabbing, and killing him. Using his knife, he pinned a letter to van Gogh's chest in which he threatened the life of a Somali-born member of the Dutch Parliament, Ayaan Hirsi Ali.

DATE OF ARREST
November 2, 2004

CIRCUMSTANCES OF THE ARREST
Police found Bouyeri shortly after he had murdered van Gogh. A brief gun battle ensued, during which Bouyeri was wounded in the leg.

THE CHARGES
Murder, attempted murder, and illegal possession of firearms

THE SENTENCE
The court found Bouyeri guilty of the murder of van Gogh, the attempted murder of the police officers and bystanders, and the weapons charge. He was sentenced to life in prison with no chance of parole.

AFTERWARD
Mohammed Bouyeri has never expressed any remorse for killing Theo van Gogh.

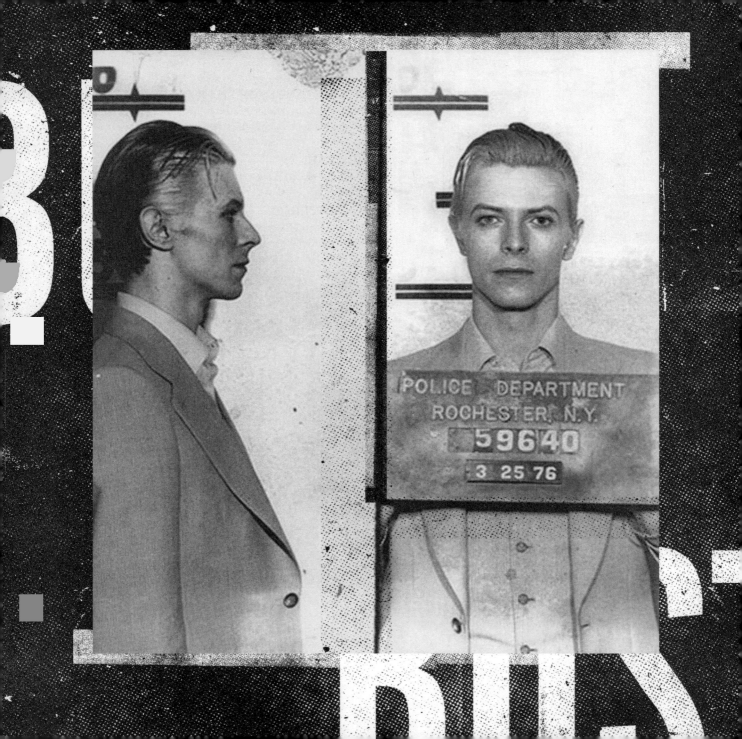

POLICE DEPARTMENT
ROCHESTER, N.Y.
59640
3 25 76

DAVID BOWIE

(1947–)

NATIONALITY
English

WHO IS HE?
David Bowie is a rock megastar whose song "Fame" (which he co-wrote with John Lennon) became a number-one hit single. He has had many hit singles and hit albums and won countless awards. He is hailed as an innovator in glam rock, art rock, and blue-eyed soul.

WHAT DID HE DO?
Bowie had half a pound of marijuana in his suite at the Americana Rochester Hotel in Rochester, New York.

DATE OF ARREST
March 21, 1976

CIRCUMSTANCES OF THE ARREST
Bowie was arrested with three other people, including Iggy Pop. The four were released after each posted $2,000 bail. Bowie's mug shot was not taken until four days later, when he came to Rochester City Court to plead innocent.

THE CHARGE
Drug possession

THE SENTENCE
The case was adjourned, and a year later the charges were dropped.

NAME CHANGE
Bowie was born David Jones, and he originally appeared as Davy Jones. He was often confused with the other Davy Jones, of the Monkees, so he renamed himself David Bowie.

BELLE BOYD, "THE CLEOPATRA OF THE SECESSION"

(1843–1900)

NATIONALITY
American

WHO WAS SHE?
Belle Boyd was a Confederate patriot who was distantly related to George Randolph, the Confederacy's secretary of war. She grew up in Martinsburg, Virginia (now West Virginia), where her father operated a store and a tobacco farm.

WHAT DID SHE DO?
In 1861, Boyd began spying for the Confederacy, reporting on activities of the Union army in the Shenandoah Valley. She obtained most of her information by flirting with Union officers. She wrote her messages in code and enclosed them inside a large pocket watch, which she entrusted to an elderly slave. He delivered the messages either to General Stonewall Jackson or General Jeb Stuart.

DATE OF ARREST
July 1863

CIRCUMSTANCES OF THE ARREST
Boyd was arrested on orders from the U.S. Secretary of War Edwin Stanton. She was taken from her family's home in Martinsburg to Carroll Prison, also known as the Old Capitol Prison, in Washington, D.C. In prison, she antagonized her guards by singing "Dixie" and flying a Confederate flag from the window of her cell.

THE CHARGE
Espionage

RELEASE
Boyd was never tried. After three months' imprisonment, she fell seriously ill with typhoid fever. She was released and given a pass through the Union lines to Richmond, Virginia.

AFTERWARD
In 1864, while sailing to England, Boyd's ship was stopped and boarded by a Union vessel. Boyd was recognized and arrested as a Confederate courier. She escaped by seducing Union Lieutenant Sam Hardinge, who brought her to safety in Canada; several weeks later they married. After the war, Boyd published her memoirs, which exaggerated her adventures as a Confederate spy. She went on the lecture circuit, billing herself as "the Cleopatra of the Secession."

ways exercising the greatest caution that no one should learn of the connection between us. To the world we

[newspaper clipping text, partially legible:]

chief of the secret service, and McDonald to aid me. With these two I went over the plan of capture, al...

...large sum of counterfeit money, day following counterfeit money resenting $117,437 was found hidde the heavy woods seven miles nortl Centralia, where Driggs had conce it just before being taken into cust

Ben Boyd was tried before Ju Blodgett in the United States dist court, in Chicago, and was defer by Judge Tuley. He was sentence ten years in the Joliet penitenti Driggs was tried in Springfield be Judge Treat and was sentenced t years in the penitentiary. The co terfeiters' wives were released; Cha Stadtfeldt received an eight-year tence, Nicholas Lange, a helper the printing press, was sentenced four years, and old man Stadtfeldt released. The "backbone of coun feiting" in the country was broken

PART II.

In order to give the actors in Lincoln tomb robbing plot their pl er places before my readers it wil necessary again to wander briefly f the straight path of my story. In early '70's it was as easy for a se service operative to find traces counterfeiters as it is for a fisher to get a bite in a Wisconsin fish l It was sometimes as difficult to l the "koniacker" as it is for the fis man to land his bass; but the cen west teemed with "coney men," n or less known to the secret serv The custom of intermarriage am

BENJAMIN BOYD.

BENJAMIN BOYD

(1834– ?)

NATIONALITY
American

WHO WAS HE?
Benjamin Boyd was the son of a legitimate master engraver who apprenticed him to one of the best engravers in their hometown, Cincinnati, Ohio. While still in his teens, Boyd became acquainted with counterfeiters. At age 21, he engraved his first counterfeit plate; it was of such high quality that Boyd never returned to legitimate engraving.

WHAT DID HE DO?
In the 1870s, Boyd was in Illinois, engraving top-quality plates for counterfeit currency for an Irish immigrant crime boss named Big Jim Kennally. By 1875, he was one of the most notorious counterfeiters in the United States. From just one plate he printed 6,000 counterfeit $50 bills. Boyd's success made him a target of the Secret Service (in the 1870s, the Secret Service hunted down counterfeiters; it did not provide security to the president).

DATE OF ARREST
October 21, 1875

CIRCUMSTANCES OF THE ARREST
Detective Patrick Tyrrell, with several other Secret Service agents, surrounded Boyd's house, then entered it unannounced. Inside, Tyrrell and his fellow agents found $117,000 in counterfeit currency and a treasure trove of engraved plates.

THE CHARGE
Counterfeiting

THE SENTENCE
Boyd was sentenced to ten years in the prison in Joliet, Illinois.

THE PLOT
In an effort to spring his best engraver from prison, Big Jim Kennally plotted to steal the body of Abraham Lincoln from its grave, then make the governor of Illinois an offer: In exchange for a full pardon for Benjamin Boyd—and $200,000 in cash—Big Jim would return Lincoln's body, safe and unharmed. And the scheme almost worked.

AFTERWARD
Benjamin Boyd served his full term in Joliet, then he vanishes from the historical record. It was commonplace among criminals in the 19th century to move to a different part of the country, assume an alias, and begin a new life; very likely, this is what Boyd did after his release.

CHRISTIAN BRANDO
(1958–2008)

NATIONALITY
American

WHO WAS HE?
Christian Brando was the eldest of the nine children of acting legend Marlon Brando. He was a high school dropout who had tried careers as an actor, a welder, a tree trimmer, and a barge pilot.

WHAT DID HE DO?
Brando's half-sister, Cheyenne, claimed that her lover, Dag Drollet, was beating her. Brando took a gun and confronted Drollet. When Drollet made a move to grab the gun, it went off and killed him.

DATE OF ARREST
May 17, 1990

THE CHARGE
Murder

THE TRIAL
Marlon Brando took the witness stand to appeal for clemency for his son. Weeping, he told the court, "I think that perhaps I failed as a father. I'm certain that there were things that I could have done differently, had I known better at the time. But I didn't."

THE SENTENCE
Brando pled guilty to voluntary manslaughter. He was sentenced to ten years in prison. After serving five years, he was released and placed on three years' probation.

AFTERWARD
In 1995, Cheyenne Brando hanged herself in Tahiti. In the late 1990s, Brando had an affair with Bonny Lee Bakley, the future wife of actor Robert Blake. In 2000, when Bakley gave birth to a daughter, Bakley claimed the baby was Christian Brando's child; a paternity test proved that Robert Blake was the father. Marlon Brando died in 2004; Christian Brando died in 2008 of pneumonia.

CHRIS BROWN

(1989–)

NATIONALITY
American

WHO IS HE?
Chris Brown is a singer, songwriter, dancer, and actor. At age 16, his single, "Run It!" from his debut album *Chris Brown*, spent five weeks in the number-one spot on Billboard's Hot 100.

WHAT DID HE DO?
Brown and his girlfriend, Rihanna, quarreled about a lengthy text message he received from one of his employees with whom he had a fling. According to the search warrant affidavit, Brown shouted, "I'm going to beat the shit out of you when we get home." When Brown put Rihanna in a headlock, she responded by trying to gouge out his eyes, then he bit her fingers.

DATE OF ARREST
February 8, 2009

CIRCUMSTANCES OF THE ARREST
When a stranger, who overheard the fight called 911, Brown drove off. Later he turned himself in at the Los Angeles Police Department's Wilshire station.

THE CHARGE
Felony assault

THE SENTENCE
Brown was sentenced to six months of community labor, such as removing graffiti, and five years probation. He was ordered to attend domestic violence classes for a year, and was forbidden to have any contact with Rihanna for five years.

AFTERWARD
Brown was conscientious about fulfilling the terms of his sentence. He apologized publicly for assaulting Rihanna, and the judge who sentenced him declared that she was pleased with his progress. However, in December 2009, Brown had a major meltdown, via his Twitter account, when he entered a Walmart in Wallingford, Connecticut, and could not find his new CD, *Graffiti*. "I'm tired of this shit," he tweeted. "Major stores r blackballing my CD. Not stockin the shelves and lying to costumers. What the fuck do I gotta do." Walmart's management released a statement saying that all their stores stocked *Graffiti*, and the Wallingford store had sold out of all its copies.

ONE YEAR LATER
In 2010, one year after Chris Brown assaulted her, Rihanna won two Grammys for "Run This Town."

FOXY BROWN

(1979–)

NATIONALITY
American

WHO IS SHE?
Born and raised in Brooklyn, New York, Foxy Brown is a rapper whose albums include *Ill Na Na* and *Brooklyn's Don Diva*. She has had many run-ins with the law.

WHAT DID SHE DO?
Brown got into an argument with a woman who wanted Brown to reduce the volume of her car stereo. The argument escalated to a fight, with Brown striking the woman with a cell phone. The assault violated the terms of Brown's probation, dating from another fight three years earlier between Brown and two manicurists in a New York City salon.

WHAT ELSE DID SHE DO?
Without notifying or gaining the permission of her probation officer, Brown moved from Brooklyn to Mahwah, New Jersey. She failed to report to her probation officer and she dropped out of a court-ordered anger management program.

DATE OF ARREST
August 14, 2007

THE CHARGES
Assault and probation violation

THE SENTENCE
The judge sentenced Brown to one year in jail.

ANOTHER CASE PENDING
In February 2007, while on a trip to Florida, Brown threw hair glue at a beauty salon employee who informed her that the store was closing.

LEGAL TROUBLES
Foxy Brown has been arrested in Raleigh, North Carolina for spitting on two hotel workers. After using obscene language during a concert in Trinidad and Tobago, police escorted her off the stage. In Jamaica, she punched a policewoman in the stomach; Jamaican authorities did not arrest her, but banned her from the country.

JAMES BROWN

(1933–2006)

NATIONALITY
American

WHO WAS HE?
"The Godfather of Soul," James Brown had a music career that spanned almost half a century. His Top Ten hits included "Papa's Got a Brand New Bag" and "I Feel Good," which became his signature songs.

WHAT DID HE DO?
Police responded to a complaint that Brown had disrupted an insurance class that was in progress in a building he owned in Augusta, Georgia. When Brown spotted the police, he sped away in his pickup truck. During the chase, which began in Georgia, crossed the Savannah River into South Carolina, then returned to Georgia again, police alleged that Brown tried to ram their patrol cars with his truck.

DATE OF ARREST
September 24, 1988

CIRCUMSTANCES OF THE ARREST
The police brought the chase to an end by shooting out two of Brown's tires.

THE CHARGES
In Georgia, Brown was charged with assault, illegal possession of a weapon (he had a shotgun in his truck), and traffic violations. In South Carolina, Brown was charged with assault and battery with intent to kill, drunk driving, and traffic violations.

THE SENTENCE
Brown was convicted of aggravated assault and failing to stop for a police officer. He was sentenced to six years and six months in prison, but was released after serving three years.

AFTERWARD
After his release, Brown had further run-ins with the law, including several arrests for domestic violence. His third wife, Adrienne Rodriguez, filed four complaints against him, and his girlfriend, Tomi Rae Hynie, brought one.

JOHN BROWN

(1800–1859)

NATIONALITY
American

WHO WAS HE?
John Brown was a fanatical abolitionist. In 1856, he led a small, armed party of followers to the homes of five proslavery families who lived along Pottawatomie Creek near Lawrence, Kansas. In the middle of the night, Brown's crew dragged five men from their homes and murdered them in cold blood. But this is not the crime for which Brown was arrested.

WHAT DID HE DO?
On October 16, 1859, Brown led 21 men—5 blacks, 16 whites, among whom were two of Brown's sons—on a raid against the arsenal in Harper's Ferry, Virginia. Brown's intention was to distribute the arsenal's weapons among slaves in the region, setting off a war of libera-tion against white Southern slaveowners. But the slaves in the area did not rise up against their masters, and Brown and his men were trapped inside the arsenal by a detachment of U.S. Marines commanded by Colonel Robert E. Lee.

DATE OF ARREST
October 18, 1859

CIRCUMSTANCES OF THE CAPTURE
The Marines stormed the arsenal, killing or mortally wounding ten of Brown's men, including both of his sons. Brown himself was badly wounded in the attack.

THE CHARGES
Sedition, murder, and conspiracy to foment a slave insurrection

THE TRIAL
The court was convened on October 26, only eight days after Brown and his surviving men were captured. His injuries made it impossible for Brown to sit in a chair, so he was carried into the courtroom on a cot. On November 2, the day sentence was pronounced, Brown had recovered sufficiently to stand and address the court. "Now, if it is deemed necessary that I should forfeit my life for the furtherance of the ends of justice," he said, "and mingle my blood farther with the blood of my children and with the blood of millions in this slave country whose rights are disregarded by wicked, cruel, and unjust enactments, I say let it be done."

THE SENTENCE
Brown was found guilty and sentenced to be hanged. He was executed on December 2.

SPECTATORS
Among the 1,500 spectators were Professor Thomas J. Jackson of the Virginia Military Institute (he would earn the nickname "Stonewall" at the First Battle of Bull Run) and a celebrated actor, John Wilkes Booth.

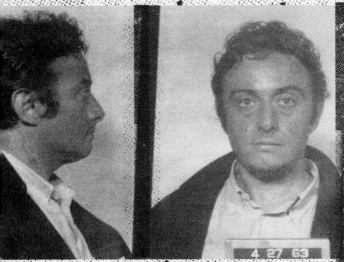

CIRCUMSTANCES OF THE ARREST
When Bruce performed his 10:00 p.m. show at the Café Au Go Go, four officers of New York City's vice squad were in the audience. After the show, they arrested Bruce and the club's owner, Howard Solomon.

THE CHARGE
Public obscenity

THE SENTENCE
The court found Bruce guilty and sentenced him to four months in the workhouse.

AFTERWARD
Bruce appealed the sentence, but before a verdict had been rendered, Bruce was found dead in his home from a morphine overdose.

THE PARDON
After Bruce's death, the appeal was dismissed and his conviction remained on the books. In 2003, Robin Williams and a group of comic actors, legal scholars, and lawyers petitioned New York's governor, George Pataki, to pardon Lenny Bruce. Governor Pataki granted the pardon on December 23, 2003.

LENNY BRUCE
(1925–1966)

NATIONALITY
American

WHO WAS HE?
In the mid-to-late 1950s, Lenny Bruce was an iconoclastic comedian whose nightclub act was laced with vulgar and obscene language. His shocking, innovative stand-up routines won him a huge audience—in 1961, he appeared at Carnegie Hall before a packed house.

WHAT DID HE DO?
During his stand-up routine at the Café Au Go Go in Greenwich Village, Bruce praised Eleanor Roosevelt's "nice tits," described the Lone Ranger sodomizing Tonto, and stated that St. Paul had given up "fucking" for Lent.

DATE OF ARREST
April 1, 1964

KOBE BRYANT

(1978–)

NATIONALITY
American

WHO IS HE?
Kobe Bryant joined the National Basketball Association (NBA) at age 18. Between 2000 and 2002, Bryant and his teammate, Shaquille O'Neal, led the Los Angeles Lakers to three NBA championships. As of 2010, Bryant was a 12-time NBA All-Star, three times an NBA All-Star Game MVP, and twice an NBA Finals MVP.

WHAT DID HE DO?
On July 1, 2003, Bryant had a sexual encounter with Katelyn Faber, an employee of the Lodge and Spa at Cordillera in Cordillera, Colorado. Faber accused Bryant of rape; Bryant insisted that the sex was consensual.

DATE OF ARREST
July 4, 2003

CIRCUMSTANCES OF THE ARREST
On July 1, 2003, Faber filed a complaint with the police, accusing Bryant of sexual assault. Three days later Bryant turned himself in, and was released after posting a $25,000 bond.

THE CHARGE
Sexual assault

THE DISMISSAL
In September 2004, while jury selection was under way, Faber informed prosecutors that she would not testify in the trial. Without her participation, prosecutors could not proceed against Bryant, so the case was dismissed.

THE SETTLEMENT
Shortly after he was accused of rape, Bryant admitted before a bank of television cameras that he had cheated on his wife, Vanessa Bryant. In 2004, he sent a letter of apology to Faber, saying, "Although I truly believe this encounter between us was consensual, I recognize now that she did not and does not view this incident the same way I did." The other terms of the settlement between Bryant and Faber have never been made public.

TED BUNDY
(1946–1989)

NATIONALITY
American

WHO WAS HE?
Ted Bundy was born in a home for unwed mothers in Burlington, Vermont. He was a quiet boy, but he appeared to blossom in college where he had a girlfriend, did volunteer work, and worked on Republican political campaigns. Bundy was accepted into law school and became engaged, but in 1974 he ditched both law school and his fiancée.

WHAT DID HE DO?
It is believed that between 1974 and 1978, Bundy murdered 36 young women and teenage girls in Colorado, Oregon, Utah, Florida, and Washington.

DATE OF ARREST
February 15, 1978

CIRCUMSTANCES OF THE ARREST
Early in the morning of February 15, 1978, Officer David Lee saw a Volkswagen Beetle parked behind a restaurant in the Brownsville neighborhood of Pensacola, Florida. As Lee approached the car, the driver pulled out into the street. Lee followed, and ran a check on the license plate number, which revealed that the car had been reported stolen. When he pulled the car over, Bundy leapt out, attacked Lee, and tried to grab his pistol. Lee subdued Bundy and placed him under arrest.

THE CHARGE
Murder and rape

THE CONFESSION
Bundy's attorneys arranged a plea bargain in which Bundy confessed to the murders of two college sorority sisters, Lisa Levi, 20 years old, and Margaret Bowman, 21 years old, and the murder of Kimberly Leach, 12 years old. In exchange, he would receive a sentence of 75 years in prison. Once he was in court, however, Bundy rejected the deal, saying, "I'm not going to do it."

THE SENTENCE
Bundy was convicted of the murders of Levi and Bowman and the rape and murder of Leach. He was sentenced to death.

THE EXECUTION
Ted Bundy was put to death by electrocution on January 24, 1989 at the Florida State Prison. Outside the prison walls, a crowd of about 200 people had gathered; when they received word that Bundy was dead, the crowd cheered.

PLAXICO BURRESS

(1977–)

NATIONALITY
American

WHO IS HE?
Plaxico Burress is a wide receiver who has played for the Pittsburgh Steelers and the New York Giants. At the 2008 Super Bowl, Burress caught the winning touchdown pass for the Giants.

WHAT DID HE DO?
While at a Manhattan nightclub, Burress accidentally shot himself in the thigh—with his own handgun.

DATE OF ARREST
December 1, 2008

CIRCUMSTANCES OF THE ARREST
The incident took place about 1:30 in the morning of Saturday, November 29, 2008. After being treated at a hospital, Burress went home. Twice on Saturday, police attempted to speak with him, both times unsuccessfully. On Sunday, Burress spoke with his lawyer. Monday morning, December 1, Burress turned himself in to the police. He was released after posting a $100,000 bond.

THE CHARGE
Criminal possession of a weapon

THE SENTENCE
Burress pled guilty to the weapons charge and was sentenced to two years in prison.

IN PRISON
Twice Plaxico Burress applied for work release, which would permit him to work outside the prison for limited periods. Both requests were denied. The Department of Correctional Services explained its decision: "[The] dangerous nature of the weapon discharging in a public place renders him unsuitable for work release."

JOEY BUTTAFUOCCO

(1956–)

NATIONALITY
American

WHO IS HE?
In 1991, Joey Buttafuocco, then the 35-year-old owner of a Long Island auto body shop, began an affair with 16-year-old Amy Fisher. In May 1992, Fisher went to the Buttafuocco home and shot Joey's wife, Mary Jo, in the face. Mary Jo Buttafuocco survived the shooting, and was able to identify her assailant—Amy was wearing a Buttafuocco Auto Body & Fender T-shirt.

WHAT DID HE DO?
Since Amy was only 16 years old at the time, Joey's affair with her was a crime. Nonetheless, throughout 1992, Joey insisted that he had never had sex with Amy Fisher. And his wife, Mary Jo, backed up his story.

DATE OF ARREST
April 15, 1993

CIRCUMSTANCES OF THE ARREST
Amy Fisher was already in prison, serving a 5-to-15-year sentence for assault. Police arrested Joey after an employee at the Buttafuocco auto body shop reported that Joey had bragged about having sex with Amy.

THE CHARGES
Statutory rape of a minor, sodomy, and endangering the welfare of a child

THE SENTENCE
In October 1993, Joey Buttafuocco pled guilty to one count of statutory rape. Joey's attorney, Dominic Barbera, tried to spin his client's "confession" by hinting broadly that Joey had committed perjury to spare his family further pain and humiliation. "That's the man he is," Barbera said. "He did what he had to do in that courtroom so everybody else's life could go on." The judge sentenced Joey to six months in prison, five years' probation, and a $5,000 fine. He was released after 129 days. Mary Jo threw him a massive welcome home party, with hundreds of guests.

AFTERMATH
Joey and Mary Jo Buttafuocco divorced in 2003. Amy Fisher served seven years in prison, during which the tabloids churned out stories that her prison guards raped her (the charges were dropped) and that she had begun a lesbian affair with a fellow prisoner (that story was never proven). In 2007, Joey and Amy announced that they were about to get married (they did not).

UNUSUAL FACTS
Joey Buttafuocco has appeared in nine movies, including *Finding Forrester*, and has appeared on eight television programs, including *Saturday Night Live*. Mary Jo Buttafuocco also appeared in a film, *Beat Boys Beat Girls*, and has made five TV appearances, including on *Oprah*. In 2007, Amy Fisher released a sex tape she made with her husband; it sold 200,000 copies.

WILLIAM CALLEY

(1943–)

NATIONALITY

American

WHO IS HE?

William Calley was a second lieutenant in the U.S. Army during the Vietnam War. He earned a Purple Heart and a Bronze Star with clusters, although there are reports that Calley's men and superiors considered him a bungler. There are rumors that his men considering "fragging" Calley ("fragging" is the killing of an officer by his own troops, typically by attack with a grenade).

WHAT DID HE DO?

On March 16, 1968, Calley led his men into the village of My Lai on a search for Viet Cong. Finding none, Calley ordered his men to kill the villagers. A museum built on the site by Vietnam's Communist government claims that the American troops massacred 504 men, women, and children: The youngest victim was 1 year old, the oldest was 82.

DATE OF INDICTMENT

September 5, 1969

THE CHARGE

Murder

THE SENTENCE

Calley was tried before a court-martial at Fort Benning, Georgia. The jury of six army officers deliberated for 13 days before rendering a guilty verdict on 22 counts of murder. Calley was sentenced to life imprisonment at hard labor. After three days in prison, he was released and placed under house arrest at Fort Benning. In 1974, he was paroled.

AFTERWARD

In 2009, William Calley made a public apology while addressing the Kiwanis Club of Greater Columbus in Columbus, Ohio. "There is not a day that goes by that I do not feel remorse for what happened that day in My Lai," he said. "I feel remorse for the Vietnamese who were killed, for their families, for the American soldiers involved and their families. I am very sorry."

GLEN CAMPBELL

(1936–)

NATIONALITY
American

WHO IS HE?
Glen Campbell had an immensely successful career in the 1960s and 1970s, with such pop and country hits as "Rhinestone Cowboy," "Gentle on My Mind," and "Wichita Lineman." He won a Grammy for "By the Time I Get to Phoenix."

WHAT DID HE DO?
While driving drunk, Campbell hit another vehicle, then sped off. At the police station, Campbell kneed one of the officers in the thigh (the officer was not hurt).

DATE OF ARREST
November 24, 2003

CIRCUMSTANCES OF THE ARREST
A witness to the accident followed Campbell and called police, who arrested him at his home in Phoenix.

THE CHARGES
Drunk driving, leaving the scene of an accident, and assaulting a police officer

THE SENTENCE
Campbell pled guilty, and was sentenced to ten days in jail and ordered to perform 75 hours of community service.

AFTERWARD
In 2005, Glen Campbell was inducted into the Country Music Hall of Fame.

JOSE CANSECO
(1964–)

NATIONALITY
Cuban-born American

WHO IS HE?
Jose Canseco began his major league baseball career in 1986, when he was signed by the Oakland Athletics. He hit 33 home runs and was named American League Rookie of the Year. In his 17-year career in MLB, he won an MVP award, a World Series ring, and became the first man in baseball history to hit 40 home runs and steal 40 bases in the same season.

THE BOOK
In 2005 Canseco published *Juiced: Wild Times, Rampant 'Roids, Smash Hits, and How Baseball Got Big.* In this tell-all memoir, Canseco confessed to having used steroids and claimed that 85 percent all of major league baseball players used performance enhancing drugs, too. And he named names, including Mark Maguire, Rafael Palmiero, and Ivan Rodriguez.

WHAT DID HE DO?
Canseco tried to smuggle human chorionic gonadotropin from Tijuana, Mexico, into the United States. The drug is said to remedy two side effects of steroid use—the body's failure to produce testosterone, and the shrinking of the testicles. Possession of human chorionic gonadotropin is illegal in the United States without a prescription. The drug is also banned by the World Anti-Doping Agency.

DATE OF ARREST
October 14, 2008

CIRCUMSTANCES OF ARREST
Customs and Border Protection agents at the border crossing stopped Canseco and his girlfriend, Heidi Northcott. During a search of Northcott's BMW, agents found six vials of human chorionic gonadotropin and ten syringes. He was detained at the San Isidro border crossing, then taken to the courthouse in downtown San Diego for indictment, after which he was released.

THE CHARGE
Introduction into interstate commerce of a misbranded drug

THE SENTENCE
Canseco pled guilty and was sentenced to 12 months of unsupervised probation.

AFTERWARD
Following his retirement from baseball, Canseco dabbled in celebrity boxing matches, mixed martial arts, and reality TV. In August 2010, he signed with the independent, professional Laredo Broncos as bench coach and a designated hitter.

AL CAPONE
(1899–1947)

NATIONALITY
American

WHO WAS HE?
Alphonse "Scarface" Capone was one of the most successful and notorious crime bosses of the 1920s. He was head of the Colosimo mob in Chicago, where he made a fortune in bootlegging and racketeering. It is widely believed that Capone was responsible for the 1929 St. Valentine's Day Massacre, in which seven members of the rival Bugs Moran gang were machine-gunned inside a Chicago garage by killers dressed as police officers.

WHAT DID HE DO?
Since the FBI could never pin any murder, bootlegging, or racketeering charges on Capone, the Treasury Department began to collect evidence against him of tax evasion.

DATE OF ARREST
June 16, 1931

THE CHARGE
Tax evasion

THE SENTENCE
Capone was tried and found guilty. The judge sentenced him to 11 years in prison and ordered him to pay a fine of $50,000, $7,692 for court costs, and $215,000 plus interest on back taxes. Capone served his sentence at Alcatraz.

AFTERWARD
Having paid all fines and back taxes and served 7 years of his sentence, Capone was released from prison. He was suffering from paresis, or loss of movement of the limbs, and a deteriorating mental condition—both brought on by syphilis. Capone retired to his estate on Palm Island, Florida where he lived with his wife and family. At the time of his death, Al Capone was said to have the mentality of a 12-year-old child.

"CARLOS THE JACKAL"
ILICH RAMIREZ SANCHEZ
(1949–)

NATIONALITY
Venezuelan

WHO IS HE?
Ilich Ramirez Sanchez, better known by his name in the underworld, Carlos the Jackal, was one of the most notorious terrorists of the 1970s and 1980s. He claimed that he was working for the Popular Front for the Liberation of Palestine.

WHAT DID HE DO?
Ramirez is believed to have masterminded the murder of the Israeli athletes at the 1972 Munich Olympics. In 1975, he seized 70 hostages during a meeting of OPEC oil ministers in Vienna. He is also believed to have been responsible for a series of bombings and attacks in Paris and London.

DATE OF ARREST
August 14, 1994

CIRCUMSTANCES OF THE ARREST
Ramirez had traveled to a private hospital in Khartoum, Sudan, for a minor surgical procedure. While Ramirez was recovering, in a private home, French security burst into the house and transported him to Paris where he was placed in solitary confinement while awaiting trial.

THE CHARGE
Murder

THE SENTENCE
Ramirez was found guilty of killing two French intelligence agents in 1975. He was sentenced to life in prison.

WHAT'S IN A NAME?
Ramirez was born in Venezuela. His father was a millionaire with a taste for left-wing politics; he named his three sons Vladimir, Ilich, and Lenin.

THE NOVELS
"Carlos the Jackal" appears as a character in Robert Ludlum's best-selling novels, *The Bourne Identity* and *The Bourne Ultimatum*.

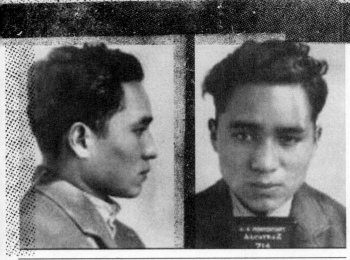

CLARENCE "THE CHOCTAW KID" CARNES

(1927–1988)

NATIONALITY
American

WHO WAS HE?
Clarence Carnes was born in Oklahoma. His family belonged to the Choctaw tribe, which in time would give him his nickname. At age 16, he quit school.

WHAT DID HE DO?
Carnes and a friend tried to hold up a gas station. When the attendant refused to hand over the money, Carnes shot and killed him.

DATE OF ARREST
1943

THE CHARGE
Murder

THE SENTENCE
Carnes was found guilty and, in spite of his youth, was sentenced to life in prison.

AFTERWARD
After nearly two years in prison at Leavenworth, Carnes escaped with two other inmates. The three escaped convicts committed several crimes, including kidnapping. They were captured and tried, and Carnes had 99 years added to his sentence. Once again he escaped and once again he was captured; this escape brought him an additional 5 years. In July 1945, 19-year-old Carnes was transferred to Alcatraz, a prison considered escapeproof; he was the youngest prisoner ever sent to Alcatraz.

PSYCHIATRIC EVALUATION
Upon arriving at Alcatraz, Carnes was turned over to Dr. Romney M. Ritchey, a psychiatrist. In his psychiatric evaluation Dr. Ritchey reported, "[Clarence Carnes] is impulsive and aggressive and heedless of the rights of others. Very self-centered in all he does and has never developed any social responsibility. He is of normal intelligence but emotionally unstable so that his conduct has always been erratic and poorly planned. He is still only 18 years of age and has never submitted himself to any social restrictions. He will require considerable supervision for an indefinite time. It is possible he may develop emotional maturity as time goes by, but this cannot be counted on with any certainty."

THE BATTLE OF ALCATRAZ
In 1946, Carnes joined an escape attempt. The escape failed, degenerating into a hostage crisis. In a shootout between prison guards and convicts, two guards and three convicts were killed and several guards were wounded. Two of the would-be escapees were executed, but Carnes was not because he had spared the lives of several guards he had been ordered to kill.

CIRCUMSTANCES OF THE ARREST

Carter, 17 years old, was among approximately 100 demonstrators protesting apartheid outside South Africa's embassy. Her older brother, Chip, was among the demonstrators, but was not one of those arrested.

THE CHARGE

No charges were filed against Carter or the other arrested demonstrators because Washington's mayor, Marion Berry, refused to prosecute anyone protesting peacefully outside the South African embassy.

A SUBSEQUENT ARREST

In 1987, Carter joined career activist Abbie Hoffman and other demonstrators to bar CIA recruiters from the campus of the University of Massachusetts. Carter, Hoffman, and 113 other demonstrators were charged with trespassing and disorderly conduct. After a highly publicized trial in Northampton, Massachusetts, Carter and her fellow defendants were acquitted.

AMY CARTER
(1967–)

NATIONALITY
American

WHO IS SHE?
Amy Carter is the daughter of former President and First Lady of the United States, Jimmy and Rosalyn Carter. In her late teens and early twenties, she was an outspoken activist for human rights.

WHAT DID SHE DO?
Carter was arrested for trespassing at the South African Embassy in Washington, D.C.

DATE OF ARREST
April 8, 1985

"BUTCH CASSIDY"
ROBERT LEROY PARKER

(1866–C.1908)

NATIONALITY
American

WHO WAS HE?
Robert LeRoy Parker was the eldest son of a Mormon family who had a ranch near Centerville, Utah. In his teens, he left home to work odd jobs on ranches; he was about 20 when he adopted the alias "Butch Cassidy." His life of crime ranged from taking a pair of jeans from a clothing store to robbing the San Miguel Valley Bank of $21,000.

WHAT DID HE DO?
Butch stole a horse belonging to a man named Richard Ashworth. The horse was valued at $5.

DATE OF ARREST
April 11, 1893

CIRCUMSTANCES OF THE ARREST
Butch was lying on his bed in the bunkhouse; his gunbelt was slung over a chair. Deputy Bob Calverly shouted that he had a warrant for Butch's arrest. Butch replied, "Well, get to shooting." Calverly charged Butch with his revolver drawn and pulled the trigger, but the gun misfired. The deputy fired again and the bullet grazed Butch's forehead, stunning him so he could be subdued.

THE CHARGE
Horse stealing

THE SENTENCE
Butch was found guilty and sentenced to two years in prison. After Butch served 18 months, the governor of Wyoming released him, with the understanding that Butch would commit no more crimes in the state.

AFTERWARD
After his release from prison, Butch formed the Wild Bunch, a gang of robbers and killers that included Harry Longabaugh, "the Sundance Kid." After they stole $60,000 in cash from a Union Pacific train, the gang became the target of a major manhunt. Butch and Sundance, along with Sundance's lover, Etta Place, escaped to New York City, then took a steamship to Argentina, where they operated a ranch before moving to Bolivia. The historical record is not certain what happened next: Butch and Sundance may have become bandits. It is certain that on November 6, 1908, in the town of San Vicente, there was a shootout between soldiers and police and two foreigners holed up in a lodging house. The strangers killed in the gun battle may have been Butch Cassidy and the Sundance Kid.

THE MOVIE
The movie, *Butch Cassidy and the Sundance Kid*, starring Paul Newman, Robert Redford, and Katharine Ross, premiered in 1969. It won four Academy Awards, including Oscars for Best Writing, Story, and Screenplay.

EDITH CAVELL

(1865–1915)

NATIONALITY
English

WHO WAS SHE?
Beginning in 1907, Edith Cavell directed a nurse training program in Brussels, Belgium. During World War I, her clinic became a Red Cross hospital where Cavell and her nurses cared for Allied and German troops.

WHAT DID SHE DO?
Cavell hid Allied soldiers and other refugees from the Germans, forged identification papers for them, and arranged for them to be transported secretly to England.

DATE OF ARREST
August 5, 1915

CIRCUMSTANCES OF THE ARREST
On July 31, the Germans arrested several individuals who had helped Cavell smuggle English soldiers out of Belgium. Five days later, Cavell was arrested. She admitted freely that she had helped fugitives escape to safety.

THE CHARGE
Treason

THE SENTENCE
Under German law, which was in force in occupied Belgium, assisting enemy troops constituted treason. Cavell was found guilty and sentenced to be executed by firing squad.

THE EXECUTION
Some accounts of Cavell's execution state that one member of the firing squad refused to shoot a woman. He was executed on the spot, then the squad shot and killed Cavell.

AFTERWARD
In May 1919, Edith Cavell's body was exhumed from its grave in Belgium and taken to England for a memorial service in Westminster Abbey, which was attended by King George V. Cavell's body was buried in Norwich, and a statue of her was erected in St. Martin's Place, London. Mount Edith Cavell in Jasper National Park, Canada, was named in her honor.

NICOLAE CEAUESCU
(1918–1989)
ELENA CEAUESCU
(1919–1989)

NATIONALITY
Romanian

WHO WERE THEY?
For 24 years, Nicolae Ceauescu was the absolute dictator of Communist Romania. His wife, Elena Ceauescu, was deputy prime minister—in fact, approximately 40 members of the Ceauescus' extended family held government office.

WHAT DID THEY DO?
The Ceauescus enforced ruinous economic programs that deprived much of the country of meat, electricity, and gasoline. They bulldozed more than a dozen churches and other culturally significant buildings to erect Communist Party office complexes, and they had planned to level more than half of Romania's 13,000 villages and replace them with "agroindustrial complexes." In December 1989, when striking workers and others demonstrated against the government, Nicolae Ceauescu ordered the army to fire on the marchers—100 were killed.

DATE OF ARREST
December 22, 1989

CIRCUMSTANCES OF THE ARREST
As antigovernment rallies spread across Romania, the Ceauescu government collapsed. On December 22, as crowds rampaged through Communist Party headquarters, Nicolae and Elena fled from Bucharest by helicopter. The army, which had sided with the revolutionaries, forced the helicopter to land, and the Ceauescus were taken to a military base at Tergoviste.

THE CHARGES
Genocide, destruction of state buildings, and undermining the economy

THE TRIAL
A military court convened on Christmas Day, and, after a one-hour trial, the Ceauescus were found guilty on all charges and sentenced to immediate execution by firing squad.

THE EXECUTION
The soldiers of the firing squad shot the couple repeatedly. After they were dead, others at the military base shot the bodies.

THE CONSPIRACY THEORY
In July 2010, the bodies of Nicolae and Elena Ceauescu were exhumed for a DNA test. It was hoped that the test results would put to rest theories that the couple's marked grave did not actually contain their bodies, that they were buried in a secret location, or that the Ceauescus had not been killed—that at the last moment their body doubles were shot in their place. The DNA tests proved that the graves contained the bodies of Nicolae and Elena Ceauescu.

ROBERT CHAMBERS
"THE PREPPIE KILLER"

(1966–)

NATIONALITY
American

WHO IS HE?
Robert Chambers was the son of a nurse. He attended several elite prep schools in Manhattan on scholarship, since his mother could not afford the tuition. From an early age, he was involved in petty thefts and drug abuse.

WHAT DID HE DO?
On the evening of August 25, 1986, Chambers was at Dorrian's Red Hand, an Irish pub on New York's Upper East Side popular with preppies and yuppies. His girlfriend broke up with him at the bar, and at about 4:30 in the morning Chambers was seen leaving Dorrian's with a former girlfriend, 18-year-old Jennifer Levin. They went to Central Park, where they had sex. Chambers would claim that he killed Levin accidentally during rough sex. The medical examiner who examined Levin's body reported that she had died of "asphyxia by strangulation," and that the bruises and injuries to her neck were consistent with strangulation and the victim clawing with her fingers to release her killer's grip.

THE INVESTIGATION
Levin's body was discovered the next morning behind the Metropolitan Museum of Art. By chance, a photographer covering the story took a picture that showed Chambers sitting on a wall watching the police investigate the scene of the crime.

DATE OF ARREST
August 26, 1986

CIRCUMSTANCES OF THE ARREST
Detectives investigating Levin's death came to Chambers's home. When he walked out of his bedroom, they saw deep, bloody scratches on both sides of his face. Initially, he said that the cat had scratched him, but as the interview with the police continued Chambers admitted that he had killed Jennifer Levin.

THE CHARGE
Murder

THE SENTENCE
The trial lasted three months. After nine days of deliberation, the jury still had not arrived at a verdict, so the prosecutor made a deal with the defense: The charge would be lowered to first-degree manslaughter, and Chambers would plead guilty and admit in court that he had intended to harm Jennifer Levin. The judge accepted the plea bargain and sentenced Chambers to 15 years in prison.

AFTERWARD
In 2008, Chambers was convicted of drug dealing. Through a plea bargain agreement, he was sentenced to 19 years in prison.

ROBERT CHAMBLISS

(1904–1985)

NATIONALITY
American

WHO WAS HE?
Robert Chambliss was a truck driver and a member of the Ku Klux Klan. In the 1940s, he was part of a Klan hit squad that flogged blacks who moved into the Center Street neighborhood in Birmingham, Alabama. Sometimes Chambliss and his fellow hit men blew up a black family's home.

WHAT DID HE DO?
On Sunday morning, September 15, 1963, Robert Chambliss climbed out of his white-and-turquoise Chevrolet and placed a box under the steps of Birmingham, Alabama's 16th Street Baptist Church. Then he climbed back in his car and drove away. At 10:22 a.m., an explosion rocked the church. Four young black girls, Adde Mae Collins, 14; Denise McNair, 11; Carole Robertson, 14; and Cynthia Wesley, 14, were attending Sunday school when the bomb went off. They were killed, and more than 20 people were injured.

CASE CLOSED
In the weeks after the bombing, FBI investigators gathered evidence to suggest that Robert Chambliss was involved in the bombing, but none of the witnesses would risk the wrath of the Klan by testifying against Chambliss in court. In 1968, the FBI closed the case.

DATE OF ARREST
September 24, 1977

CIRCUMSTANCES OF THE ARREST
Birmingham police officers arrested Chambliss at his home. As he was led to the squad car, Chambliss shouted to reporters, "This is all politics!"

THE CHARGE
Murder

THE TRIAL
Chambliss's niece, Elizabeth Cobb, testified that before the bombing her uncle had said, "Just wait until after Sunday morning and they'll beg us to let them segregate."

THE SENTENCE
Chambliss was found guilty of murder and sentenced to life in prison. At his sentencing, he declared, "Judge, I swear to God, I did not bomb that church. I never bombed nothing." Eight years later, Chambliss died in prison. He never acknowledged his guilt or implicated anyone else in the bombing.

AFTERWARD
In 2001, one of Chambliss's accomplices, Thomas Blanton Jr., was tried and convicted of murder. In 2002, another accomplice, Bobby Frank Cherry, was also found guilty of murder. Both men were sentenced to life in prison.

CHARLIE CHAPLIN
(1889–1977)

NATIONALITY
English

WHO WAS HE?
Charlie Chaplin was one of the stars of the silent screen, famous for his "Little Tramp" character. In 1919, with Douglas Fairbanks, Mary Pickford, and D. W. Griffiths, he founded United Artists studios. His 1940 spoof, *The Dictator*, in which he lampooned Adolf Hitler, was his biggest box office hit, earning $5 million. It was banned in Germany.

WHAT DID HE DO?
In 1941 and 1942, Chaplin had an affair with Joan Barry, an aspiring Hollywood starlet, 31 years younger than he was. They often traveled together between his home in California and hers in New York. Under the terms of the Mann Act, it was a crime for a man to transport a woman who was not his wife across state lines "for immoral purposes."

THE PATERNITY SUIT
By 1944, Chaplin's affair with Barry was over. She was pregnant and claimed that Chaplin was the father. A blood test of Chaplin, Barry, and the baby proved that Chaplin had not fathered Barry's child.

DATE OF INDICTMENT
February 10, 1944

CIRCUMSTANCES OF THE ARREST
The police invited the press, including photographers, to cover Chaplin's arrest and fingerprinting.

THE CHARGES
Violation of the Mann Act and conspiracy

THE SENTENCE
Chaplin pled not guilty. After deliberating for three hours, the jury acquitted him of all charges.

THE FBI FILE
For years, the FBI kept Chaplin, an outspoken Communist sympathizer, under surveillance. Eventually, Chaplin's file ran to 2,000 pages. In 1952, the U.S. Attorney General revoked Chaplin's permit to enter the United States.

HENRI "PAPILLON" CHARRIÈRE
(1906–?)

NATIONALITY
French

WHO WAS HE?
Henri Charrière was a French sailor who mangled his own thumb to get a discharge from the navy. He entered the Paris criminal underworld, where he received the nickname Papillon, for the butterfly tattoo on his chest.

WHAT DID HE DO?
In 1931, Charrière murdered a pimp named Roland Le Petit.

DATE OF CONVICTION
October 26, 1931

THE CHARGE
Murder

THE SENTENCE
Charrière was found guilty and sentenced to life in prison. He was sent to Devil's Island, a prison colony off the coast of French Guiana.

THE ESCAPES
Charrière claimed in his autobiography, *Papillon*, that he attempted to escape from the prison nine times, and ultimately was successful. Using a large bag filled with coconuts as a flotation device, he leapt off a cliff into the sea and was carried by the current to the mainland. From French Guiana, he made his way to Venezuela, where he married, had children, and became a successful restauranteur.

THE BOOK AND THE MOVIE
Papillon, Charrière's account of his life, was published in 1970. Because some of his stories appeared far-fetched, it was generally described as an autobiographical novel. Nonetheless, it became a bestseller and the inspiration for the 1973 movie, *Papillon*, starring Steve McQueen and Dustin Hoffman.

AFTERWARD
In his autobiography, Charrière described the brutal prison conditions he endured, including two years in solitary confinement. He also told of his nine escape attempts, and insisted that he was wrongly convicted of the pimp's murder. An examination of the police and the prison records showed that it is very likely that it was Charrière who killed the pimp, and that he never attempted a single prison break.

THE RETURN OF PAPILLON
In 1973, it was widely reported that Henri Charrière had died of throat cancer. Then, in 2005, he turned up alive in Venezuela. No one knows why he decided to vanish from the public eye in 1973.

CÉSAR CHÁVEZ
(1927–1993)

NATIONALITY
American

WHO WAS HE?
César Chávez was a labor activist and founder of the United Farm Workers (UFW) union. In imitation of Mahatma Gandhi, Chávez used nonviolent tactics to pressure landowners and corporations to improve the pay and working conditions of farm workers.

WHAT DID HE DO?
In August 1970, Chávez led approximately 6,000 members of the UFW in a strike against lettuce growers in Salinas Valley, California. As the strike virtually shut down the lettuce industry in the valley,

violence erupted across the region. A state judge issued a court order banning the UFW, and Chávez by name, from picketing. Chávez refused to obey the order.

DATE OF ARREST
December 4, 1970

THE CHARGE
Contempt of court

IN JAIL
During the two weeks he was in jail, Chávez was visited by Coretta Scott King, the widow of Dr. Martin Luther King, Jr., and Ethel Kennedy, the widow of Senator Bobby Kennedy.

THE RELEASE
The Supreme Court of California reviewed the circumstances of Chávez's arrest and ordered him released. He walked out of jail on December 23.

AFTERWARD
At Chávez's death in 1993, 50,000 mourners attended the funeral. In 1994, President Bill Clinton awarded César Chávez the Medal of Freedom, presenting it to Chávez's widow, Helen Chávez.

STYLLOU PANTOPIOU CHRISTOFI
(?–1954)

NATIONALITY
Greek Cypriot

WHO WAS SHE?
Styllou Pantopiou Christofi emigrated from her native Cyprus to England. In 1954, she was living with her son, Stavros, her daughter-in-law, Hella, and her three grandchildren in the Hampstead district of London. Styllou and Hella did not get along, arguing most often about how Hella raised the children, which Styllou considered too permissive.

WHAT DID SHE DO?
Stavros worked nights as a waiter. After he left the house on July 29, 1954, Styllou used a heavy can to knock Hella unconscious. Then she strangled her and dragged her body into the backyard, where she set Hella's body on fire. The fire spread to the house, so Styllou ran out into the street and flagged down a passing car. Firefighters rescued the children and extinguished the fire before much damage was done.

DATE OF ARREST
July 29, 1954

CIRCUMSTANCES OF THE ARREST
Styllou told police that she had been in bed when the sound of male voices in the house awakened her. She went downstairs and saw the body burning in the yard, but the men escaped. The police didn't buy it and arrested Styllou at once.

THE CHARGE
Murder

THE SENTENCE
Stavros tried to persuade his mother to plead insanity as her defense. "I am a poor woman of no education," Styllou replied, "but I am not a madwoman." She was found guilty of murder and sentenced to be hanged.

AFTERWARD
After Styllou Pantopiou Christofi had been executed, it was learned that in 1925, in Cyprus, she had been tried for the murder of her mother-in-law. She was acquitted.

GALEAZZO CIANO
(1903–1944)

NATIONALITY
Italian

WHO WAS HE?
Count Galeazzo Ciano was a well-to-do playboy and diplomat whose family were ardent supporters of Italy's Fascist Party. In 1930, Ciano married Edda Mussolini, the daughter of Il Duce, Benito Mussolini, the Fascist dictator of Italy. Mussolini propelled his son-in-law's political career, appointing him foreign minister when Ciano was only 33 years old.

WHAT DID HE DO?
As the Allies invaded Italy, Ciano and other members of the Fascist Grand Council voted to depose Mussolini and withdraw Italy from the war.

DATE OF ARREST
October 19, 1943

CIRCUMSTANCES OF THE ARREST
Adolf Hitler sent Nazi troops to rescue Mussolini and reinstate him as ruler of Italy. Edda Ciano escaped with her three children to Switzerland, but Galeazzo Ciano was arrested by the Nazis.

THE CHARGE
Treason

THE SENTENCE
Ciano and four other Fascists who had voted to depose Mussolini were found guilty of treason and sentenced to death. On January 11, 1944, the five men were led outside the medieval walls of Verona, seated in chairs, and shot in the back of the head.

AFTERWARD
Edda Ciano had pleaded with her father for her husband's life. When that failed, she tried blackmail, threatening to publish Galeazzo Ciano's diaries. That threat did not move Mussolini, either. After Ciano's execution, Edda published the diaries, but they were not packed with sensational revelations about Il Duce's inner circle. Edda never spoke to her father again.

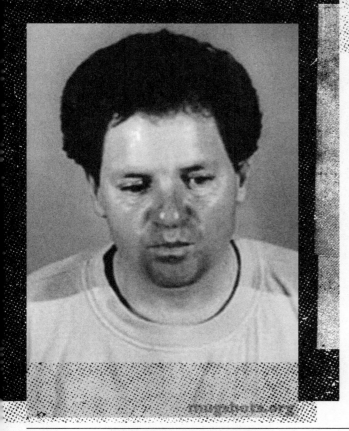

ROGER CLINTON

(1956–)

NATIONALITY
American

WHO IS HE?
Roger Clinton is the younger half-brother of former U.S. president Bill Clinton. In the 1990s he became an actor, appearing in nearly two dozen movies and television programs, including the animated series of *The Blues Brothers*, in which he played President Clinton.

WHAT DID HE DO?
While driving through Hermosa Beach, California, police observed Clinton's car drifting back and forth over the center line of the road. Earlier in the night, Clinton had allegedly tried to provoke a fight with the doorman at the nearby Lighthouse nightclub.

DATE OF ARREST
February 17, 2001

CIRCUMSTANCES OF THE ARREST
After failing the breathalyzer and balance and coordination tests, Clinton was arrested.

THE CHARGE
Drunk driving and disturbing the peace

THE SENTENCE
Clinton pled guilty to reckless driving, a reduced charge. He was fined $1,350, sentenced to two years' probation, and ordered to stay at least 100 yards from the Lighthouse nightclub.

INTERESTING FACT
Less than a month earlier, President Clinton had granted his brother a presidential pardon for a 1985 drug conviction that sent Roger Clinton to jail for a year. The pardon expunged the conviction and jail time from Roger Clinton's record.

GARY COLEMAN

(1968–2010)

NATIONALITY
American

WHO WAS HE?
Gary Coleman was a promising child star who played Arnold Jackson on the sitcom *Diff'rent Strokes* from 1978 to 1986. Coleman was paid $100,000 per episode; later, he would discover that his parents and his advisers misappropriated most of his money. He sued them and was awarded $1.3 million. After *Diff'rent Strokes*, his acting career faded away. In 2003, he made an unsuccessful run for governor of California.

WHAT DID HE DO?
The details of what happened between Coleman and his wife, Shannon Price, were not released. The couple had a tempestuous relationship, and Coleman had been arrested once before on a domestic violence charge.

DATE OF ARREST
January 24, 2010

CIRCUMSTANCES OF THE ARREST
Coleman had financial difficulties. At the time of his arrest, he remained in jail because he could not raise the bail of $1,725. A fan came forward and posted bail for him.

THE CHARGE
Domestic violence

THE OUTCOME
The 2010 domestic violence case was never resolved in court. In May 2010, Gary Coleman fell in his home, struck his head, and died of a brain hemorrhage.

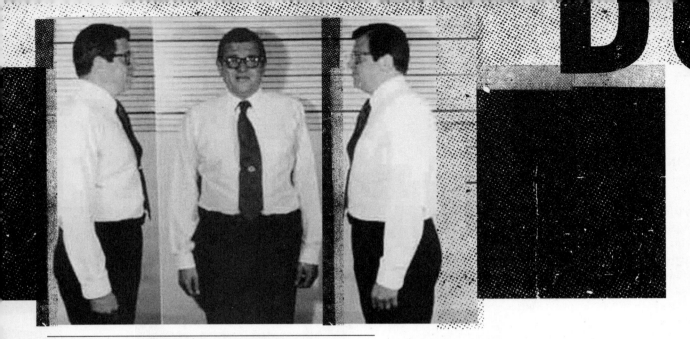

CHARLES COLSON

(1931–)

NATIONALITY
American

WHO IS HE?
Charles Colson was a Republican and an attorney. In 1969, Richard Nixon appointed him as counsel to the president. He became an active member of the Committee to Re-elect the President.

WHAT DID HE DO?
Colson was regarded by some in the Nixon administration as an "evil genius." He plotted to discredit Daniel Ellsberg, who had leaked to the *New York Times* and other newspapers the top-secret Pentagon Papers that detailed the U.S. government's strategy in Vietnam. Colson even considered firebombing the Brookings Institution, a public policy think tank that opposed the Nixon administration.

DATE OF INDICTMENT
March 8, 1974

THE CHARGE
Obstruction of justice

THE SENTENCE
Colson pled guilty and received a sentence of one-to-three years in prison. He was released after serving seven months.

AFTERWARD
Shortly before his arrest, Colson had a religious conversion experience. In 1976, he founded the Prison Fellowship Ministries to bring the consoling message of Christianity to inmates and their families. In 1983, he founded the Justice Fellowship to advocate for prison reform. For his work, Colson received the 1993 Templeton Prize for Progress in Religion.

ROBERT CONRAD

(1930–)

NATIONALITY
American

WHO IS HE?
Robert Conrad is an actor, best remembered for his starring roles in the television series *The Wild Wild West* and *Baa Baa Black Sheep*.

WHAT DID HE DO?
On March 31, 2003, near Arnold, California, he crashed his Jaguar head-on into a Subaru. Conrad's blood alcohol level was 0.20 percent, nearly three times the state's legal limit. The driver of the other car, 26-year-old Kevin Burnett, suffered a broken leg and a broken wrist. Conrad suffered partial paralysis and temporary memory loss.

DATE OF ARREST
March 31, 2003

THE CHARGE
Drunk driving

THE CONTINUANCE
In consideration of Conrad's injuries, the judge postponed the DUI hearing for a month.

THE SENTENCE
Conrad was found guilty and sentenced to six months' house arrest. He lost his driver's license for one year. He was placed on five years' probation and ordered to attend an alcohol counseling program.

AFTERWARD
Two years later, Kevin Burnett died of perforated ulcers. His family claimed that his death was a result of the injuries he sustained in the accident. Since the accident, Conrad has stayed out of the public eye.

THE BIRTH DATE
Hollywood biographies of Robert Conrad listed his birth date as 1935. Court records revealed that he was born in 1930.

JOSEPH CORBETT JR.

(1928–2009)

NATIONALITY
American

WHO WAS HE?
As a boy, Joseph Corbett had been a science prodigy, but he never developed his gifts. In 1951, he was found guilty of the murder of a 20-year-old hitchhiker. In prison, psychiatrists examined Corbett and found him to be "markedly schizoid" with a potential for "violent, uncontrolled emotion." In 1955, he escaped from prison and traveled to Denver, where he worked as a chemist for the Benjamin Moore Paint Co. He lived under an alias—Walter Osborne. In 1959, for unknown reasons, he quit his job.

WHAT DID HE DO?
Corbett plotted to kidnap Adolph Coors III, the heir to the Coors Company brewery fortune. He would demand between $250,000 and $500,000, then leave Denver to begin a new life elsewhere. Corbett confronted Coors on the morning of February 9, 1960. Coors resisted, and Corbett shot him twice, killing him. He dumped the body in a re-mote landfill, then fled to Canada. In September 1960, FBI agents and sheriff's deputies found Coors's body.

PLANNING THE KIDNAPPING
Corbett purchased leg irons, a pair of handcuffs, and a tent—he planned to camp out with Coors in some isolated location until the ransom was paid.

DATE OF ARREST
October 29, 1960

CIRCUMSTANCES OF THE ARREST
FBI agents traced Corbett to a Vancouver hotel. Corbett had told the desk clerk he was expecting the delivery of a typewriter; about 9:00 a.m. there was a knock on his door and a voice called out, "Typewriter ordered for Mr. Wainwright [the alias Corbett was using in Vancouver]." Corbett opened the door, saw the FBI agents with their guns drawn, and said, "I'm your man."

THE CHARGE
Murder and kidnapping

THE SENTENCE
After a 13-day trial, Corbett was found guilty and sentenced to life in prison.

AFTERWARD
Corbett was a model prisoner. In 1980, after serving almost 20 years, he was paroled. He found a job driving a truck for the Salvation Army.

MARY ANN COTTON

(1832–1873)

CIRCUMSTANCES OF THE ARREST

Since evidence of poisoning could not be proved conclusively in the other cases, Cotton was arrested and charged with poisoning her seven-year-old stepson, Charles Edward Cotton, whose body contained significant levels of arsenic.

THE CHARGE

Murder

THE SENTENCE

Cotton was found guilty and sentenced to be hanged. Her execution was bungled; the drop did not break her neck, so she dangled from the end of the rope, writhing and kicking, as she slowly strangled to death.

NATIONALITY

English

WHO WAS SHE?

To her friends and neighbors, Mary Ann Cotton appeared to be a lovely, compassionate, nurturing soul, who suffered the loss of 16 members of her family: her mother, three husbands, nine children, and three stepchildren—all of whom died of painful stomach ailments.

WHAT DID SHE DO?

Cotton is believed to have administered arsenic, in small doses, to her mother, husbands, children, and stepchildren, as well as one of her lovers. After her arrest, the bodies of several of her victims were exhumed, and traces of arsenic were found in them.

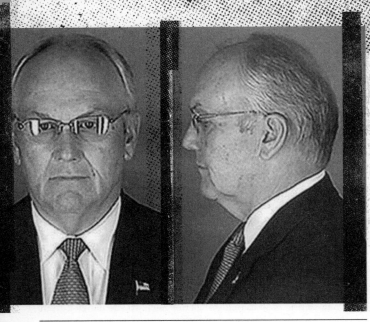

LARRY CRAIG
(1945–)

NATIONALITY
American

WHO IS HE?
Larry Craig is a Republican politician who represented Idaho for 28 years in Congress, 18 of them in the U.S. Senate.

WHAT DID HE DO?
About 12:15 on the afternoon of June 11, 2007, Craig stood outside a men's room stall occupied by Sgt. Dave Karsnia. Peering through the crack between the door and the frame, Craig made fidgeting gestures with his fingers. Then he occupied the stall beside Karsnia where, according to the complaint, Craig tapped his right foot several times, "which Sergeant Karsnia recognized as a signal often used by persons communicating a desire to engage in sexual conduct."

DATE OF ARREST
June 11, 2007

CIRCUMSTANCES OF THE ARREST
Sgt. Karsnia had been assigned to a sting operation at a men's room in the Minneapolis–St. Paul International Airport that had a reputation as a sexual cruising ground.

THE CHARGES
Disturbing the peace, interference with privacy, and disorderly conduct.

THE PLEA
On August 1, 2007, Craig entered a plea of guilty to the disorderly conduct charge.

THE SENTENCE
Craig received a $575 fine, which included court fees, and a suspended sentence of ten days in the county workhouse.

AFTERWARD
Craig tried to keep his arrest and guilty plea quiet, but on August 27, the Washington, D.C. newspaper, *Roll Call*, broke the story. The next day the senator stood before a crowd of reporters to say that when he pled guilty to the disorderly conduct charge he had "overacted and made a poor decision." Then he said, "Let me be clear: I am not gay and never have been." In 2008, the Minnesota Court of Appeals refused to toss out Craig's guilty plea. In 2009, after completing his term as senator, Craig returned home to Idaho. He did not run for reelection.

A DESTINATION
According to a story published in 2007 in the *Idaho Statesman*, "the Larry Craig men's room" in the Minneapolis–St. Paul Airport had become a tourist destination.

CHERYL CRANE

(1943–)

NATIONALITY
American

WHO IS SHE?
Cheryl Crane is the daughter of Hollywood bombshell Lana Turner and Joseph Stephenson Crane, a sometime actor and successful restauranteur.

WHAT DID SHE DO?
On the evening of April 4, 1958, Lana Turner had a violent argument with her lover, Johnny Stompanato, a gigolo and gangster wannabe. Through the door, 14-year-old Cheryl heard Stompanato swear that he would cut up Turner's face, and kill her mother and daughter. Cheryl ran to the kitchen, got a large knife, and returned to her mother's bedroom. When Stompanato stepped out of the bedroom, Cheryl stabbed him, piercing his aorta.

DATE OF ARREST
April 4, 1958

CIRCUMSTANCES OF THE ARREST
Turner called Jerry Geisler, a high-powered Hollywood attorney who had successfully defended Errol Flynn and Charlie Chaplin. Geisler called the police, and he, Turner, and Cheryl rode to the police station in Geisler's limo.

THE CHARGE
Murder

THE SENTENCE
After deliberating for thirty minutes, the jury returned a verdict of justifiable homicide. The jury believed that Crane had killed Stompanato because she feared that he would kill her mother, or herself, or both of them. She was sent to a girls' boarding school, but was eventually placed in the custody of her grandmother.

AFTERWARD
The media attention prompted by the murder and the subsequent trial renewed interest in Lana Turner as an actress; she made a comeback in *Imitation of Life*. Cheryl Crane went into the restaurant business with her father, then became a real estate agent. In 1988, she published her autobiography, *Detour: A Hollywood Story*.

THOMAS NEILL CREAM, "THE LAMBETH POISONER"

(1850–1892)

NATIONALITY
Scots

WHO WAS HE?
When he was a child, Thomas Neill Cream's family emigrated from Scotland to Canada, where Cream studied medicine. He completed his medical studies in Edinburgh where he was licensed as a physician and a surgeon. Between 1878 and 1891, he practiced medicine in Edinburgh; London, Ontario; Chicago; and London, England.

FIRST CONVICTION
In 1881, while living in Chicago, Cream used strychnine to kill his lover's husband. Cream was arrested, convicted of murder, and sentenced to life in prison at the penitentiary in Joliet. After serving ten years, he was paroled. Immediately, he traveled to England.

WHAT DID HE DO?
Cream found a house on Lambeth Palace Road in London. In the evenings, he walked the city's streets; when he encountered a prostitute, he introduced himself as a physician and offered her "medication," often saying it would improve the woman's complexion. The medicine was strychnine; Cream is believed to have poisoned at least five prostitutes.

DATE OF ARREST
June 3, 1892

THE CHARGE
Murder

THE SENTENCE
The trial lasted five days, and the jury retired for only ten minutes before reaching a guilty verdict. In sentencing the prisoner, Justice Henry Hawkins said Cream's crimes were "so diabolical in [their] character, fraught with so much cold-blooded cruelty [that they could] be expiated only by your death."

THE EXECUTION
Cream was hanged privately, inside the prison. But an enormous crowd had gathered outside. When he was dead, a black flag was flown over the prison walls. The crowd cheered.

THE RUMOR
It is said that as the hood was slipped over his head, Cream tried to confess to other murders. According to this story, his last words were, "I am Jack the..."

HAWLEY HARVEY CRIPPEN

(1862–1910)

NATIONALITY
American

WHO WAS HE?
Hawley Harvey Crippen was an American practitioner of homeopathetic medicine who married Cora Turner, a music hall starlet who went by the stage name Belle Elmore. They moved to London, England, where Crippen was not permitted to bill himself as "Dr. Crippen," which made it difficult for him to earn a living. To supplement their income, Crippen and his wife took in boarders.

THE LADY VANISHES
After a party at their home on January 31, 1910, Cora Crippen vanished—friends and neighbors never saw her again. Later, Crippen told friends that Cora had gone back to America, where she died. Soon afterward, Ethel "Le Neve" Neave moved into the house. Alerted by suspicious neighbors, Chief Inspector Walter Dew of Scotland Yard called on the couple. He interviewed them and searched the house, but found nothing incriminating. Nonetheless, Dew's visit panicked Crippen and Neave. They sailed to Belgium and traveled to Antwerp, where they booked passage to Canada aboard the *SS Montrose*. Le Neve cut her hair short and dressed as boy so she could pass as Crippen's teenage son.

WHAT DID HE DO?
Crippen and Le Neve's disappearance renewed police suspicions. They searched the house more thoroughly and under the basement floor found human remains they believed were those of Cora Crippen. Investigators concluded that Crippen poisoned his wife, then cut off her head, removed her genitals, and sliced her flesh away from her bones.

DATE OF ARREST
July 31, 1910

CIRCUMSTANCES OF THE ARREST
The captain of the *Montrose* recognized his passengers as Crippen and Le Neve, and sent a wireless cable to Scotland Yard. As the *Montrose* steamed toward Quebec, a ship bearing Chief Inspector Dew caught up with it. Dew came aboard and confronted Crippen. "Thank God it's over," he said. Crippen was handcuffed because, during a search of the prisoner's pockets, Dew had found a suicide note.

THE CHARGES
Murder and mutilation

THE SENTENCE
Crippen was found guilty and hanged.

AFTERWARD
In 2007, a team of American scientists compared the DNA of a portion of the tissue said to be Cora Crippen with tissue samples taken from individuals who said they were her relatives. After comparing the two, the scientists concluded that the tissue sample that had been preserved for nearly a century in the Royal London Hospital had not been taken from the body of Cora Crippen. However, there is evidence that Cora had no family, so the DNA test might have been inconclusive.

DAVID CROSBY

(1941–)

NATIONALITY
American

WHO WAS HE?
A famous singer, songwriter, and guitarist inducted into the Rock and Roll Hall of Fame twice—for being a member of the Byrds and Crosby, Stills & Nash.

WHAT DID HE DO?
After a number of run-ins with the law over drug possession, Crosby was arrested.

DATE OF ARREST
April 13, 1982

CIRCUMSTANCES OF THE ARREST
In March, on his way to sing at a demonstration at a nuclear power plant, Crosby crashed his car into the median of a freeway in California. Rescuers who pulled him from the wreckage also found Quaaludes, cocaine, and an unlicensed .45.

In April, Crosby was arrested again after freebasing cocaine in this dressing room of Cardi's nightclub in Dallas.

THE SENTENCE
In 1983, Crosby appeared in a Texas court. According to the *Dallas Times Herald*, "Several times he fell asleep and snored loudly, his head tilted back and his mouth open. When the snoring became too loud, one of his attorneys leaned over and shook him awake." Crosby was sentenced to five years in prison but was admitted into a drug rehabilitation instead.

AFTERWARD
While appealing the verdict, Crosby is arrested in 1984 for possession of drugs, including heroin, cocaine, pot and codeine. In 1985, he enters and escapes from a stint in a court-ordered New Jersey treatment facility. He is then is sent to jail in Huntsville Texas, where he spends nine months of a five-year sentence. He later thanked the judge who sentenced him for helping him kick his $1000-a-day habit. "I wrote him a letter saying, 'Listen, you know, I thought you were a bad guy, but the truth is you did your job really well and I'd like you to know that I'm one of those rare successes that you wish you had more of,'" Crosby said.

RUSSELL CROWE
(1964–)

NATIONALITY
New Zealander

WHO IS HE?
Russell Crowe is an Academy Award–winning actor and leading man, the star of *Gladiator*, *Cinderella Man*, *A Beautiful Mind*, and *Master and Commander*, among other films. He has a reputation for a violent temper.

WHAT DID HE DO?
At 4:00 a.m. on June 6, 2005, Crowe tried to call his family in Australia. The phone in his $3,000-a-night suite at New York's Mercer Hotel was not operating properly. Crowe called the front desk for assistance, but Nestor Estrada, the clerk, did not solve the problem. Crowe disconnected the phone, went down to the lobby, and hurled the phone at Estrada, striking him in the face and leaving an inch-long cut on his cheek.

DATE OF ARREST
June 6, 2005

CIRCUMSTANCES OF THE ARREST
New York police arrested Crowe at the hotel. Estrada was treated at a hospital near the hotel and released.

THE CHARGES
Assault and criminal possession of a weapon (the telephone)

THE SENTENCE
Crowe pled guilty to a lesser charge of third-degree assault and was given a conditional discharge, which spared him jail time as long as he was not arrested again in the following year.

ALTERCATIONS
Between 1999 and 2005, Crowe was involved in at least five violent altercations: a bar fight in Australia; a shoving-and-shouting match with a BBC producer who cut short Crowe's acceptance speech at the BAFTA awards ceremony; a fight with a fellow diner at a London restaurant; a loud argument with a waitress at the release party for *Master and Commander*; and a fistfight that included biting his bodyguard on the set of *Cinderella Man*.

LEON CZOLGOSZ

(1873–1901)

DATE OF ARREST
September 6, 1901

THE PRESIDENT'S CONDITION
The wound in President McKinley's chest was superficial; the one in his abdomen was critical, but doctors expected him to recover. Tragically, the stomach wound became gangrenous: William McKinley died on September 14, 1901.

THE CHARGE
Murder

THE SENTENCE
At his trial, Czolgosz admitted that he had assassinated President McKinley. The judge sentenced him to be electrocuted at Auburn Prison. He was executed on October 29, 1901, 54 days after he shot the president.

LAST WORDS
Before he was executed, Leon Czolgosz stated, "I killed the president because he was the enemy of the good people—the good working people. I am not sorry for my crime."

EMMA GOLDMAN
Under interrogation, Czolgosz admitted that the speeches of Emma Goldman had inspired him to assassinate McKinley. Goldman was arrested and imprisoned briefly. Upon her release, she said, "[Leon Czolgosz] had committed the act for no personal reasons or gain. He did it for what is his ideal: the good of the people. That is why my sympathies are with him."

NATIONALITY
American

WHO WAS HE?
Leon Czolgosz was born in Detroit, the son of Polish immigrants. As a young man he worked in a wire mill in Cleveland. After suffering a mental breakdown, he returned to his family's farm outside Cleveland. In 1900, he began to read anarchist newspapers, and became particularly interested in the case of an Italian anarchist who assassinated King Umberto of Italy.

WHAT DID HE DO?
After hearing the prominent anarchist Emma Goldman speak in Cleveland and Chicago, Czolgosz bought a pistol and traveled to Buffalo, New York, where President William McKinley was scheduled to visit the Pan-American Exposition. After the president had addressed the audience assembled in the exposition's Temple of Music, Czolgosz walked up to McKinley and shot him twice.

JEFFREY DAHMER

(1960–1994)

NATIONALITY
American

WHO WAS HE?
Jeffrey Dahmer was a social misfit who was discharged from the U.S. Army for his heavy drinking. He found a job at a chocolate factory in Milwaukee, Wisconsin.

WHAT DID HE DO?
Beginning in 1978, Dahmer kidnapped, tortured, raped, and murdered perhaps as many as 17 teenage boys and young men. Usually he dismembered the corpses; sometimes he committed acts of cannibalism. Most of his victims were Asian or African-American.

DATE OF ARREST
July 22, 1991

CIRCUMSTANCES OF THE ARREST
On July 22, Dahmer's next victim, Tracy Edwards, escaped from Dahmer's apartment. Edwards flagged down a patrol car and told the police that Dahmer had tried to handcuff him and had threatened him with a knife (the handcuffs were still dangling from one of Edwards's wrists). The police returned with Edwards to Dahmer's apartment, where they found photographs of mutilated human bodies, and three human heads in the refrigerator.

THE CHARGE
Murder

THE SECURITY PREPARATIONS
Public outrage was so intense that an eight-foot-high wall of bulletproof glass was erected between the part of the courtroom where the judge, jury, attorneys, and defendant sat, and the portion of the courtroom reserved for spectators.

THE SENTENCE
While in police custody, Dahmer admitted to the killings, but at his trial, on the advice of his attorney, he changed his plea to guilty by reason of insanity. The jury found Dahmer guilty on 15 counts of murder; the judge sentenced him to 15 consecutive life sentences.

AFTERWARD
Initially, prison authorities kept Jeffrey Dahmer isolated from the rest of the prison population—for his own protection. Dahmer, however, asked to spend at least some time among other inmates. On November 28, 1994, Dahmer was assigned to a work detail with two other killers: Jesse Anderson, a white supremacist, and Christopher Scarver, a schizophrenic. When the guards were not present, Scarver used a broom handle to bludgeon Anderson and Dahmer to death.

THE EVIDENCE
After Dahmer was killed, the city of Milwaukee collected all his photographs, dissection tools and torture implements, and his refrigerator and burned them.

D'ANGELO
(1974–)

NATIONALITY
American

WHO IS HE?
Michael Eugene Archer, who goes by the stage name D'Angelo, is an R&B singer-songwriter whose 2000 album, *Voodoo*, sold over 1 million copies. He created a sensation with his video, "Untitled (How Does I Feel)" where he showed off his newly chiseled body. D'Angelo won a Grammy for best R&B Vocal and *Voodoo* won a Grammy for Best R&B Album. Then he virtually vanished from the music scene.

WHAT DID HE DO?
Police alleged that at about 2:30 in the morning of March 6, 2010, while driving through New York City's West Village, D'Angelo pulled his Range Rover up beside a woman on the sidewalk and offered her $40 for oral sex.

DATE OF ARREST
March 6, 2010

CIRCUMSTANCES OF THE ARREST
The woman D'Angelo thought was a prostitute was an undercover police officer. When arresting officers searched D'Angelo's Range Rover, they found he was carrying $12,000 in cash.

THE CHARGE
Soliciting sex

THE SENTENCE
As of November 2010, D'Angelo's case had not come to court.

MIKE DANTON

(1980–)

NATIONALITY
Canadian

WHO IS HE?
Mike Danton is a Canadian hockey player who played for the New Jersey Devils and the St. Louis Blues before his conviction. After his release, he was signed by the St. Mary's Huskies of Halifax, Nova Scotia.

WHAT DID HE DO?
Danton tried to hire a hit man to kill his agent, David Frost. The man to whom he offered $10,000 to do the contract killing was actually a police dispatcher.

DATE OF ARREST
April 16, 2004

CIRCUMSTANCES OF THE ARREST
FBI agents arrested Danton at the airport in San Jose, California, hours after his team, the St. Louis Blues, were eliminated from the Stanley Cup playoffs.

THE CHARGE
Conspiracy to commit murder

THE SENTENCE
Danton pled guilty and was sentenced to 90 months in prison.

AFTERWARD
Mike Danton was paroled after serving 63 months of his sentence. Once he was released, he explained to the press and his fans that he had never intended to have his former agent, David Frost, killed—his real target was Steve Jefferson, his father.

NAME CHANGE
Danton was born Michael Jefferson. After a contentious relationship with his family, he legally changed his name.

ANGELA DAVIS

(1944–)

NATIONALITY
American

WHO IS SHE?
Angela Davis is a political activist, author, and college professor. She was born in Alabama; as a teenager she was involved in the civil rights movement. In the 1960s, while studying at the University of California, San Diego, she joined the Black Panthers and the Che-Lumumba Club, which was affiliated with the Communist Party. She also befriended George Jackson, one of three Soledad Prison inmates accused of killing a prison guard.

WHAT DID SHE DO?
In August 1970, while on trial in the Marin County Courthouse, Jackson and several other inmates attempted to escape. Four people were killed in the escape attempt, including the judge, Harold J. Haley. Police found that Davis had purchased the weapons used in the escape attempt, including the shotgun used to kill Judge Haley.

DATE OF ARREST
October 13, 1970

CIRCUMSTANCES OF THE ARREST
For two months, Davis eluded the FBI (she was on the Ten Most Wanted List). She traveled with a fellow Communist, David Poindexter. In New York, they registered at a Howard Johnson Motor Lodge as Mr. and Mrs. George Gilbert. Five days later, the FBI tracked Davis and Poindexter to the motel and arrested them.

THE CHARGES
Accomplice to conspiracy, kidnapping, and murder

THE SENTENCE
An all-white jury acquitted Davis on all counts. She had spent 18 months in prison.

AFTERWARD
After her trial, Davis emigrated to Cuba. Later, she returned to the United States, where she continued her work as a political activist, calling for the abolition of prisons.

UNUSUAL FACT
In 1972, John Lennon and Yoko Ono wrote "Angela" in Davis's honor. That same year, Mick Jagger wrote "Sweet Black Angel" for her.

JEFFERSON DAVIS

(1808–1889)

NATIONALITY
American

WHO WAS HE?
Jefferson Davis was a Southern aristocrat, a graduate of West Point, a veteran of the Blackhawk and Mexican War, and a senator from the state of Mississippi.

WHAT DID HE DO?
In 1861, when Mississippi seceded from the Union, Davis left the U.S. Senate. He was named the first and only president of the Confederate States of America by the Confederate Congress (later, the appointment was ratified by the voters). He served as president and commander-in-chief of the Confederacy throughout the Civil War.

DATE OF ARREST
May 10, 1865

CIRCUMSTANCES OF THE ARREST
In April 1865, with Richmond ready to fall to Union General Ulysses S. Grant, Davis fled south. Federal troops caught up with him in Irwinville, Georgia. In his haste to escape capture, he grabbed his wife's overcoat instead of his own, which led to a rumor in the North that Davis had been captured while attempting to escape disguised as a woman.

THE CHARGE
Treason

THE SENTENCE
Davis's case never came to trial. After almost two years of imprisonment in Fort Monroe, Virginia, Davis was released on bail and the U.S. government dropped the charges against him.

AFTERWARD
After his release, Davis tried his hand at several businesses, but they all failed. He wrote a history, *The Rise and Fall of the Confederate Government*, which was published in 1881. He died in New Orleans in 1889 and was buried in Richmond, Virginia, the former capital of the Confederacy.

THE BAIL BONDSMEN
Davis did not have the $100,000 bail the federal government required, so the money was put up by several Northerners who sympathized with his case, including the newspaperman Horace Greeley and the robber baron Cornelius Vanderbilt.

EUGENE V. DEBS

(1855–1926)

DATE OF ARREST
June 30, 1918

THE CHARGE
Sedition

THE SENTENCE
Debs served as his own defense attorney during his trial. He was found guilty and sentenced to ten years imprisonment.

IN PRISON
Debs served time in a state prison in Moundsville, West Virginia, before being transferred to a federal prison in Atlanta. In 1920, the Socialist Party nominated him again as its candidate for the presidency. Although Debs was still in prison, he received 1 million votes. On Christmas Day 1921, President Warren G. Harding commuted Debs's sentence to time served and ordered his release.

AFTERWARD
Debs returned to his home in Terre Haute, Indiana. He was a sick man, but he still wrote and occasionally gave speeches. In 1926, he entered a sanitarium outside Chicago, where he died.

NATIONALITY
American

WHO WAS HE?
Eugene V. Debs was the founder of the American Railway Union, a four-time nominee of the Socialist Party for president of the United States, and an outspoken opponent of World War I and America's involvement in the war.

WHAT DID HE DO?
On June 16, 1918, Debs delivered a speech in Canton, Ohio, in which he condemned the war and called for the overthrow of the capitalist system in the United States. Debs said, "Yes, in good time we are going to sweep into power in this nation and throughout the world. We are going to destroy all enslaving and degrading capitalist institutions and re-create them as free and humanizing institutions. The world is daily changing before our eyes. The sun of capitalism is setting; the sun of socialism is rising."

WHAT DID HE DO?
DeLay was accused of trying to skirt Texas law by funneling through Republican national campaign committees $190,000 in contributions from corporations to state legislative candidates.

DATE OF ARREST
October 20, 2005

CIRCUMSTANCES OF THE ARREST
The day after an arrest warrant was issued for DeLay, he turned himself in at the Harris County Sheriff's Office. He was released after posting $10,000 bail.

THE CHARGES
Conspiracy and money laundering

THE SENTENCE
The DeLay trial was scheduled for October 26, 2010.

DELAY THE DANCER
In September 2009, DeLay was a competitor on the reality TV program *Dancing with the Stars*. He survived for three weeks before leaving the show because of stress fractures in his feet.

TOM DELAY
(1947–)

NATIONALITY
American

WHO IS HE?
Tom DeLay is a member of the Republican Party who represented Texas' 22nd Congressional District in the House of Representatives from 1984 to 2006. From 2003 to 2005, he was House Majority Leader. After he left Congress, he wrote his memoirs, *No Retreat, No Surrender: One American's Fight*, and founded First Principles, a political consulting organization.

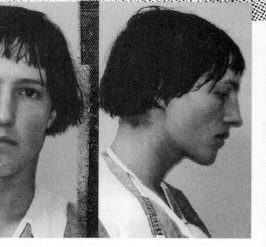

whipped his horse and sped off down the road. The deputies chased him in their police car for nearly a mile, until Detweiler tried to make a sharp turn up a driveway; he lost control of his buggy and ran it into a ditch. Detweiler scrambled out of the wreckage and ran away. Two Amish men who lived in the neighborhood helped the police get the horse out of the ditch. Inside the buggy, the officers found alcohol. A short time later they apprehended Detweiler.

THE CHARGES

Fleeing the scene of arrest, underage possession of alcohol, reckless endangerment, failure to yield to an emergency vehicle, and overdriving an animal

THE SENTENCE

Bail was set at $500, and Detweiler was remanded to the county jail.

LEVI DETWEILER

(1993–)

NATIONALITY

American

WHO IS HE?

Levi Detweiler is the son of an Amish farm family who live near Leon, New York.

WHAT DID HE DO?

At 1:30 a.m. on July 12, 2010, Levi Detweiler was driving his horse and buggy on Cherry Creek Hill Road. Deputies of the Cattaraugus County Sheriff's Office saw him cruise past a stop sign without bringing his vehicle to a halt.

DATE OF ARREST

July 12, 2010

CIRCUMSTANCES OF THE ARREST

The sheriff's deputies ordered Detweiler to pull over. Instead, he

EAMON DE VALERA

(1882–1975)

NATIONALITY
Irish

WHO WAS HE?
Eamon de Valera was born in New York City, the son of an Irish mother and a Cuban father. At age two, his uncle took him to Ireland to be raised by his grandmother. As a young man, he became involved in Irish nationalist organizations and participated in the failed Easter Rising of 1916.

WHAT DID HE DO?
Toward the end of Ireland's Civil War, de Valera advocated a general ceasefire, with all parties laying down their weapons. The Irish Free State government, which wanted to fight on until all of Ireland, including the province of Ulster, was free from British rule, considered such sentiments treasonous.

DATE OF ARREST
August 15, 1923

CIRCUMSTANCES OF THE ARREST
De Valera had been in hiding, but emerged in August. He was in Ennis, County Clare, about to give a speech when he was arrested for violating the Public Safety Act.

THE CHARGE
Sedition

THE SENTENCE
De Valera was sentenced to a year in prison

AFTERWARD
Eamon de Valera spent his life immersed in Irish politics. He was an advocate of Ireland's first constitution; resisted pressure from Winston Churchill to bring Ireland into World War II on the side of the Allies (Ireland remained neutral throughout the war); served as Taoiseach, or prime minister, of Ireland; and was president of Ireland from 1959 until 1973, when he retired at age 90.

WHAT DID HE DO?

Dick was at a club called Rum Runners in Huntington, West Virginia. When a security guard asked him to comply with the rules of the club and wear a wristband, Dick grabbed the guard's crotch. Later that evening, while talking with a patron, Dick repeatedly grabbed the man's crotch and kissed him.

DATE OF ARREST

January 23, 2010

THE CHARGE

Sexual abuse

JAIL TIME

Police took Dick to the Western Regional Jail in Barboursville, West Virginia, where he remained until a friend posted $60,000 bail.

TROUBLE WITH THE LAW

At the time of his arrest in West Virginia, there was another case pending against Dick: In July 2008, while leaving a Buffalo Wild Wings chicken joint in Murrietta, California, he pulled down the tank top and bra of a 17-year-old girl. Dick was arrested and charged with sexual battery.

ANDY DICK

(1965–)

NATIONALITY

American

WHO IS HE?

Andy Dick is a comedian, actor, producer, and lead singer in a comic band called Andy Dick and the Bitches of the Century.

ANDY

JOHN DILLINGER
(1903–1934)

NATIONALITY
American

WHO WAS HE?
John Dillinger was a troubled boy who grew up to be a violent man. During a ten-month period in 1933–1934, Dillinger and his gang went on a crime spree, robbing banks, killing 11 men and wounding 12. Yet at the time many Americans looked on Dillinger as a romantic, dashing, Robin Hood–style desperado.

WHAT DID HE DO?
In 1924, Dillinger attempted to rob a grocery store in his hometown, Mooresville, Indiana. On his father's advice, he pled guilty, and was sentenced to 10 to 20 years in prison. He was released after serving 8 1/2 years. He had been out of prison four months when he robbed a bank in Bluffton, Ohio.

DATE OF ARREST
September 22, 1933

THE ESCAPE
Police incarcerated Dillinger in Lima, Ohio. Meanwhile, eight of Dillinger's friends escaped from the Indiana State Prison; four of the escapees traveled to Lima to bust Dillinger out of jail. They locked the sheriff's wife and a deputy in a cell, and shot and killed the sheriff.

THE CHARGE
Bank robbery

DILLINGER AND HIS GANG
The Dillinger gang went on a crime spree, robbing banks, stealing weapons from police arsenals, and killing two police officers. In March 1934 the cops caught up with Dillinger in East Chicago, but he busted out of jail again, using a wooden gun he had whittled.

THE ALLEY
The FBI took up the Dillinger case. In July 1934, FBI agents tracked him to Chicago. On July 24, 1934, as Dillinger and two female companions watched a movie at the Biograph Theatre, three FBI agents set up a stakeout outside. When Dillinger and the women emerged from the theater, the agents moved in. Dillinger drew his pistol and ran down an alley. The FBI agents fired five shots—three of them struck John Dillinger, killing him.

PETE DOHERTY
(1979–)

DATE OF ARREST
March 19, 2010

CIRCUMSTANCES OF THE ARREST
The Whitehead case was the 21st time Doherty had been arrested. He was released on bail.

THE CHARGE
Suspicion of supplying controlled drugs

PREVIOUS ARRESTS
Between February 2005 and March 2010, Pete Doherty was arrested for robbery, blackmail, drug possession, driving under the influence, car theft, and assault.

NATIONALITY
English

WHO IS HE?
Pete Doherty is a singer and musician. With Carl Barât he formed the Libertines, which was active from 1997 to 2004; in 2010, Doherty and Barât re-formed the Libertines. Doherty appears regularly in the tabloids for his relationship with model Kate Moss, his heroin addiction, and his arrest record.

WHAT DID HE DO?
London police alleged that Doherty supplied narcotics to his friend, Robin Whitehead, a documentary filmmaker and heiress. Whitehead died of a suspected drug overdose.

NANNIE "THE JOLLY BLACK WIDOW" DOSS

(1905–1965)

NATIONALITY
American

WHO WAS SHE?
Nannie Doss appeared to be a friendly, outgoing, down-to-earth wife, mother, and grandmother, who had a weakness for romance and true confession magazines. But if members of her family "got on her nerves," as she put it, she poisoned them.

WHAT DID SHE DO?
Between 1927 and 1954, Doss murdered her mother, four of her five husbands, her sister Dovie, her grandson Robert, and one of her mothers-in-law. In 1954, she put rat poison in the coffee of her husband, Samuel Doss; the dose made him sick enough to see the family's doctor, W. D. Hidy, but it didn't kill him. Nannie Doss tried again, lacing a bowl of prunes with rat poison, which did kill Sam. His pa-tient's sudden death made Dr. Hidy suspicious, and he asked Nannie's permission to perform an autopsy. She gave her consent. The autopsy found that Samuel Doss had died of arsenic poisoning.

DATE OF ARREST
November 26, 1954

THE CHARGE
Murder

THE SENTENCE
The state of Oklahoma put Doss through a battery of psychological tests to establish that she was competent to stand trial. She was found to be sane. Prosecutors focused on the murder of Doss's fifth husband, Samuel Doss, because that case had the most evidence. Doss pled guilty and was sentenced to life in prison—Oklahoma had never executed a woman, and the judge stated that he did not want to set the precedent. Ten years later she died of leukemia in the penitentiary hospital.

AFTERWARD
In prison, Doss remained good-natured, and was delighted when *Life* magazine purchased the rights to publish her life story. When a visiting reporter asked Doss about her life at the penitentiary, she told him, "When they get shorthanded in the kitchen here, I always offer to help out, but they never do let me."

THE SIXTH MAN
At the time she was preparing to kill Samuel Doss, Nannie was corresponding with a man she met through a personal ad. She baked him a cake and mailed it to him. The cake was not poisoned.

ALFRED DREYFUS

(1859–1935)

NATIONALITY
French

WHO WAS HE?
Alfred Dreyfus was educated in military academies in preparation for a career in the French army. He studied at the École Superieure de Guerre, and was accepted as a trainee for the French army's General Staff. Dreyfus was the only Jewish candidate in the program.

WHAT DID HE DO?
In 1894, the French intelligence agency discovered that someone on the General Staff was passing military secrets to the Germans. Captain Dreyfus was suspected of being the traitor.

DATE OF ARREST
October 15, 1894

THE CHARGE
Treason

THE SENTENCE
Less than three months after his arrest, Dreyfus was tried before a court-martial and found guilty. He was stripped of his rank and sentenced to life imprisonment on Devil's Island, a prison colony in French Guiana.

THE REVELATION
In 1896, French military intelligence had a new chief, Lt. Col. Marie Georges Picquart. He reexamined the Dreyfus case and found that the most likely suspect was Major Ferdinand Walsin Esterhazy. Picquart's superiors rejected his findings, and reassigned him to service in southern Tunisia. The story of the Dreyfus–Picquart–Esterhazy affair was leaked to the press, setting off an intense public debate about anti-Semitism in France's government, military, and daily life. The author Émile Zola published a celebrated article titled, "J'accuse," in which he denounced the cover-up that kept an innocent man in prison.

A NEW TRIAL
In 1899, under pressure from public opinion, the army held a second trial, although even this was believed to be tainted—shortly before the trial began, forged documents that established Dreyfus's guilt were found in his file. Lt. Col. Hubert Henry came under suspicion and committed suicide. Nonetheless, the court confirmed the guilty verdict, but modified Dreyfus's sentence to ten years in prison. In September 1899, Émile Loubet, president of France, pardoned Dreyfus.

AFTERWARD
In 1906, Dreyfus was exonerated and restored to the rank of captain. In 1908, Dreyfus attended the interment of Émile Zola in the Pantheon in Paris. During the ceremony a right-wing journalist named Louis Gregori fired two shots at Dreyfus, wounding him slightly. Gregori was tried for attempted murder and acquitted.

DAVID DUKE

(1950–)

NATIONALITY
American

WHO IS HE?
David is a former Republican legislator in Louisiana who ran twice for the presidency of the United States. He also ran, unsuccessfully, for governor of Louisiana, the Louisiana State Senate, the U.S. Senate, and the U.S. House of Representatives. He is a former grand wizard of the Knights of the Ku Klux Klan.

WHAT DID HE DO?
Duke wrote a book titled, *My Awakening*, in which he denies that the Holocaust took place. In the Czech Republic, Holocaust denial is a crime punishable by three years in prison.

DATE OF ARREST
April 24, 2009

CIRCUMSTANCES OF THE ARREST
Duke had come to the Czech Republic at the invitation of Czech neo-Nazis to promote the Czech translation of his book. He was also scheduled to speak at Prague's Charles University on the subject of extremism, but university administrators canceled his lecture.

THE CHARGE
Holocaust denial

THE RESOLUTION
Rather than press charges, the Czech government released Duke, ordering him to leave the country.

A DIFFERENT KIND OF RECEPTION
In 2006, Duke was invited to Tehran to attend a conference on the Holocaust sponsored by Mahmoud Ahmadinejad, president of Iran. In an interview with the *Associated Press*, Duke said, "The Holocaust is the device used as the pillar of Zionist imperialism, Zionist aggression, Zionist terror, and Zionist murder."

FRANCISCO MARTIN DURAN
(1968–)

NATIONALITY
American

WHO IS HE?
Francisco Martin Duran was an upholsterer from Colorado.

WHAT DID HE DO?
On October 29, 1994, Duran stood outside the fence on the north side of the White House and fired a semiautomatic rifle at a group of men standing on the lawn—he believed that one of the men was President Bill Clinton.

DATE OF ARREST
October 29, 1994

CIRCUMSTANCES OF THE ARREST
As Secret Service agents sprinted across the White House lawn toward Duran, three passerbys tackled and held him down until law enforcement arrived.

THE CHARGES
Attempted assassination of a U.S. president and assault on a federal officer

THE DEFENSE
Duran's attorneys employed the insanity defense for their client. Duran stated that in the mountains of Colorado he encountered an alien being that was using an evil mist to control the U.S. government and eventually the entire world. Duran believed it was his mission to destroy the mist. Psychiatrists and psychologists who testified for the prosecution said that Duran's insanity was a ruse.

THE SENTENCE
The jury found Duran guilty of attempting to assassinate President Clinton, and guilty of assaulting four Secret Service agents, illegal possession of firearms, using the firearms in the commission of a crime of violence, and causing $3,400 of damage to the White House. Duran was sentenced to 40 years in prison.

WHERE WAS THE PRESIDENT?
President Clinton was not on the lawn at the time of the shooting, but in the First Family's residence, watching a football game.

MONK EASTMAN

(C.1875–1920)

NATIONALITY
American

WHO WAS HE?
After working as a bouncer at a nightclub, Monk Eastman started his own gang on New York's Lower East Side. Eastman specialized in robbery and extortion.

WHAT DID HE DO?
At 3:00 in the morning of February 2, 1903, near Broadway and 42nd Street in New York City, Eastman and an accomplice tried to rob a wealthy young man.

DATE OF ARREST
February 2, 1903

CIRCUMSTANCES OF THE ARREST
The young man was being shadowed by two Pinkerton detectives who, unbeknownst to him, had been hired by his family to keep him out of trouble. When the detectives intervened, Eastman and his accomplice fired at the Pinkertons, then ran off, but were intercepted by a New York City police detective.

THE CHARGE
Felonious assault with attempt to kill

THE SENTENCE
Eastman was found guilty and sentenced to ten years in prison.

AFTERWARD
After serving five years in Sing Sing, Eastman was released. In 1917, he enlisted in the army to fight in World War I. During his physical, the army physician asked Eastman where he had gotten the bullet and knife scars. Eastman replied, "Oh, a lot of little wars around New York." After serving in France, Eastman went back to his life of crime. In 1920, at 4:00 in the morning on a dark street in Lower Manhattan, a rival gangster shot and killed Monk Eastman.

ADOLF EICHMANN
(1906–1962)

NATIONALITY
German

WHO WAS HE?
Adolf Eichmann was born in Germany but grew up in Linz, Austria, where his father operated a small mining business. Eichmann was an unsettled young man who abandoned his studies for a degree in engineering, worked for his father for a time, took a job in an electrical construction company, then became a traveling salesman for an oil company. He joined the Austrian Nazi Party in 1932, went to work for Heinrich Himmler's Security Service (SD) in Germany in 1934, and gradually rose ever higher in the Nazi Party.

WHAT DID HE DO?
From 1941 to 1945, Eichmann was head of the Gestapo's Department for Jewish Affairs—in other words, he was responsible for sending 3 million Jews to the death camps. He visited several of the camps to see firsthand how efficiently camp officials exterminated their prisoners.

CAPTURED
At the end of the war, American troops captured Eichmann and placed him in an internment camp. Eichmann escaped the camp and fled to Argentina, where he lived under an alias, Ricardo Klement.

DATE OF ARREST
May 2, 1960

CIRCUMSTANCES OF THE ARREST
Two agents of the Mossad, Israel's secret service, tracked Eichmann to his apartment in a suburb of Buenos Aires. They smuggled him out of the country to stand trial in Jerusalem.

THE CHARGE
Crimes against humanity

THE DEFENSE
At his trial, Eichmann defended his actions, saying, "Why me? Everybody killed the Jews."

THE SENTENCE
Adolf Eichmann was found guilty and sentenced to death. He was hanged in Ramleh prison on May 31, 1962.

THE BANALITY OF EVIL
Hannah Arendt, a German Jew who left the country before Hitler took power, covered the Eichmann trial for the *New Yorker*. She observed that he was not a fanatical anti-Semite, but an ordinary bureaucrat who committed horrible crimes because it was his job. Arendt said that Eichmann epitomized what she called, "the banality of evil."

DATE OF ARREST
June 4, 2000

CIRCUMSTANCES OF THE ARREST
The judge permitted Eminem to continue his tour, but if he left the state of Michigan he was required to supply his itinerary to police. Eminem was released after posting a $100,000 bond.

THE CHARGES
Carrying a concealed weapon and assault with a deadly weapon.

THE SENTENCE
In a plea deal, Eminem pled guilty to carrying a concealed weapon. In return, he would do no jail time. The judge sentenced Eminem to two years' probation, also ordering him to avoid excessive drinking and "assaultive behavior," and to undergo counseling. Furthermore, he was forbidden to own any weapon.

EMINEM (MARSHALL MATHERS)
(1972–)

NATIONALITY
American

WHO IS HE?
Marshall Bruce Mathers III (better known by his stage name, Eminem) is a rapper, record producer, and actor, whose first album, *The Slim Shady*, won a Grammy for Best Rap Album. He would go on to win 11 Grammys, plus an Oscar for Best Original Song, "Lose Yourself."

WHAT DID HE DO?
Outside a nightclub in Warren, Michigan, Eminem saw a man kissing his wife, Kim. Eminem pulled out an unloaded pistol and hit the man in the head.

PABLO ESCOBAR

(1949–1993)

NATIONALITY
Colombian

WHO WAS HE?
Pablo Escobar was a lifelong criminal who became chief of the notorious Medellín drug cartel. Eventually, 80 percent of cocaine shipped for sale to the United States was manufactured by Escobar's cartel. Nonetheless, he fashioned for himself an image as a Colombian Robin Hood by giving generously to the poor, especially in Medellín.

WHAT DID HE DO?
In addition to smuggling cocaine into the United States, Escobar was believed to be responsible for the kidnapping and murder of many of his enemies and rivals, as well as police officers and government officials.

DATE OF ARREST
November 18, 1986

THE CHARGE
Drug smuggling and racketeering

THE SENTENCE
After Escobar's arrest, his associates began to murder people associated with the upcoming trial. As a result of this terror campaign, the charges against Escobar were dropped.

PRISON TIME
In 1991, Escobar and the Colombian government reached an agreement: He would agree to serve a five-year prison sentence, but it must be in a prison of his construction. In return, the government would not extradite him to the United States. Escobar's prison resembled a luxury hotel, where he was visited by friends and prostitutes, and received a steady supply of gourmet meals, drugs, and alcohol. In 1992, the government insisted that Escobar move to a state prison, but during the transfer he escaped.

THE MANHUNT
For 16 months, Colombian police and Search Bloc agents, aided by Delta Force from the United States, searched for Escobar, who retaliated by killing over 600 police officers. A vigilante group, called Los Pepes, joined the fight, blowing up Escobar's facilities and killing his senior aides as well as his relatives. In 1993, Search Bloc agents caught up with Escobar; in the shootout that ensued, Escobar was shot and killed.

THE FORBES LIST
In 1989, *Forbes* magazine listed Escobar as the seventh richest man in the world, with a personal fortune estimated at $24 billion.

MICHAEL JUDE FAY

(1951–2009)

NATIONALITY
American

WHO WAS HE?
Michael Jude Fay was a Catholic priest, pastor of St. John's Church in the affluent town of Darien, Connecticut.

WHAT DID HE DO?
Fay embezzled at least $1 million from his parish, spending the money on lavish vacations, Cartier jewelry, designer clothes, expensive furnishings for the rectory, a condo in Florida, and an apartment on New York's Upper East Side.

DATE OF ARREST
May 17, 2006

CIRCUMSTANCES OF THE ARREST
When the parish bookkeeper and the assistant pastor became suspicious of Fay's high living, they hired a private investigator.

THE CHARGE
Interstate transportation of money obtained by fraud

THE SENTENCE
Fay pled guilty and was sentenced to 37 months in prison. The judge ordered him to repay the $1 million he stole from his parish. Fay asked the judge to spare him from going to prison, as he had been diagnosed with terminal prostate cancer. The judge declined the request.

AFTERWARD
Michael Jude Fay died in prison of prostate cancer in August 2009. St. John's bookkeeper claimed that the Diocese of Bridgeport punished her for her role as a whistle-blower by cutting her benefits and creating a hostile work environment. She sued, and the diocese settled out of court. The associate pastor left the priesthood, claiming that William Lori, the bishop of Bridgeport, unjustly blamed him for bringing the scandal to light.

RONALD DE FEO JR.

(1951–)

NATIONALITY
American

WHO IS HE?
Ronald De Feo Jr., is the eldest son of a Long Island, New York, family. He was a troubled kid who ran away from home three times and hung out with a rough bunch of kids.

WHAT DID HE DO?
About 3:00 in the morning of November 13, 1974, De Feo shot and killed his parents, Ronald and Louise De Feo; his sisters, Dawn, 18, and Allison, 13; and his brothers Marc, 12, and John, 9.

DATE OF ARREST
November 14, 1974

CIRCUMSTANCES OF THE ARREST
At 6:30 in the evening of November 13, 1974, De Feo ran into Henry's Bar in Amityville, shouting, "You got to help me! I think my mother and father are shot!" Several people from the bar followed De Feo to his family's house, where they found Ronald and Louise dead in their bed. When the police arrived, De Feo claimed that his family were the victims of a mob hit; the police took him to the station for his own safety. At the station, De Feo confessed that he had murdered his parents and siblings. "Once it started, I just couldn't stop," he told the police. "It went so fast."

THE CHARGE
Murder

THE SENTENCE
De Feo was found guilty and given six consecutive life sentences in prison.

THE AMITYVILLE HORROR
Thanks to Jay Anson's 1977 novel, *The Amityville Horror*, the murder of the De Feos has become linked to tales that the family's house was built on an ancient Indian burial ground and that angry spirits urged Ronald De Feo to murder. The Lutz family, who bought the De Feo house in 1977, claimed that they were terrorized by evil spirits and abandoned the house only 28 days after they moved in (the Lutzes' story became the basis for Anson's novel and the subsequent movies).

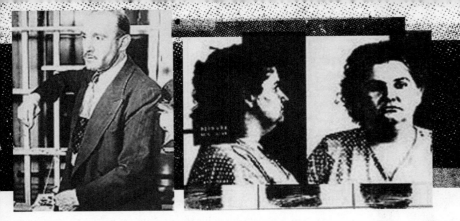

RAYMOND FERNANDEZ

(1914–1951)

MARTHA BECK

(1920–1951),
"THE LONELY HEARTS KILLERS"

NATIONALITY
American

WHO WERE THEY?
Raymond Fernandez was a gigolo and con man who targeted female members of "lonely hearts clubs," winning their love, then stealing their money and jewelry. Martha Beck was a nurse and a single mother of two whom Fernandez had initially targeted as his next victim. Instead, they became partners—but only after Beck abandoned her children at the Salvation Army.

WHAT DID THEY DO?
In 1949, Beck caught Fernandez in bed with their current mark, 66-year-old Janet Fay. In a fit of jealous rage, Beck struck Fay's head with a hammer; Fernandez finished her off by strangling. Their next victim was Delphine Downing, a widow with a two-year-old daughter. Fernandez drugged Downing then shot her; Beck drowned the little girl. When neighbors did not see the Downings for a time, they called the police.

DATE OF ARREST
February 28, 1949

CIRCUMSTANCES OF THE ARREST
The police had no trouble tracking down Fernandez and Beck—they were living in the Downings' house.

THE CHARGE
Murder

THE TRIAL
Fernandez and Beck had signed a 73-page confession, assuming that they would be tried in Michigan, which did not have the death penalty. But they were extradited for trial to New York, their state of residence, which did have the death penalty. Newspapers published lurid accounts of the couple's bizarre sexual practices (Fernandez dabbled in the occult) and commented on Beck's size (she weighed 200 pounds).

THE SENTENCE
Raymond Fernandez and Martha Beck were found guilty and sentenced to the electric chair on August 22, 1949. They were executed on March 8, 1951.

JACQUES FESCH
(1930–1957)

NATIONALITY
French

WHO WAS HE?
Jacques Fesch was the wastrel son of a well-to-do Parisian family. At age 21, he married Pierrette Polack, who was pregnant with his child. Shortly after Pierrette gave birth to a daughter, Fesch abandoned them and had affairs with several women. One of these affairs produced a son—Fesch abandoned the boy and his mother, too. In 1954, Fesch decided to start a new life—in the South Pacific. And he wanted his father to buy him a yacht so he could sail to his new home in style. Fesch's father refused.

WHAT DID HE DO?
During the evening rush hour on February 25, 1954, Fesch entered a currency exchange shop near the Paris Stock Exchange. Pulling a pistol from his briefcase, Fesch ordered the currency dealer, Alexandre Silberstein, to hand over all the cash in the till. When Silberstein protested, Fesch pistol-whipped him, grabbed 300,000 francs, and ran out into the street.

DATE OF ARREST
February 25, 1954

CIRCUMSTANCES OF THE ARREST
Silberstein stumbled out of his shop, calling for help. A police officer, 35-year-old Jean Vergne, ran after Fesch, shouting for him to surrender. Instead, Fesch pulled out his pistol and fired, killing Vergne instantly. Officer Vergne was a widower and the father of a four-year-old girl. Fesch tried to escape, but he was pursued by a large crowd that held him until more police arrived.

THE CHARGE
Murder

THE SENTENCE
Fesch was found guilty of murder and sentenced to the guillotine.

AFTERWARD
In prison, Fesch was surly and unrepentant. He mocked his devoutly Catholic defense attorney and sent away the prison chaplain. But in February 1955, he claimed to have had a dramatic conversion experience. He called for the chaplain, made his confession, reconciled with his wife and parents, and began to spend long periods praying. His conversion did not mitigate his sentence. Jacques Fesch was beheaded on October 1, 1957. Just before the blade fell, he prayed, "Holy Virgin, have pity on me!"

UNUSUAL FACT
In 1987, the archbishop of Paris, Cardinal Jean Marie Lustiger, began the process that could lead to Jacques Fesch being declared a saint of the Roman Catholic Church.

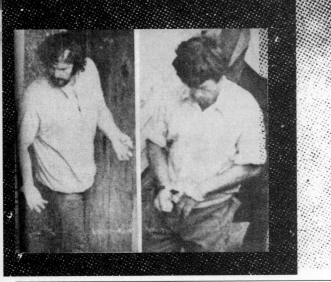

JAMES RICHARD FINCH
(1944–)

JOHN ANDREW STUART
(1940–1979)

NATIONALITY
Australian

WHO WERE THEY?
James Richard Finch and John Andrew Stuart were career criminals. Finch had already served 14 years in prison, Stuart had served 12, in addition to several stints in mental health institutions.

WHAT DID THEY DO?
At approximately 2:00 in the morning of March 8, 1973, Finch and Stuart went to the Whiskey Au Go Go nightclub in Brisbane, Australia. They poured two drums of gasoline into the club, then set it on fire. Fifteen people died in the fire.

DATE OF ARREST
March 8, 1973

CIRCUMSTANCES OF THE ARREST
When the police arrived, Stuart became violent—it took six detectives to restrain him. Finch remained calm.

THE CHARGES
Arson and murder

THE SENTENCE
During the trial both men insisted that they were innocent. Nonetheless, they were both convicted of arson and murder and sentenced to life in prison.

AFTERWARD
In 1979, Stuart went on a hunger strike; he was found dead in his cell on the sixth day. Finch appealed his conviction for 15 years; in 1988, he was released, but was required to leave the country. In England, Finch admitted that he had firebombed the club.

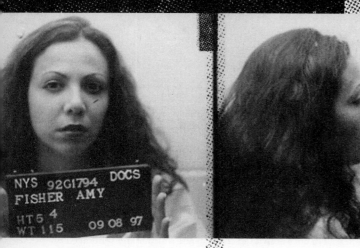

NYS 92G1794 DOCS
FISHER AMY
HT 5 4
WT 115   09 08 97

AMY FISHER

(1974–)

NATIONALITY

American

WHO IS SHE?

At age 16, Amy Fisher began an affair with Joey Buttafuocco, the owner of an auto body repair shop. Buttafuocco was 35 years old and married at the time.

WHAT DID SHE DO?

On May 13, 1992, Fisher asked a friend to drive her to the Buttafuoccos' house in Massapequa, New York. When Mary Jo Buttafuocco came to the door, Fisher shot her in the head. Mary Jo survived the shooting.

DATE OF ARREST

May 21, 1992

CIRCUMSTANCES OF THE ARREST

When Mary Jo described her attacker, Joey realized that it was Amy. He confessed to his wife that he had been having an affair, and notified the police. Amy Fisher was arrested at her parents' home in Merrick, New York. The case became a media sensation—the press christened Amy "the Long Island Lolita."

THE CHARGE

Attempted murder

THE SENTENCE

Fisher pled guilty to first-degree assault and was sentenced to 5 to 15 years in prison. She was released on parole after serving 7 years.

AFTERWARD

Amy Fisher married, had two children, wrote two books, and became a porn star.

HEIDI FLEISS, "THE HOLLYWOOD MADAM"

(1965–)

NATIONALITY
American

WHO IS SHE?
Heidi Fleiss operated a call-girl agency that catered to Hollywood celebrities. The women in Fleiss's agency, many of whom had been fashion models, commanded up to $10,000 per assignment.

WHAT DID SHE DO?
Fleiss was accused of laundering at least $300,000.

DATE OF ARREST
June 8, 1993

CIRCUMSTANCES OF THE ARREST
Fleiss was taking out the garbage when the police arrived at her home with a warrant for her arrest.

THE CHARGES
Conspiracy, income tax evasion, and money laundering

THE SENTENCE
Fleiss was found guilty and sentenced to 37 months in prison.

AFTERWARD
After her release from prison, Fleiss wrote two books, *Pandering* and *The Player's Handbook*, and released a DVD titled *Sex Tips*. In an interview with CNN, she said of her days as the Hollywood Madam, "I took the oldest profession on earth and I did it better than anyone on earth."

CHARLES "PRETTY BOY" FLOYD
(1904–1934)

NATIONALITY
American

WHO WAS HE?
Charles "Pretty Boy" Floyd was born in Georgia; his father was a tenant farmer and occasional bootlegger. At age 21, Charles Floyd moved to St. Louis, where he held up stores and warehouses and served his first prison term. In 1930, while being escorted to prison once again, Floyd escaped.

WHAT DID HE DO?
On June 17, 1933, Floyd and two accomplices, Adam Richetti and Vernon Miller, tried to rescue a friend, Frank Nash, whom law enforcement officers were returning to prison in Leavenworth, Kansas. As two police officers and five FBI agents escorted Nash to a car outside Union Station in Kansas City, Floyd and his accomplices opened fire, killing the two police officers, two of the FBI agents, and Nash.

THE GETAWAY
Floyd, Miller, and Richetti escaped—Miller to Detroit, where he was killed by a mobster; Floyd and Richetti to Buffalo, where they lived for several months with their girlfriends, Rose and Beulah Baird. In October 1934, they decided to move to Oklahoma.

DATE OF ARREST
October 22, 1934

THE CHARGE
Murder

CIRCUMSTANCES OF THE ARREST
Outside Wellsville, Ohio, Floyd drove his car into a telephone pole. While the women took the car to a repair shop, Floyd and Richetti hid on the outskirts of town. They were spotted by local residents who called the police; when police went out to investigate, Floyd and Richetti opened fire. The police snagged Richetti, but Floyd got away. Two days later, the FBI tracked Floyd to a farm in eastern Ohio. There was another shootout, and Floyd was wounded. The FBI agents placed Floyd under arrest and called for an ambulance, but he died before it arrived.

AFTERWARD
When the Baird sisters learned that Richetti had been arrested and Floyd was dead, they hurried out of Wellsville and headed to Kansas City, Missouri. They arrived in time to attend Floyd's funeral in Sallinaw, Oklahoma. Richetti was tried for murder, found guilty, and was executed in the gas chamber of the Missouri State Penitentiary in Jefferson City.

THE NICKNAME
Floyd acquired his nickname from a witness to one of his holdups. She described the robber as "a pretty boy."

ERROL FLYNN
(1909–1959)

NATIONALITY
Australian-born American citizen

WHO WAS HE?
Errol Flynn was one of the most popular actors in Hollywood, renowned for his swashbuckling performances in such classics as *Captain Blood* and *The Adventures of Robin Hood*. He was also a notorious womanizer.

WHAT DID HE DO?
In September 1942, Flynn met Betty Hansen at a Hollywood dinner party—Hansen was 17 years old. The next day, Hansen told her sister that Flynn had taken her upstairs and they had had sex. When Hansen's family filed a complaint, the district attorney already had another complaint on file against Flynn for having sex with a minor aboard his yacht.

DATE OF ARRAIGNMENT
November 23, 1942

CIRCUMSTANCES OF THE ARRAIGNMENT
Florabel Muir, one of the newspaper reporters who covered the arraignment, wrote, "If Errol was panicky, he managed to conceal it. He was courteous and dreadfully serious while he was being fingerprinted."

THE CHARGE
Statutory rape

THE TRIAL
In jury selection, Flynn's defense attorney chose nine women, hoping they would be dazzled by Flynn's good looks. On the witness stand, the young women sounded confused while Flynn eloquently denied all charges. He was acquitted.

A NEW PHRASE
After Errol Flynn's acquittal, a new phrase became popular—"In like Flynn." Originally it meant to be lucky, or for everything to be going well. Later, it acquired a sexual connotation.

139813
C LEVELAND
32 5 8 126
NOV 3 1970

BUSTED

JANE FONDA

(1937–)

NATIONALITY
American

WHO IS SHE?
The daughter of renowned actor Henry Fonda, Jane Fonda began her own acting career in the 1960s, which included starring in *They Shoot Horses Don't They*, for which she was nominated for an Academy Award. In the '60s, Fonda was also politically active, particularly in the anti–Vietnam War movement.

WHAT DID SHE DO?
Fonda had been in Ontario giving an anti–Vietnam War speech. As she reentered the United States at Cleveland's Hopkins International Airport, U.S. customs officials stopped her, searched her luggage and purse, and found 105 bottles of pills, which Fonda identified as vitamins. After being held for several hours, Fonda got up to use the bathroom; an FBI agent tried to stop her, so she shoved him aside.

DATE OF ARREST
November 2, 1970

THE HEARING
From the security room at the airport, Fonda was taken to Cuyahoga County Jail. The next morning police led her, past a crowd of reporters and TV cameras, to the courthouse. She was released on $5,500 bail.

THE CHARGES
Assaulting an officer and smuggling narcotics

THE SENTENCE
When it was found that the pills actually were vitamins, the charges for drug smuggling and assaulting an officer were dropped.

JANE FONDA IN JAIL
At the county jail, a fellow prisoner told her, "They ought to throw you in jail. We don't want no Commies running around loose in this country." When Fonda asked what he was in for, he replied, "Murder."

JOHN T. FORD

(1829–1894)

NATIONALITY
American

WHO WAS HE?
John T. Ford was one of the most successful theatrical entrepreneurs in 19th-century America. He and his brothers, Frank and Harry Clay Ford, owned Ford's Theatre in Washington, D.C. They were also good friends with the celebrated actor, John Wilkes Booth.

WHAT DID HE DO?
On April 14, 1865, when President Abraham Lincoln and his wife, Mary, along with two friends came to the theater, none of the Ford brothers were present. John was in Richmond, the one-time capital of the newly defeated Confederacy, which government investigators considered particularly suspicious.

DATE OF ARREST
April 18, 1865

CIRCUMSTANCES OF THE ARREST
John was arrested at his home in Baltimore. His brothers were also rounded up and, together, they were confined in the Old Capitol Prison in Washington. In prison, John wrote twice to Secretary of War Edwin Stanton, who was leading the investigation, protesting his innocence and offering to help the government identify and arrest the real conspirators. Stanton never replied to Ford's letters.

THE CHARGE
Conspiracy to assassinate the president

THE OUTCOME
After 39 days in prison, the charge was dismissed and the three brothers were released. The government, however, did not return the theater to the Ford brothers; instead, they received a payment of $100,000.

AFTERWARD
From 1866 to 1931, the federal government used Ford's Theatre as office space and as a warehouse. In 1893, part of the building collapsed, killing 22 clerks and injuring 68. From 1931 until 1964, the building stood empty; then Congress funded a complete restoration of the theater, which reopened as a tourist attraction in 1968.

PETER FOSTER

(1962–)

NATIONALITY
Australian

WHO IS HE?
Peter Foster has been called "the International Man of Mischief" and the "the World's Greatest Living Con Man." Since age 14, he has been a wildly successful entrepreneur who has made millions on everything from leasing pinball machines to selling weight-loss products to producing television programs. He was also an international playboy, who has been linked to such beauties as pop star Samantha Fox.

WHAT DID HE DO?
After the year 2000, Foster became involved in politics in Fiji, donating more than $1 million (Fiji) to the New Labour Unity Party, which antagonized the government in power. In 2006, the Fijian government accused Foster of forging a police clearance certificate in order to obtain a Fijian work permit.

DATE OF ARREST
October 25, 2006

CIRCUMSTANCES OF THE ARREST
At the time of Foster's arrest, Fijian police beat him so severely that he required hospitalization for several days before he could be taken into custody.

THE CHARGES
Forgery, passing forged documents, and obtaining a work permit on forged documents

CONDITIONS OF HIS ARREST
Initially, Foster was kept under house arrest at a hotel, but he asked—and received permission—to relocate to his home in Fiji. In January 2007, Foster skipped bail and fled aboard a private boat crewed by Australians to Vanuatu.

THE SENTENCE IN VANUATU
For entering Vanuatu illegally, Foster was fined $1,400 (Australian) and sentenced to six weeks in jail. He served three weeks, was released, then flew home to Australia in spite of the Fijian government's demand that he be extradited for trial.

AFTERWARD
In 2009, Peter Foster signed a $1.2 million contract with a British publisher for the story of his life—the largest advance a British publisher has ever paid to an Australian.

JOE FRANCIS

(1973–)

NATIONALITY
American

WHO IS HE?
Joe Francis is the founder of the *Girls Gone Wild* DVD franchise, and its spin-off, *Guys Gone Wild*. His business is said be worth hundreds of millions of dollars.

WHAT DID HE DO?
During spring break, Francis filmed seven young women, all of whom were minors, in sexually compromising situations. The girls sued. During the settlement negotiation, Francis shouted obscenities and then went to the media: He described the judge mediating the negotiation as a "judge gone wild." The judge ordered Francis to settle the case; Francis refused, and was cited for contempt of court.

DATE OF ARREST
April 10, 2007

CIRCUMSTANCES OF THE ARREST
At 6:30 in the morning of April 10, 2007, police at Florida's Panama City Airport recognized Francis and arrested him. Francis claimed that he was on his way to turn himself in.

THE CHARGE
Contempt of court

MORE TROUBLE
The day after Francis was taken into custody in Panama City, a federal grand jury indicted him for tax evasion, citing $20 million worth of allegedly bogus business deductions he had taken.

EVEN MORE TROUBLE
The day after he was charged with tax evasion, Francis was charged with bribing a public servant, possessing a controlled substance, and introducing contraband into a detention facility. Allegedly, while in jail, Francis offered a guard $100 for a bottle of water. When the guard refused, Francis offered him $500. When guards searched his cell, they found 16 prescription medications. Inmates are not permitted to keep cash in jail.

THE SENTENCE
Francis pled guilty to the contempt charge and was sentenced to 35 days in jail.

AFTERWARD
As for the bribery and contraband charges, Francis pled guilty to the contraband charge, was sentenced to time served, and fined $60,000. In 2009, the Internal Revenue Service filed a tax lien against Francis for more than $33 million.

ANTOINETTE FRANK

(1971–)

NATIONALITY
American

WHO IS SHE?
Antoinette Frank was a New Orleans police officer who worked as a security guard at a Vietnamese restaurant in East New Orleans.

WHAT DID SHE DO?
On March 4, 1995, after the restaurant had closed and the owner, Chau Vu, was counting cash in the kitchen, Frank entered the restaurant dining room and at gunpoint demanded that an employee hand over the money. Chau hid the cash in the microwave, then, with another employee, took refuge inside the restaurant's walk-in refrigerator. In the dining room, three of the restaurant's employees told Frank they did not know where the money was—she shot and killed them.

DATE OF ARREST
March 4, 1994

CIRCUMSTANCES OF THE ARREST
The police arrived as Frank was hunting for Chau and the other restaurant employee. Frank identified herself as a police officer, but Chau yelled that Frank was the killer. At police headquarters, Frank confessed to the crime.

THE CHARGE
Murder

THE SENTENCE
Frank was found guilty and sentenced to death. She was scheduled to be executed in December 2008, but received a stay of execution.

TELEVISION
Frank's crime was the inspiration for the "Saigon Rose" episode of the television crime drama, *Homicide: Life on the Street*.

LEO FRANK

(1884–1915)

NATIONALITY
American

WHO WAS HE?
Leo Frank had moved from Brooklyn to Atlanta to manage the National Pencil Company factory there. He became president of the city's Jewish fraternal organization, B'nai B'rith.

WHAT DID HE DO?
Frank was accused of murdering Mary Phagan, a 13-year-old girl who, until recently, had worked at the factory.

DATE OF ARREST
April 29, 1913

CIRCUMSTANCES OF THE ARREST
The day of the murder, April 27, 1913, was a Sunday, and the factory was closed. The only employees in the building were Frank, who was working in his office, Jim Conley, the factory janitor, and Newt Lee, the factory watchman. Frank came under suspicion after police discovered what they believed to be bloodstains and hair they believed to be Mary's in the workroom across from Frank's office.

THE CHARGE
Murder

THE TRIAL
Jim Conley, the factory janitor, testified that Frank had admitted to murdering Mary Phagan, and together they hid the body in the factory's basement. Throughout the trial, a large, hostile, anti-Frank crowd stood outside the courthouse.

THE SENTENCE
Frank was found guilty and sentenced to be hanged. For his part in the crime, Conley was sentenced to one year on a chain gang.

AFTERWARD
William Smith, the attorney who represented Conley, made a public declaration that he believed his client had murdered Mary Phagan. Frank hired a new defense team to appeal his case. Meanwhile, John Slaton, governor of Georgia, reviewed the evidence from the trial. When word leaked out that Slaton was considering commuting Frank's sentence to life imprisonment, 1,000 people signed a declaration that if the governor granted Frank a commutation, they would avenge Mary Phagan's murder by killing Slaton and his wife. In spite of the threat, Slaton commuted Frank's sentence, and sent him to the Milledgeville prison farm, 100 miles from Atlanta, where he hoped Frank would be safe.

THE LYNCHING
On August 16, 1915, 25 men stormed the prison, overpowered the guards, and seized Frank. He was pushed into the back seat of a car and driven to a wooded area outside Marietta, where he was lynched. A Marietta newspaper editorialized, "We regard the hanging of Leo M. Frank in Cobb County as an act of law-abiding citizens."

MARTIN FRANKEL

(1954–)

NATIONALITY
American

WHO IS HE?
Martin Frankel was a Connecticut financier who claimed to invest the assets of insurance companies.

WHAT DID HE DO?
Through a trust, Frankel purchased small insurance companies in Arkansas, Mississippi, Oklahoma, Missouri, and Tennessee. Instead of investing the companies' assets, however, he pocketed the money—at least $200 million. He used the money to buy a four-acre estate in Greenwich, Connecticut, and a fleet of 30 black Mercedes and BMWs, among other high-end luxury items.

THE DISAPPEARANCE
In 1999, insurance regulators in Mississippi began asking Frankel uncomfortable questions about his insurance companies. As he prepared to leave the country, he told his assistant to destroy the company's files. She filled large plastic garbage bags with shredded files, and tried to burn others. The fire set off the smoke detector, which brought firefighters to Frankel's estate.

FRANKEL'S NOTES
Among Frankel's papers, police found a "to-do" list that included "Launder money" and "Get $ to Israel." There was also an astrological chart that purported to answer the question, "Will I go to prison?"

DATE OF ARREST
September 4, 1999

CIRCUMSTANCES OF THE ARREST
Frankel was arrested at a hotel in Hamburg, Germany. A search of his room uncovered nine phony passports and a stash of hundreds of diamonds. Eventually, Frankel would also turn over $118 million in assets, including $30 million from his Swiss bank accounts.

THE CHARGES
Insurance fraud, racketeering, and money laundering

THE SENTENCE
Frankel was found guilty and sentenced to 17 years in prison.

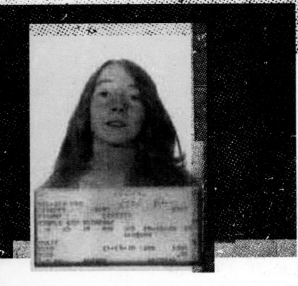

LYNETTE "SQUEAKY" FROMME
(1948–)

NATIONALITY
American

WHO IS SHE?
In 1967, Lynette "Squeaky" Fromme joined the "family" of Charles Manson, the mastermind of the infamous 1969 Sharon Tate killings. Fromme did not participate in the murders, but she remained loyal to Manson even after his conviction and imprisonment.

WHAT DID SHE DO?
On 1975 in Sacramento, California, Fromme pointed a gun at President Gerald Ford. Before she could fire, Secret Service agents tackled her. An inspection of the gun found that, although it had a full clip, no bullet was in the chamber.

DATE OF ARREST
September 5, 1975

THE CHARGE
Attempted assassination of the president

THE SENTENCE
Fromme was found guilty and sentenced to life in prison. Under the sentencing guidelines in place in 1975, she was eligible for parole, and in 2009 Fromme was released.

LIFE IN PRISON
In 1979, Fromme attacked a fellow inmate with a clawhammer. In 1987, she escaped from Alderson Federal Penitentiary in Alderson, West Virginia, but was apprehended two days later. Both incidents resulted in additional prison time being tacked onto her sentence.

NICKNAME
Manson and his followers lived on the Spahn Ranch. It is said that Fromme got the name Squeaky because she squeaked whenever the ranch's owner, George Spahn, tried to grope her.

SATARO FUKIAGE

(1889–1926)

THE CHARGE
Murder

SENTENCE
Fukiage was found guilty of murder and sentenced to be hanged.

NATIONALITY
Japanese

WHO WAS HE?
Sataro Fukiage was something of a sexual, criminal, and intellectual prodigy. He lost his virginity at age 11 to a 17-year-old girl. He was first arrested for theft at age 12. During his stints in jail, he studied mathematics and classical Chinese.

WHAT DID HE DO?
Beginning at age 17, Fukiage went on a rape-and-killing spree, murdering at least 7 girls and raping perhaps as many as 100 women and girls.

DATE OF ARREST
July 28, 1924

CIRCUMSTANCES OF THE ARREST
Initially, Fukiage confessed to the murders of 13 girls. Later, he retracted his confession, saying that he had been tricked by the police; he now claimed that he had only killed six girls.

WHAT DID SHE DO?

Beverly Hills police officer Paul Kramer pulled Gabor over for a traffic violation. Gabor claimed that he was obscene and rude to her, so she slapped Kramer across the face.

DATE OF ARREST

June 14, 1989

THE CHARGE

Assault

THE SENTENCE

Gabor was found guilty and sentenced to three days in the El Segundo jail. She was also required to pay $13,000 in court costs and perform 120 hours of community service at a women's shelter.

THE JURY

Gabor objected to the individuals selected for her jury, saying they were not her peers because none of them were actors, directors, or film producers.

ZSA ZSA GABOR

(1917?–)

NATIONALITY

Hungarian-born American citizen

WHO IS SHE?

Zsa Zsa Gabor (her given name is Sari) was Miss Hungary of 1936 before she came to America and became an actress. Beginning in 1952, she had a busy career as a supporting actress in films, including *Moulin Rouge* and *Lili*, and as a guest star on such television programs as *The Danny Thomas Show*, *Bonanza*, and *Batman*. Her sister, Eva Gabor, also emigrated to America and became an actress.

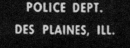

JOHN WAYNE GACY

(1942–)

NATIONALITY
American

WHO WAS HE?
John Wayne Gacy was a successful contractor. He was involved in local politics, and was popular with his neighbors, for whom he threw block parties. Dressed in full clown costume and makeup, he visited children in area hospitals.

WHAT DID HE DO?
Gacy abducted and murdered 33 teenage boys and young men. Most of the bodies he buried in the crawl space beneath his house in Norwood Park Township, a Chicago suburb; two bodies he buried in his backyard and four he dumped into the Des Plaines River.

DATE OF ARREST
December 22, 1978

CIRCUMSTANCES OF THE ARREST
In December 1978, police learned that Gacy was the last person to see Robert Piest, a 15-year-old boy who had disappeared days earlier. They obtained a warrant and searched Gacy's house. Among the evidence they collected was a ring that belonged to a teenage boy who had disappeared a year earlier. The police returned to Gacy's house for a more thorough search and discovered the bodies of 29 of Gacy's victims.

THE CONFESSION
Gacy told police that there were four John Gacys: John the contractor; John the clown; John the local politician; and John or Jack Hanley, who was the killer.

THE CHARGE
Murder

THE SENTENCE
After deliberating for 2 hours, the jury found Gacy guilty of 33 murders. He was sentenced to death and executed in 1994.

LAST WORDS
Before he was executed by lethal injection, Gacy said to the prison guards and officials, "Kiss my ass."

MAHATMA GANDHI

(1869–1948)

WHAT DID HE DO?

Beginning in 1920, Gandhi urged Indians to refuse to perform any task that in any way helped to sustain the British Raj in India. Millions of Indians joined Gandhi's Non-Cooperation Movement, thereby virtually shutting down the British colonial administration in the country.

DATE OF ARREST

March 10, 1922

THE CHARGE

Sedition

THE SENTENCE

Gandhi was found guilty and sentenced to six years in prison.

AFTERWARD

Following his release from prison in 1924, Gandhi continued his nonviolent campaign for the independence of India, which was achieved in 1947. Tragically, violent riots erupted across India, between Hindus and Muslims, in which thousands were killed. Gandhi, himself, was assassinated by a Hindu extremist in 1948.

NATIONALITY

Indian

WHO WAS HE?

Born in India but trained as a lawyer in England, Mahatma Gandhi became the preeminent figure in the Indian independence movement during the first half of the 20th century. He was jailed several times for his political activities.

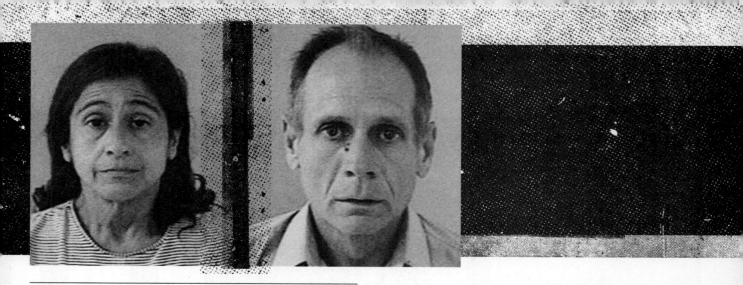

PHILLIP GARRIDO
(1951–)

NANCY GARRIDO
(1955–)

NATIONALITY
American

WHO ARE THEY?
Phillip and Nancy Garrido's neighbors considered them to be a friendly, helpful couple who cared for Phillip's ailing mother.

WHAT DID THEY DO?
In 1991, Phillip Garrido kidnapped 11-year-old Jaycee Lee Dugard as she stood waiting for her school bus. Phillip and his wife, Nancy, kept the girl in tents and sheds they erected in the backyard of their home in Antioch, California. During the 18 years the Garridos kept Dugard captive, Philip fathered two daughters with her.

THE COMPOUND
From the street, the Garridos' house looked no different from those of their neighbors. When a parole officer visited (Phillip had a previous conviction for kidnapping and rape), he did not see the backyard compound because it was screened by shrubs, garbage cans, and a tarp.

DATE OF ARREST
August 26, 2009

CIRCUMSTANCES OF THE ARREST
Phillip Garrido caught the attention of campus police at the University of California, Berkeley, where he was seen with two young girls trying to enter the university library. The police notified Garrido's parole officer, who arranged a meeting. Garrido brought his wife, his daughters, and a woman he introduced to the parole officer as "Allissa." Allissa was Jaycee Lee Dugard.

THE CHARGES
Kidnapping, forcible rape, lewd acts on a child, and false imprisonment

THE LAWSUIT
The Dugard family sued the state of California, claiming that Jaycee would have been found sooner if Phillip Garrido had been properly supervised by the parole board. The state paid the family $20 million to settle the claim.

BILL GATES
(1955–)

NATIONALITY
American

WHO IS HE?
Bill Gates is one of the leaders of the personal computer revolution; with Paul Allen, he cofounded Microsoft. Thanks to the success of Microsoft, Gates has become one of the wealthiest men in the world.

WHAT DID HE DO?
In Albuquerque, New Mexico, Gates was pulled over for speeding and running a red light (he was driving a Porsche). Gates was found to be driving without a license. This was at least the second time that Gates had been pulled over for a traffic violation.

DATE OF ARREST
December 13, 1977

THE CHARGES
Running a red light, and driving without a license

THE VANISHING RECORDS
In spite of an exhaustive search of their criminal records, the Albuquerque police have not found any documentation regarding Gates's arrest or the final disposition of his case.

MICROSOFT'S SPOKESMAN
When asked about the arrest, a spokesman for Microsoft said that Gates remembers the incident in 1977. Then the spokesman added, "It is well-known that when Bill was young he didn't have a very good driving record."

HENRY LOUIS GATES JR.

(1950–)

NATIONALITY
American

WHO IS HE?
Henry Louis Gates is director of the W.E.B. Du Bois Institute for African and African American Research at Harvard University, and the author of many books, including *The Future of Race* and *The Trials of Phillis Wheatley.*

WHAT DID HE DO?
Upon returning from a trip to China, Gates could not get into his house—the door was jammed. He asked the driver of the car he'd rented to bring him from the airport to help him. A neighbor saw two men trying to force open the door, assumed it was a burglary, and called the police.

DATE OF ARREST
July 16, 2009

CIRCUMSTANCES OF THE ARREST
Police arrested Gates at his home. According to the police report, Gates exhibited "loud and tumultuous behavior," accused the arresting officer of being a racist, warned him that he had "no idea who he was messing with," and asserted that he was being arrested because "I'm a black man in America."

THE CHARGE
Disorderly conduct

THE SENTENCE
Gates was released on a $40 bail. Prosecutors dropped the charges.

THE PRESIDENT WEIGHS IN
During a news conference shortly after the Gates affair, President Barack Obama, responding to a reporter's question about the case said, "The Cambridge police acted stupidly."

THE BEER SUMMIT
To settle the matter, President Obama invited Professor Gates and Police Sgt. James Crowley to the White House for a conversation over beers about the situation. The men met in the Rose Garden, where they were joined by Vice President Joe Biden.

THE SENTENCE

Genet and Pelta were acquitted of the vagrancy charge, but they were found guilty of the invalid ticket charge. Furthermore, Genet was found guilty of swindling. He was sentenced to a month in jail and a fine of 50 francs; Pelta was fined 50 francs and released.

AFTERWARD

Genet's writing career began in 1939. His best-known works are *Our Lady of the Flowers* and *Querelle of Brest*. He continued his life of crime, primarily as a thief. In 1947, he was arrested again and sentenced to life in prison. Through the influence of Sartre, Gide, and Cocteau, Genet was pardoned by the president of France. In 1966, he stopped writing and spent the rest of life as a lecturer and advocate of radical political causes.

JEAN GENET

(1910–1986)

NATIONALITY

French

WHO WAS HE?

Jean Genet was a writer and founder of avant-garde theater. Although he was befriended by literary lights Jean-Paul Sartre, André Gide, and Jean Cocteau, Genet was most at ease in the sleazy underworld of criminals, pimps, and male prostitutes.

WHAT DID HE DO?

Genet and a friend, Leon Pelta, used invalid tickets to travel from Paris to Auxerre.

DATE OF ARREST

May 7, 1939

THE CHARGES

Vagrancy, swindling, and using an invalid train ticket

JOHN GEOGHAN

(1935–2003)

NATIONALITY
American

WHO WAS HE?
John Geoghan was ordained a priest for the Roman Catholic Archdiocese of Boston in 1962. At his first parish and at every subsequent parish, church officials received complaints that Geoghan molested children. The archdiocese sent him for treatment to St. Luke's Institute in Maryland, the Institute of Living in Connecticut, and Southdown Institute, Ontario. He was also treated by several psychoanalysts and psychotherapists. None of these treatments were successful. In 1998, the Catholic Church defrocked John Geoghan.

WHAT DID HE DO?
Geoghan was accused of molesting more than 130 children over a period of 30 years.

DATE OF INDICTMENT
December 2, 1999

THE CHARGES
Indecent assault and battery, rape, and molestation

THE SENTENCE
Geoghan was convicted of indecently touching a ten-year-old boy. He could not be convicted on the graver charges because under Massachusetts law, the statute of limitations for such cases had expired. The judge gave Geoghan the maximum sentence—ten years in prison.

INCARCERATED
Geoghan was sent to Concord Prison, where he was mocked and harassed by other convicts as well as some of the guards. In 2003, he was moved to a maximum security prison in Shirley, Massachusetts. In his unit was a convicted murderer, Joseph Druce. On August 23, 2003, Druce attacked Geoghan in his cell, strangling him and stomping on him until he was dead.

AFTERWARD
As the sex abuse scandal grew, Cardinal Bernard Law, Archbishop of Boston, resigned and retired to Rome. Joseph Druce was convicted of murder and given an additional life sentence.

RICHARD GERE

(1949–)

NATIONALITY
American

WHO IS HE?
Richard Gere is a Golden Globe–winning actor whose films include *An Officer and a Gentleman, Pretty Woman,* and *Chicago.* In 1999, he founded a humanitarian organization in India, the Gere Foundation India Trust.

WHAT DID HE DO?
At an HIV/AIDS awareness event in Delhi, Gere embraced Bollywood star Shilpa Shelty, bent her over backwards, and kissed her several times on the cheek.

THE RIOTS
After photos of the clench were published in newspapers across India, mobs turned out in several Indian cities to burn Gere in effigy.

DATE ARREST WARRANT WAS ISSUED
April 26, 2007

THE CHARGE
Public obscenity

THE FUGITIVE
Gere did not wait for the police to arrest him—he left India immediately.

THE RESOLUTION
In March 2008, two justices of India's Supreme Court reviewed the case and declared the complaint to be "frivolous." The chief justice of India, K. G. Balakrishnan, announced to the court, "Richard Gere is free to enter the country. This is the end of the matter."

GERONIMO

(1829–1909)

NATIONALITY
Chiricahua Apache

WHO WAS HE?
Goyahkia (Geronimo was the name the Mexicans and the Americans called him) was a Chiricahua Apache who dedicated his life to defending his tribe's lands and way of life after a Mexican army unit massacred his wife, his three children, and his mother in a raid.

WHAT DID HE DO?
For 30 years, Geronimo fought Mexican and American settlers who encroached on his tribe's land in Arizona and northern Mexico. In 1874, the U.S. government moved the Apaches to a reservation, where they lived as virtual prisoners. Geronimo and some followers escaped from the reservation and for the next 12 years fought a guerrilla war against U.S. troops and white settlers.

DATE OF SURRENDER
September 4, 1886

CIRCUMSTANCES OF THE ARREST
By September 1886, Geronimo's band of approximately 150 Apache concluded that further resistance was futile. Geronimo surrendered to General Nelson Miles near Fort Bowie on the Arizona/New Mexico border. Geronimo was treated as a prisoner of war, and was imprisoned first in Florida, then Alabama.

THE RESERVATION
Eventually, Geronimo was sent to live on the Comanche and Kiowa reservation near Fort Sill in Oklahoma.

AFTERWARD
At Fort Sill, Geronimo took up farming and converted to Christianity. In 1905, he was a guest at President Theodore Roosevelt's inauguration.

SKULL AND BONES
There is a persistent rumor that in 1918 Prescott Bush—father of former president George H. W. Bush and grandfather of former president George W. Bush—opened Geronimo's grave and stole his skull and several other bones, which have been on display in the clubhouse of Skull and Bones, an elite secret society of Yale University students. In 2009, Geronimo's heirs sued Skull and Bones for the return of their ancestor's remains.

MEL GIBSON
(1956–)

NATIONALITY
American

WHO IS HE?
Born in America but raised in Australia, Mel Gibson is an actor with a string of blockbuster hits, including *Mad Max* (1979), *Lethal Weapon* (1987) and the *Lethal Weapon* sequels, *Hamlet* (1990), *Braveheart* (1995), and *The Patriot* (2000). He also wrote, produced, and directed *The Passion of the Christ*, one of the highest-grossing films of all time.

WHAT DID HE DO?
Gibson was drunk and driving erratically along the Pacific Coast Highway in Malibu, California. Deputy James Mee of the Los Angeles County Sheriff's Office pulled him over and gave Gibson field sobriety and alcohol breath tests—which the actor failed.

DATE OF ARREST
July 28, 2006

CIRCUMSTANCES OF THE ARREST
Gibson tried to run away, but Mee caught him, cuffed him, and got him into the back seat of the patrol car. Inside the patrol car, Gibson threatened to "f**k" the arresting officer. Next, Gibson launched into a rant against Jews: "F*****g Jews ... The Jews are responsible for all the wars in the world." Then he asked Deputy Mee, "Are you a Jew?"

THE CHARGE
Drunk driving

THE APOLOGY
The day after his arrest, Gibson issued a public apology that read in part, "The arresting officer was just doing his job and I feel fortunate that I was apprehended before I caused injury to any other person. I acted like a person completely out of control when I was arrested, and said things that I do not believe to be true and which are despicable. I am deeply ashamed of everything I said. Also, I take this opportunity to apologize to the deputies involved for my belligerent behavior."

THE SENTENCE
In court, Gibson pled no contest to the charge. He was sentenced to three years' probation and ordered to attend an alcohol education program and pay $1,608 in fines and court costs.

AFTERWARD
In 2006, after Gibson had completed three years of probation, he petitioned to have his DUI conviction expunged from his record. Since Gibson had never violated the rules of his probation, a judge in Malibu granted his request.

JOHN GIELGUD
(1904–2000)

NATIONALITY
English

WHO WAS HE?
John Gielgud was an English actor best known originally for his Shakespearean roles. He went on to appear in many films, including *Murder on the Orient Express, Gandhi, Chariots of Fire, The Elephant Man,* and, most famously, *Arthur,* for which he won an Oscar for best Supporting Actor.

WHAT DID HE DO?
Late one evening in 1953, Gielgud went to one of London's underground public restrooms to pick up a man, as he had done many times before.

DATE OF ARREST
October 21, 1953

CIRCUMSTANCES OF THE ARREST
The evening of October 21, 1953, Gielgud approached a good-looking young man loitering in the lavatory. The young man was a member of Scotland Yard's "Pretty Police," handsome men who went undercover to arrest homosexuals.

THE CHARGE
Importuning for immoral purposes

THE SENTENCE
At the police station, Gielgud gave his name as Arthur Gielgud (Arthur was, in fact, his real first name) and his occupation as a clerk. Such subterfuges were commonplace among well-known individuals who wanted to keep their arrest out of the newspapers. Gielgud pled guilty and was fined £10.

THE PRESS
As it happened, a reporter for the *Evening Standard* was in the courtroom at his arraignment and recognized Gielgud. The story of Gielgud's arrest was published that afternoon. Gielgud feared that his acting career was over; however, that night, when he returned to the theater where he was performing in *A Day by the Sea*, the audience gave him a standing ovation. The press and the public at large were not so accepting, yet Gielgud continued to find work as an actor.

AFTERWARD
The scandal did not hurt Gielgud's career. He toured for ten years, performing *The Ages of Man,* a collection of excerpts from Shakespeare. In 1994, the Globe Theatre in the West End of London was renamed the Gielgud Theatre. And in 1996, he was appointed to Britain's Order of Merit.

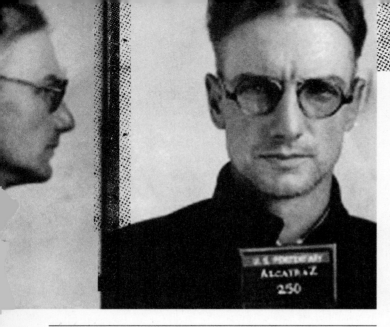

CIRCUMSTANCES OF THE ARREST
Unfortunately for Giles, the boat was not going to San Francisco, but to a military installation on nearby Angel Island. On the island Giles was spotted immediately, arrested, and taken back to Alcatraz.

THE CHARGES
Impersonating a soldier and attempted escape

THE SENTENCE
Three years were added to the life sentence Giles was already serving.

A PHILOSOPHICAL FRAME OF MIND
The warden of Alcatraz told a reporter for the *San Francisco Chronicle* that, upon his return to the prison, Giles had said "that time means nothing to him—that he had everything to gain by trying to escape and nothing to lose. And he also said he had been planning a getaway since his imprisonment here in 1935."

JOHN K. GILES
(1895–1979)

NATIONALITY
American

WHO WAS HE?
John K. Giles was a convicted murderer who was sent to Alcatraz to serve a life sentence. He worked at the prison's dock, where supplies were unloaded and searched for contraband. From these searches, he assembled, piece by piece, a complete U.S. Army uniform, including dog tags.

WHAT DID HE DO?
On July 31, 1945, after the supply boat arrived, he slipped away from the work detail, put on his uniform, then joined the soldiers aboard the boat.

DATE OF ARREST
July 31, 1945

GARY GILMORE
(1940–1977)

NATIONALITY
American

WHO WAS HE?
From his early teens, Gary Gilmore was a career criminal who did jail time for assault and armed robbery. In April 1976, he was put on conditional parole. He went to Provo, Utah, where he lived with a cousin, Brenda Nicol, who tried to help him go straight.

WHAT DID HE DO?
On July 19, 1976, in Orem, Utah, Gilmore robbed then shot and killed a gas station attendant. The following day he robbed then shot and killed a motel clerk.

DATE OF ARREST
July 21, 1976

CIRCUMSTANCES OF THE ARREST
While trying to dispose of the murder weapon, Gilmore accidentally shot himself in the hand. He called his cousin Brenda, told her what he had done, and asked for bandages and painkillers. Brenda Nicol contacted the police. When Gilmore was arrested, Nicol told him, "You commit a murder Monday, and commit a murder Tuesday. I wasn't waiting for Wednesday to come around."

THE CHARGE
Murder

THE SENTENCE
Gilmore was found guilty and sentenced to death.

THE EXECUTION
Gary Gilmore refused to appeal his conviction and asked to be executed by firing squad. His request was granted, and he was shot inside an unused building within the Utah State Prison. He was the first person to be executed in the United States in a decade. It is said that his last words were "Let's do it."

THE BOOKS
Gary Gilmore was the inspiration for Norman Mailer's Pulitzer Prize–winning novel *The Executioner's Song* (1979). In 1995, Mikal Gilmore, Gary's brother, published a family memoir, *Shot through the Heart*.

THE GLEN RIDGE RAPISTS

CHRISTOPHER ARCHER (1972-), BRYANT GROBER (1972-), KEVIN SCHERZER (1971-), KYLE SCHERZER (1971-)

NATIONALITY
American

WHO ARE THEY?
Christopher Archer, Bryant Grober, Kevin Scherzer, and Kyle Scherzer were high school athletes in Glen Ridge, New Jersey.

WHAT DID THEY DO?
On March 1, 1989, Archer lured Susan Fisher into the rec room in the basement of the Scherzer family's home. Fisher's IQ had been measured at 64, giving her the intellectual development of an eight-year-old child. In the rec room were about a dozen athletes from the high school. A handful of boys induced Fisher to take off her clothes and perform fellatio on Grober. Afterwards, the boys raped her with a broomstick, a baseball bat, and a wooden rod. Then Fisher masturbated each boy in the room.

THE SECRET
The boys swore Fischer to secrecy, but she revealed what happened to her swimming coach. The boys, in the meantime, bragged about the incident to their friends. As word spread through the town, the high school principal called the police.

DATE OF ARREST
May 24, 1992

CIRCUMSTANCES OF THE ARREST
The accused were arrested in their homes, almost simultaneously, by four teams of detectives.

THE CHARGES
Conspiracy to commit sexual assault, aggravated sexual assault, and aggravated criminal sexual contact

THE FIRST PLEA BARGAIN
The six arrested were Christopher Archer, Paul Archer, Bryant Grober, Peter Quigley, Kevin Scherzer, and Kyle Scherzer. In exchange for their testimony, Paul Archer and Quigley were sentenced to perform 60 hours of community service.

THE SENTENCE
After deliberating for 12 days, the jury found all four guilty. After their appeal, Kyle Scherzer was sentenced to 7 years, and Christopher Archer and Kevin Scherzer were sentenced to 15 years. Bryant Grober was put on 3 years' probation.

AFTERWARD
Kyle Scherzer was paroled in 2000; Christopher Archer and Kevin Scherzer were paroled in 2001. The case was detailed in Bernard Lefkowitz's book, *Our Guys: The Glen Ridge Rape and the Secret Life of the Perfect Suburb*.

AMON GOETH

(1908–1946)

NATIONALITY
Austrian

WHO WAS HE?
By age 17, Amon Goeth was an ardent Nazi—although at the time the Nazi Party was illegal in his native Austria. At age 22, he traveled to Germany where he joined the SS and began a stellar military career. In 1942, he was assigned to Poland as part of the SS operation to exterminate the country's Jews. In Poland, he was made commandant of Plaszow concentration camp.

WHAT DID HE DO?
Goeth supervised the closing of the Cracow ghetto, during which operation 2,000 Jews were killed and 10,000 sent to Plaszow. At the camp, he and the SS men under his command tortured and killed inmates on a daily basis. On Yom Kippur 1943, Goeth had 50 Jews selected at random and shot. It is estimated that Goeth was responsible for the deaths of 8,000 men, women, and children.

DATE OF ARREST
August 29, 1945

CIRCUMSTANCES OF THE ARREST
Goeth was captured by American troops, who handed him over to the Poles for trial.

THE CHARGES
Crimes against humanity

THE SENTENCE
Poland's postwar Communist government found Goeth guilty and sentenced him to be hanged. He was taken to Plaszow where a gallows had been erected near the concentration camp. The hangman bungled the job, and it took three attempts before Goeth died.

THE FILM
Amon Goeth was played by Ralph Fiennes in Steven Spielberg's 1994 Academy Award–winning film *Schindler's List*.

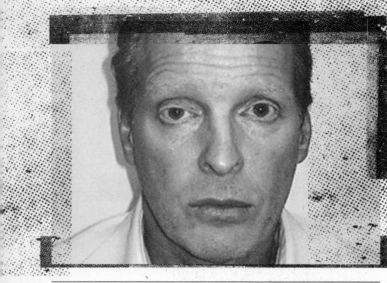

ALAN GOLDER, "THE DINNERTIME BANDIT"

(1955–)

NATIONALITY
American

WHO IS HE?
Golder grew up in poverty on Long Island—his father was a two-bit criminal and his mother was a waitress at a bowling alley. As a child, he shoplifted toys and baseball cards from Woolworth's; later he stole bicycles from kids in better-off neighborhoods. At age 16, he dropped out of high school to become a full-time criminal.

WHAT DID HE DO?
Between 1975 and 1997, Golder burglarized hundreds of homes of wealthy families, such as the Kennedys, and celebrities, such as Johnny Carson. Typically, he entered homes at dinnertime, climbing in through a second-story window dressed as a ninja. While the family was eating downstairs, Golder looted jewelry and other valuables. His lifetime haul is believed to have totaled at least $5 million.

THE FUGITIVE
In 1997, as investigators closed in on him, Golder fled to Europe, ultimately settling in Belgium.

DATE OF ARREST
December 14, 2006

CIRCUMSTANCES OF HIS ARREST
When Belgian government officials discovered that Golder was in the country, they ordered his arrest and extradited him to the United States in November 2007.

THE CHARGES
Burglary, larceny, and kidnapping

THE SENTENCE
Golder was found guilty and sentenced to two 10-year sentences for burglary, plus 12 years for larceny and 15 years for kidnapping. The sentences would run concurrently.

THE MANUSCRIPT
After Golder fled the United States, investigators entered his home in Queens, where they found the manuscript of his autobiography, titled *Precious Metal: Confessions of a Rock 'n' Roll Jewel Thief.*

JULIO GONZALEZ

(1954–)

THE CHARGES
Murder, arson, and assault

THE SENTENCE
Gonzalez was found guilty and sentenced to 4,350 years in prison—the longest sentence ever handed down by a New York judge.

NATIONALITY
Cuban-born American citizen

WHO WAS HE?
Julio Gonzalez came to the United States from Cuba during the 1980 Mariel boatlift. He worked as a packer in a warehouse in Queens. On March 25, 1990, the night he went to the Happy Land nightclub in the Bronx, he was unemployed. At the club, he got into an argument with his girlfriend, Lydia Feliciano; she dumped him. The club's bouncer threw Gonzalez out.

WHAT DID HE DO?
Gonzalez returned to Happy Land with a container of gasoline, which he poured on the club's only stairway, then set it on fire. Happy Land had no fire alarm and no sprinkler system. Eighty-seven patrons and employees were killed in the fire—either trampled to death or killed by smoke inhalation. Lydia Feliciano was among those who escaped the fire.

DATE OF ARREST
March 26, 1990

DWIGHT GOODEN

(1964–)

NATIONALITY
American

WHO IS HE?
Dwight Gooden entered major league baseball at age 19, when he joined the New York Mets. In the 1980s, he was a pitching phenom, but trouble with drugs and alcohol derailed his career.

WHAT DID HE DO?
At about 8:30 in the morning of March 23, 2010, Dwight Gooden was in a two-car crash in Franklin Lakes, New Jersey.

DATE OF ARREST
March 23, 2010

CIRCUMSTANCES OF THE ARREST
At the time, the police would not say what "controlled dangerous substance" Gooden was on, or in whose car the child was. It was revealed later that at the time of his arrest, Gooden's 5-year-old son was in the back seat of his car.

THE CHARGES
Driving under the influence of a controlled dangerous substance, leaving the scene of an accident, and endangering the welfare of a child

THE SENTENCE
Dwight Gooden's case has not yet gone to trial.

WHAT DID HE DO?

In October 1895, Miura sent assassins to kill the Korean empress Myeongseong, also known as Queen Min (at the time, Japan was attempting to expand its influence into Southeast Asia).

DATE OF ARREST

January 20, 1896

CIRCUMSTANCES OF THE ARREST

In response to worldwide public outrage, the Japanese government arrested Miura and others accused of conspiracy to assassinate Queen Min.

THE CHARGE

Attempted assassination

THE SENTENCE

Miura Gor and the other defendants in the case were acquitted, the court citing "lack of evidence." Outside of Japan, the trial and the verdict were regarded as a farce.

MIURA GOR

(1847–1926)

NATIONALITY

Japanese

WHO WAS HE?

Miura Gor was an officer and later a lieutenant general in Japan's Imperial Army. In the 1870s he played a leading role in putting down several rebellions against the Imperial government. In 1890, Miura was named a viscount (shishaku) and joined Japan's House of Peers.

JOHN GOTTI
(1940–2002)

NATIONALITY
American

WHO WAS HE?
John Gotti was a New York crime boss renowned as one of the most powerful mobsters in the United States. For his fashion sense, he was known as the "the Dapper Don." He was also known as "the Teflon Don": Although prosecutors repeatedly brought charges against Gotti, they couldn't make any of them stick.

WHAT DID HE DO?
Gotti built his criminal empire by having his boss, Paul Castellano, murdered outside Spark's Steak House in Manhattan in 1985. The FBI tapped his phone and heard Gotti speak about many other murders and other criminal activity.

DATE OF ARREST
December 11, 1990

CIRCUMSTANCES OF THE ARREST
Detectives arrested Gotti at his hangout, the Ravenite Social Club on Mulberry Street in New York's Little Italy.

THE CHARGES
Murder, conspiracy to murder, illegal gambling, loan sharking, obstruction of justice, bribing a public official, and tax evasion

THE SENTENCE
After deliberating for 11 hours, the jurors found Gotti guilty of all charges. After the verdict was read, the chief of the FBI's New York office said to reporters, "The don is covered with Velcro, and every charge stuck." Gotti was sentenced to life in prison.

AFTERWARD
John Gotti died in prison of throat cancer.

THE REALITY SERIES
In 2004, A&E premiered *Growing Up Gotti*, a reality show that followed the lives of Victoria Gotti, John Gotti's daughter, and her three children, Carmine, John, and Frank Agnello.

HUGH GRANT

(1960–)

NATIONALITY
English

WHO IS HE?
Hugh Grant is an English actor who achieved stardom in the 1994 film *Four Weddings and a Funeral*. He went on to star in *Sense and Sensibility* and *Bridget Jones' Diary*.

WHAT DID HE DO?
On June 27, 1995, near Sunset Boulevard, Grant solicited the services of a Hollywood prostitute.

DATE OF ARREST
June 27, 1995

CIRCUMSTANCES OF THE ARREST
At about 1:30 in the morning, two Los Angeles police officers saw a woman speak briefly with the driver of a white BMW, then climb into the front seat. The car drove down a side street and parked. When the officers approached the car, they found Grant and the prostitute engaging in "lewd conduct."

THE CHARGE
Lewd conduct

THE SENTENCE
Grant pled guilty, was fined $1,180, given two years' probation, and was ordered to attend AIDS education classes.

GRANT ON LENO
Grant had been scheduled to appear on *The Tonight Show* with Jay Leno. Rather than cancel his appearance, he fulfilled his commitment. Speaking of his arrest just days earlier, Grant said, "I think you know in life what's a good thing to do and what's a bad thing, and I did a bad thing. And there you have it." Grant was praised in the press for taking responsibility for his actions and not trying to spin the incident.

ROSE O'NEAL GREENHOW

(1817–1864)

NATIONALITY
American

WHO WAS SHE?
Rose O'Neal Greenhow was a prominent Washington, D.C. society hostess—intelligent, attractive, and well-connected. She numbered several presidents and many members of Congress as her friends. One of her closest associates was Senator John C. Calhoun, from whom she acquired a passion for the cause of Southern independence.

WHAT DID SHE DO?
At the beginning of the Civil War, Greenhow operated a spy ring that collected intelligence about the Union Army and forwarded it to Confederate General P.G.T. Beauregard. It is said that the Confederacy owed its victory at the First Battle of Bull Run to the information Greenhow supplied.

DATE OF ARREST
August 23, 1861

CIRCUMSTANCES OF THE ARREST
For several months, Greenhow was kept under arrest in her home, with soldiers posted there full-time. In January 1862, she was transferred, along with her eight-year-old daughter, Rose, to the Old Capitol Prison.

THE CHARGE
Espionage

THE HEARING
At her hearing, Greenhow defended herself, saying, "If Mr. Lincoln's friends will pour into my ear such important information, am I to be held responsible for all that?" The judge decided that putting a woman on trial might inflame public opinion in the North as well as the South.

THE SENTENCE
In lieu of a trial, the court exiled Greenhow to the Confederacy. She left prison with a Confederate flag draped over her shoulders.

AFTERWARD
Jefferson Davis sent Greenhow to Europe to win French and British support for the Confederate cause. Emperor Napoleon III and Queen Victoria received her, but they were not persuaded to join forces with the South. On the journey home, while she was being rowed ashore in a storm, the boat overturned and Rose O'Neal Greenhow drowned.

IRMA "THE BEAUTIFUL BEAST" GRESE

(1923–1945)

NATIONALITY
German

WHO WAS SHE?
Irma Grese was Senior SS Supervisior at the Auschwitz/Bergen-Belsen concentration camp, where she was in charge of 30,000 women prisoners.

WHAT DID SHE DO?
Grese treated prisoners with extreme cruelty, whipping them, beating some to death, releasing her attack dogs on others. It is said that, after her arrest, three lampshades, made from the skin of prisoners, were found in her quarters.

DATE OF ARREST
April 15, 1945

CIRCUMSTANCES OF THE ARREST
Grese and 44 others, including the commandant of Bergen-Belsen, Josef Kramer, were arrested by the British liberators of the camp.

THE CHARGES
Crimes against humanity

THE SENTENCE
Grese was found guilty and hanged.

CHARLES GUITEAU

(1841–1882)

NATIONALITY
American

WHO WAS HE?
Charles Guiteau spent six years living in the Oneida Community, a utopian society that practiced what its members described as "Bible Communism." After leaving Oneida and moving to New York, Guiteau filed suit against the community, demanding $9,000 for the work he had performed for them. Guiteau's irrational claims led his attorney to drop the case. He married, but after five years his wife—whom he abused almost daily—divorced him. He became obsessed with politics and offered to campaign for the Republican candidate for president, James A. Garfield; noting Guiteau's odd behavior, party officials declined. Nonetheless, Guiteau became convinced that Garfield owed him a diplomatic post, preferably in Vienna or Paris. After being rebuffed repeatedly by Garfield's secretary of state, Guiteau decided to avenge himself on the president.

WHAT DID HE DO?
On July 2, 1881, Guiteau waited at the Baltimore and Potomac Station in Washington, D.C. for President Garfield. As Garfield walked down the platform toward his train, Guiteau pulled out a pistol and shot the president twice.

DATE OF ARREST
July 2, 1881

CIRCUMSTANCES OF THE ARREST
Guiteau was seized immediately by police. On the way to jail, Guiteau asked one police officer if he was a Republican. The officer said yes, and Guiteau promised to make him Washington's chief of police.

THE PRESIDENT
Garfield lingered for more than two months, dying on September 19.

THE CHARGE
Assassination

THE TRIAL
Guiteau insisted on acting as his own attorney. He argued that he wasn't responsible for the death of Garfield; it was the president's inept physicians who killed him (the argument could be made). He insisted that while he might be "legally insane," he was not "actually insane," a distinction no one else in the courtroom understood. And Guiteau declared that the court lacked jurisdiction because Garfield had died at his summer home in New Jersey, rather than in the White House in Washington.

THE SENTENCE
After deliberating for one hour, the jury found Guiteau guilty. Spectators in the courtroom applauded the verdict. Guiteau was sentenced to be hanged.

THE PRESIDENT'S BENEFACTOR
In prison, Guiteau expected to be pardoned by the new president, Chester A. Arthur. He believed that Arthur must feel grateful to Guiteau—if he hadn't killed Garfield, Arthur would have remained vice president.

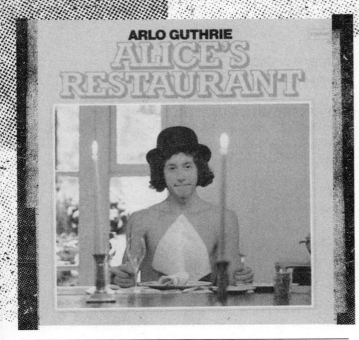

ARLO GUTHRIE

(1947–)

NATIONALITY
American

WHO IS HE?
Arlo Guthrie is a singer/songwriter and social activist. His father was the folk singer Woody Guthrie; his mother was Maria Mazia Guthrie, a member of the Martha Graham Dance Company.

WHAT DID HE DO?
On Thanksgiving Day 1965, Guthrie was spending the holiday with Ray and Alice Brock and their hippie houseguests in Great Barrington, Massachusetts. Alice asked Guthrie and another guest to take the trash to the dump. Since the dump was closed, the two dumped the trash down a hill.

DATE OF ARREST
November 28, 1965

CIRCUMSTANCES OF THE ARREST
The police officer who discovered the unauthorized dumping found in the garbage an envelope bearing the Brocks' name and address. He arrested the two men at the Brocks' house and put them in jail until Alice Brock bailed them out.

THE CHARGE
Littering

THE SENTENCE
Guthrie and his friend were found guilty, fined $25 each, and ordered to clean up the mess and dispose of it properly.

AFTERWARD
The incident became the inspiration for Arlo Guthrie's 18-minute-long hit single, "Alice's Restaurant Massacree."

MERLE HAGGARD

(1937–)

NATIONALITY
American

WHO IS HE?
Merle Haggard is one of the most influential performers of country music. In the 1960s, he developed a distinctive style, rooted in country but influenced by blues, jazz, and folk. Haggard has had at least 38 hit singles and won three Grammys. In his teens and early twenties, Haggard had a series of run-ins with the law, ranging from petty crimes to more serious charges.

WHAT DID HE DO?
On Christmas Eve 1957, Haggard and two friends tried to rob a restaurant in Bakersfield, California. The three were drunk, and thought it was about 3:00 in the morning; in fact, it was 10:30 at night. So when they entered the restaurant through the back door, they found the place full of employees and patrons. They upgraded their plans from burglary to armed robbery.

DATE OF ARREST
December 24, 1957

CIRCUMSTANCES OF THE ARREST
Police picked up Haggard that night, but he escaped from jail and went home to explain to his wife what he had done. He was captured by the police the next day.

THE CHARGE
Armed robbery

THE SENTENCE
Haggard was found guilty and sentenced to three years in San Quentin.

AFTERWARD
Once he got out of prison, Haggard worked manual labor jobs by day and sang at local clubs at night. It was the beginning of a musical career that would make him a country music legend.

ANNA MARIE HAHN

(1906–1938)

NATIONALITY
German-born American

WHO WAS SHE?
Anna Marie emigrated from Bavaria to Cincinnati, where she lived in the city's German neighborhood. She worked as a private nurse, tending elderly German men.

WHAT DID SHE DO?
Between 1932 and 1937, Hahn poisoned at least four men. She ingratiated herself with her victims so that they would make generous bequests to her in their wills. Then she poisoned them.

DATE OF ARREST
August 11, 1937

CIRCUMSTANCES OF THE ARREST
Hahn and her son had traveled to Denver with her latest client, George Obendorfer. After killing Obendorfer, Hahn tried, unsuccessfully, to pawn his jewelry and withdraw $1,000 from his bank account. The suspicious pawnbroker and bank manager alerted the police. Initially, the police charged her with grand larceny; after an autopsy of Obendorfer's body, and the exhumation of two of Hahn's other "patients," the charge was changed to murder.

THE CHARGE
Murder

THE SENTENCE
Anna Marie Hahn was found guilty and sentenced to the electric chair.

THE ONE WHO GOT AWAY
While caring for George Heiss, Hahn served him a mug of beer. Before he could take a sip, several flies landed in the beer and died. Heiss fired Hahn, but did not call the police.

ROBERT J. HALDERMAN

(1957–)

NATIONALITY
American

WHO IS HE?
Robert J. Halderman was a producer for *48 Hours*, the CBS news-magazine program.

WHAT DID HE DO?
Halderman demanded $2 million from late-night night talk show host David Letterman. If Letterman refused to pay up, Halderman threatened to expose Letterman's sexual relationships with several of his female employees.

DATE OF ARREST
October 1, 2009

THE CHARGE
Attempted grand larceny

THE SENTENCE
Halderman pled guilty and was sentenced to six months in prison and 1,000 hours of community service.

AFTERWARD
Halderman was released two months early, for good behavior. At the time of his release, he had been nominated for an Emmy for his work on a *48 Hours* episode about an exchange student accused of murder.

LETTERMAN'S APOLOGY
Letterman admitted his affairs on the air, telling his viewers, "I have had sex with women who work for me on this show." During a subsequent appearance on *Live with Regis and Kelly*, Letterman characterized his affairs as "stupid behavior."

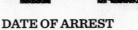

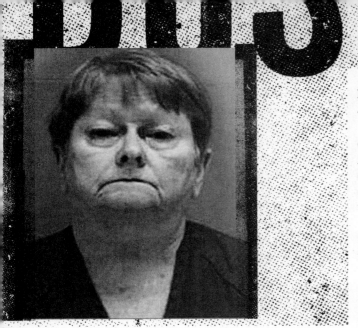

MARY NANCE HANSON

(1939–)

NATIONALITY
American

WHO IS SHE?
Mary Nance Hanson, 71 years old, had a stormy relationship with her daughter-in-law, Tetyana Nikitina. In 2005, Nikitina divorced Hanson's son; the court awarded her custody of the two children. Hanson and her son had tried, unsuccessfully, to have the custody arrangement overturned.

WHAT DID SHE DO?
Hanson went to the preschool in Millcreek, Utah, where her former daughter-in-law worked as a teacher. In the parking lot, Hanson shot and killed Nikitina as she sat in her car.

DATE OF ARREST
January 29, 2010

CIRCUMSTANCES OF THE ARREST
After murdering Nikitina, Hanson called 911 to report what she had done. When the 911 operator asked her why she did such a thing, Hanson replied, "I don't know, and that's all I'm going to say." She waited for the police in the school parking lot.

THE CHARGE
Murder

THE SENTENCE
Hanson pled guilty, then asked the judge to sentence her to death by lethal injection. The judge replied that her crime did not merit the death penalty. "Well, then," Hanson said, "I guess I didn't do a good enough job."

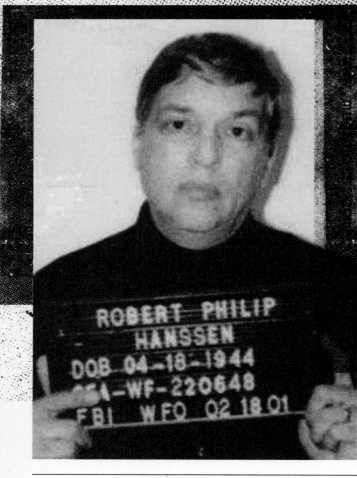

WHAT DID HE DO?

The FBI alleged that Hanssen had left at least 20 packages full of classified information for Russian agents. In exchange, he received approximately $1.4 million in diamonds and cash.

DATE OF ARREST

February 18, 2001

CIRCUMSTANCES OF THE ARREST

FBI agents caught Hanssen in the act of leaving classified material for his Russian handlers at a drop site in Foxstone Park in Vienna, Virginia.

THE CHARGES

Espionage and conspiracy

THE SENTENCE

Hanssen pled guilty and was sentenced to life in prison without parole. At his sentencing, he said, "I apologize for my behavior. I am shamed by it. Beyond its illegality, I have torn the trust of so many. Worse, I have opened the door for calumny against my totally innocent wife and our children. I hurt them deeply. I have hurt so many deeply."

ROBERT HANSSEN

(1944–)

NATIONALITY

American

WHO IS HE?

Robert Hanssen was a special agent of the FBI with 25 years of service in counterintelligence.

NAVEED AFZAL HAQ

(1975–)

NATIONALITY
American

WHO IS HE?
Naveed Afzal Haq is of Pakistani descent. Although his father was one of the founders of the local mosque in Richland, Washington, after high school, Haq rarely attended. In 2005, he was baptized in an evangelical church, but after several months he stopped attending services.

WHAT DID HE DO?
Holding a gun to the head of a 13-year-old girl, Haq forced his way into the offices of the Jewish Federation of Greater Seattle. Shouting, "I am a Muslim American, angry at Israel," he opened fire, killing one woman and wounding five others.

DATE OF ARREST
July 27, 2006

CIRCUMSTANCES OF THE ARREST
Haq shot Dayna Klein, 17 weeks pregnant, in the arm: As he fired, she turned to protect her unborn child. She called 911 and persuaded Haq to speak to the dispatcher. A SWAT team arrested Haq at the Jewish center; he was held on $50 million bail.

THE CHARGES
Murder, attempted murder, kidnapping, burglary, and hate crime

THE SENTENCE
Haq's first trial ended with a hung jury. In the second trial, he was found guilty on all counts and sentenced to life in prison, plus an additional 120 years, with no chance of parole.

PULLED OVER
Thirty minutes before he attacked the women at the Jewish Federation, police pulled Haq over for a minor traffic violation. He did not appear strange or dangerous, so police let him continue on his way.

TONYA HARDING
(1970–)

NATIONALITY
American

WHO IS SHE?
Tonya Harding is a champion figure skater, the first American woman to complete a triple axel. She won the 1991 U.S. Figure Skating Championships.

WHAT DID SHE DO?
Harding was part of a scheme that involved her ex-husband, Jeff Gillooly, and her former bodyguard, Shawn Richardson, and two other confessed conspirators, Shane Stant and Derrick Smith, to injure rival skater Nancy Kerrigan so she could not compete. On January 6, 1994, while Kerrigan was at a practice session in Detroit, Stant struck her above the knee with a police baton, bruising her leg but not breaking it.

DATE OF ARRESTS
Richardson, Stant, and Smith were arrested on January 14, 1994. Gillooly was arrested on January 19.

THE "CONFESSION"
On January 27, at a press conference, Harding admitted that a week after Kerrigan was attacked, she knew that her rival had been the subject of conspiracy, but she did not come forward with the information.

THE SENTENCE
As part of a plea bargain, Harding pled guilty to conspiracy to hinder prosecution. She was sentenced to three years probation, obliged to pay $110,000 in fines and court costs, donate $50,000 to the Special Olympics, and perform 500 hours of community service. She was also ordered to resign from the U.S. Figure Skating Association.

THE OLYMPICS
Harding was permitted to compete in the Olympics in Lillehammer, Norway, where she faced off against Kerrigan. An estimated 120 million viewers tuned in to see Kerrigan take home the silver; Harding placed eighth.

AFTERWARD
Tonya Harding was banned from skating for life. Since then, her life has lurched from one scandal to another: the release of a sex tape; being ordered by a judge to give up alcohol and stay away from her boyfriend; calling the cops to report that a stranger was threatening her with a knife, or that intruders were trying to steal her car. In 2003–2004, she tried a new career as a professional woman boxer.

DATE OF ARREST
February 13, 1917

CIRCUMSTANCES OF THE ARREST
Mata Hari was arrested after French military intelligence intercepted a German transmission and was able to decode Mata Hari's code name.

THE CHARGE.
Espionage

THE SENTENCE
Mata Hari was found guilty and sentenced to be executed by firing squad.

THE GREAT GARBO
In 1931, Greta Garbo played the exotic dancer-turned-spy in the film *Mata Hari*. It was a highly romanticized biopic, and very successful, grossing nearly $1 million in the United States alone (an enormous sum at the time).

MATA HARI
(1876–1917)

NATIONALITY
Dutch

WHO WAS SHE?
Margaretha Geertruida Zelle MacLeod (Mata Hari was her stage name; it is Javanese for "eye of the morning") was born in what is now Indonesia, the daughter of a Dutch colonist and a Javanese woman. She was renowned for her string of lovers, most of them prominent members of the British, German, or French governments, and her salacious dance performances, typically in very skimpy costumes.

WHAT DID SHE DO?
During World War I, Mata Hari was living in Paris, but her political sympathies were with Germany. In 1916, she learned that the British and the French were about to introduce a new weapon—the tank. How she acquired this information is unknown, but it is suspected that one of her lovers, who worked in the French government, may have told her. She was also seen around Paris with a British officer wearing the insignia of the new tank battalion, so he may have been her source. Mata Hari passed this information along to Berlin, in time for the Germans to manufacture an antitank weapon.

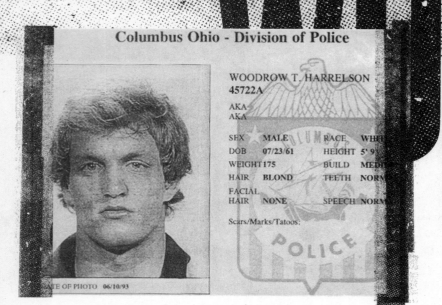

Columbus Ohio - Division of Police

WOODROW T. HARRELSON
45722A
AKA-
AKA

SEX   MALE   RACE   WHI
DOB   07/23/61   HEIGHT   5' 9'
WEIGHT 175   BUILD   MEDI
HAIR   BLOND   TEETH   NORM
FACIAL
HAIR   NONE   SPEECH NORM

Scars/Marks/Tatoos:

POLICE

DATE OF PHOTO 06/10/93

WOODY HARRELSON

(1961–)

NATIONALITY
American

WHO IS HE?
Woody Harrelson is an American actor who got his first big break on the TV sitcom *Cheers*—he played the lovable but not very bright bartender, Woody. Harrelson went on to star in such films as *Natural Born Killers, The People vs. Larry Flynt,* and *Wag the Dog.* He also appeared in several episodes of the TV sitcom *Will & Grace.*

WHAT DID HE DO?
In Columbus, Ohio, neighbors and passers-by called the police to report that a young man was drunk and dancing in the middle of the street.

DATE OF ARREST
October 12, 1982

CIRCUMSTANCES OF THE ARREST
The police loaded Harrelson into the back of their police van, but Harrelson escaped. The cops chased him on foot; when they caught up with him, Harrelson slugged one of the police officers.

THE CHARGES
Disorderly conduct, assault, and resisting arrest

THE SENTENCE
Harrelson was found guilty of assault and resisting arrest, and was fined $390.

MORE RUN-INS WITH THE LAW
In 1996, Harrelson was arrested for planting hemp in Kentucky; that same year he was arrested for climbing the Golden Gate Bridge to protest logging in California's redwood forests. In 2002, he was arrested in London and charged with damaging the back door and ashtray of a taxi.

WHAT DID SHE DO?

In 1980, Harris was suicidal. She drove from Washington to Tarnower's home in Purchase, New York, where she planned to see him one last time, then kill herself. Once she arrived, he ignored her. Then Harris spotted Tryforos's negligee and flew into a rage. Tarnower slapped her across the face; Harris took out her pistol and held it to her own head. Tarnower tried to grab the gun. What happened next is still debated. The prosecution argued that Harris shot Tarnower five times in cold blood; the defense insisted that the shooting was accidental.

DATE OF ARREST

March 10, 1980

CIRCUMSTANCES OF THE ARREST

After the shooting, Harris called the police, admitted that she had shot Tarnower, and told the police that they would find the gun in her car.

THE CHARGE

Murder

THE SENTENCE

After deliberating for eight days, the jury found Harris guilty of second-degree murder. She was sentenced to 15 years to life in prison.

IN PRISON

While serving her sentence, Jean Harris published three books, including her memoirs. After 12 years behind bars, Harris was granted clemency by New York Governor Mario Cuomo.

JEAN HARRIS

(1923–)

NATIONALITY

American

WHO IS SHE?

Jean Harris was a divorced mother of two boys, the headmistress of the prestigious Madeira School for Girls in Washington, D.C., and the sometime mistress of Dr. Herman Tarnower, a cardiologist and author of the best seller, *The Complete Scarsdale Medical Diet*. Harris and Tarnower had been lovers since 1967, but he would never commit to her. During the 14 years that Harris and Tarnower were more or less together, he dated other women. Harris became especially jealous of Lynne Tryforos, Tarnower's assistant.

COLTON HARRIS-MOORE, "THE BAREFOOT BANDIT"
(1991–)

NATIONALITY
American

WHO IS HE?
Colton Harris-Moore is a six-foot-five-inch 19-year-old accused of a rash of robberies in Washington State, Idaho, British Columbia, and the Bahamas. According to Harris-Moore's mother, by the time he was 13, he had four convictions for possession of stolen property.

WHAT DID HE DO?
Harris-Moore is alleged to have burglarized dozens of homes and businesses, and stolen at least five planes, one of which he flew to the Bahamas. He committed some of his crimes barefoot, once mocking police by leaving a chalk outline of his bare foot on the floor of a store he burglarized.

DATE OF ARREST
July 11, 2010

CIRCUMSTANCES OF THE ARREST
Bahamanian police caught up with Harris-Moore off the coast of Eleuthera Island. When he saw the police cruiser, Harris-Moore gunned his stolen motorboat. Police put an end to the high-speed boat chase by shooting the motor of Harris-Moore's boat. He was barefoot at the time of his arrest.

THE CHARGES
In the Bahamas: entering the Bahamas illegally, and illegally landing a plane

In the United States: burglary

THE SENTENCE
Harris-Moore pled guilty to the Bahamas charges, was sentenced to three months in prison, and fined $300. Then he was extradited to the United States.

AFTERWARD
Harris-Moore is in jail awaiting trial.

THE BANDIT ON FACEBOOK
Colton Harris-Moore's 18 months on the lam made him a folk hero among some. Tens of thousands of fans joined his Facebook page.

ROBERT HARRISON
(1905–1978)

DATE OF INDICTMENT
May 15, 1957

THE CHARGES
Criminal libel and distributing obscene materials

THE WITNESSES
Fearful of being called to the witness stand and obliged to swear to tell the truth in court, many Hollywood stars and other celebrities decided to take a long ocean voyage or travel outside the United States during the trial. Except for Maureen O'Hara, who had sued Harrison for libel. She became a witness for the prosecution.

THE TRIAL
The case ended with a hung jury. The prosecutor said that he intended to retry the case. Subsequently, Harrison announced a shift in the editorial focus of *Confidential*, from Hollywood sex scandals to politics.

THE MOVIE
Harrison and his scandal sheet were the inspiration for the 1997 film *L.A. Confidential*.

NATIONALITY
American

WHO WAS HE?
Robert Harrison, a publisher of girlie magazines, made the switch to publishing *Confidential*, a celebrity scandal magazine, in 1952.

WHAT DID HE DO?
Confidential ran stories about the indiscretions of Hollywood stars, such as a Tab Hunter's all-male pajama party, Maureen O'Hara's tryst in the balcony of Grauman's Chinese Theatre, Robert Mitchum exposing himself at a dinner party, and Joe DiMaggio asking Frank Sinatra to help him find some "muscle" to take care of his wife, Marilyn Monroe's, latest lover.

NIDAL MALIK HASAN

(1970–)

NATIONALITY
American

WHO IS HE?
Nidal Malik Hasan is a major in the U.S. Army who served as a psychiatrist at the Fort Hood army base in Texas. Although he was heard to express extremist Islamic views, which were reported to his superiors at Fort Hood and to the FBI, Hasan was never investigated.

WHAT DID HE DO?
On November 5, 2009, Hasan entered the Soldier Readiness Center, shouting "Allahu akbar!" or "God is greatest!" He opened fire, killing 13 and wounding 32 soldiers.

DATE OF ARREST
November 5, 2009

CIRCUMSTANCES OF THE ARREST
Sgt. Kimberly D. Munley and Sgt. Mark Todd returned fire. As Hasan fell to the ground, wounded, Munley ran over, kicked the pistol from Hasan's hand, and handcuffed him. Hasan's wounds left him partially paralyzed.

THE CHARGES
Premeditated murder and attempted murder

THE LEGAL PROCEEDING
The U.S. Army is assembling evidence to court-martial Hasan. If he is found guilty, he could face the death penalty.

BRUNO HAUPTMANN

(1899–1936)

NATIONALITY
German

WHO IS HE?
During World War I, Bruno Hauptman served as a machine gunner for the German army. After the war, he supported himself by burglary and armed robbery—he was arrested and served four years in prison. In 1923, using false papers, he emigrated to the United States, where he married and found work as a carpenter.

WHAT DID HE DO?
Hauptmann was accused of kidnapping and murdering Charles A. Lindbergh Jr., the 20-month-old son of the aviator Charles Lindbergh and Anne Morrow Lindbergh.

THE RANSOM
The Lindbergh family agreed to pay $50,000 in ransom for their child. Dr. John F. Condon, a retired school principal, agreed to deliver the ransom. In return, Condon received instructions as to where to find the baby—in Martha's Vineyard, Massachusetts. The child was not found in Martha's Vineyard, but on May 13, 1932, the baby's body was found near Mount Rose, New Jersey, about five miles from his parents' home.

DATE OF ARREST
September 24, 1934

CIRCUMSTANCES OF THE ARREST
In 1935, a $10 gold certificate from the ransom turned up in a bank near Hauptmann's home in the Bronx. Written on the back was the license plate number of Hauptmann's car. Police searched Hauptmann's house and garage, and found $15,000 of the ransom money, as well as a wooden board with Condon's address and phone number written on it.

THE CHARGES
Murder and extortion

THE SENTENCE
After a five-week trial, Hauptmann was found guilty and sentenced to death. He was electrocuted on April 3, 1936.

THE ORIENT EXPRESS
The Lindbergh case was the inspiration for Agatha Christie's murder mystery novel, *Murder on the Orient Express*, which was made into a movie in 1974 with an all-star cast that included Albert Finney, John Gielgud, Ingrid Bergman, Sean Connery, and Vanessa Redgrave.

ILLINOIS.—PORTRAITS OF THE CONDEMNED CHICAGO ANARCHISTS.
FROM CENTRAL PHOTOS BY MOSHER.—SEE PAGE 000.

THE HAYMARKET RIOT ANARCHISTS

GEORGE ENGEL (1836-1887),
ADOLPH FISCHER (1858-1887),
SAMUEL FIELDEN (1847-1922),
LOUIS LINGG (1864-1887),
OSCAR NEEBE (1850-1922),
ALBERT PARSONS (1848-1887),
MICHAEL SCHWAB (1853-1898),
AUGUST SPIES (1855-1887)

NATIONALITY
German; Neebe and Parsons were American-born

WHO WERE THEY?
All eight were political and labor activists, all of whom were involved in socialist or anarchist movements.

WHAT DID THEY DO?
On May 4, 1886, an outdoor public meeting was held at Chicago's Haymarket Square, where approximately 1,000 people assembled to show their support for an eight-hour workday. Among the spectators was Carter Harrison, the mayor of Chicago, who supported labor reform legislation. When the meeting concluded, most of the crowd dispersed peacefully, but a few stragglers remained in the square. As Chicago police moved in to hurry the stragglers along, someone threw a bomb. The blast killed seven police officers and injured many bystanders.

DATE OF ARREST
Various dates in May 1886

THE CHARGE
Murder

THE EVIDENCE
There was no evidence that any of the men charged had thrown the bomb in Haymarket Square. The thrower has never been positively identified.

THE SENTENCE
After a trial that lasted a little more than a month, all the defendants were found guilty. They were all sentenced to death, except Neebe, who was sentenced to 15 years in prison at hard labor.

AFTERWAR
Attorneys for the Haymarket Anarchists appealed the case all the way to the U.S. Supreme Court, but without success. On November 10, 1887, Illinois Governor Richard Oglesby commuted Fielden and Schwab's sentences to life in prison. Lingg committed suicide by biting a dynamite cap. Spies, Parsons, Fischer, and Engel were hanged at noon on November 11, 1887. In 1893, Illinois Governor John Peter Altgeld pardoned Fielden, Schwab, and Neebe.

SAN MATEO SHERIFF
HEARST   P C
9 1975   106284

PATTY HEARST

(1954–)

NATIONALITY
American

WHO IS SHE?
Patty Hearst is the daughter of Randolph Hearst, managing editor of the *San Francisco Examiner*, and granddaughter of the media mogul and art collector, William Randolph Hearst. On February 4, 1974, armed members of the Symbionese Liberation Army (SLA), a political extremist organization, broke into the apartment Hearst shared with her fiancé, Steven Weed. They beat up Weed, and kidnapped Hearst. Fifty-nine days into her kidnapping, Hearst announced to the world via audiotape that she had joined the SLA and taken the name Tania.

WHAT DID SHE DO?
On April 15, 1974, Hearst participated in a bank robbery that netted the SLA over $10,000. On May 16, 1974, when two of her SLA com-rades, William and Emily Harris, were stopped at Mel's Sporting Goods store on suspicion of shoplifting, Hearst, who was waiting in a van across the street, sprayed the store with bullets so the Harrises could escape.

DATE OF ARREST
September 18, 1975

CIRCUMSTANCES OF THE ARREST
Hearst and the Harrises were on the lam for more than a year. Authorities finally tracked them down at their apartment in the Mission District of San Francisco.

THE CHARGE
Armed robbery

THE TRIAL
Hearst's defense was that she had been brainwashed by the SLA. On the witness stand she tried to explain that she could not be held liable for any of her actions during the time she was with the SLA.

THE SENTENCE
The jury did not believe Hearst or accept the brainwashing defense. She was found guilty and sentenced to seven years in prison. In 1979, President Jimmy Carter commuted her sentence to time served (she had been in prison for 22 months). In 2001, President Bill Clinton granted Patty Hearst a full pardon. Two months after leaving prison, Hearst married Bernard Shaw, her bodyguard.

NEVILLE HEATH

(1917–1946)

NATIONALITY
British

WHO WAS HE?
Neville Heath was a handsome young veteran of World War II. He was also convicted of theft and fraud, and was court-martialed for wearing military decorations to which he was not entitled.

WHAT DID HE DO?
Heath murdered three women, mutilating the bodies of his victims.

DATE OF ARREST
July 6, 1946

CIRCUMSTANCES OF THE ARREST
On July 3, 1946, Heath met 21-year-old Doreen Marshall at her hotel in Bournemouth and took her to dinner. Two days later, the manager of the hotel called the police to report that Marshall had never returned after her date. Heath, who was posing as Group Capt. Rupert Brooke, was asked to come to the police station to assist with the investigation. One of the Bournemouth police officers recognized Heath from a Scotland Yard wanted flyer. A search of Heath's jacket produced Marshall's return railway ticket to London, a pearl from her necklace, and a cloakroom ticket for the Bournemouth West train station. After claiming Heath's luggage from the railway cloakroom, the police found inside the luggage clothing stained with blood of another of Heath's victims, Margery Gardner.

THE CHARGE
Murder

THE SENTENCE
At his trial, Heath pled insanity, a defense that two physicians disputed. After deliberating for one hour the jury returned a verdict of guilty. About three weeks later, Neville Heath was hanged.

RICHARD HEENE
(1961–)
MAYUMI IIZUKA HEENE
(1964–)

NATIONALITY
American

WHO ARE THEY?
Richard Heene and Mayumi Iizuka Heene are the parents of the "Balloon Boy," a six-year-old child who on October 15, 2009, supposedly was swept away in a large, homemade, helium balloon.

WHAT DID THEY DO?
The Heenes' call to the authorities for help resulted in dozens of emergency responders and two Colorado National Guard helicopters fanning out across the area to search for the little boy. The incident also attracted international media attention. But the child wasn't in the balloon; he was safe at home, hiding in the garage. The "emergency" was a hoax generated by the Heenes to attract publicity in the hopes of scoring a reality TV program.

DATE OF ARREST
October 21, 2009

CIRCUMSTANCES OF THE ARREST
Once the hoax was exposed, the Heenes turned themselves in to the police.

THE CHARGES
Falsely influencing authorities and filing a false report

THE ENTENCE
Richard Heene was found guilty of falsely influencing authorities and was sentenced to 90 days in jail. Mayumi Heene was found guilty of filing a false report and sentenced to 20 days in jail. The Heenes were also ordered to reimburse the authorities $36,000 (the agencies that had responded to the "crisis" wanted $48,000).

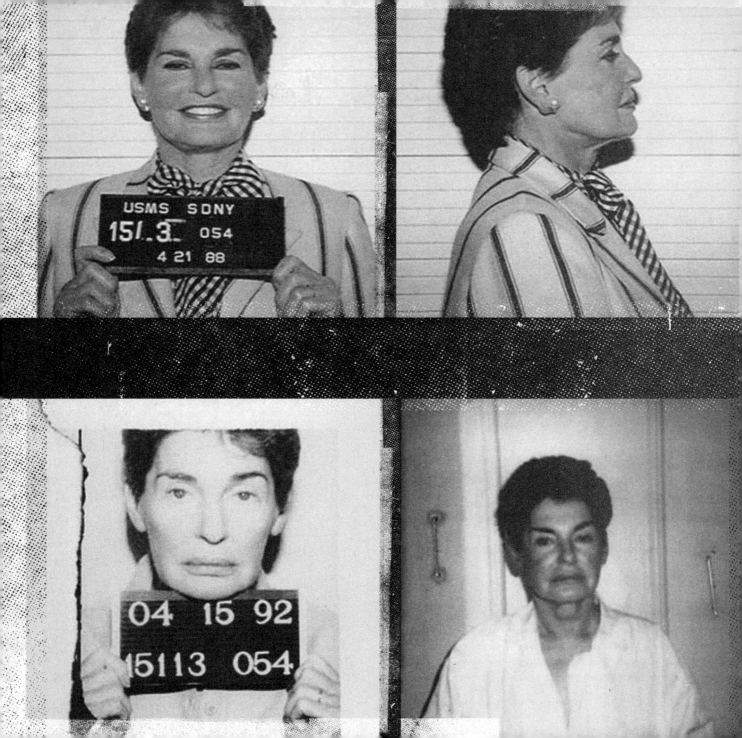

LEONA HELMSLEY

(1920–2007)

NATIONALITY
American

WHO WAS SHE?
With her husband Harry, Leona Helmsley managed a real estate empire worth $5 billion: The Empire State Building was among their properties. They had four homes, including a luxurious penthouse apartment overlooking New York's Central Park and an estate in Greenwich, Connecticut.

WHAT DID SHE DO?
Although the Helmsleys paid about $50 million in taxes annually, they were not forthcoming about all their assets. Harry's health was so poor that he was judged unfit to stand trial, so Leona was tried alone.

DATE OF ARREST
April 21, 1988

THE CHARGE
Tax evasion

THE TRIAL
Witnesses for the prosecution included Helmsley employees who described Leona as "the queen of mean"—terrorizing her staff, cheating contractors, and, most memorably, saying. "We don't pay taxes. Only little people pay taxes."

THE ENTENCE
Helmsley was found guilty and sentenced to four years in prison and 750 hours of community service. After 21 months, she was released, but an additional 150 hours of community service were added to her sentence after the judge learned that she had sent members of her staff to do the work for her.

AFTERWARD
Harry Helmsley died in 1997; Leona Helmsley died ten years later. In her will, she established a trust for the care of dogs, endowing it with billions of dollars. A judge ruled that the trustees of the Helmsley estate could use their own discretion to determine how much money should go to the canine trust fund.

GLENN HELZER

(1970–)

JUSTIN HELZER

(1972–)

NATIONALITY

American

WHO ARE THEY?

Glenn and Justin Helzer are brothers who dreamed of starting an organization that would spread the gospel message of peace and harmony and hasten Christ's second coming to earth. To fund their organization they planned to embezzle funds from two of Glenn's clients, Ivan and Annette Stineman.

WHAT DID THEY DO?

The brothers murdered the Stinemans, as well as Selina Bishop (Glenn's girlfriend); her mother, Jennifer Villarin; and Villarin's friend, James Gamble. They were assisted by their roommate, Dawn Godman.

DATE OF ARREST

August 7, 2000

CIRCUMSTANCES OF THE ARREST

After the Stinemans were reported missing, police located their minivan in Oakland, California. They found the Helzers' fingerprints on the van. When they arrested the brothers and Godman, Glenn escaped. He forced his way into a neighbor's house, where he cut off his ponytail, changed into the homeowner's clothes, then ran. Police caught him, but inside the patrol car, Glenn smashed the rear window and escaped a second time. Again the police recaptured him.

THE CHARGES

Murder, extortion, and kidnapping

THE SENTENCE

Both brothers were found guilty and each received five death sentences. Dawn Godman was sentenced to 37 years in prison.

AFTERWARD

Since their conviction, the Helzers have been sitting on death row in San Quentin prison.

RUSSELL HENDERSON
(1977–)

AARON MCKINNEY
(1976–)

NATIONALITY
American

WHO ARE THEY?
Russell Henderson and Aaron McKinney dropped out of high school and worked as roofers in Laramie, Wyoming. Henderson had been arrested twice for drunk driving; McKinney was charged with stealing $2,500 from a Kentucky Fried Chicken franchise. Around Laramie, McKinney had a reputation for brawling.

WHAT DID THEY DO?
On the night of October 6, 1998, Henderson and McKinney were in a bar in Laramie. They approached Matthew Shepard, a 21-year-old college freshman. When he told them he was gay, they said they were gay, too. Henderson and McKinney offered Shepard a ride home. Once he was inside their truck, Henderson and McKinney drove to a remote section of Laramie, where they beat Shepard, robbed him, tortured him, then took him outside town where they left him tied to a ranch fence. Eighteen hours later, a passing bicyclist discovered Shepard comatose and hanging from the fence. Matthew Shepard died in the hospital six days later.

LATER THAT NIGHT
After abandoning Matthew Shepard to die, Henderson and McKinney returned to Laramie where they got into a fight with two Hispanic men. McKinney suffered a hairline fracture and was hospitalized four rooms away from Shepard.

DATE OF ARREST
October 9, 1998

THE CHARGES
Kidnapping, aggravated robbery, and attempted murder

THE TRIAL
During the trial, Henderson and McKinney's attorneys mounted what became known as "the gay panic defense"—that Shepard's sexual advances to the men set off a period of temporary insanity.

THE SENTENCE
Henderson and McKinney were found guilty and could have been executed by lethal injection. Before sentencing, however, Matthew Shepard's parents petitioned the court to sentence their son's killers to life in prison. The judge granted the family's request.

AFTERWARD
In December 1998, Matthew Shepard's parents, Dennis and Judy Shepard, established the Matthew Shepard Foundation to promote tolerance, especially among young people.

O. HENRY
(WILLIAM SYDNEY PORTER)
(1862–1910)

NATIONALITY
American

WHO WAS HE?
O. Henry is the pen name of William Sydney Porter, a short story writer famous for his unexpected plot twists and surprise endings.

WHAT DID HE DO?
Between October and November 1894, O. Henry embezzled $854.08 from the First National Bank of Austin, Texas, where he worked as a teller. In December 1894, he resigned from the bank. When a warrant was issued for his arrest, Henry bolted, taking a cruise around South America.

DATE OF ARREST
February 5, 1897

CIRCUMSTANCES OF THE ARREST
When O. Henry learned that his wife was seriously ill, he returned to Austin and turned himself in to the police. He was released on bail.

THE CHARGE
Embezzlement

THE SENTENCE
O. Henry was found guilty and sentenced to five years in prison. After serving three years and three months, he was released.

AFTERWARD
In prison, O. Henry began jotting down notes and abbreviated character sketches of his fellow inmates. He used these in the short stories he published after he got out of prison.

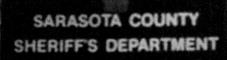

PEE WEE HERMAN (PAUL REUBENS)

(1952–)

NATIONALITY
American

WHO IS HE?
Paul Reubens is a comedian, actor, writer, and producer who created the character Pee Wee Herman. His popular children's program, *Pee Wee's Playhouse*, ran on Saturday mornings from 1986 to 1990.

WHAT DID HE DO?
At a triple-X adult theater in South Florida, Herman was observed masturbating.

DATE OF ARREST
July 26, 1991

THE CHARGE
Indecent exposure

THE SENTENCE
Herman pled no contest to the charge. He was fined $50 and ordered to perform 70 hours of community service.

THE FALLOUT
CBS canceled reruns of *Pee Wee's Playhouse*. Disney–MGM Studios pulled the backstage tour video narrated by Herman. Pee Wee Herman dolls disappeared from toy stores.

THE RECOVERY
In spite of the scandal, Reubens continued to find work in show business, including guest spots on programs such as *30 Rock*. He is making a new movie, *Pee Wee's Playhouse: The Movie*.

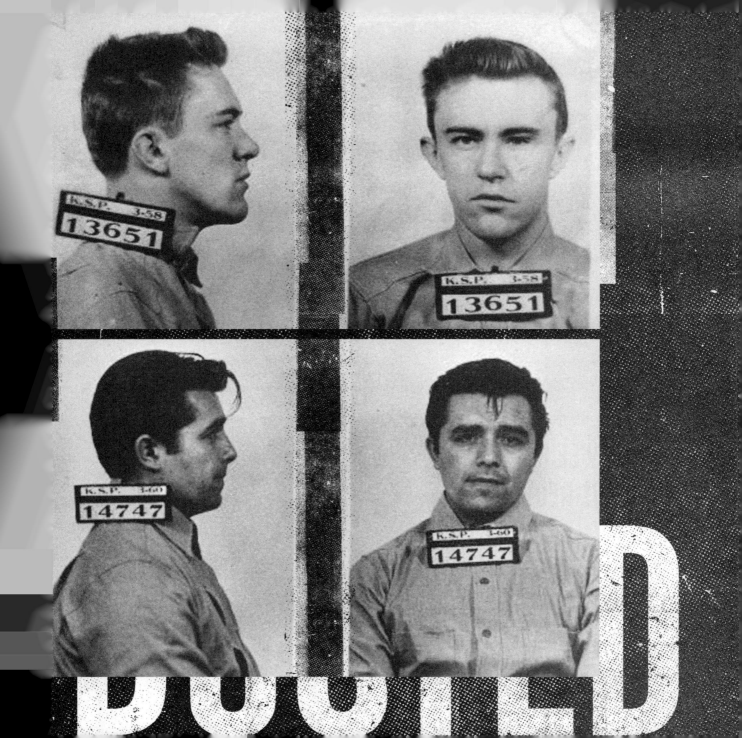

RICHARD HICKOCK
(1931–1965)

PERRY SMITH
(1928–1965)

NATIONALITY
American

WHO WERE THEY?
Richard Hickock enjoyed a stable childhood, growing up on his family's farm in Kansas. Perry Smith's parents tried to support the family as rodeo performers. When Smith's parents split up, his mother put him in an orphanage. Hickock and Smith both drifted into a life of crime that included stealing cars and passing bad checks. They met in 1958 when they were both doing time in the Kansas State Penitentiary.

WHAT DID THEY DO?
On November 15, 1959, Hickock and Perry drove to the farm of the Clutter family outside Holcomb, Kansas. In prison, an inmate had told Hickock that Herbert Clutter was a successful farmer and businessman, who often kept $10,000 in cash in the house. Hickock and Smith entered the house through an unlocked door, tied up the family, then went looking for the money—all they found was about $50. Smith slit Herbert Clutter's throat, then shot him in the head. He shot 15-year-old Kenyon Clutter in the face. Bonnie Clutter (Herbert's wife) and Nancy Clutter, 16, were also shot in the head, although Smith and Hickock gave conflicting accounts of who killed the women.

DATE OF ARREST
December 30, 1959

CIRCUMSTANCES OF THE ARREST
Hickock and Smith were picked up by police in Las Vegas, Nevada, where they had passed bad checks.

THE CHARGE
Murder

THE SENTENCE
The jury deliberated for only 40 minutes before rendering a guilty verdict. Hickock and Smith laughed as they walked out of the courtroom and back to their cells. They were both hanged.

THE BOOK AND THE MOVIE
Truman Capote traveled to Garden City, Kansas, to write a story about the murders for the New Yorker. His lifelong friend, Harper Lee, author of *To Kill a Mockingbird*, came with him. Capote befriended the people of Garden City, including the detective investigating the murders, and eventually Hickock and Smith, too. The article became *In Cold Blood*, a best-selling book and then a movie.

DATE OF ARREST
December 13, 2009

THE CHARGES
Disorderly conduct and resisting arrest

THE SENTENCE
Hill pled guilty and was sentenced to two years' probation.

HENRY HILL

(1943–)

NATIONALITY
American

WHO IS HE?
Henry Hill was a New York mobster who turned FBI informant. He was the inspiration for Ray Liotta's character in Martin Scorsese's 1990 film, *Goodfellas*. In December 2009, Hill traveled to St. Louis, where his art was to be exhibited in a local gallery, and to sign autographs at a Larry Flynt strip club.

WHAT DID HE DO?
Hill was drunk and, as he put it, "caused a little commotion" in the lobby of the Drury Inn in Fairview Heights, Illinois. When police came to arrest him, Hill became belligerent.

PARIS HILTON

(1981–)

NATIONALITY
American

WHO IS SHE?
The great-granddaughter of Conrad Hilton, founder of the Hilton Hotel chain, Paris Hilton is arguably the world's foremost "celebutante," a person who possesses no great talent but becomes famous because of her wealth, beauty, and association with genuine celebrities.

WHAT DID SHE DO?
Hilton was pulled over in Los Angeles on suspicion of drunk driving.

DATE OF ARREST
September 7, 2006

THE CHARGE
Drunk driving

IN HER OWN DEFENSE
The next morning Hilton called Ryan Seacrest's KIIS-FM radio program to discuss her arrest. "So maybe I was speeding a little bit and I got pulled over," she said. "I was just really hungry and wanted an In-And-Out Burger."

THE SENTENCE
Hilton pled no contest to the drunk driving charge. Her license was suspended and she was placed on three years' probation.

AFTERWARD
In February 2007, Hilton was pulled over for driving with her headlights off. When police discovered that her license had been suspended, they impounded her car, a $190,000 Bentley. Originally, she was sentenced to 45 days in jail for violating probation, but the judge reduced her sentence to 23 days. She was ordered to begin her jail term on June 3, 2007, but was permitted to attend the 2007 MTV Movie Awards first.

JOHN HINCKLEY JR.

(1955–)

NATIONALITY
American

WHO IS HE?
John Hinckley Jr.'s parents and older brother and sister were successful, affectionate, and outgoing. He was a recluse, a college dropout. In 1976, he moved to Hollywood where he invented an imaginary girlfriend for himself and became obsessed with the movie *Taxi Driver*, the story of a mentally unhinged cabbie who stalks a politician. Hinckley became particularly enamored of one of the film's stars, Jodie Foster. In 1980, when Foster entered Yale University, Hinckley did, too, sending her letters and poems and phoning her repeatedly.

WHAT DID HE DO?
In March 1981, Hinckley sent a letter to Foster in which he declared that, for her sake, he planned to assassinate President Ronald Reagan. On March 30, 1981, Hinckley waited outside the Washington Hilton, where the president had delivered a speech to members of labor unions. As Reagan walked toward his limo, Hinckley stepped out of the crowd and fired his handgun six times. Hinckley wounded the president, his press secretary James Brady, police officer Thomas Delahanty, and Security Agent Timothy McCarthy.

DATE OF ARREST
March 30, 1981

CIRCUMSTANCES OF THE ARREST
Secret Service agents and police officers tackled Hinckley and took him into custody at the scene.

THE CHARGE
Attempted assassination

THE SENTENCE
During the seven-week-long trial, the jury heard testimony regarding Hinckley's mental instability. After deliberating for the three days, the jury found John Hinckley Jr., not guilty by reason of insanity. The judge committed Hinckley to the St. Elizabeth Mental Hospital in Washington, D.C.

AFTERWARD
As of 1999, Hinckley was permitted to leave the hospital, under the supervision of hospital staff members, to go shopping or to see a movie. In 2003, the court permitted Hinckley to leave the hospital unsupervised to visit his parents.

9137 NE

ALGER HISS
(1904–1996)

NATIONALITY
American

WHO WAS HE?
Alger Hiss was a protégé of Supreme Court Justice Felix Frankfurter and the private secretary to Supreme Court Justice Oliver Wendell Holmes. He joined the administration of Franklin D. Roosevelt, and often went to court to defend the constitutionality of FDR's New Deal initiatives. After World War II, Hiss helped found the United Nations.

WHITTAKER CHAMBERS
In 1948, during testimony before the House Un-American Activities Committee, Whittaker Chambers, a former member of the Communist Party who had spied for the Soviet Union, denounced Hiss as a clandestine Communist.

WHAT DID HE DO?
Chambers charged that Hiss had given him secret State Department documents, instructing him to pass the papers along to Soviet agents. Hiss denied the allegation and sued Chambers for libel. Appearing before a grand jury, Hiss denied, under oath, that he was a Soviet spy; the grand jury did not believe him and charged him with perjury.

DATE OF INDICTMENT
December 15, 1948

THE CHARGE
Perjury

THE SENTENCE
Hiss's first trial ended with a hung jury. In the second trial, he was convicted of perjury and sent to prison for five years. After serving 44 months, he was released.

AFTERWARD
The state of Massachusetts had disbarred Hiss, so he found work as a salesman. He always maintained his innocence, and wrote a book, *In the Court of Public Opinion*, in which he defended himself against the government's charges. In the 1970s, the FBI declassified 40,000 pages of documents related to Hiss's case, which indicated that Hiss was innocent. He filed a petition to have his guilty verdict overturned, but a federal Appeals Court refused. Nonetheless, in 1975 the state of Massachusetts readmitted Hiss to the bar. After the fall of the Soviet Union, Hiss's name appeared in several Soviet documents, which suggested that Hiss had worked for the KGB.

THE PUMPKIN PAPERS
Whitaker Chambers claimed that he had concealed government documents and rolls of film given to him by Hiss inside a hollowed-out pumpkin on his family's farm. A judge ordered Chambers to hand over the documents and film to Hiss's lawyers, but Chambers refused, giving them instead to members of the House Un-American Activities Committee, thereby setting off a controversy about the authenticity of "the Pumpkin Papers."

ADOLF HITLER

(1889–1945)

NATIONALITY
Austrian

WHO WAS HE?
Adolf Hitler was a failed artist, a veteran of World War I, and an ardent German nationalist. In the years after the war, he became prominent in political organizations that opposed Socialism and Communism, and rejected the humiliating terms of the Treaty of Versailles, which stripped Germany of its military and required the country to pay war reparations to the Allies.

WHAT DID HE DO?
On November 8, 1923, Hitler held several Bavarian government officials captive in a beer hall in Munich (the coup became known as "the Beer Hall Putsch"). The next day he was among 3,000 putschists who tried to take over Germany's Weimar Republic. When police blocked the marchers' way, a gunfight erupted in the streets that left 14 putschists and 4 policemen dead. The insurgents fled, but many, including Hitler, were arrested in the following days.

DATE OF ARREST
November 11, 1923

CIRCUMSTANCES OF THE ARREST
Police tracked Hitler to the home of friends in a Munich suburb.

THE CHARGE
Treason

THE SENTENCE
Hitler was found guilty and sentenced to five years in prison. In prison he began to formulate his political and social philosophies, dictating them to his fellow inmate, Rudolf Hess (future Deputy Führer of the Third Reich). The result was his autobiography, titled *Mein Kampf (My Struggle)*, which sold 10 million copies between 1925 and 1945.

AFTERWARD
Adolf Hitler founded the Nazi Party and became the supreme leader, or Führer, of the German people. He dreamed of conquering the world, exterminating Jews, Communists, Gypsies, and homosexuals, and reducing races he considered inferior, such as the Slavs, to the status of permanent slave laborers. Hitler is responsible for the deaths of at least 50 million soldiers and civilians during the war, including 11 million Jews and gentiles who were murdered in Nazi concentration camps.

MARK HOFMANN
(1954–)

NATIONALITY
American

WHO IS HE?
Mark Hofmann is a sixth-generation Mormon who secretly renounced his faith sometime in his teens. Nonetheless, he maintained the façade of a devout, practicing Mormon.

WHAT DID HE DO?
Hofmann forged documents related to the history of the Mormon Church, including the so-called "Salamander Letter," which described an encounter Joseph Smith, the founder of the Mormon religion, had with a talking salamander that was transfigured into an angel. Hofmann sold 446 bogus documents for large sums to the leaders of the Mormon Church in Salt Lake City. Hofmann also forged and sold other documents, including a letter allegedly written by Betsy Ross and allegedly lost poems by Emily Dickinson.

In spite of the hefty fees he received for his documents (the Salamander Letter alone sold for $40,000), Hofmann was deep in debt in 1985. For reasons that still are not clear, Hofmann decided to kill several individuals who collected antique documents. Using homemade bombs, Hofmannn killed document collector Steve Christensen and Kathy Sheets, the wife of Christensen's former employer. A third bomb went off in Hofmann's car, badly injuring him.

DATE OF ARREST
February 1986

THE CHARGES
Murder and forgery

THE SENTENCE
Hofmann was found guilty and sentenced to life in prison. The first time he appeared before a parole board, he showed no remorse for the deaths of Christensen and Sheets.

IN CIRCULATION
Mark Hofmann produced countless bogus historical documents, some of which have not been detected and are still in circulation among collectors.

BILLIE HOLIDAY

(1915–1959)

NATIONALITY
American

WHO WAS SHE?
In her teens, Billie Holiday began singing in Harlem nightclubs. At age 18, she was discovered by music producer John Hammond, who gave her a recording contract—she cut her first album with Benny Goodman. She went on to record with Count Basie and Artie Shaw.

WHAT DID SHE DO?
Holiday's addiction to heroin was well-known in the music community and to the New York police. While performing in New York, police searched her hotel room and found heroin.

DATE OF ARREST
May 16, 1947

THE CHARGE
Possession of illegal narcotics

THE SENTENCE
Holiday was found guilty and sentenced to a year in prison.

AFTERWARD
Eleven days after her release, Holiday performed before a sold-out crowd at Carnegie Hall. She never overcame her drug addiction. In 1959, while on her deathbed at a New York hospital, police found heroin in her room and tried to arrest her. She was kept under guard until her death on July 17, 1959.

HOLLYWOOD TEN

ALVAH BESSIE (1904-1985), HERBERT J. BIBERMAN (1900-1971), LESTER COLE (1904-1985), EDWARD DYMTRYK (1908-1999), RING LARDNER JR. (1915-2000), JOHN HOWARD LAWSON (1894-1977), ALBERT MALTZ (1908-1985), SAMUEL ORNITZ (1890-1957), ADRIAN SCOTT (1912-1973), AND DALTON TRUMBO (1905-1976)

NATIONALITY
American

WHO WERE THEY?
The Hollywood Ten were screenwriters: Bessie and Cole had worked on *Objective Burma*; Dymtryk had written *Ruggles of Red Gap* and *Back to Battaan*; Lardner wrote *Woman of the Year* and contributed to *A Star Is Born*; Lawson wrote *Algiers* and *Cry the Beloved Country*; Maltz wrote *Destination Tokyo*; Ornitz and Scott worked almost entirely on B movies, such as *Imitation of Life*; Trumbo wrote *Kitty Foyle*; Herbert Biberman directed *Salt of the Earth* and wrote *The Master Race*.

WHAT DID THEY DO?
On the political spectrum, all of the Hollywood Ten leaned to the left. Some were Communist sympathizers, and some had been active in Communist organizations. When they were called before the House Un-American Activities Committee (HUAC), which was investigating Communist influence in the film industry, all ten men refused to cooperate.

DATE OF INDICTMENT
November 24, 1947

THE CHARGE
Contempt of Congress

THE SENTENCE
All ten were convicted and were sentenced to prison terms ranging from six to twelve months. They were all blacklisted from the movie industry.

THE FRIENDLY WITNESS
After his release from prison, Dymtryk went to England, where he directed several films. In 1951, he returned to the United States and offered to testify before HUAC. This time he answered all the committee's questions and named 26 other members of the movie industry whom he suspected were involved in leftist and/or Communist organizations. HUAC declared him a "friendly witness" and removed his name from the blacklist.

AFTERWARD
Alvah Bessie never wrote another screenplay, although he did write a novel about his experiences with HUAC, *Inquisition in Eden*. Herbert J. Biberman produced two independent films, Salt of the Earth and *Slaves*, both of which were more popular in Europe than in the United States. Lester Cole wrote screenplays under a pseudonym. Edward Dymtryk had a successful career as a screenwriter, writing such films as *The Caine Mutiny* and *The Young Lions*. Ring Lardner Jr., worked under pseudonyms until 1970 when he wrote the screenplay for *M*A*S*H*. John Howard Lawson moved to Mexico where he wrote books on film. Albert Maltz collaborated on screenplays anonymously until 1970, when he received credit for *Two Mules for Sister Sara*. Samuel Ornitz never worked in Hollywood again, and spent the rest of his life writing novels, including *Bride of the Sabbath*. Adrian Scott also left the film industry. Donald Trumbo worked anonymously on screenplays until 1960 when he was credited for his work on *Exodus* and *Spartacus*.

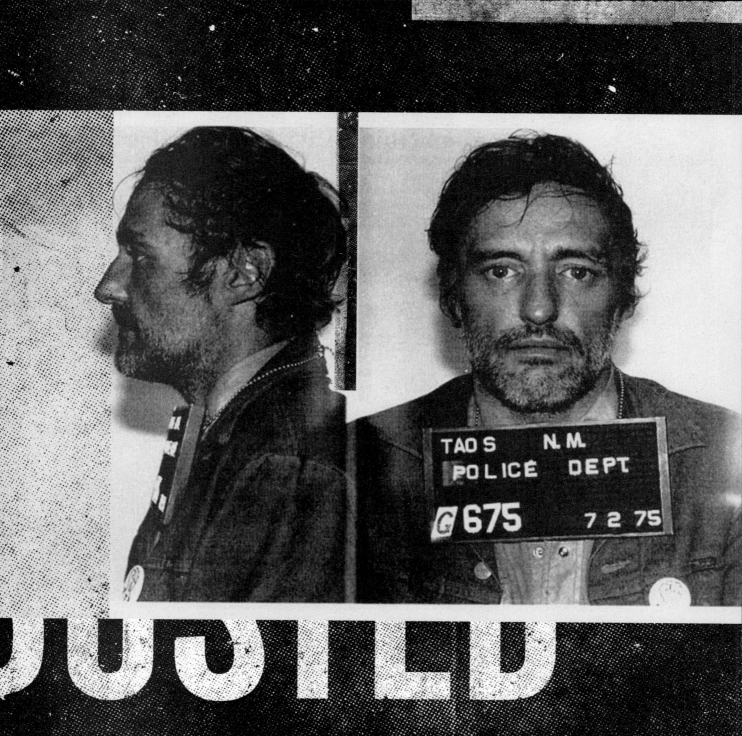

TAOS   N. M.
POLICE   DEPT
675   7 2 75

BUSTED

DENNIS HOPPER

(1936–2010)

NATIONALITY
American

WHO WAS HE?
After getting bit parts in movies and television programs in the 1950s and 1960s, Dennis Hopper's career skyrocketed in 1969 with the release of *Easy Rider*. He went on to star in *Apocalypse Now*, *Blue Velvet*, and *Speed*.

WHAT DID HE DO?
While driving in Taos, New Mexico, Hopper caused a traffic accident. He fled the scene, but was tracked down by the police and arrested.

DATE OF ARREST
July 2, 1975

THE CHARGES
Reckless driving, leaving the scene of an accident, and evading arrest

THE SENTENCE
Hopper was found guilty and fined $250.

AFTERWARD
In the 1970s and 1980s Hopper's career stalled, in large part because of his addictions to drugs and alcohol.

THE MARRYING MAN
Hopper married five times. Of his eight-day marriage to Michelle Phillips, he said, "The first seven were pretty good."

TOM HORN JR.
(1860–1903)

NATIONALITY
American

WHO WAS HE?
Tom Horn was a sharpshooter who was hired by the Pinkerton Detective Agency to hunt down outlaws. After four years with the Pinkertons, Horn took a job as a hired killer for the Wyoming Cattlemen's Association. The organization sent him out to gun down farmers, sheep ranchers, or anyone else who got in the cattlemen's way.

WHAT DID HE DO?
Horn shot and killed Willie Nickell, the 14-year-old son of a sheep rancher. If the Wyoming Cattlemen's Association hired Horn to kill young Nickell, no record of such a "hit" survives, and no other motive for the killing has ever been established.

DATE OF ARREST
January 13, 1902

CIRCUMSTANCES OF THE ARREST
Joe LeFors, the famous deputy U.S. marshall who tracked Butch Cassidy and the Hole in the Wall Gang, found Horn sleeping in a chair in the back of a Cheyenne saloon. Horn was drunk when he confessed to killing Willie Nickell.

THE CHARGE
Murder

THE SENTENCE
Horn was found guilty and hanged.

AFTERWARD
Horn's defense attorney and friends filed more than a dozen appeals with the governor of Wyoming for a retrial or a stay of execution. He refused every appeal, including one made just hours before Horn went to the gallows.

THE SEND-OFF
On the morning of the execution, two of Horn's friends, Charles and Frank Irwin, stood near the gallows and sang a hymn:

Life is like a mountain railroad
With an engineer so brave
We must make this run successful
From the cradle to the grave
Watch the curves, the fill the tunnels
Never falter, never fail
Keep your hand upon the throttle
And your eye upon the rail.

JEREMY JASON HULL

(1983–)

NATIONALITY
American

WHO IS HE?
By age 24, Jeremy Jason Hull had a long criminal record, including stealing a truck and forging checks. In 2007, five counties in Minnesota had arrest warrants out for Hull.

WHAT DID HE DO?
On April 29, 2007, Lewis Wilczek, a 21-year-old entrepreneur who owned a vehicle exhaust repair business, drove to St. Cloud, Minnesota, to collect $2,500 that Hull owed him. When Lewis arrived at Hull's apartment, Hull strangled him to death. He took Wilczek's body to a gravel pit, set it on fire, then dumped the charred remains into a grave. Then Hull assumed Wilczek's identity, transferring $50,000 from his victim's savings account.

DATE OF ARREST
May 2, 2007

CIRCUMSTANCES OF THE ARREST
On May 2, 2007, Norine Wilczek was driving through St. Cloud when she spotted her brother's distinctive truck—a silver 2004 F-350 with red stripes, oversized exhaust pipes, 33-inch all-terrain tires, and a body lift. She called the police. When the police arrived, Hull identified himself as Lewis Wilczek.

THE CHARGE
Murder

THE SENTENCE
Hull was found guilty of murder and sentenced to life in prison without parole. At the sentencing, District Court Judge Steven Anderson told Hull, "These actions are just unbelievable."

THE ACCOMPLICE
Hull's girlfriend, Casey Jo Oldenburg, helped Hull dispose of Wilczek's body. After Hull's arrest, she entered his apartment—which had been sealed by the police—and removed Hull's computer and his diary, Wilczek's cell phone, and other items. Some she destroyed; the rest she eventually turned over to the police. For her part in the crime, Oldenburg was sentenced to seven years and two months in prison.

SADDAM HUSSEIN

(1937–2006)

NATIONALITY
Iraqi

WHO WAS HE?
Saddam Hussein came from a peasant family in the town of Tikrit in northern Iraq. At age 20 he joined the Ba'ath Party and two years later participated in the attempted assassination of Iraq's prime minister, Abd al-Karm Qsim, and the overthrow of his government. The coup failed. In the 1960s and 1970s, Saddam became a leader of the Ba'athists. In 1979 he came to power as president, which was a stepping-stone to becoming dictator of Iraq.

WHAT DID HE DO?
Saddam led Iraq into a bloody ten-year-long war against Iran, which ended in a stalemate. His 1990 invasion of Kuwait proved to be a military disaster. He crushed uprisings among the Kurds and Shi'ite Muslims by murdering thousands in his prisons and using biological weapons against the Kurds, killing approximately 25,000. His development of chemical and biological weapons prompted repeated sanctions from the United Nations. Saddam's refusal to cooperate with UN weapons inspectors in 2002 led to the U.S. and British invasion of Iraq in 2003.

DATE OF CAPTURE
December 13, 2003

CIRCUMSTANCES OF THE ARREST
Approximately 24 hours after receiving a tip about Saddam's whereabouts, 60 U.S. troops cordoned off an area around a farmhouse outside Tikrit. Saddam was found hiding in an underground cellar outside the farmhouse.

THE CHARGE
Crimes against humanity

THE SENTENCE
Throughout his nine-month trial, Saddam continually interrupted the proceedings, denouncing the tribunal as stooges of the Americans. He was found guilty and hanged.

CLIFFORD IRVING

(1930–)

NATIONALITY
American

WHO IS HE?

Clifford Irving was a not-terribly-successful novelist. He fared better with his nonfiction work, Fake!, the biography of the art forger Emory de Hory.

WHAT DID HE DO?

In 1970, Irving and his friend, children's author Richard Suskind, hatched a scheme to write the "autobiography" of the eccentric, reclusive multimillionaire, Howard Hughes. Suskind gained access to news archives and unpublished manuscripts about Hughes, while Irving forged letters purportedly written by Hughes and produced "interviews" he claimed he had had with Hughes over several years. The publisher McGraw-Hill paid Irving an advance of $100,000 for the book.

DATE OF INDICTMENT

March 13, 1972

CIRCUMSTANCES OF THE ARREST

Hughes learned of the publication of his "autobiography" through advance publicity for the book. He held a telephone press conference in which he stated that the book was a fraud, and that he had never met Irving. Then Hughes's lawyers sued McGraw-Hill and Irving.

THE CHARGE

Fraud

THE SENTENCE

Irving and Suskind were found guilty. Irving was sentenced to 17 months in prison, Suskind received a sentence of six months.

AFTERWARD

In 1981, Irving published an account of the fraud in a book titled *The Hoax*. In 2005, the book was made into a movie starring Richard Gere and Alfred Molina.

KHALID ISLAMBOULI

(1955–1982)

NATIONALITY
Egyptian

WHO WAS HE?
Khalid Islambouli was a graduate of the Egyptian Military Academy who enlisted in the Egyptian army, where he rose to the rank of lieutenant. Soon thereafter, he joined the terrorist organization, Egyptian Islamic Jihad.

WHAT DID HE DO?
During a military parade, Islambouli and three accomplices charged the reviewing stand where Egyptian President Anwar Sadat was watching the parade with Egyptian and foreign dignitaries. The assassins hurled grenades at Sadat; when Islambouli reached the stand, he fired his assault rifle into Sadat at point-blank range.

DATE OF ARREST
October 6, 1981

CIRCUMSTANCES OF THE ARREST
Egyptian troops seized Islambouli and his accomplices at the scene of the crime.

THE CHARGE
Assassination

THE SENTENCE
Khalid Islambouli and his three accomplices were found guilty and sentenced to public execution by firing squad.

AFTERWARD
The government of Iran, which had despised Sadat for offering asylum to the deposed shah, Mohammad Reza Pahlavi, and for making peace with Israel in 1979, named a Tehran street in Khalid Islambouli's honor. In 1995, Ahowqi Islambouli, Khalid's younger brother, made an unsuccessful attempt to assassinate Egyptian president Hosni Mubarak.

AN INSPIRATION
The al-Islambouli Brigade of Al Qaeda and the al-Islambouli Brigade in Chechnya revere Khalid Islambouli as a martyr.

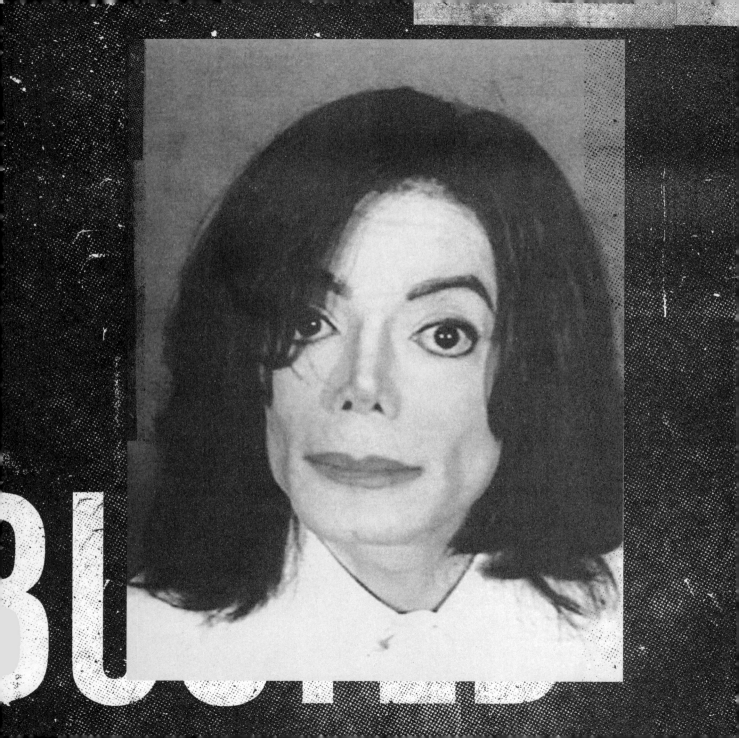

MICHAEL JACKSON

(1958–2009)

NATIONALITY
American

WHO WAS HE?
"The King of Pop," Michael Jackson reached fame as a child, performing with his brothers as "The Jackson Five." In the early 1980s, he was famous for his music videos, such as "Beat It," "Billie Jean," and "Thriller." His 1982 album, *Thriller*, was the best-selling album of all time. By 2003, it was estimated that Jackson had amassed a fortune worth half a billion dollars.

WHAT DID HE DO?
The parents of a 12-year-old boy suffering from cancer accused Jackson of sexually molesting their son. In 1993, the family of a 13-year-old boy charged Jackson with child molestation, but the case was dropped after Jackson and the family reached an out-of-court settlement in which, it was said, Jackson paid the family $20 million.

DATE OF ARREST
November 20, 2003

CIRCUMSTANCES OF THE ARREST
Santa Barbara police served the arrest warrant in Las Vegas, where Jackson was making a music video. Jackson flew back to California where he was booked, photographed, and fingerprinted. After posting $3 million bail, he was released; he flew back to Las Vegas.

THE CHARGES
Lewd conduct with a child younger than 14, attempted lewd conduct, administering alcohol to facilitate child molestation, and conspiracy to commit child abduction, false imprisonment, or extortion.

THE TRIAL
The most damning piece of evidence in the trial was a clip from a documentary film that Jackson had authorized, showing the star and the boy holding hands and discussing their sleeping arrangements. The boy in question testified in detail as to how Jackson had molested him, but later retracted his testimony.

THE VERDICT
The trial lasted 14 weeks. After deliberating for seven days, the jury exonerated Jackson of all charges.

AFTERWARD
Following the trial, Michael Jackson left the United States to take up residence in Bahrain. In 2009, Jackson announced that he was preparing a series of comeback concerts. On June 25, 2009, Jackson died at a mansion he was renting in Los Angeles. The coroner concluded that the singer died from a lethal mixture of prescription medications. Jackson's personal physician was charged with manslaughter.

MICK JAGGER

(1943–)

NATIONALITY
English

WHO IS HE?
Mick Jagger is the lead singer for the Rolling Stones, one of the greatest and most enduring rock 'n' roll bands. Since the band's inception in 1962, it has produced 29 studio albums, 10 live albums, and 92 singles, including such hits as "[I Can't Get No] Satisfaction," "Brown Sugar," and "Sympathy for the Devil." For almost 50 years, Jagger has been a rock superstar.

WHAT DID HE DO?
Jagger, Keith Richards, and three members of their entourage got in a fight with a photographer in Warwick, Rhode Island.

DATE OF ARREST
July 18, 1972

THE CHARGES
Assault and obstructing the police

THE SENTENCE
After Jagger pled guilty, he and the others were released and the charges against them were dropped.

AFTERWARD
From Warwick they drove to Boston, where they were four hours late for a concert. Jagger apologized to the crowd, saying he had been "thrown in jail a bit."

CIRCUMSTANCES OF THE ARREST
Rahum's disappearance set off a nationwide manhunt coordinated by the Israeli army and the police. Jawad Mona was arrested in the Palestinian village of Bir Nabala.

THE CHARGE
Murder

THE SENTENCE
An Israeli military court found Jawad Mona guilty and sentenced her to life in prison.

AMANA JAWAD MONA
(1974–)

NATIONALITY
Palestinian

WHO IS SHE?
Amana Jawad Mona worked as an administrator for a Palestinian fashion and entertainment magazine.

WHAT DID SHE DO?
Online, Jawad Mona befriended Ofir Rahum, a 16-year-old Jewish Israeli. She persuaded him to meet her in a Jerusalem bus station for a romantic encounter. In Jerusalem, Rahum was met by members of the Tanzim, a militant Palestinian organization, who shot and killed him, then buried his body in Ramallah.

DATE OF ARREST
January 20, 2001

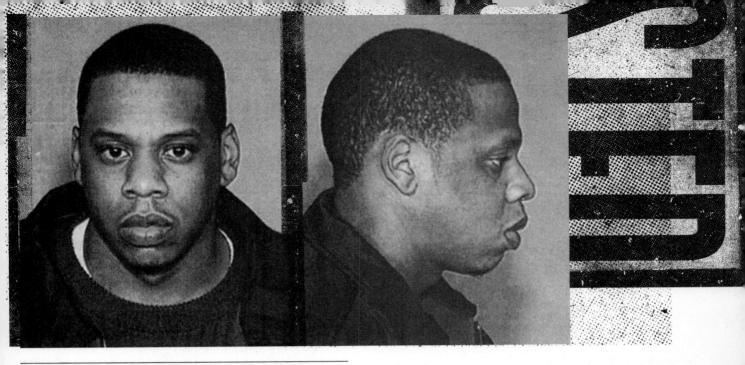

JAY-Z (SHAWN COREY CARTER)

(1969–)

NATIONALITY
American

WHO IS HE?
Jay-Z is a rapper whose albums have sold 50 million copies around the world. He has won ten Grammys and he is the solo artist who has had the most number-one albums on the Billboard 200. A successful business tycoon with his own line of clothing (Rocawear), Jay-Z is also part owner of the NBA's New Jersey Nets.

WHAT DID HE DO?
On December 1, 1999, during a party at a New York nightclub, Jay-Z confronted Lance "Un" Rivera, accusing him of selling pirated copies of his music. The argument escalated, and Jay-Z stabbed Rivera twice—once in the abdomen, once in the shoulder—with a five-inch knife.

DATE OF ARREST
December 2, 1999

CIRCUMSTANCES OF THE ARREST
Jay-Z turned himself in to New York police. At his arraignment, he pled not guilty.

THE CHARGE
Assault

THE SETTLEMENT
Rivera did not file charges against Jay-Z. Instead, the case was settled out of court for a sum reported to be between $500,000 and $1 million. A judge sentenced Jay-Z to three years' probation.

WILLIAM J. JEFFERSON

(1947–)

NATIONALITY
American

WHO IS HE?
William J. Jefferson is a Democratic politician who represented Louisiana's 2nd Congressional District in the House of Representatives from 1991 to 2009. He was Louisiana's first black representative in Congress since the end of Reconstruction in the 1870s.

WHAT DID HE DO?
In 2005, the FBI filmed Jefferson taking $100,000 in cash from an informant who was posing as a business executive seeking Jefferson's influence to help the "executive" establish business contracts in Nigeria. Jefferson said he would need $500,000 to "motivate" the president of Nigeria.

THE RAIDS
The FBI raided Jefferson's home, where they found $90,000 in cash in the freezer. Then the FBI raided his congressional office—believed to be the first time law enforcement agents had searched the office of a Member of Congress.

DATE OF INDICTMENT
June 4, 2007

THE CHARGES
Bribery, conspiracy, money laundering, obstruction of justice, racketeering, and wire fraud

THE SENTENCE
During the trial, prosecutors produced evidence that Jefferson had received between $400,000 and $1 million in bribes. He was found guilty and sentenced to seven years and three months in prison.

CONGRESS AND THE VOTERS
Once the scandal broke, Democratic leaders in the House expelled Jefferson from the Ways and Means Committee—he charged that he was a victim of racism. In 2006, with the scandal still raging, the voters of the 2nd Congressional District reelected Jefferson.

JUSTIN S. JOHNSON
(1989–)

NATIONALITY
American

WHO IS HE?
A rather dim handyman

WHAT DID HE DO?
At the drive-through window of a local bank in Bloomfield, Indiana, Johnson tried to cash a check for $1 million. When the teller asked for identification, Johnson turned over his driver's license (the teller made a photocopy of it). Then she explained that the check was not valid, that she could not cash it, and she could not return it to Johnson.

DATE OF ARREST
July 24, 2010

CIRCUMSTANCES OF THE ARREST
After Johnson drove away, the teller telephoned the police, who arrested Johnson at his home.

THE CHARGE
Forgery

THE RATIONALE
Johnson told the police that he had received a blank check from a man for whom he had done some work. He had filled in the $1 million amount, forged the man's signature, and taken it to the bank. Later, police discovered that the signature had been forged by Johnson's wife, Sarah Johnson.

JAIL TIME
Justin Johnson was held on $10,000 bail.

CHIEF JOSEPH

(1840–1904)

NATIONALITY
Nez Percé

WHO WAS HE?
Joseph was chief of the Nez Percé tribe. His home was the Wallowa Valley in northeastern Oregon, but his tribal lands, by treaty with the U.S. government, stretched from Oregon into Idaho. In 1863, the U.S. government reneged on the treaty, seizing all the land except a tiny portion in Idaho, and insisted that the Nez Percé settle on the Idaho reservation. Joseph appealed the decision until 1877, when he and his people were threatened with a cavalry attack. As he led 200 warriors and about 500 women, children, and elderly to Idaho, about 20 young warriors broke away and attacked nearby settlements, killing several Americans.

WHAT DID HE DO?
Chief Joseph sided with the war leaders of his tribe. In an attempt to escape from U.S. control, he led his people on a 1,400-mile march, fighting off 2,000 U.S. troops and their Indian allies. General William Tecumseh Sherman said of Chief Joseph's march, "[The Nez Percé] fought with almost scientific skill, using advance and rear guards, skirmish lines, and field fortifications."

DATE OF ARREST
October 5, 1877

CIRCUMSTANCES OF THE ARREST
At his surrender, Chief Joseph addressed the Nez Percé and the American troops: "I am tired of fighting. Our chiefs are killed. . . . It is cold, and we have no blankets. The little children are freezing to death. My people, some of them, have run away to the hills, and have no blankets, no food. No one knows where they are—perhaps freezing to death. I want to have time to look for my children, and see how many of them I can find. Maybe I shall find them among the dead. Hear me, my chiefs! I am tired. My heart is sick and sad. From where the sun now stands I will fight no more forever."

THE CHARGE
Prisoner of war

THE SENTENCE
Chief Joseph and the surviving members of his band were taken to a reservation in Oklahoma. He was never permitted to return to his home in the Wallowa Valley.

AFTERWARD
In his final years, Chief Joseph served as an activist, demanding that the U.S. government recognize that the Indian tribes were also entitled to the protections and guarantees of the U.S. Constitution.

AHN JUNG-GEUN

(1879–1910)

NATIONALITY
Korean

WHO WAS HE?
Ahn Jung-geun was an advocate for Korean independence from Japan, an expert in martial arts, and a superb marksman.

WHAT DID HE DO?
On October 26, 1909, Jung-geun went to the train station in Harbin, Manchuria, with a pistol concealed in a lunchbox. As Ito Hiobumi, Japan's resident-general in Korea and a supporter of Japan's policy to colonize Korea, stepped off the train, Jung-geun fired, hitting Ito three times and wounding three other Japanese who were part of his entourage.

DATE OF ARREST
October 26, 1909

CIRCUMSTANCES OF THE ARREST
After firing every round in his pistol, Jung-geun called for Korean independence while waving a Korean flag.

THE CHARGE
Assassination

THE SENTENCE
Jung-geun was found guilty and sentenced to death.

AFTERWARD
Ahn Jung-geun was acclaimed as a hero and martyr of the Korean independence movement. He was also revered by Chinese nationalists, who were also resisting Japan's incursion into their country. Both North and South Korea consider Jung-geun a national hero.

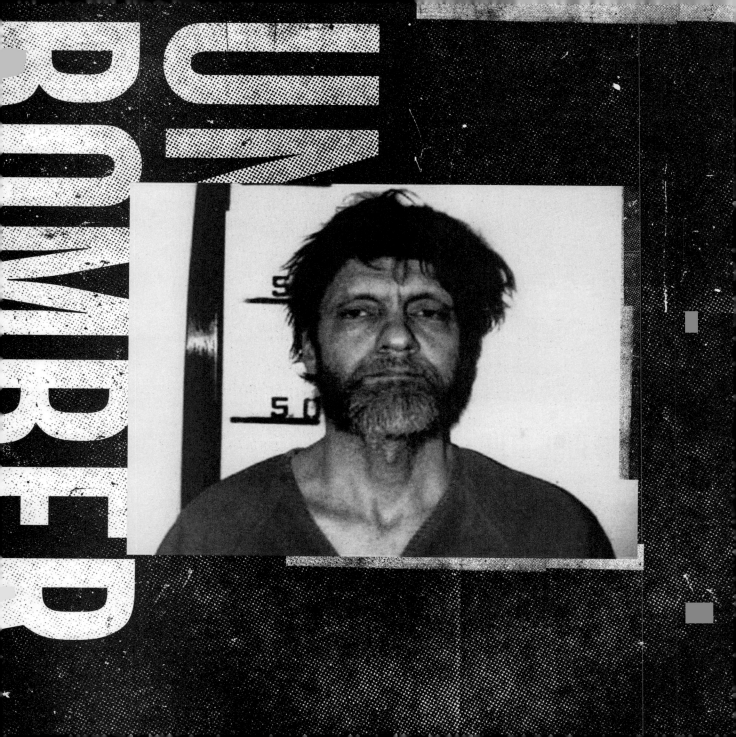

TED KACZYNSKI, "THE UNABOMBER"

(1942–)

NATIONALITY
American

WHO IS HE?
Ted Kaczynski trained as a mathematician. For years he lived as a recluse in a cabin in the remote village of Lincoln, Montana.

WHAT DID HE DO?
Over a period of about 20 years, Kaczynski sent bombs through the mail, killing 3 people and wounding 22. He smuggled a bomb onto an American Airlines flight from Chicago to Washington, D.C., and although it detonated, it only set off a small fire, rather than blowing up the aircraft, as he intended. Because he targeted universities and airlines, authorities nicknamed the unknown killer "the Unabomber."

DATE OF ARREST
April 3, 1996

CIRCUMSTANCES OF THE ARREST
Kaczynski often sent letters to survivors of his bombs and to the media, but law enforcement officials were never able to trace the origin of the correspondence. In 1995, Kaczynski released a 35,000-word denunciation of technology—his so-called "Manifesto"— which the *New York Times* and the *Washington Post* agreed to publish if he stopped sending bombs. Several of Kaczynski's acquaintances and colleagues recognized the ideas as his, but it was Ted Kaczynski's brother David who turned him in to the authorities.

THE CHARGES
Murder and illegally transporting, mailing, and using bombs

THE TRIAL
Kaczynski pled not guilty, claiming the government's case against him was political. He showed no remorse for the people he had killed or wounded.

THE SENTENCE
Ted Kaczynski was found guilty and sentenced to life in prison with no chance of parole.

AFTERWARD
David Kaczynski received a $1 million reward for turning in the Unabomber. He said he would use the money to assist his brother's victims.

UNUSUAL FACT
In 2010, a real estate company put Kaczynski's homestead in Montana up for sale, marketing it as a piece of "infamous U.S. history." The asking price was $69,500.

NATIONALITY
Russian

WHO WAS SHE?
Fanya Yefimovna Kaplan was a Russian revolutionary. At age 16, she was involved in a bomb plot against the government of Tsar Nicholas II. Kaplan was arrested and sentenced to life in a forced labor camp. She was released in 1917, following the February Revolution that brought down the tsarist government.

WHAT DID SHE DO?
As a member of the Socialist Revolutionaries, Kaplan disapproved of Lenin's Bolshevik politics. On August 30, 1918, Kaplan went to a factory where Lenin was to address the workers. After the speech, Kaplan shot Lenin, wounding him in the shoulder and the jaw.

DATE OF ARREST
August 30, 1918

HER CONFESSION
She was arrested on the spot. During her interrogation she made a statement: "Today I shot at Lenin. I did it on my own. I will not say from whom I obtained my revolver. I will give no details. I had resolved to kill Lenin long ago. I consider him a traitor to the Revolution."

THE SENTENCE
On September 3, 1918, Fanya Kaplan was shot without trial.

AFTERWARD
Hours after Kaplan's execution, a Bolshevik decree called for a "merciless mass terror against all enemies of the revolution." In the Red Terror that followed, thousands were arrested and executed.

FANYA YEFIMOVNA "FANNI" KAPLAN
(1890–1918)

RADOVAN KARADZIC

(1945–)

NATIONALITY
Serbian

WHO IS HE?
Radovan Karadzic trained as a psychiatrist and dabbled in poetry. During the 1992–1995 civil war in the former Yugoslavia, Karadzic emerged as an ultranationalist leader of the Serbs.

WHAT DID HE DO?
It is widely believed in the international community that Karadzic is responsible for the deaths of 8,000 Bosnian Muslims in the city of Srebenica, and that he authorized the killing of civilians in Sarajevo.

THE FUGITIVE
In 1997, after U.S. president Bill Clinton brokered a peace deal in the former Yugoslavia, Karadzic went into hiding. It is believed that a network of police, intelligence agents in Serbia and Montenegro, and certain elements in the Serbian Orthodox Church kept Karadzic safe for 11 years.

DATE OF ARREST
July 21, 2008

THE CHARGES
Genocide and crimes against humanity

THE TRIAL
Karadzic was taken to The Hague in the Netherlands for trial before the International Criminal Tribunal. He insisted on conducting his own defense.

IMMUNITY
Radovan Karadzic claims that Richard C. Holbrooke of the U.S. State Department promised him immunity from prosecution if, after the war, Karadzic stayed out of politics. Holbrooke, who died in December 2010, denied making such a promise, but the judges of the tribunal have asked the U.S. State Department for clarification.

MOHAMMED AJMAL AMIR KASAB
(1987–)

NATIONALITY
Pakistani

WHO IS HE?
Ajmal Kasab is the son of poor laborers from a remote village in the Punjab district of Pakistan. He worked for a time as a laborer in Lahore, then supported himself as a petty criminal before enlisting in the Islamic terrorist organization, Lashkar-e-Taiba.

WHAT DID HE DO?
In 2008, Kasab was one of ten jihadists selected by the Lashkar-e-Taiba leadership to launch terror attacks in Mumbai, India, whose targets included luxury hotels, a railway station, a restaurant, and a Jewish center. In the attacks, 166 people were killed and hundreds were injured.

DATE OF ARREST
December 1, 2008

CIRCUMSTANCES OF THE ARREST
Kasab was the only one of the ten terrorists to survive the attacks. Police caught him in Mumbai as he was trying to flee the city in a stolen car.

THE CHARGES
Murder, waging war against India, conspiracy, and terrorism

THE TRIAL
Initially, Kasab confessed to the terrorist attacks, claiming that he joined Lashkar-e-Taiba in order to get money for his family. Later he recanted his confession, stating that he had been framed by the police.

THE SENTENCE
Kasab was found guilty and sentenced to death by hanging.

WHAT DID HE DO?

Keach and his assistant, Deborah Steele, were arrested by customs officials at Heathrow Airport in London. Each of them had in their possession about $7,500 worth of cocaine.

DATE OF ARREST

April 4, 1984

CIRCUMSTANCES OF ARREST

Keach and Steele were taken into custody and released after paying bail of $100,000.

THE CHARGE

Importing cocaine

THE SENTENCE

Keach was found guilty and sentenced to nine months in prison. Steele was given three months, but the sentence was thrown out upon appeal. Keach also appealed, but Britain's Lord Chief Justice ruled that the sentence was "correct in principle and cannot be criticized as being too long."

STACY KEACH

(1941–)

NATIONALITY

American

WHO IS HE?

Stacy Keach is a star of the stage and screen who has appeared in such films as *The New Centurions*, *The Long Riders*, and *American History X*. At the time of his arrest, Keach was starring in a popular TV series, Mickey Spillane's *Mike Hammer*.

against Keating was that his salesmen at the Lincoln Savings & Loan sold junk bonds to elderly and retired Americans, assuring them that the bonds were federally insured. They were not, and when the junk bond market collapsed, those who had bought the bonds lost everything they had invested in those bonds.

DATE OF ARREST
September 18, 1990

THE CHARGES
Securities fraud, racketeering, conspiracy, transporting stolen property, wire fraud, and bankruptcy fraud

THE SENTENCE
Keating pled guilty to wire fraud and bankruptcy fraud, but pled innocent to the other charges. He was found guilty on all counts, sentenced to ten years in prison, and fined $250,000. Five years later, on appeal, the guilty convictions were overturned on a technicality.

THE JUDGE
The judge at the Keating trial was Lance A. Ito, who would become a minor celebrity while presiding over the first O. J. Simpson murder trial.

CHARLES KEATING
(1923–)

NATIONALITY
American

WHO IS HE?
Charles Keating was an antipornography crusader who later entered the field of real estate development and banking.

WHAT DID HE DO?
Charles Keating was involved in the securities fraud that brought about the collapse of savings and loan institutions in the United States, wiping out the savings of thousands of bank customers, and costing U.S. taxpayers $2.6 billion. One of the most egregious charges

GEORGE "MACHINE GUN" KELLY

(1895–1954)

NATIONALITY

American

WHO WAS HE?

George Kelly came from a well-to-do family in Memphis, Tennessee. He dropped out of college, became a bootlegger, and began hanging around small-time gangsters. His girlfriend (later his wife) Kathryn Thorne—she had an impressive criminal record that ranged from prostitution to robbery to suspected murder—created the image of "Machine Gun" Kelly, encouraging him to use the gun in bank hold-ups, and then handing out the spent shells as souvenirs to other gangsters.

WHAT DID HE DO?

In July 1933, Kelly and his wife planned to kidnap a wealthy oilman, Charles Urschel. Urschel and his wife were playing bridge with friends when Kelly and Thorne burst into the house and dragged Charles away.

THE RANSOM

Kelly and Thorne drove Urschel to a ranch in Texas where they kept him blindfolded. They demanded $200,000 in ransom, which the Urschel family paid. After the drop, Kelly released Urschel outside Norman, Oklahoma.

THE FUGITIVES

Kelly and Thorne drove around the Midwest, stayed for a time in Chicago, then went to a friend's place in Memphis. The FBI had been trailing them the whole time.

DATE OF ARREST

September 26, 1933

CIRCUMSTANCES OF THE ARREST

As FBI agents stormed into the house in Memphis, Kelly cried, "G-men! Please don't shoot!"

THE CHARGE

Kidnapping

THE SENTENCE

Kelly and Thorne were found guilty and sentenced to life in prison. Thorne was sent to a federal prison in Cincinnati; Kelly was sent to Alcatraz.

AFTERWARD

Kelly wrote several letters to Charles Urschel, begging his forgiveness and appealing to him to use his influence to get himself and Thorne out of prison. Urschel never replied.

PATRICK J. KENNEDY II

(1967–)

NATIONALITY
American

WHO IS HE?
Patrick J. Kennedy II is the son of the late Senator Edward "Ted" Kennedy and the nephew of the late President John F. Kennedy. Since 1995, he has represented Rhode Island's 1st Congressional District in the House of Representatives.

WHAT DID HE DO?
At 2:45 in the morning on May 4, 2006. Kennedy crashed his car into a barrier on Capitol Hill in Washington, D.C. When police arrived, they thought Kennedy appeared drunk, but the officers did not administer a field sobriety test.

DATE OF CITATION
May 4, 2006

CIRCUMSTANCES OF THE ARREST
Kennedy told the police that he was "headed to the Capitol to make a vote." (The last vote had been taken in the House six hours earlier.) Kennedy later released a statement that he had been suffering from the effects of two prescription medications.

THE CHARGES
Failure to keep in the proper lane, driving at an unreasonable speed, and failure to give full time and attention to his vehicle

THE SENTENCE
Kennedy's attorney's cut a deal with prosecutors: He pled guilty to driving under the influence of prescription drugs. He was sentenced to one-year probation and fined $350. He was also ordered to enter a rehabilitation program that included attendance at AA meetings and twice-weekly drug tests.

AFTERWARD
In 2010, Patrick Kennedy announced that he would not seek reelection to the House of Representatives.

WHAT DID HE DO?
During the vetting process for the Homeland Security position, Kerik made a series of false statements to White House officials, which raised so many red flags that within a week of his nomination, Kerik withdrew his name from consideration. He was also charged with accepting $225,000 worth of construction and renovation work for his home from a vendor with links to the mob who wanted to obtain contracts with the city of New York.

DATE OF ARREST
November 9, 2007

CIRCUMSTANCES OF THE ARREST
Kerik surrendered to authorities the day after a New York grand jury indicted him.

THE CHARGES
Conspiracy, mail fraud, wire fraud, and lying to the Internal Revenue Service

THE SENTENCE
In a plea bargain, Kerik pled guilty to 8 of the 16 counts in his indictment and was sentenced to four years in prison.

BERNARD KERIK
(1955–)

NATIONALITY
American

WHO IS HE?
The former police commissioner of New York City, Bernard Kerik rose to international fame after the September 11, 2001 attacks. In 2003, he went to Iraq to train Iraqi police. In 2004, President George W. Bush chose Kerik to lead the Department of Homeland Security.

KEN KESEY

(1935–2001)

NATIONALITY
American

WHO WAS HE?
Ken Kesey was an author best known for his novel, *One Flew Over the Cuckoo's Nest*. In the 1960s, Kesey was famous/notorious for his LSD-laced parties, which were later described by Tom Wolfe in *The Electric Kool-Aid Acid Test*.

WHAT DID HE DO?
Police arrested Kesey for possession of marijuana.

DATE OF ARREST
January 6, 1965

CIRCUMSTANCES OF THE ARREST
To avoid a trial and a likely prison sentence, Kesey faked his own suicide by leaving his truck parked beside a cliff, then he had friends drive him to Mexico. Eight months later, an anonymous source tipped off police that Kesey was back in the United States. Police spotted him driving on the Bayshore Freeway in California. Kesey tried to escape—unsuccessfully—first in his vehicle, then on foot.

THE CHARGE
Possession of marijuana

THE SENTENCE
Kesey served five months in prison.

AFTERWARD
Once out of jail, Kesey retired to his family's farm in Oregon's Willamette Valley. He wrote many articles for magazines, such as *Rolling Stone*, appeared occasionally at rock festivals, and traveled with his friends, who called themselves the Merry Pranksters.

THE MOVIE
One Flew Over the Cuckoo's Nest won Oscars for Best Film, Best Actor (Jack Nicholson), Best Actress (Louise Fletcher), Best Director (Milos Forman), and Best Screenplay (Lawrence Hauben and Bo Goldman).

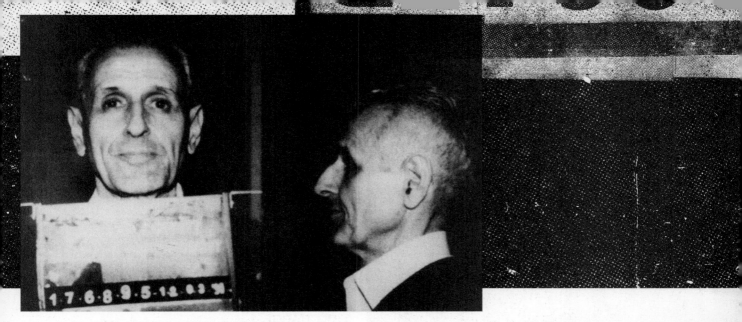

JACK KEVORKIAN

(1928–)

NATIONALITY
American

WHO IS HE?
Dr. Jack Kevorkian is a pathologist and advocate of physician-assisted suicide. He is said to have helped at least 130 patients take their own lives.

WHAT DID HE DO?
In 1998, Kevorkian gave a lethal injection to a terminally ill patient, Thomas Youk, whose consent he had obtained. Kevorkian filmed the entire process, then dared prosecutors to stop him. He released the tape to the CBS newsmagazine *60 Minutes*, which aired it on November 12, 1998.

DATE OF ARREST
March 26, 1999

CIRCUMSTANCES OF THE ARREST
The state of Michigan had revoked Kevorkian's license to practice medicine, so he was barred from having in his possession prescription medications.

THE CHARGES
Murder and administering a controlled substance

THE SENTENCE
Kevorkian was found guilty and sentenced to 10–25 years in prison.

AFTERWARD
After Kevorkian had served eight years and two months in prison, the governor of Michigan paroled him. Since his release from prison, Kevorkian has continued to advocate for the decriminalization of physician-assisted suicide. In 2008, he ran in Michigan as an independent for the House of Representatives; Kevorkian lost, receiving only 2.6 percent of the votes.

WHAT DID HE DO?

Outside a Waffle House restaurant in the Atlanta area, Kid Rock and members of his entourage got into a fight with Harlen Akins, who, it was alleged, had said something insulting to a woman traveling with the rapper.

DATE OF ARREST

October 20, 2007

CIRCUMSTANCES OF THE ARREST

Police pulled over Kid Rock's tour bus, arresting him and several members of his entourage. He posted $1,000 bond and was released. On his way out of the jail, he signed autographs for fans.

THE CHARGE

Battery

THE SENTENCE

Kid Rock was found guilty, sentenced to one year probation, and fined $1,000. A jury awarded Akins compensatory damages of $40,000.

KID ROCK
(ROBERT JAMES RITCHIE)
(1971–)

NATIONALITY

American

WHO IS HE?

Kid Rock is a singer/songwriter and rapper with multiple platinum albums and five Grammy nominations.

SANTE KIMES
(1934–)
AND
KENNY KIMES
(1975–)

NATIONALITY
American

WHO ARE THEY?
Sante and Kenny Kimes are a mother-and-son team of con artists and murderers.

WHAT DID THEY DO?
On July 5, 1998, Sante and Kenny Kimes dragged their landlady, Irene Silverman, a wealthy, 83-year-old socialite, into their suite in Mahattan. The old woman put up a fight, so Sante immobilized her with a stun gun, then Kenny strangled her. They wrapped the body in several plastic garbage bags, stuffed it into a large duffel bag, and dumped it in a trash bin in Hoboken, New Jersey. They planned to return to the Silverman mansion, which Sante would say she had just purchased from her dear friend Irene, who had gone off to a Europe on a long, extended vacation.

DATE OF ARREST
July 8, 1998

CIRCUMSTANCES OF THE ARREST
New York City police arrested Sante and Kenny at the New York Hilton. A search of their Lincoln Town Car (which they had stolen) produced Irene Silverman's passport and the keys to her mansion, real estate transfer papers, a notebook in which Sante had practiced writing Silverman's signature, and two loaded pistols—a Glock 9mm and a .22 Berretta.

THE CHARGES
The Kimeses were charged with murder, robbery, burglary, conspiracy, grand larceny, illegal weapons possession, forgery, and eavesdropping. The jury found them guilty of 118 different crimes; speaking to reporters afterward, Sante Kimes characterized the guilty verdicts as "a temporary setback."

THE SENTENCE
After describing Sante as a woman of "unremitting malevolence," and her son Kenny as "a remorseless predator," Judge Rena K. Uviller of the New York State Supreme Court sentenced Sante to 120 2/3 years to life in prison and Kenny to 126 1/3 to life in prison.

AFTERWARD
In 2004, the Kimeses were extradited to California to stand trial for the murder of a business associate, David Kazdin. Sante and Kenny were found guilty and sentenced to life in prison with no chance of parole.

UNUSUAL FACT
Sante Kimes had a previous conviction—for keeping slaves. In the 1980s, she kept several illegal immigrant women locked in her homes in Nevada and Hawaii and forced them to work as her domestic servants. She was convicted and sentenced to three years in prison.

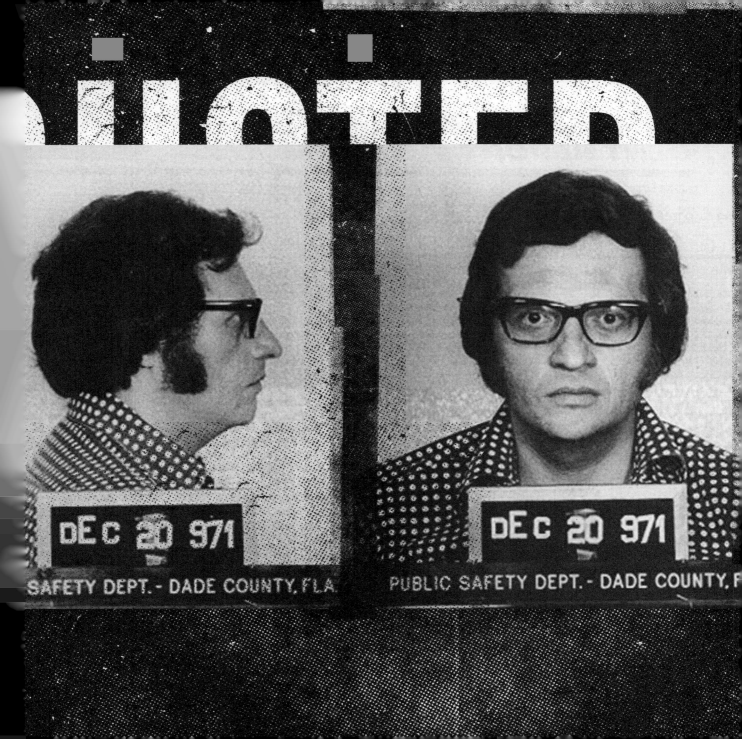

WANTED

DEc 20 971

DEc 20 971

SAFETY DEPT. - DADE COUNTY, FLA.

PUBLIC SAFETY DEPT. - DADE COUNTY, F

LARRY KING

(1933–)

NATIONALITY
American

WHO IS HE?
Larry King first went on the air in 1957 in Miami at a radio station where he had been working as a gopher and office cleaner. (The program's regular host had quit unexpectedly, and, given a choice between a rookie and dead air, the station chose the rookie.) In 1985, King joined CNN, interviewing politicians, celebrities, and newsmakers, and taking calls from viewers. In fall 2010, King retired from the program.

WHAT DID HE DO?
The details of this case are difficult to pin down. In 1971, King was arrested for passing a bad check. Various versions as to why he did so are in circulation—that he was living beyond his means and needed cash, that he made a loan to an associate of Jim Garrison, a New Orleans district attorney, who was investigating the John F. Kennedy assassination, that he used the check to cover a loan he could not repay, and that he had defrauded his business partner.

DATE OF ARREST
December 20, 1971

THE CHARGE
Grand larceny

THE SENTENCE
King pleaded no contest to the charge. What sentence he received from the court is unknown, but for several years after the incident he could not get a job in broadcasting. During that period, King worked as an announcer at a racetrack.

THE BROOKLYN YEARS
King grew up in the same Brooklyn neighborhood as Sandy Koufax, the legendary left-handed pitcher who spent his entire major league baseball career playing for the Dodgers, first in Brooklyn, then in Los Angeles. King and Koufax (their names were Lawrence Zeiger and Sanford Braun in those days) were boyhood friends.

MARTIN LUTHER KING JR.

(1929–1968)

NATIONALITY
American

WHO WAS HE?
A Baptist minister from Atlanta, Georgia, Dr. Martin Luther King Jr., was the founder of the Southern Christian Leadership Conference, an organization dedicated to ending racial segregation and extending civil rights to all Americans.

WHAT DID HE DO?
On Good Friday 1963, King joined demonstrators in Birmingham, Alabama, who called for the desegregation of schools and all public facilities, such as restaurants.

DATE OF ARREST
April 12, 1953

THE CHARGE
Demonstrating without a permit

THE MANIFESTO
During the eleven days he was incarcerated, King wrote his *Letter from Birmingham Jail*, calling upon the clergy of Birmingham to support the civil rights movement.

THE SENTENCE
City government officials in Birmingham agreed to desegregate schools, stores, and restaurants, and to put an end to racially discriminatory hiring practices. In the wake of this new city ordinance, The charges against King were dropped.

AFTERWARD
Dr. Martin Luther King Jr., became the leader of the civil rights movement in the United States. In recognition of his nonviolent campaign to achieve racial equality, he won the 1964 Nobel Peace Prize. As Congress passed the Civil Rights Acts and the Voting Rights Act, King called for an end to discrimination in housing and employment, and for decent housing for the poor. Dr. King was assassinated in Memphis, Tennessee, on April 4, 1968.

RODNEY KING POLICE OFFICERS:

STACEY KOON (1950-), LAURENCE POWELL (1962-), TIMOTHY WIND (1960-), AND THEODORE BRISENO (1950-)

NATIONALITY
American

WHO ARE THEY?
Stacey Koon, Laurence Powell, Timothy Wind, and Theodore Briseno were officers of the Los Angeles Police Department who were on patrol the night of March 2–3, 1991.

WHAT DID THEY DO?
The four officers arrested Rodney King, who was drunk and had been speeding on the 210 Freeway. After they had King cuffed and lying on the ground, the police beat him with metal batons. King's injuries were so severe that he was taken to a hospital by ambulance.

THE VIDEO
From his apartment nearby, George Holliday videotaped the beating of Rodney King. Holliday gave the tape to the Los Angeles television station, KTLA. The tape was picked up by CNN, which led to an FBI investigation of the beating.

DATE OF INDICTMENT
March 14, 1991

THE CHARGES
Powell, Wind, and Brisenio: excessive use of force; Koon: willfully permitting and failing to take action to stop the unlawful assault

THE SENTENCES
Koon, Wind, and Brisenio were acquitted of all charges, but in Powell's case the jury could not reach a verdict.

AFTERWARD
About two hours after the verdict was announced, rioting erupted in Los Angeles. The riots took the lives of 53 people and caused more than $1 billion in property damage. More than 7,000 people were arrested.

THE SECOND TRIAL
President George H. W. Bush ordered the Justice Department to examine the evidence to determine if the four LAPD officers violated Rodney King's civil rights. A federal grand jury indicted all four officers. Koon and Powell were found guilty and sentenced to two years in prison; Wind and Brisenio were acquitted. Later, Wind and Brisenio were both dismissed from the LAPD.

JULIAN KNIGHT

(1968–)

NATIONALITY
Australian

WHO IS HE?
Julian Knight was ten days old when he was adopted by an Australian military family. At age 14, Knight joined the Army Cadets and at age 17, he enlisted in the Army Reserves where he soon became especially proficient in the use of a variety of weapons. At age 19, Knight stabbed a sergeant; he was released on bail and expelled from the Royal Military College.

WHAT DID HE DO?
On the evening of August 9, 1997, Knight took a pump-action shotgun, a .22-caliber rifle, and an M14 automatic rifle, climbed onto a platform behind a billboard overlooking Hoddle and Ramsden Streets in Melbourne, and opened fire on passing cars. He killed 6 people and wounded 19.

DATE OF ARREST
August 10, 1997

CIRCUMSTANCES OF THE ARREST
Once the police arrived, Knight fled on foot through the streets of Melbourne until he was cornered by a police detective.

THE CHARGE
Murder

THE SENTENCE
Knight was found guilty and sentenced to seven consecutive life sentences, but he could be eligible for parole in May 2014, after serving 27 years.

REGINALD KRAY
(1933–2000)
AND
RONALD KRAY
(1933–1995)

NATIONALITY
English

WHO WERE THEY?
Reginald and Ronald Kray were twins, extremely close and extremely violent. They were both arrested for assault at age 17, but the charge was dropped for lack of evidence. In their 20s, the Krays started a crime organization that controlled a number of pubs and nightclubs.

WHAT DID THEY DO?
During a gang war, they murdered a rival, George Cornell, in the middle of a crowded pub. When a hit man, Jack "the Hat" McVitie, failed to finish a job, Ronald stabbed McVitie repeatedly in the face, stomach, and neck while Reginald cheered him on. These and other crimes were well known in the London underworld, but the Krays' reputation for brutality made any potential witnesses think twice before going to the police.

DATE OF ARREST
May 9, 1968

CIRCUMSTANCES OF THE ARREST
Once the Krays were in police custody, witnesses came forward to give evidence against them.

THE CHARGE
Murder

THE SENTENCE
The twins were found guilty and sentenced to life in prison, with no chance of parole until they had served a minimum of 30 years.

AFTERWARD
Ronald died of a heart attack in 1995 while incarcerated in a hospital for the criminally insane. In 2000, Reginald was diagnosed with inoperable bladder cancer and was released on compassionate grounds; he died several weeks later. The brothers are buried side by side.

GENE KRUPA
(1909–1973)

NATIONALITY
American

WHO WAS HE?
Gene Krupa was the first jazz drummer soloist. In the 1930s, he played with such jazz legends as Tommy Dorsey, Bix Beiderbecke, and Benny Goodman. In 1938, he started his own orchestra. Krupa's theatrical performance on the drums and his good looks attracted the attention of Hollywood, and he was cast as a drummer in several films, including *Some Like it Hot*.

WHAT DID HE DO?
Police alleged that Krupa sent a 17-year-old boy to his hotel room to retrieve some marijuana cigarettes.

DATE OF ARREST
January 20, 1943

THE CHARGES
Drug possession and contributing to the delinquency of a minor

THE SENTENCE
Krupa was found guilty and sentenced to 90 days in jail. He served 84 days and was released.

AFTERWARD
When he got out of jail, Krupa was certain his career was over, but Dorsey and Goodman helped him land new gigs. He found renewed success with his arrangements of be-bop and with the release of a studio recording featuring Krupa and drummer Buddy Rich. He retired in 1967, playing in public only occasionally. A reunion of the Benny Goodman Quartet, in August 1973, was his final performance. Gene Krupa died eight weeks later.

BUSTED

JAN KUBIS
(1913–1942)
AND
JOZEF GABÍK
(1912–1942)

NATIONALITY
Czech

WHO WERE THEY?
Jan Kubis and Jozef Gabík were Czechs who escaped to England when Adolf Hitler seized Czechoslovakia. They joined the Free Czechs, a fighting force trained by the British for the ultimate liberation of their homeland.

WHAT DID THEY DO?
The British recruited Kubis and Gabík to fly into Czechoslovakia and assassinate Reinhard Heydrich, chief of the Third Reich's Main Security Office and effectively the governor of Bohemia and Moravia. Heydrich was responsible for rounding up Jews, and others the Nazis considered undesirable, for extermination in concentration camps. On May 1942, Kubis and Gabík and several other Czech patriots waited for Heydrich along his usual daily route to his office in Prague Castle. As the car drove by, the Czechs opened fire, and Kubis threw an antitank grenade into the car. Heydrich was mortally wounded and died soon after the attack.

THE ESCAPE
Kubis, Gabík, and the other men involved in the assassination were hidden in the homes of friends and then in Sts. Cyril and Methodius Orthodox Church.

THE ROUNDUP
Hitler ordered the Gestapo to find the assassins and carry out reprisals throughout Czechoslovakia. Ultimately, 13,000 individuals were arrested and hundreds were tortured and killed. One of the assassins' associates, Karel Curda, betrayed Kubis and Gabík to the Gestapo.

DATE OF ATTEMPTED ARREST
June 18, 1942

THE CHARGE
Assassination

THE AFTERMATH
The seven Czechs barricaded themselves inside the church as the Nazis hurled grenades and pumped tear gas inside. Kubis was killed in the gun battle. Gabík and the six others took their own lives.

KONRAD KUJAU
(1938–2000)
AND
GERD HEIDEMANN
(1931–)

NATIONALITY
German

WHO ARE THEY?
Since 1955, Gerd Heidemann had been a reporter for the German newsmagazine, *Stern*. He was also a collector of Nazi memorabilia. In 1980, while visiting a fellow collector, Heidemann was shown a volume purported to be the diary of Adolf Hitler for the period January through June 1935. Using the alias "Herr Fischer," Konrad Kujau passed himself off as a dealer in antiques; in fact, he was a forger who manufactured and sold fake Nazi artifacts—often complete with bogus certificates of authenticity—to gullible collectors.

WHAT DID THEY DO?
Heidemann tracked the 1935 volume to "Herr Fischer," who assured the reporter that he had Hitler's complete diaries from 1932 to 1945. At this time Germany was divided between East and West—Heidemann was in the West, Kujau in the East. Kujau said the diaries could only be smuggled out one volume at a time—which gave him time to forge the complete set. Heidemann, without any authority from his superiors at *Stern*, offered 85,000 marks ($57,000) for each volume of the Hitler diaries. Although *Stern* made Heidemann the agent for the transaction, giving him a generous advance and promising him royalties on the sales of the diaries, Heidemann got greedy: He told the editors at *Stern* that Kujau had raised his fee to 200,000 marks ($135,000) per volume. He hadn't, and Heidemann pocketed the extra cash. Ultimately, Heidemann kept more than 6 million marks ($4.05 million) of the 9 million marks ($6.08 million) *Stern* paid out.

THE DIARIES DEBUNKED
In 1983, to counter skepticism in the international press regarding the diaries, *Stern* sent out all the volumes for analysis. Tests revealed that the ink, paper, and even the glue with which the volumes were bound had been made within the previous 24 months.

DATE OF ARREST
May 14, 1983

CIRCUMSTANCES OF ARREST
Heidemann turned himself in and confessed everything. West German police caught Kujau as he tried to cross the border into Austria.

THE CHARGE
Fraud

THE SENTENCE
Heidemann and Kujau were convicted, and each was sentenced to four years in prison.

AFTERWARD
In 1988, Konrad Kujau opened a gallery in Stuttgart, where he sold his reproductions, which he advertised as "authentic fakes" of paintings by Rembrandt, Monet, Dali, and even Hitler. In 2002, researchers studying the files of the former East German intelligence service found that, from 1953 until the late 1980s, Gerd Heidemann had worked for the Stasi, the East German secret police. Heidemann adamantly denied that he was ever a Stasi agent.

BERGEN COUNTY, N.J.
SHERIFF'S OFFICE

NO. 80066 B DATE 12 17

NAME KUKLIINSKI RICHARD

WT 270 HT 6 4 TOWN 72

D.O.B. 4-11-35 IDM09

BUSTED

RICHARD "THE ICEMAN" KUKLINSKI

(1936–2006)

NATIONALITY
American

WHO WAS HE?
Richard Kuklinski came from a violent, abusive Jersey City, New Jersey, family—his father beat to death Richard's brother, Florian. Kuklinski would claim that he committed his first murder at age 13, killing the leader of a local street gang who was bullying him. As a young man he enjoyed killing homeless men, especially those who resembled his father. Later, Kuklinski became a hit man for the Gambino crime family.

WHAT DID HE DO?
Kuklinski is said to have killed perhaps as many as 250 people. Through an undercover agent who had infiltrated the mob, and the testimony of one of Kuklinski's friends in the crime organization, federal and state of New Jersey authorities believed they had enough evidence to convict Kuklinski of the murders of at least 5 individuals.

DATE OF ARREST
December 17, 1986

CIRCUMSTANCES OF THE ARREST
Federal agents and police blocked off the street where Kuklinski lived to reduce his chances of escaping. Even so, Kuklinski put up such a struggle that it took several officers to physically subdue him.

THE CHARGE
Murder

THE SENTENCE
Kuklinksi was found guilty and given five consecutive life sentences. In prison he confessed to the murder of New York police detective Peter Calabro, which added an additional 30 years to his sentence.

AFTERWARD
In prison, Kuklinski granted interviews to journalists, psychiatrists, and filmmakers. He claimed that if he ever lost his temper and beat his wife to death, he would have to kill his three children, too. He said that sometimes he left his victims to be eaten alive by rats. He claimed that once he tested a crossbow by firing it at a stranger—the arrow struck the man in the skull, killing him instantly.

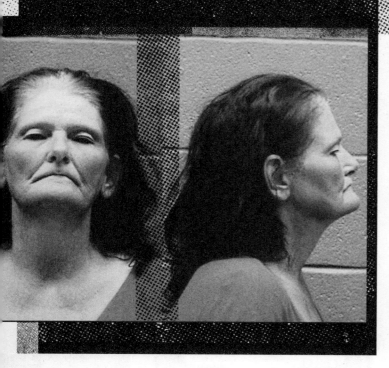

DATE OF ARREST
July 20, 2010

CIRCUMSTANCES OF THE ARREST
Lain was taped by the restaurant's security cameras. About three in the morning, police arrested her at her home, where they found methamphetamine and marijuana.

THE CHARGES
Burglary, possession of a controlled dangerous substance, possession of paraphernalia, and illegal trespass.

SHARON LAIN
(1959–)

NATIONALITY
American

WHO IS SHE?
Sharon Lain, a native of Midwest City, Oklahoma, had been fired from her job as manager of the night shift at a local McDonald's.

WHAT DID SHE DO?
Dressed in a wig and using a girdle as a mask, Lain approached the drive-through window of the McDonald's where she once worked, reached in, and using her cash register key took money from the till.

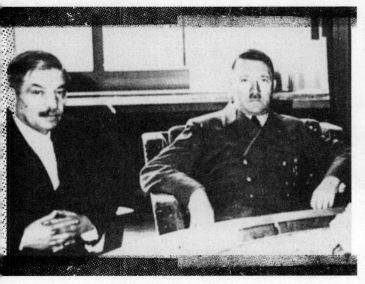

PIERRE LAVAL

(1883–1945)

NATIONALITY
French

WHO WAS HE?
A sharp-tongued, short-tempered, argumentative man, Laval was a career politician whose determination to stay in power often led him to switch from one party to another. In his lifetime, he would migrate from Marxism to independent to conservative.

WHAT DID HE DO?
In 1940, Laval accepted the office of minister of state in Vichy France, a puppet government under the control of the Nazis. Laval's frequent contacts with the Nazis, including Adolf Hitler, led to the charge that he was a collaborator—an accusation that gained more strength after he surrendered to the Germans the Bor copper mines and the gold of the Belgian government. He negotiated a deal with the Nazis in which the Third Reich would release one French prisoner of war for every three Frenchmen or women Laval sent to Germany as forced laborers. Laval was also accused of sending Jewish children under the age of 16 to Nazi death camps—although his anti-Semitic activities are still debated.

DATE OF ARREST
August 1, 1945

CIRCUMSTANCES OF THE ARREST
Laval and his wife had sought refuge in Spain, but the Spanish government turned them over to the French. The Lavals were flown to Paris, where Madame Laval was released and Pierre Laval was formally arrested.

THE CHARGE
Treason

THE SENTENCE
Laval was found guilty and sentenced to be executed by firing squad. In prison he tried to kill himself by swallowing poison, but the poison's shelf life had expired—it only made him sick. After the prison doctors pumped his stomach, Pierre Laval was taken to the prison yard and shot.

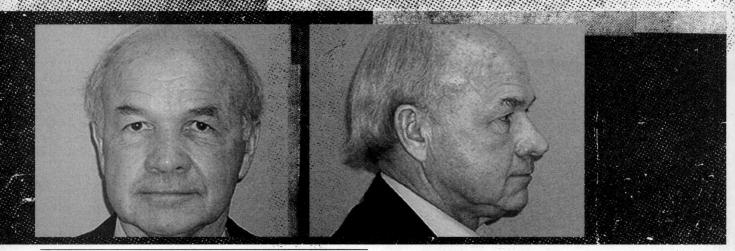

KENNETH LAY

(1942–2006)

NATIONALITY
American

WHO WAS HE?
Kenneth Lay was the CEO of Enron, a large energy company with corporate headquarters in Texas. He was an advocate for energy deregulation, and a friend of and fund-raiser for George W. Bush. For a time, pundits suggested that Lay might be named secretary of energy in President Bush's cabinet, but nothing came of that.

WHAT DID HE DO?
It was widely believed that Lay had made Enron one of the most successful and innovative companies in the United States. In fact, Enron cooked its books, concealing its debt and exaggerating its profits (auditors from the accounting firm of Arthur Andersen were implicated in the fraud). In 2001, the house of cards collapsed and billions in Enron employee pensions vanished.

DATE OF ARREST
July 8, 2004

CIRCUMSTANCES OF THE ARREST
After being indicted by a grand jury, Lay turned himself into to authorities in Houston.

THE CHARGES
Conspiracy, fraud, and lying to banks

THE SENTENCE
After deliberating for six days, the jury found Lay guilty. He was liable to a sentence of life in prison and fines amounting to more than $43 million.

AFTERWARD
Six weeks after the trial, and four months before he was to be sentenced, Kenneth Lay suffered a massive heart attack at his home in Aspen, Colorado, and died.

WHAT DID HE DO?

Leary attempted to cross from Laredo, Mexico, to Texas with his girl-friend, Rosemary Woodruff, his 15-year-old son Jack, and his 17-year-old daughter Susan, who was concealing marijuana in her underwear. The family was stopped and searched.

DATE OF ARREST

December 20, 1965

CIRCUMSTANCES OF THE ARREST

Although the marijuana was found on Susan's person, Leary took responsibility for it and was arrested.

THE CHARGE

Possession of marijuana

THE SENTENCE

Leary was found guilty, sentenced to 30 years in prison, and fined $30,000.

AFTERWARD

Leary appealed his conviction all the way to the U.S. Supreme Court, which ruled that the narcotics law under which Leary had been convicted violated his Fifth Amendment protections. His conviction was quashed and he was freed.

UNUSUAL FACT

In 1969, Leary ran for governor of California under the slogan, "Come together, join the party." The slogan became the inspiration for John Lennon's song, "Come Together."

TIMOTHY LEARY

(1920–1996)

NATIONALITY

American

WHO WAS HE?

Timothy Leary was a psychologist who became one of the icons of the counterculture movement of the 1960s and 1970s. He advocated experimentation with psychedelic drugs, and coined the phrase, Turn on, tune in, drop out.

TOMMY LEE
(1962–)

NATIONALITY
American citizen

WHO IS HE?
Tommy Lee is the drummer for the band Mötley Crüe. His on again/off again relationship with *Baywatch* bombshell Pamela Anderson made headlines, as did their sex tape, which became the number-one-selling adult video of 1998.

WHAT DID HE DO?
During a concert in Greensboro, North Carolina, Lee and Mötley Crüe bassist Nikki Sixx poured a drink over the head of John Allen, a black security guard. Sixx shouted racist epithets at Allen, then he and Lee urged fans to attack the security guard.

DATE OF ARREST
October 11, 1999

CIRCUMSTANCES OF THE ARREST
After dodging the law for almost two years, Lee turned himself in to police in Greensboro, North Carolina. Lee posted $5,000 bail and was released on his own recognizance.

THE CHARGES
Assault and attempting to incite a riot

THE SENTENCE
Lee and Sixx both pled no contest and received 18 months' probation.

LEGAL TROUBLES
Even before the assault and riot incident, Tommy Lee had been in trouble with the law, including charges of indecent exposure, domestic violence, and unlawful possession of a firearm.

FERNAND LEGROS

(1931–1983)

NATIONALITY

French

WHO WAS HE?

Fernand Legros was a frustrated ballet dancer who became an art dealer. In the 1950s in Miami, Florida, Legros met Elmyr de Hory, a Hungarian artist who had no luck selling his own paintings, but found success forging the works of Picasso, Matisse, and Renoir, among other great masters. Legros became de Hory's agent for these bogus paintings

WHAT DID HE DO?

Legros sold de Hory's forged paintings—sometimes with forged certificates of authenticity—to art collectors. To Texas art collector Algur Meadows alone, Legros sold $1.5 million in forged paintings.

DATE OF ARREST

1979

CIRCUMSTANCES OF THE ARREST

After running to Switzerland and then Brazil, Legros was arrested on the Spanish island of Ibiza.

THE CHARGE

Fraud

THE SENTENCE

Legros was found guilty, sentenced to two years in prison, and fined $3,000.

AFTERWARD

Elmyr de Hory committed suicide. Fernand Legros died of throat cancer.

KEN LEISHMAN, "THE GENTLEMAN BANDIT"

(1931–1979)

NATIONALITY
Canadian

WHO WAS HE?
Ken Leishman of Manitoba was a mechanic, a salesman, and a pilot who became one of Canada's most notorious—and successful—robbers. Charming, well-dressed, and unfailingly polite to his victims, Leishman was nicknamed "the Gentleman Bandit."

WHAT DID HE DO?
On March 1, 1966, Leishman and four accomplices stole $385,000 in gold bullion. In a stolen Air Canada truck, dressed in Air Canada coveralls, the men drove onto the tarmac of Winnipeg Airport to the TransAir plane carrying the gold. They told the TransAir flight crew that they had been sent to transport the gold shipment to an Air Canada aircraft. Without asking any questions, the TransAir crew handed over the gold.

DATE OF ARREST
March 1966

CIRCUMSTANCES OF THE ARREST
The Royal Canadian Mounted Police arrested Leishman and his accomplices within days of the gold heist. All the bullion was recovered but one gold bar.

THE CHARGE
Robbery

THE SENTENCE
Leishman was found guilty and sentenced to nine years in prison.

AFTERWARD
After his release, Leishman settled in Red Lake, Ontario, where he became deputy mayor. In 1979, during a Medevac mercy flight, Ken Leishman's plane went down in northern Ontario. His remains were found in the wreckage a year later.

VLADIMIR LENIN

(1870–1924)

NATIONALITY
Russian

WHO WAS HE?
Born Vladimir Ilyich Ulyanov, Lenin's family were members of the middle class. For his government service, Lenin's father was elevated to the Russian nobility. Lenin's elder brother Alexander was hanged in 1887 for attempting to assassinate Tsar Alexander III. In the 1890s, Lenin joined the revolutionary movement.

WHAT DID HE DO?
In 1895, Lenin participated in a plot to kill Tsar Alexander III.

DATE OF ARREST
December 7, 1895

THE CHARGE
Plotting against the tsar

THE SENTENCE
Lenin was found guilty and sentenced to 14 months in a St. Petersburg prison before being sent to Siberia for three years.

AFTERWARD
From 1907 until 1917 Lenin lived in exile in Western Europe, writing, lecturing, and planning for a revolution he at times was not certain would actually take place. The appalling casualties of World War I, combined with shortages of food and fuel in the cities, sparked the Russian Revolution of 1917. The tsar was overthrown and Lenin returned to Russia to lead the fledgling Soviet Union (1917–1924).

LENIN'S BODY
After his death, Lenin's body was embalmed and placed on display in a specially built mausoleum in Moscow's Red Square. In 1941, the Soviet government, fearing that Moscow would fall to the Nazis, moved Lenin's body to Siberia. Since the collapse of the Soviet Union, there has been ongoing discussion in Russia as to whether Lenin's body should continue on permanent exhibit or whether it should be buried.

JERRY LEE LEWIS

(1935–)

NATIONALITY
American

WHO IS HE?
Jerry Lee Lewis was a child piano prodigy who developed a raw, wild performance style that was influenced by gospel, folk, and R&B. His hit singles included "Whole Lot of Shakin' Going On" and "Great Balls of Fire." In 1957, Lewis sold more records than Elvis Presley. In 1986, Lewis was the first artist inducted into the Rock and Roll Hall of Fame.

WHAT DID HE DO?
At about two in the morning on November 23, 1976, Lewis parked his white Lincoln Continental in front of the gates of Graceland, Elvis Presley's home in Memphis, Tennessee. The night guard (Elvis's cousin, Harold Lloyd) observed Lewis staggering in the driveway, waving a pistol, and demanding to see Elvis.

DATE OF ARREST
November 23, 1976

CIRCUMSTANCES OF THE ARREST
By the time the police arrived, Lewis had climbed back into his car, where he had the pistol on his lap. Police arrested Lewis and confiscated the weapon.

THE CHARGE
Public drunkenness and possession of a firearm

THE SENTENCE
After a brief trial in Memphis, Lee was acquitted of all charges.

UNUSUAL FACT
A few days before his 71st birthday in 2006, Lewis released *Last Man Standing*, an album of 21 rock classics, including duets with Mick Jagger, Rod Stewart, and Bruce Springsteen.

G. GORDON LIDDY

(1930–)

NATIONALITY
American

WHO IS HE?
After graduating from law school, G. Gordon Liddy joined the FBI, where at age 29 he became the youngest bureau chief in the history of the organization. After the election of Richard Nixon in 1968, Liddy became part of the administration. In 1971, he worked on the Committee to Re-elect the President, devising a variety of schemes to embarrass the Democrats and neutralize the administration's opponents.

WHAT DID HE DO?
Liddy was the supervisor of the five men who broke into the Democratic National Committee offices at the Watergate Hotel to plant bugs.

DATE OF INDICTMENT
September 15, 1972

THE CHARGES
Conspiracy, burglary, and illegal wiretapping

THE SENTENCE
Liddy was found guilty, fined $40,000, and sentenced to 20 years in prison.

AFTERWARD
In 1977, President Jimmy Carter commuted Liddy's sentence; he was released on parole four months later. In 1980, Liddy published his autobiography, *Will*, which became a best seller. He appeared in Oliver Stone's film, *Nixon*, and guest-starred on *Miami Vice*, *MacGyver*, and other television programs.

UNUSUAL FACT
In the 1980s, Liddy went on the college circuit, participating in a popular series of debates with Timothy Leary.

RUSH LIMBAUGH

(1951–)

DATE OF ARREST
April 28, 2006

CIRCUMSTANCES OF THE ARREST
Limbaugh turned himself in to Palm Beach County, Florida. He was released on $3,000 bail.

THE CHARGE
Prescription fraud

THE SENTENCE
In a plea-bargain arrangement, the charge against Limbaugh was dropped; in exchange, he agreed to receive treatment for substance abuse.

NATIONALITY
American

WHO IS HE?
Rush Limbaugh is a conservative commentator whose radio program, *The Rush Limbaugh Show,* reaches more than 14 million listeners each week.

WHAT DID HE DO?
Police alleged that Limbaugh had gone "doctor shopping," acquiring 2,000 prescription painkillers from four different doctors during a six-month period.

JOHN WALKER LINDH
(1981–)

NATIONALITY
American

WHO IS HE?
John Walker Lindh grew up in Maryland and California. At age 16, he converted to Islam. In 2000, he went to Yemen and then to Pakistan, where he studied at a madrassa, or Islamic school. In 2001, he joined the Taliban in Afghanistan.

WHAT DID HE DO?
After the attacks of September 11, 2001, when the United States allied itself with the Northern Alliance (Afghan forces fighting to drive the Taliban out of Afghanistan), Lindh remained with the Taliban.

DATE OF ARREST
November 25, 2001

CIRCUMSTANCES OF THE ARREST
Lindh was captured by Northern Alliance forces. During his interrogation at Qala-i-Jangi, a military prison, Taliban inmates mounted a uprising in which 73 Afghanis and one American—Johnny "Mike" Spann, the CIA officer who was interrogating Lindh—were killed.

THE CHARGES
Conspiracy to murder U.S. citizens, providing material support and resources to terrorist organizations, and using and carrying firearms and other destructive devices during crimes of violence

THE SENTENCE
The U.S. Department of Justice offered Lindh a plea deal: a sentence of 20 years (instead of the three life sentences he could receive if convicted) in exchange for Lindh's guilty plea to serving with the Taliban and carrying weapons he intended to use against Americans. Furthermore, Lindh agreed never to claim that he had been abused or tortured while in the custody of the U.S. military.

AFTERWARD
Lindh, his family, and his friends are all subject to the "Son of Sam law," which forbids them to profit from any book or movie deal about Lindh's life. If a book or movie based on his life is ever produced, any profits would go directly to the federal government.

JOHN LIST

(1925–2008)

THE CHARGE
Murder

THE SENTENCE
List was tried in New Jersey and found guilty. He was sentenced to five consecutive life terms in prison.

AFTERWARD
List died of pneumonia while in prison.

UNUSUAL FACT
A year after List killed his family, arsonists burned down the List house in Westfield. It is rumored that a signed Tiffany stained-glass skylight, worth $100,000, was destroyed in the fire.

NATIONALITY
American

WHO WAS HE?
A religious accountant who was slowly going bankrupt.

WHAT DID HE DO?
On November 9, 1971, List murdered his mother, his wife, and his three children in the family home in Westfield, New Jersey.

DATE OF ARREST
June 1, 1989

CIRCUMSTANCES OF THE ARREST
List vanished after the killings, eluding investigators for 18 years. In 1989, the television program *America's Most Wanted* aired an episode about the List case, including a bust of what he might look like at that time. List was living in Virginia at the time, where he worked as an accountant. A neighbor thought the bust bore a striking resemblance to List, and called the police.

HEATHER LOCKLEAR

(1961–)

NATIONALITY
American

WHO IS SHE?
Heather Locklear is an actress best known for her roles on the television drama series, *Dynasty* and *Melrose Place*.

WHAT DID SHE DO?
Locklear was driving on a California highway while under the influence of prescription drugs.

DATE OF ARREST
September 27, 2008

CIRCUMSTANCES OF THE ARREST
A California Highway Patrol officer found Locklear in her parked car, which was blocking traffic on a highway in Montecito.

THE CHARGE
Driving under the influence of prescription drugs

THE SENTENCE
In exchange for Locklear pleading guilty to reckless driving, the more serious charge against her was dismissed. She was fined $700 and ordered to attend a driver's education course. She was also placed on informal probation.

AFTERWARD
In April 2010, Heather Locklear was arrested in Ventura, California, and charged with getting into a collision, then leaving the scene of the accident. The charges were dropped because the police did not have sufficient evidence to determine who was driving the car at the time of the accident.

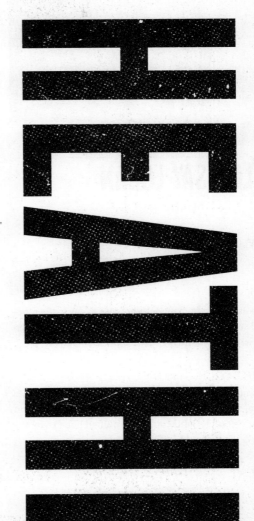

LINDSAY LOHAN

(1986–)

NATIONALITY
American

WHO IS SHE?
Lindsay Lohan was a child fashion model whose big break in the movie business arrived at age 11 with the remake of *The Parent Trap*. She went on to star in Robert Altman's *A Prairie Home Companion*.

WHAT DID SHE DO?
Two months after another arrest for drunk driving and just days after being released from rehab, while still wearing an alcohol-detection ankle bracelet, Santa Monica, California, police pulled Lohan over for suspicion of drunk driving.

DATE OF ARREST
July 24, 2007

CIRCUMSTANCES OF THE ARREST
Breathalyzer tests registered Lohan's blood alcohol level as .12 and .13 (the legal limit is .08). Police found a "small" amount of cocaine in her pocket.

THE CHARGE
Drunk driving

THE SENTENCE
Lohan was tried for both DUI cases simultaneously. She pled guilty to driving while under the influence of cocaine, and no contest to driving while under the influence of alcohol. She was sentenced to 24 hours in jail and 10 days of community service.

AFTERWARD
Lindsay Lohan continues to have trouble with drugs, alcohol, and the law. She has had repeated stints in rehab, some of them court-ordered. In 2010, a judge issued a bench warrant for her arrest after she failed to appear at a DUI progress report hearing. In the summer of 2010, she served 14 days of a 90-day jail sentence (she was released early because she was not a violent offender, and the jail was over-crowded).

JACK LONDON
(1876–1916)

NATIONALITY
American

WHO WAS HE?
In his time, Jack London worked as an oyster fisherman, a gold prospector, a sailor, and a high school janitor. He had long periods when he was a drifter. He was drawn to Socialist political causes. But he is best remembered as a novelist and short story writer, the author *The Call of the Wild* and *The Sea Wolf.*

WHAT DID HE DO?
After quitting his job in California, London drifted across country, visited the Columbian Exposition in Chicago, stopped for a time with relatives in Michigan, then went on the road again. Unemployed and without a home, he was arrested in Buffalo, New York.

DATE OF ARREST
June 29, 1894

THE CHARGE
Vagrancy

THE SENTENCE
London was found guilty and sentenced to 30 days in jail.

AFTERWARD
London's writing brought him fame and financial security. He was invited to speak at Yale University and Carnegie Hall. He ran (unsuccessfully) for mayor of Oakland, on the Socialist Party ticket.

JARED L. LOUGHNER

(1989–)

NATIONALITY
American

WHO IS HE?
Jared L. Loughner lived with his parents in Tucson, Arizona. He attempted to join the U.S. Army but was rejected. He attended two community colleges in Arizona where he often disrupted classes with bizarre outbursts. Acquaintances suspected that Loughner suffered from emotional or mental health problems

WHAT DID HE DO?
On Saturday January 8, 2011, Loughner fired a semi-automatic weapon into a crowd that had come to meet Congresswoman Gabrielle Giffords. He killed six people, including a 9-year-old girl and a federal judge, and wounded 15, including Giffords.

DATE OF ARREST
January 8, 2011

CIRCUMSTANCES OF THE ARREST
Three bystanders were instrumental in Loughner's arrest: Patricia Maisch grabbed the weapon's magazine and Roger Sulzgeber and Joseph Zimudie tackled Loughner and pinned him to the ground.

THE CHARGE
Attempted assassination of a member of Congress, killing an employee of the federal government, and attempting to kill federal employees

THE SENTENCE
As of mid-January 2011, Loughner had not yet been indicted by a grand jury.

UNUSUAL FACT
During a search of the Loughner family's home, authorities found an envelope bearing Jared Loughner's signature, the phrases "I planned ahead" and "My assassination," and the name "Giffords."

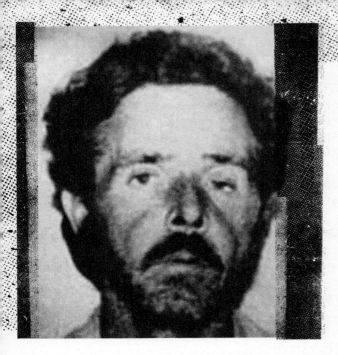

HENRY LEE LUCAS

(1936–2001)

NATIONALITY
American

WHO WAS HE?
As a child, Henry Lee Lucas was brutally abused by his mother. He ran away from home when he was about 13 years old, supporting himself as a thief and a burglar.

WHAT DID HE DO?
He claimed that he murdered his first victim when he was 17. He would later confess to having killed approximately 600 people.

DATE OF ARREST
June 11, 1983

CIRCUMSTANCES OF THE ARREST
Lucas was arrested in Texas for unlawful possession of a weapon. Soon after his arrest, Texas police determined that he was involved in the murders of a 12-year-old girl and an 82-year-old woman.

THE CHARGE
Murder

THE SENTENCE
By the time Lucas came to trial, he had been charged with 11 murders. He was found guilty and sentenced to death, but Governor George W. Bush commuted the sentence to life in prison. Lucas died of heart failure in prison.

AFTERWARD
Henry Lee Lucas had a habit of confessing to hundreds of killings, then retracting his confessions. Exactly how many people he killed is unknown, but the number ranges from 40 to 350.

cheni Louis 5855

LUIGI LUCHENI

(1873–1910)

NATIONALITY
Italian

WHO WAS HE?
Luigi Lucheni was abandoned by his mother and raised in an orphanage. As a young man, he served in the Italian military. After being honorably discharged, he moved to Switzerland, where he was strongly influenced by the anarchist movement. He longed to strike a blow for the common people by killing a member of the aristocracy.

WHAT DID HE DO?
On September 10, 1898, at the pier in Geneva, Switzerland, Lucheni knocked down Empress Elisabeth of Austria, stabbing her with a thin, sharp blade. Not realizing that she was hurt, the empress got up and hurried aboard a steamship. Minutes later she fell to the deck, dead.

DATE OF ARREST
September 10, 1898

CIRCUMSTANCES OF THE ARREST
Police arrested Lucheni near the scene of the crime. Rather than try to escape, Lucheni expressed pride in having killed the empress.

THE CHARGE
Assassination

THE SENTENCE
Lucheni confessed his crime in open court and was sentenced to life in prison.

AFTERWARD
After Lucheni's arrest, a conference of anarchists met in Rome, where they established a legal defense fund for comrades in trouble with the law. Twelve years into his life sentence, Luigi Lucheni hanged himself in his cell, using his belt as a noose.

CHARLES "LUCKY" LUCIANO
(1897–1962)

NATIONALITY
Italian-born American citizen

WHO WAS HE?
In 1907, Lucky Luciano emigrated with his family from Sicily to New York City. He began his life of crime in his teens. Luciano would go on to establish the "Five Families," the five Mafia crime organizations in New York (Luciano was the first boss of the Genovese family). During Prohibition, he made millions each year bootlegging. Eventually, his criminal empire would include gambling, narcotics, prostitution, and loan sharking; he also controlled the labor unions on the Manhattan waterfront.

WHAT DID HE DO?
New York Special Prosecutor Thomas E. Dewey could not assemble enough evidence to indict Luciano on his more nefarious activities, but he did have enough to charge him with operating one of the largest prostitution rings in the United States.

DATE OF ARREST
April 1, 1936

CIRCUMSTANCES OF THE ARREST
Luciano was in Hot Springs, Arkansas; Dewey sent detectives to arrest him there and bring him back to New York for trial.

THE CHARGE
Prostitution

THE SENTENCE
Luciano was found guilty and sentenced to 30–50 years in prison.

AFTERWARD
During World War II, the U.S. Army asked Luciano to use his influence with the Mafia in Sicily to undermine Axis forces and collect intelligence for the Allies. In return, Luciano was permitted to run his crime empire from his jail cell. After the war, Luciano was paroled, but required to return to Italy. Luciano settled in a 60-room villa in Naples, where he and his mistress enjoyed the high life. After his death, the U.S. government permitted Luciano's family to bring his body back to the United States for burial in St. John's Cemetery in Queens.

Kurt Frederick Ludwig

KURT FREDERICK LUDWIG

(1903–?)

NATIONALITY
American-born German citizen

WHO WAS HE?
Kurt Frederick Ludwig was a small child when his parents decided to leave Ohio and return to Germany. By 1938, he had been recruited as a spy by the Nazis, who sent him to New York.

WHAT DID HE DO?
Ludwig collected information about New York harbor, U.S. Army installations, and aircraft plants. He sent this information to Heinrich Himmler, Reinhard Heydrich, and other top officials of the Third Reich.

DATE OF ARREST
August 23, 1941

CIRCUMSTANCES OF THE ARREST
In 1941, the FBI had Ludwig under surveillance. When he realized he was being followed, he fled across the country, hoping to get to Japan and from there back to Germany. The FBI caught up with him in Cle Elum, Washington.

THE CHARGES
Treasonable conspiracy and espionage

THE SENTENCE
Ludwig was found guilty and sentenced to 20 years in prison. If his acts of espionage had taken place after the United States had entered World War II, he probably would have been executed.

AFTERWARD
In 1953, Ludwig was released from Alcatraz and deported. No one knows what became of him.

PATRICE LUMUMBA
(1925–1961)

NATIONALITY
Congolese

WHO WAS HE?
Patrice Lumumba was a civil servant in the Belgian colony of the Congo. In his early twenties, he joined the Congolese independence and Pan-African movements, which called for the abolition of all European colonies in Africa.

WHAT DID HE DO?
Lumumba was accused of starting an anticolonial riot in Stanleyville (now Kisangani), in which 30 people were killed.

DATE OF ARREST
October 1959

THE CHARGE
Inciting a riot

THE SENTENCE
Lumumba was found guilty and sentenced to six months in prison.

AFTERWARD
Lumumba was released early so he could travel to Brussels to attend a conference on the Congo's independence. After independence, Lumumba was elected prime minister of the Congo. During a period of civil unrest, Lumumba turned to the Soviet Union for assistance, thereby alienating Belgium and the United States. In 1960, he was deposed in a coup and kept under house arrest until he was transported to an isolated spot outside Lubumbashi, where he was executed by firing squad.

BELGIAN AND U.S. INVOLVEMENT
After the death of Patrice Lumumba, it was rumored that the Belgian and American governments had been complicit in his overthrow and execution. In 2002, the Belgian government admitted that it had been responsible, in part, for the death of Lumumba. The U.S. government released documents stating that the CIA had been aware of Belgium's role in the affair, but that the agency had not been involved in his overthrow or execution.

BERNIE MADOFF
(1938–)

NATIONALITY
American

WHO IS HE?
Bernie Madoff is a former Long Island lifeguard who built one of the major investment houses on Wall Street. His clients included banks, such as HSBC, as well as celebrities, such as Steven Spielberg. He promised investors steady, even astronomical annual returns on their money. In some cases, he claimed he could bring in a 46 percent annual return on investment.

WHAT DID HE DO?
Madoff put together an investment Ponzi scheme—possibly the biggest in the history of Wall Street—in which institutional and private investors lost at least $65 billion.

DATE OF ARREST
December 11, 2008

CIRCUMSTANCES OF THE ARREST
Federal agents arrested Madoff at his posh Manhattan penthouse on the Upper East Side after his sons had turned him in.

THE CHARGES
Fraud, perjury, making false filings with the Securities and Exchange Commission (SEC), and theft from an employee benefit plan

THE SENTENCE
Madoff pled guilty to all charges and received the maximum sentence—150 years in prison.

AFTERWARD
As of May 2010, investors had filed 2,085 claims for compensation. The claims total $5.45 billion, but the reimbursement fund contains only $1.5 billion. The widow of one of Madoff's earliest investors, Jeffry Picower, returned $7.2 billions in profits to help pay for claims.

Madoff's son Mark, distraught at being tarnished by the scandal, commited suicide in 2011, two years to the day of his father's arrest.

NORMAN MAILER
(1923–2007)

NATIONALITY
American

WHO WAS HE?
Norman Mailer was a novelist and journalist who won two Pulitzer Prizes and one National Book Award. His novels include *The Naked and the Dead* and *The Executioner's Song*. He also wrote the still-controversial essay, "The White Negro."

WHAT DID HE DO?
To launch his campaign for mayor of New York, Norman Mailer threw a party, inviting New York power brokers, literary types, and street people to his apartment. The literary crowd and the street people came, but the power brokers did not. As the night wore on, Mailer became drunk and belligerent. He argued with his wife, Adele Morales. Supposedly, she told him he was not as good as Dostoyevsky; he grabbed a pen knife and stabbed her twice. One of the wounds damaged Morales's heart.

DATE OF ARREST
November 20, 1960

THE CHARGE
Felonious assault

THE SENTENCE
Morales refused to press charges, but Mailer was still brought into court to determine if he was in his right mind. Appealing to the judge, he said, "It is important to me not to be sent automatically to some mental institution because for the rest of my life my work will be considered as the work of a man with a disordered mind. My pride is that as a sane man I can explore areas of experience that other men are afraid of." The judge sent Mailer to Bellevue Hospital for 17 days of psychiatric evaluation. Morales recovered.

UNUSUAL FACT
In 1980, Mailer championed the cause of Jack Abbott, a convicted killer who wanted to be paroled. Thanks in part to Mailer's influence, Abbott was paroled. Six weeks after his release, he killed a man.

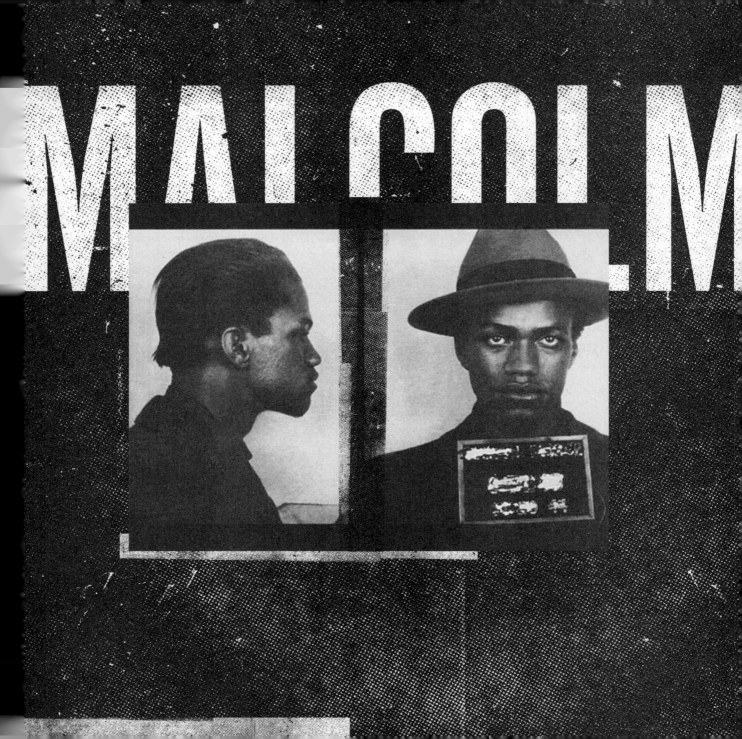

MALCOLM X (MALCOLM LITTLE)

(1925–1965)

NATIONALITY
American

WHO WAS HE?
Malcolm Little was one of eight children. His mother was a home-maker. His father was a Baptist preacher and an avid supporter of Marcus Garvey's Black Nationalist movement. His father's political activities attracted the attention of the white supremacist organization, the Black Legion, which burned down the Little family's home and murdered Malcolm's father.

WHAT DID HE DO?
In his teens, Little moved to Harlem where he became involved in drugs, gambling, and prostitution. Later he moved to Boston where he broke into and stole from homes and businesses.

DATE OF ARREST
January 12, 1946

CIRCUMSTANCES OF THE ARREST
Little had dropped off for repair a watch he had stolen. It was a much more expensive piece than anyone in the Roxbury section of Boston could afford, so the jeweler called the police. When Little came by the shop to pick up the watch, the police were waiting for him.

THE CHARGE
Burglary

THE SENTENCE
Little was found guilty and sentenced to ten years in prison. After serving eight years, he was released.

AFTERWARD
In prison, Little became interested in the Nation of Islam and the writings of the NOI's leader, Elijah Muhammad, who called for black Americans to live apart from their white neighbors. Little joined the NOI and took a new name, Malcolm X—X representing the tribal name his ancestors had lost when they were brought as slaves to America. Malcolm became one of the NOI's most effective speakers, attracting thousands of new members to the movement. In 1964, after a series of conflicts with Muhammad, Malcolm founded his own religious organization, the Muslim Mosque, which created tension between Malcolm and the NOI. His home was firebombed; he traveled with bodyguards. In 1965, as he was about to speak at the Audubon Ballroom in New York, three men charged the stage and shot him dead.

NELSON MANDELA
(1918–)

NATIONALITY
South African

WHO IS HE?
Nelson Mandela is the son of a chief of the Tembu tribe. In the 1940s, he joined the African National Congress (ANC) to overturn South Africa's apartheid policies.

WHAT DID HE DO?
In 1960, the South African government banned the ANC. Mandela's response was to argue that the ANC should establish a military wing to defend itself and perhaps force the government to abolish apartheid.

DATE OF ARREST
August 5, 1962

THE CHARGES
Sabotage and fomenting revolution

THE SENTENCE
Mandela was found guilty and sentenced to five years at hard labor. For his involvement in the military arm of the ANC, that sentence was later extended to life in prison.

AFTERWARD
In 1990, after 28 years in prison, Nelson Mandela was released. As a free man, he led the ANC in negotiating an end to apartheid in South Africa and establishing free elections. In 1993, Mandela won the Nobel Peace Prize. In 1994, he was elected president of South Africa, an office he held until 1999.

CRYSTAL GAIL MANGUM

(1979–)

NATIONALITY
American

WHO IS SHE?
Crystal Gail Mangum was a student at North Carolina Central University; she worked as an escort and stripper for the Allure Escort service. She became notorious in 2006 after she falsely accused three members of the Duke University lacrosse team of rape. The three men were exonerated, and the Durham County District Attorney, Mike Nifong, was tried and found guilty of employing deceit and misrepresentation in his handling of the case.

WHAT DID SHE DO?
During a domestic dispute with her boyfriend, Mangum set fire to her apartment. In the apartment at the time were her three children—ages ten, nine, and three, her boyfriend, and two police officers who had responded to a 911 call made by Mangum's nine-year-old daughter.

DATE OF ARREST
February 17, 2010

CIRCUMSTANCES OF THE ARREST
Before the police arrived, Mangum had tried to burn her boyfriend's clothes in the bathtub. After the police arrived, she tried to set a second fire. Police evacuated Mangum, her children, and her boyfriend from the apartment while firefighters put out the blaze.

THE CHARGES
Attempted murder, arson, simple assault, identity theft, communicating threats, damage to property, resisting arrest, and child endangerment

BAIL
Bail was set at $250,000. Mangum remained in jail until the bond could be raised, then was placed under house arrest pending trial. She was permitted only supervised visitation with her children. In August 2010, Mangum was arrested again for failing to comply with the court's directive regarding visitation.

CHARLES MANSON

(1934–)

NATIONALITY
American

WHO IS HE?
Charles Manson was a career criminal who in the late 1960s established in California a commune known as the Manson Family. Based on a misreading of the Beatles song, "Helter Skelter," Manson believed that America was on the verge of a race war.

WHAT DID HE DO?
To set off the apocalyptic race war, Manson planned the murder of actress Sharon Tate and her husband, film director Roman Polanski. On August 9, 1969, he sent four members of the Manson Family to Tate and Polanski's house, with instructions to kill everyone they met in the most gruesome manner possible. Polanski wasn't there and therefore wasn't killed. The next night Manson led six members of the Family to the home of Leno and Rosemary LaBianca, where he supervised the couple's murder.

DATE OF ARREST
October 12, 1969

CIRCUMSTANCES OF THE ARREST
Police raided the Barker Ranch, where Manson and his Family were in hiding, on a tip about a stolen car. It was while Manson was in jail on the automobile charge that police realized who they had in custody.

THE CHARGES
Murder and conspiracy

THE SENTENCE
After a trial during which members of the Family continually disrupted the proceedings, Manson was found guilty and sentenced to death. The death penalty was instantly commuted to life in prison after a 1972 Supreme Court decision banned capital punishment in California.

AFTERWARD
Under California law, Manson may request parole. Between 1978 and 2007, he requested parole 11 times; each time his petition was denied. He is eligible for parole again in 2012.

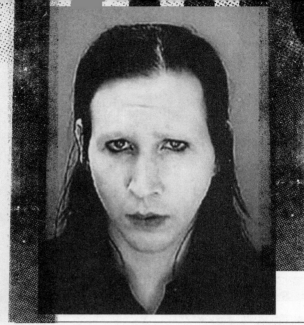

MARILYN MANSON (BRIAN HUGH WARNER)

(1969–)

NATIONALITY
American

WHO IS HE?
Marilyn Manson is a rock singer/songwriter notorious for his outrageous costumes and often sexually charged concert performances.

WHAT DID HE DO?
During a concert in Detroit, Manson, dressed in a G-string, wrapped his legs around a security guard and rubbed his crotch against him. Then he spit on the guard.

DATE OF ARREST
August 17, 2001

THE CHARGES
Assault and sexual misconduct

THE SENTENCE
The judge reduced the charges to misdemeanor disorderly conduct. Manson pled no contest and paid a $4,000 fine. He and the security guard later reached a settlement—the figure has not been disclosed to the public.

AFTERWARD
Manson's other legal woes include a complaint that Manson had supplied a woman with cocaine and encouraged her to drive while under the influence. Manson's former keyboardist sued him for $20 million in back pay. Both cases were settled out of court.

PETER MANUEL, "THE BEAST OF BIRKENSHAW"

(1927–1958)

NATIONALITY
American-born Scottish citizen

WHO WAS HE?
Peter Manuel was born in New York, but moved back to Scotland with his parents in 1932. As a boy, he was a petty thief. In his teens, he was arrested for a series of sexual assaults for which he served nine years in prison.

WHAT DID HE DO?
Between 1956 and 1958 Manuel killed at least eight people, including a ten-year-old boy. He told police he had actually committed 18 murders.

DATE OF ARREST
January 13, 1958

CIRCUMSTANCES OF THE ARREST
Police traced banknotes stolen from the Smart family—his last victims—to Manuel, who had used the cash to buy drinks in Glasgow pubs.

THE CHARGE
Murder

THE SENTENCE
Manuel was found guilty and hanged.

AFTERWARD
A 2009 BBC program, "The Mind of a Psychopath," argued that Manuel was legally insane and should have been confined to a prison for the criminally insane rather than executed.

MATTHEW MCCONAUGHEY

(1969–)

NATIONALITY
American

WHO IS HE?
Matthew McConaughey is an actor whose breakout roles came with two 1996 films, *Lone Star* and *A Time to Kill*.

WHAT DID HE DO?
At his house in Austin, Texas, McConaughey and a friend were playing music and bongo drums so loudly that the neighbors called the cops.

DATE OF ARREST
October 25, 1999

CIRCUMSTANCES OF THE ARREST
Police found McConaughey drunk, naked, playing bongos, and dancing in a room where drug paraphernalia was scattered about. When the arresting officer told the actor to put on his pants, McConaughy replied, "Fuck you" and tried to punch the officer. As he was escorted out of the house, McConaughey body-slammed the officer.

THE CHARGES
Resisting arrest and possession of marijuana and drug paraphernalia

THE SENTENCE
McConaughey pled guilty to violating a noise ordinance and was fined $50. The other charges were dropped.

AFTERWARD
After a series of dramatic roles in films such as *Amistad*, McConaughey switched almost exclusively to romantic-comedies, including *The Wedding Planner*, *Sahara*, and *Failure to Launch*.

GARY MCKINNON

(1966–)

NATIONALITY
Scottish

WHO IS HE?
Gary McKinnon is a computer systems administrator who is said to have pulled off "the biggest military computer hack of all time," according to a U.S. prosecutor. McKinnon has said that he was looking for evidence that the U.S. government has suppressed information about extraterrestrials, "free energy," and antigravity technology.

WHAT DID HE DO?
In interviews with the press, McKinnon admitted to hacking into the computers of the U.S. military and NASA. The U.S. government claims that he did $800,000 worth of damage to its computer systems.

DATE OF ARREST
March 19, 2002

CIRCUMSTANCES OF THE ARREST
British police arrested McKinnon, but at the request of the U.S. government he was questioned by Britain's National High Tech Crime Unit.

EXTRADITION
McKinnon fought extradition for seven years, appealing to the House of Lords, the European Court of Human Rights, and Britain's home secretary. The extradition was delayed again in 2010 after a new government was elected in Great Britain.

THE CHARGE
Hacking into U.S. military and NASA computers

THE SENTENCE
If found guilty in an American court, McKinnon could face 70 years in prison and $2 million in fines.

UNUSUAL FACT
In 2008, Gary McKinnon was diagnosed with Asperger's syndrome, a form of autism, and clinical depression. A psychiatrist from St. George's Hospital in London said that if McKinnon were sent to prison he would almost certainly commit suicide.

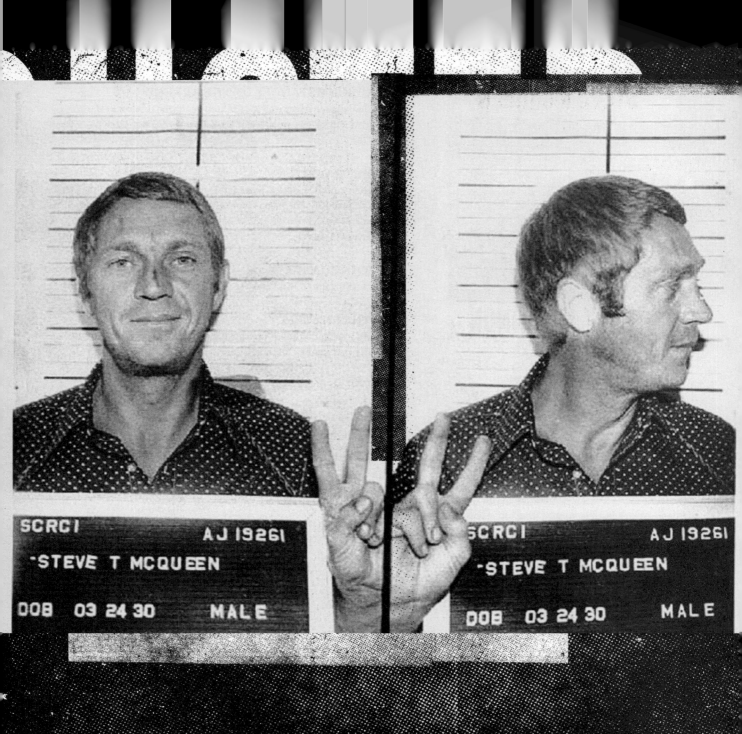

STEVE MCQUEEN

(1930–1980)

NATIONALITY
American

WHO WAS HE?
"The King of Cool," Steve McQueen was an actor famous for his antihero roles during the 1960s and 1970s. His films *The Magnificent Seven* and *The Great Escape* were popular with audiences, and he won an Oscar nomination for his role in *The Sand Pebbles*.

WHAT DID HE DO?
McQueen got drunk in Anchorage, Alaska, and drove his car at high speeds up and down the city streets.

DATE OF ARREST
June 22, 1972

THE CHARGE
Driving under the influence

THE SENTENCE
McQueen posted bail, then left town. He did not return to Anchorage for his trial and was convicted in absentia.

AFTERWARD
In the 1970s, McQueen made *The Getaway*, *The Towering Inferno*, and *Tom Horn*. He also raced cars and collected motorcycles. After being diagnosed with mesothelioma, McQueen sought nontraditional treatments in Mexico. After undergoing surgery to remove a cancerous tumor from his neck, he suffered cardiac arrest and died.

TIMOTHY MCVEIGH

(1968–2001)

AND

TERRY NICHOLS

(1955–)

NATIONALITY
American

WHO WERE THEY?
Timothy McVeigh was a college dropout who enlisted in the U.S. Army. He received a Bronze Star for his service during the Gulf War. After his honorable discharge from the army, he drifted from job to job. He began to read extremist antigovernment literature. After the siege and destruction of the Branch Davidians' compound in Waco, Texas, McVeigh decided to strike a blow against the federal government.

Terry Nichols also dropped out of college and enlisted in the army, where he and McVeigh became friends. They shared the same antigovernment views.

WHAT DID THEY DO?
McVeigh and Nichols built a bomb and placed it inside a Ryder truck. On April 19, 1995, McVeigh parked the truck outside the Alfred P. Murrah Federal Building in Oklahoma City. The building contained government offices, as well as a day care center. McVeigh lit the fuse, then ran. The subsequent explosion killed 168 and injured 450. Among the victims were 19 small children and babies.

DATES OF ARREST
McVeigh: April 19, 1995
Nichols: April 21, 1995

CIRCUMSTANCES OF THE ARRESTS
An Oklahoma state trooper stopped McVeigh's car outside Perry, Oklahoma, because the car had no license plate. When the trooper found that McVeigh was carrying a concealed weapon, he arrested him. Three days later, while McVeigh was still in jail, investigators realized that he was the Oklahoma City bomber. Nichols was arrested at his home after he permitted federal agents to search the place.

THE CHARGES
Use of a weapon of mass destruction, conspiracy, and murder

THE SENTENCE
McVeigh was found guilty and sentenced to death. In 2001, he called a halt to the appeals process and subsequently was executed by lethal injection. Nichols was convicted and sentenced to life in prison.

UNUSUAL FACT
In 1997, President Bill Clinton signed a Senate bill that barred veterans who were convicted of crimes from being buried in a military cemetery.

LYLE MENENDEZ

(1968–)
AND

ERIK MENENDEZ

(1970–)

NATIONALITY
American

WHO ARE THEY?
Lyle and Erik Menendez grew up in a wealthy family, first outside Princeton, New Jersey, then in a mansion in Beverly Hills, California.

WHAT DID THEY DO?
On August 20, 1989, they shot their parents to death as the couple sat in the den of their Beverly Hills home watching television.

DATE OF ARREST
December 8, 1992

CIRCUMSTANCES OF THE ARREST
In the six months after their parents' death, the boys went on a spending spree, squandering an estimated $1 million on penthouse apartments, jewelry, and lavish vacations. But Erik's conscience bothered him and he confessed to committing the murders to his psychiatrist, who went to the police.

THE CHARGE
Murder

THE SENTENCE
The first trial ended in two hung juries (a separate panel of jurors had been selected for each brother). The second ended with their conviction. The Menendez brothers were sentenced to life in prison.

AFTERWARD
The brothers were sent to different prisons and have not seen each other since their conviction in 1996. They have both married, although California bars convicted murderers from the privilege of conjugal visits.

THOMAS T. MEAGHER.

THOMAS FRANCIS MEAGHER

(1823–1867)

NATIONALITY
Irish-born American citizen

WHO WAS HE?
Thomas Francis Meagher was the son a well-to-do Irish Catholic merchant in Waterford, Ireland. He received a first-class education in Jesuit schools, where he studied the history of Ireland, especially its tragic experience under English rule. In his early 20s, he became active in politics, especially the Irish independence movement.

WHAT DID HE DO?
In 1848, Meagher attempted to foment a rebellion against the English. Scarcely more than a couple dozen men joined the uprising, which fizzled out.

DATE OF ARREST
August 12, 1848

CIRCUMSTANCES OF THE ARREST
Meagher could not bring himself to surrender. Instead, he let his whereabouts be known so the British could find and arrest him.

THE CHARGE
Sedition

THE SENTENCE
Meagher was found guilty. There was some anxiety in Ireland that he might be drawn and quartered. (The penalty had been outlawed in England, but not in Ireland.) Instead, he was exiled for life to Australia.

AFTERWARD
Meagher escaped from Australia and sailed to America, where he practiced law. When the Civil War broke out in 1861, Meagher formed the Irish Brigade, which served with distinction for the North (Union) at virtually every battle in the East, including Antietam and Gettysburg. After the war, Meagher served as governor of Montana.

RAMON MERCADER
(1913–1978)

NATIONALITY
Catalan

WHO WAS HE?
Ramon Mercader's mother had fought with the Communists during Spain's civil war (1936–1939) and later served as a Soviet agent. Mercader followed his mother's example, becoming an ardent Communist.

WHAT DID HE DO?
In 1940, Mercader traveled to Mexico where, on August 20, he entered the home of Leon Trotsky and killed him with an axe. Members of Trotsky's entourage captured Mercader; his accomplices, who were waiting with getaway cars outside the house, drove off when he did not appear.

DATE OF ARREST
August 20, 1940

CIRCUMSTANCES OF THE ARREST
Mercader was taken into custody at the scene of the crime.

THE CHARGE
Murder

THE SENTENCE
Mercader was convicted and sentenced to 20 years in prison.

AFTERWARD
It is likely that Joseph Stalin ordered the murder of his nemesis, Trotsky. Stalin presented Mercader's mother with the Order of Lenin for the assistance she provided to her son in planning the murder. After his release from prison, the USSR presented Mercader with the Hero of the Soviet Union medal. At his death, Mercador was buried in Moscow.

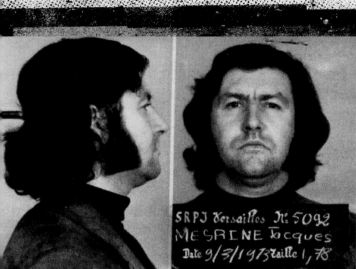

JACQUES MESRINE

(1936–1979)

NATIONALITY
French

WHO WAS HE?
Jacques Mesrine held respectable jobs—in an architectural firm, as a restauranteur, as a chauffeur—but he always returned to a life of crime in a variety of international venues, including Palma de Majorca, Geneva, and Quebec.

WHAT DID HE DO?
In 1968, in Quebec, Mesrine attempted to kidnap his millionaire employer, Georges Deslauriers. He bungled the kidnapping and fled across the border into the United States.

DATE OF ARREST
July 16, 1968

CIRCUMSTANCES OF THE ARREST
U.S. agents arrested Mesrine in Arkansas and sent him back to Quebec for trial.

THE CHARGE
Attempted kidnapping

THE SENTENCE
Mesrine was convicted and sentenced to ten years in prison.

AFTERWARD
In 1972, Mesrine and a fellow convict named Jean-Paul Mercier escaped from prison and went on a crime spree, robbing banks in Montreal and murdering two Canadian forest rangers. Before the authorities could capture them, Mesrine and Mercier fled to Venezuela. In 1973, Mesrine was back in France, robbing banks. In 1979, he kidnapped millionaire Henri Lelievre; he released his captive after receiving a ransom of 6 million francs. French police named Mesrine L'Ennemi Public Numéro Un, or Public Enemy Number One. On November 2, 1979, police ambushed Mesrine in a Paris suburb, firing 19 rounds into his car, killing Mesrine and wounding his girlfriend.

GEORGE METESKY, "THE MAD BOMBER"

(1903–1994)

NATIONALITY
American

WHO WAS HE?
George Metesky worked as a mechanic for the Consolidated Edison utility company in New York. A workplace accident permanently disabled him. He filed a claim for workman's compensation, but Con Ed's attorney's fought it and Metesky's claim was denied.

WHAT DID HE DO?
In 1941, Metesky placed a homemade bomb at a Con Ed power plant, but it was a dud. Between 1951 and 1956 he started making bombs again, planting them in places that received a lot of foot traffic, including Grand Central Station, the Port Authority Bus Terminal, and movie theaters. Of the 33 or more bombs he planted, 22 exploded, injuring 15 people.

DATE OF ARREST
January 22, 1957

CIRCUMSTANCES OF THE ARREST
New York and Waterbury, Connecticut police arrested Metesky at his home in Waterbury. In his garage, they found a cache of bombmaking materials and equipment.

THE CHARGES
Attempted murder, damaging a building by explosion, maliciously endangering life, and carrying concealed weapons

THE SENTENCE
Psychiatrists declared Metesky a hopelessly incurable paranoid schizophrenic, and therefore not competent to stand trial. He was committed to the Matteawan Hospital for the Criminally Insane in Beacon, New York.

AFTERWARD
In 1973, the U.S. Supreme Court ruled that a defendant could not be confined in a prison hospital without a trial. Psychiatrists who evaluated Metesky found him to be harmless, so he was released. He spent the rest of his life in Waterbury.

UNUSUAL FACT
The George Metesky case is the first on record in which the police developed a profile of the criminal in order track down the suspect. Working with a criminologist, they developed a profile based on letters Metesky sent to the police and the press.

JONATHAN RHYS MEYERS
(1977–)

NATIONALITY
Irish

WHO IS HE?
Jonathan Rhys Meyers is an Irish actor who has starred in *Match Point*, *Bend It Like Beckham*, and *Mission Impossible III*, but is probably best known for playing Henry VIII in the cable television miniseries *The Tudors*.

WHAT DID HE DO?
At the Dublin airport, a drunken Rhys Meyers was loud, abusive to airline employees, and refused to control himself despite repeated warnings from police.

DATE OF ARREST
November 18, 2007

THE CHARGES
Public drunkenness and breach of the peace

THE SENTENCE
Rhys Meyers was released on bail, and subsequently the charges were dropped.

AFTERWARD
In 2009, Rhys Meyers was arrested at Charles de Gaulle Airport in Paris. Rhys Meyers, who had been drinking heavily, got into an altercation with a bartender who refused to serve him. When a waiter tried to intervene, Rhys Meyers punched him in the face. In 2010, his belligerent behavior at John F. Kennedy International Airport in New York resulted in Rhys Meyers being banned for life from flying United Airlines.

GEORGE MICHAEL

(1963–)

NATIONALITY
English

WHO IS HE?
George Michael is a singer/songwriter who rose to stardom in the 1980s as part of the pop duo, Wham! In 1987, he went solo and had a series of hit singles, including "I Want Your Sex," as well as a Grammy-winning duet with Aretha Franklin for "I Knew You Were Waiting [for Me]."

WHAT DID HE DO?
Michael tried to pick up a man in a men's room in a park in Beverly Hills, California. The man he propositioned was an undercover cop.

DATE OF ARREST
April 7, 1998

THE CHARGE
Soliciting sex

THE SENTENCE
Michael pled no contest to the charge and paid a fine of $810. He was ordered to perform 80 hours of community service.

AFTERWARD
Michael made a video of his single, "Outside," which showed two men dressed as cops kissing in a public restroom. Marcelo Rodriguez, the cop who arrested Michael, sued him for $10 million, claiming that the video was intended to humiliate him, and that in postarrest interviews Michael had slandered him. The court ruled against Rodriguez.

REPEAT OFFENDER
In 2006, a photographer for the tabloid newspaper, *News of the World*, photographed Michael having sex with a man in a park in London. Since he was not spotted by the police, Michael was not arrested.

MICHAEL MILKEN

(1946–)

THE CHARGES
Racketeering and securities fraud

THE SENTENCE
Of the 98 charges listed in the original indictment, Milken pled guilty to 6 charges of tax evasion and securities violations. Milken was sentenced to ten years in prison and barred for life from ever working in the securities industry. He was fined $200 million and required to pay $900 million to investors who had been the victims of his illegal trades. Milken was released from prison after serving a little more than two years.

AFTERWARD
With his brother Lowell, Michael Milken established the Milken Family Foundation, a philanthropic organization that supports innovators in education and contributes to epilepsy and prostate cancer research.

NATIONALITY
American

WHO IS HE?
Michael Milken is a graduate of the Wharton School of Business who in the 1970s established the high-yield bond trading department at Drexel Burnham and Company.

WHAT DID HE DO?
It has been said that Milken was contemptuous of the Securities and Exchange Commission regulations, that he manipulated the securities markets, cheated stockholders, and derived huge profits from his illegal trading activities—$5.3 million from trades with Ivan Boesky alone.

DATE OF ARREST
March 29, 1989

WHAT DID HE DO?

Milosevic is charged with responsibility for the deaths of perhaps as many as 230,000 Croatians and Bosnians, and the displacement of 3 million people during the Yugoslav wars of the 1990s.

DATE OF ARREST

May 1999

THE CHARGE

War crimes

THE SENTENCE

Milosevic was taken to The Hague in The Netherlands for trial before an international tribunal. On March 11, 2006, before The trial had come to a conclusion, Milosevic died in his cell of a heart attack.

SLOBODAN MILOSEVIC

(1941–2006)

NATIONALITY

Serbian

WHO WAS HE?

Slobodan Milosevic is the son of a former Orthodox priest and a Communist schoolteacher. He joined the Communist Party of Yugoslavia in 1959. After almost three decades in Communist politics, in the late 1980s Milosevic embraced Serbian nationalism. In 1989, he was elected president of Serbia.

BRIAN MITCHELL
(1953–)
AND
WANDA BARZEE
(1945–)

NATIONALITY
American

WHO ARE THEY?
Brian Mitchell and his wife Wanda Barzee practiced a bizarre, self-invented form of Mormonism. Mitchell claimed that God wanted him to take seven more wives, and that 14-year-old Elizabeth Smart was to be the first.

WHAT DID THEY DO?
In 2002, Mitchell and Barzee broke into the Smart family home in Salt Lake City, Utah, and kidnapped Elizabeth, who was in bed sleeping at the time. For the next nine months, Mitchell raped Elizabeth daily, and sometimes more than once a day.

DATE OF ARREST
March 12, 2003

CIRCUMSTANCES OF THE ARREST
Several residents of Sandy, Utah, who had seen the Elizabeth Smart episode on *America's Most Wanted*, called the police after they spotted Mitchell with two women dressed in long robes and wearing veils, walking on State Street.

THE CHARGES
Aggravated kidnapping, aggravated sexual assault, and aggravated burglary

THE SENTENCE
In 2009, Wanda Barzee was sentenced to 15 years in prison. During his trial in 2010, Brian Mitchell frequently disrupted the proceedings, on one occasion demanding that the judge step down from the bench and grovel in the dust. He was found guilty and is expected to receive life in prison.

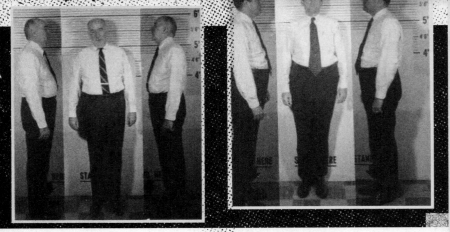

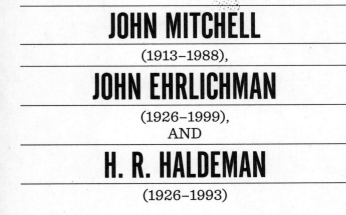

JOHN MITCHELL

(1913–1988),

JOHN EHRLICHMAN

(1926–1999),
AND

H. R. HALDEMAN

(1926–1993)

NATIONALITY
American

WHO WERE THEY?
John Mitchell was Richard Nixon's law partner and, in 1968, his campaign manager. Nixon appointed him attorney general. John Ehrlichman was a domestic political advisor to Nixon. H. R. Haldeman had been an advance man and campaign manager for Nixon's campaigns in the 1960s. He became White House chief of staff.

WHAT DID THEY DO?
Mitchell approved the plan to bug the headquarters of the Democratic National Committee at the Watergate. Ehrlichman used illegal methods to discredit opponents of the Nixon administration and sent burglars to break into the office and rifle through the files of Dr. Lewis Fielding, the psychiatrist of Daniel Ellsberg, a Vietnam-era U.S. military analyst and whistle-blower who had leaked the Pentagon Papers to the press. Haldeman discussed with Nixon the possibility of using the CIA to derail the FBI investigation of the Watergate scandal.

DATE OF INDICTMENT
March 1, 1974

THE CHARGES
Conspiracy to obstruct justice, perjury, and obstruction of justice

THE SENTENCES
Mitchell served 19 months in prison. Ehrlichman and Haldeman each served 18 months.

AFTERWARD
Mitchell retired to Georgetown and became part owner of the exclusive Jockey Club. Ehrlichman became a business consultant, a novelist, and wrote a memoir titled, *Witness to Power: The Nixon Years.* Haldeman became a real estate developer. He also wrote a memoir, *The Ends of Power.*

ROBERT MITCHUM
(1917–1997)

NATIONALITY
American

WHO WAS HE?
Robert Mitchum was an actor who specialized in tough-guy roles, particularly in the film noir genre. His films include *Night of the Hunter, Not As a Stranger, The Big Sleep,* and *Cape Fear.*

WHAT DID HE DO?
Police found Mitchum to have marijuana on his person.

DATE OF ARREST
September 1, 1948

CIRCUMSTANCES OF THE ARREST
Mitchum was arrested with actress Lila Leeds during an antinarcotics sting operation that targeted Hollywood stars.

THE CHARGE
Possession of marijuana

THE SENTENCE
Mitchum was found guilty and sentenced to 60 days at a prison farm. *Life* magazine ran a story on Mitchum in jail, complete with photos of him sweeping the jailhouse floor and milking one of the prison farm's cows.

AFTERWARD
Jail time did not derail Mitchum's career. His later films included *Ryan's Daughter; The Friends of Eddie Coyle; Farewell, My Lovely;* and the TV miniseries *The Winds of War.*

UNUSUAL FACT
Mitchum was arrested in Savannah, Georgia, at age 14 for vagrancy and sentenced to a chain gang. He escaped and returned to his family in Delaware.

HARRY "BREAKER" MORANT

(1864–1902)

NATIONALITY
Australian

WHO WAS HE?
Harry Morant was an Australian drover, especially skilled at breaking, or taming horses, which is how he acquired his nickname, "Breaker." He fought in South Africa during the Second Boer War.

WHAT DID HE DO?
In South Africa, Morant killed Boer prisoners of war. When Morant discovered that a German missionary had witnessed these summary executions, he killed the missionary, too.

DATE OF ARREST
October 24, 1901

CIRCUMSTANCES OF THE ARREST
Morant and Lieutenant Peter Joseph Handcock, who had also participated in killing the Boer prisoners, were each held in solitary confinement, pending their court martial.

THE CHARGE
War crimes

THE SENTENCE
Morant and Handcock were found guilty and sentenced to execution by firing squad.

AFTERWARD
The film *Breaker Morant*, directed by Bruce Beresford and starring Edward Woodward, was released in 1980. It won ten Australian Film Institute Awards, including Best Film, Best Director, and Best Leading Actor.

DATE OF ARREST
March 24, 1991

THE CHARGE
Domestic violence

THE SENTENCE
Richardson dropped the charges against Moore, but in 1997 she filed for divorce.

AFTERWARD
In 1998, Moore was diagnosed with progressive supranuclear palsy, an untreatable neurological condition. He died in 2002.

DUDLEY MOORE

(1935–2002)

NATIONALITY
English

WHO WAS HE?
Dudley Moore was an English comic actor who began his career as a member of the comedy troupe Beyond the Fringe. In the 1960s, he teamed up with Peter Cook in the British television comedy series, *Not Only . . But Also*. In Hollywood he starred in *10*, playing opposite Bo Derek. He is best remembered as the jovial drunk in *Arthur*, for which he was nominated for an Oscar.

WHAT DID HE DO?
Backstage at the Academy Awards, Moore got into an argument with Nicole Richardson (his fourth wife) and struck her repeatedly.

SARA JANE MOORE

(1930–)

NATIONALITY
American

WHO IS SHE?
In the 1970s, Sarah Jane Moore was a bookkeeper who became involved in revolutionary political movements, but she was also an FBI informant.

WHAT DID SHE DO?
On September 22, 1975, Moore went to the St. Francis Hotel in San Francisco where President Gerald Ford was staying. As Ford left the hotel, Moore fired her .38 caliber revolver, but missed. She was taking aim for a second shot when a U.S. Marine, Oliver Sipple, tackled her. The gun went off, injuring a cab driver but missing the president (the cabbie recovered from his wound).

DATE OF ARREST
September 22, 1975

CIRCUMSTANCES OF THE ARREST
Moore was arrested at the scene.

THE CHARGE
Attempted assassination

THE SENTENCE
Moore pled guilty and was sentenced to life in prison. In a statement to the court, she said, "Am I sorry I tried? Yes and no. Yes, because it accomplished little except to throw away the rest of my life. And, no, I'm not sorry I tried, because at the time it seemed a correct expression of my anger."

AFTERWARD
Moore was paroled in 2007, after serving 32 years. Gerald Ford had died a year earlier.

UNUSUAL FACT
Sarah Jane Moore tried to kill President Ford 17 days after Squeaky Fromme tried to do the same thing.

DATE OF ARREST
May 11, 1994

THE CHARGES
Making bombs and issuing death threats

THE SENTENCE
Morris was found guilty of making the death threats and sentenced to two years in prison. The sentence was reduced to one year.

AFTERWARD
It has never been proven that Morris detonated the bomb in the City Council building. That crime remains unsolved.

BARRY MORRIS

(1935–2001)

NATIONALITY
Australian

WHO WAS HE?
Barry Morris was a rancher, an oilman, and a real estate developer who entered politics. In 1988, he was elected to the New South Wales Legislative Assembly.

WHAT DID HE DO?
Morris is suspected of setting off a bomb in the Blue Mountains City Council building. The explosion caused significant structural damage, but injured no one. Morris also made several death threats against his political nemesis, John Pascoe.

SEP 20 1970

PUBLIC SAFETY DEPT. - DADE COUNTY, FLA

SEP 20 1970

PUBLIC SAFETY DEPT. - DADE COUNTY

JIM MORRISON

(1943–1971)

NATIONALITY
American

WHO WAS HE?
One of the founding members and the lead vocalist of The Doors, Jim Morrison was a handsome, charismatic, self-destructive god of psychedelic rock. His poetry, much of it inspired by his use of hallucinogens, formed the lyrics of The Doors' greatest hits, songs that ranged from the deeply seductive to the darkly disturbing.

WHAT DID HE DO?
The Doors were contracted to perform before a crowd of 13,000 at the Dinner Key Auditorium in Miami, Florida. Morrison appeared onstage very drunk, took the microphone, and began a 65-minute rant during which he berated the audience as "fucking idiots" and "a bunch of slaves." Then he began to strip off his clothes. Larry Mahoney, a reporter for the *Miami Herald*, reported, "Morrison appeared to masturbate in full view of his audience, screamed obscenities, and exposed himself. He also got violent, slugged several of The Image [the promoters] officials, and threw one of them offstage before he himself was hurled into the crowd."

DATE OF ARREST
March 5, 1969

CIRCUMSTANCES OF THE ARREST
Four days after the concert, the Dade County Sheriff's Office issued a warrant for Jim Morrison's arrest. When Morrison learned of the charges, he dismissed them as a joke.

THE CHARGES
Lewd and lascivious behavior: two counts of indecent exposure, two counts of public profanity, and one count of public drunkenness

THE SENTENCE
A jury convicted Morrison of one charge of public profanity and one charge of indecent exposure. Judge Murray Goodman sentenced Morrison to six months of hard labor and a $500 fine for public exposure and 60 days of hard labor for profanity. Morrison was freed after posting a $50,000 bond.

AFTERWARD
While his attorney filed an appeal, Morrison left the United States for Paris. He died there, apparently of a drug overdose.

UNUSUAL FACT
The prosecutors were willing to drop the charges if The Doors agreed to play a free concert in Miami. Morrison rejected the offer. His suviving family and bandmates also rejected the 2010 pardon by the State of Florida and the City of Miami, saying: "We don't feel Jim needs to be pardoned for anything."

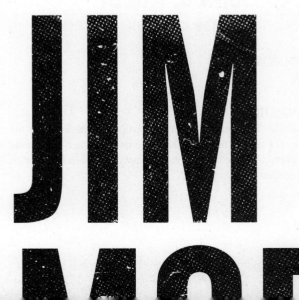

JOHN S. MOSBY

(1833–1916)

NATIONALITY
American

WHO WAS HE?
Known as "the Gray Ghost," during the Civil War, John S. Mosby led a Confederate cavalry battalion that used guerrilla tactics to strike Union targets. Mosby's Rangers eluded capture by blending in with the local civilian population.

WHAT DID HE DO?
At age 19, while a student at the University of Virginia, Mosby got into a fight with George R. Turpin, a notorious bully. During the fight, Mosby shot Turpin with a pistol, wounding but not killing him.

DATE OF ARREST
March 29, 1852

CIRCUMSTANCES OF THE ARREST
Mosby was arrested at his family's home.

THE CHARGE
Unlawful shooting and malicious shooting

THE SENTENCE
Convicted of unlawful shooting, Mosby was sentenced to one year in prison and fined $500. After serving several months of his sentence, Mosby was pardoned by the governor of Virginia and his fine was rescinded.

AFTERWARD
After General Robert E. Lee's surrender at Appomattox Court House, Virginia, Mosby disbanded his cavalry rather than surrender to the Yankees. Nonetheless, when Ulysses S. Grant ran for president in 1868, Mosby campaigned for him in Virginia. Grant appointed Mosby U.S. consul to Hong Kong. For the rest of his life, Mosby worked for the federal government, in the Department of the Interior and as an assistant attorney general in the Department of Justice.

JEAN MOULIN

(1899–1943)

NATIONALITY
French

WHO WAS HE?
During World War II, Jean Moulin led eight underground Resistance organizations in Lyon, France, and directed guerrilla activities against the Nazis and their collaborators in the Vichy government.

WHAT DID HE DO?
Moulin ordered attacks on Nazi military units; directed the destruction of bridges and railway lines; and helped downed Allied pilots escape to neutral countries, such as Spain.

DATE OF ARREST
June 21, 1943

CIRCUMSTANCES OF THE ARREST
Moulin and six other leaders of the Resistance arranged to meet at a doctor's office in a Lyon suburb. An informer betrayed them and they were all arrested by the Gestapo.

THE CHARGE
Acting as a Member of the Resistance

THE SENTENCE
Klaus Barbie, head of the Gestapo in Lyon, supervised Moulin's torture and interrogation. He was not given a trial, but was sent to Berlin for summary execution. Moulin had been so severely tortured that he died before the train reached Berlin.

AFTERWARD
In 1964, Moulin's ashes were moved to the Pantheon in Paris, France's shrine for national heroes.

ZACARIAS MOUSSAOUI

(1968–)

NATIONALITY
French

WHO IS HE?
Zacarias Moussaoui's parents emigrated from Morocco to France, where he was born. While studying for a degree in international business in London, Moussaoui became involved with extremist Islamic groups, which led to his expulsion from the moderate mosque he had been attending. Moussaoui joined Al Qaeda, trained in Afghanistan, and took flight lessons in Norman, Oklahoma.

WHAT DID HE DO?
Moussaoui was one of the conspirators of the September 11, 2001 attacks.

DATE OF ARREST
August 16, 2001

CIRCUMSTANCES OF THE ARREST
Moussaoui's ignorance of basic principles of aviation and his insistence on practicing with a flight simulator made his flight instructors suspicious. They contacted the FBI.

THE CHARGES
Conspiracy to commit acts of terrorism transcending national boundaries, conspiracy to commit aircraft piracy, conspiracy to destroy aircraft, conspiracy to use weapons of mass destruction, conspiracy to murder United States employees, and conspiracy to destroy property

THE SENTENCE
Initially, Moussaoui admitted his guilt, then denied it. After he was found guilty, he confessed once again. The jury voted against the death penalty, so Moussaoui was sentenced to life in prison, with no chance of parole.

AFTERWARD
Zacarias Moussaoui is incarcerated in the Supermax prison in Florence, Colorado.

SAMUEL MUDD

(1833–1883)

NATIONALITY
American

WHO WAS HE?
Samuel Mudd was a physician, farmer, and Confederate sympathizer who lived with his family on a farm near Bryantown, Maryland.

WHAT DID HE DO?
Mudd had met John Wilkes Booth on several occasions, and appears to have been involved in the plots to kidnap President Abraham Lincoln. He may have known of Booth's plan to assassinate Lincoln. On the night of April 14–15, 1865, Booth, who had broken his leg after shooting Lincoln, stopped at Mudd's house for medical treatment. Mudd set Booth's broken bone, but did not report him to the authorities. Mudd would say that Booth was wearing false whiskers, so he did not recognize him.

DATE OF ARREST
April 24, 1865

CIRCUMSTANCES OF THE ARREST
Mudd was arrested after several interviews with government investigators, who felt that his answers to their questions about Booth and the assassination plot were evasive.

THE CHARGE
Conspiracy to assassinate the president

THE SENTENCE
A military commission found Mudd guilty and sentenced him to life in prison at Fort Jefferson, located on an island off the coast of Florida.

AFTERWARD
Two years into his sentence, an epidemic of yellow fever broke out in the prison; among its victims was the prison's doctor. Mudd volunteered to help, and with the assistance of a doctor from Key West cared for hundreds of inmates and guards. After the epidemic, the majority of prison guards wrote to President Andrew Johnson, informing him about what Mudd had done, and entreating the president to pardon him. Johnson did pardon Mudd and ordered his release. Mudd returned home to his family. Since his death in 1883, some of Samuel Mudd's descendants have petitioned the federal government to overturn his conviction. As of 2010, the family has not been successful.

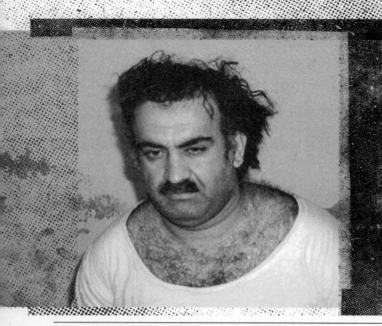

KHALID SHEIKH MOHAMMED

(1964/65–)

NATIONALITY
Pakistani

WHO IS HE?
Khalid Sheikh Mohammed is a senior member of the leadership of Al Qaeda and a close associate of Osama bin Laden.

WHAT DID HE DO?
Mohammed was the mastermind of the 1993 World Trade Center bombing, the September 11, 2001 attacks, the Bali nightclub bombings of 2002, and the murder of Wall Street Journal reporter Daniel Pearl in 2002.

DATE OF ARREST
March 1, 2003

CIRCUMSTANCES OF THE ARREST
Pakistani agents captured Mohammed, then turned him over to the Americans.

THE CHARGES
War crimes, terrorism, and murder

THE SENTENCE
Early in 2010, Attorney General Eric Holder announced that the Obama administration planned to try Mohammed before a civilian court in New York City, blocks away from the site of the World Trade Center. The announcement caused an uproar among the public and New York officials, who objected to the security risks and the disruption to the businesses and residents of Lower Manhattan.

AFTERWARD
In the face of such opposition, the prosecutors at the Department of Justice returned to their original plan, saying Mohammed would be held in a military prison while they reviewed their options. It is likely that Khalid Sheikh Mohammed will remain in prison indefinitely.

THE CONFESSIONS
Khalid Sheikh Mohammed confessed to more than two dozen terrorist plots. He said that he made these confessions after CIA interrogators subjected him to waterboarding.

TERENCE MULLEN

(1848–?)
AND

JACK HUGHES

(?–?)

NATIONALITY
Irish-born American citizens

WHO WERE THEY?
Terence Mullen and Jack Hughes were Irish immigrants living in Chicago; both men were members of a counterfeiting ring operated by James "Big Jim" Kennally. Mullen operated the Hub, a saloon he and Kennally owned on Chicago's Near West Side. Hughes was a "shover," a counterfeiter's term for a member of the gang who used bogus currency for everyday purchases in shops and other retail establishments.

WHAT DID THEY DO?
In January 1876, Big Jim's best engraver, Benjamin Boyd, had been arrested and sentenced to ten years in prison. Without Boyd to produce high-quality bogus currency, Big Jim's counterfeiting business was on the verge of collapse. To pressure the governor of Illinois to grant Boyd a pardon, Big Jim decided to steal the body of Abraham Lincoln from its tomb in Springfield, Illinois. Then he would send a message to the governor: In exchange for a pardon for Boyd and $200,000 in cash, Big Jim would return Lincoln's body, safe and unharmed. Big Jim recruited Mullen and Hughes to do the actual grave robbing, but the gang was thoroughly infiltrated by the Secret Service, who were waiting for them at the tomb on the night of the robbery. Unfortunately, as the Secret Service men were closing in to make the arrest, one of the detectives' pistols went off accidentally, and Mullen and Hughes escaped.

continued

G. W. Jorns   Springfield, Ill.

agents that the would-be grave robbers were back in town. The detectives trailed Mullen and Hughes until they were both in the Hub at the same time. On the evening of November 17, 1876, two detectives entered the saloon and ordered beers. As Mullen tapped the beer, one detective drew his pistol and arrested Mullen, while the other walked over to the stove where Hughes sat slumped in a chair, napping.

THE CHARGES
Conspiracy to steal the remains of Abraham Lincoln and attempted larceny in trying to steal the coffin

THE SENTENCE
A Springfield jury found Mullen and Hughes guilty of conspiracy and larceny. They were both sentenced to one year in the state penitentiary in Joliet—the prison where Benjamin Boyd was serving his ten-year sentence. A reporter for the *Chicago Times* wrote that there was a general consensus among the jurors and the spectators that Mullen and Hughes were not the masterminds of the plot, but were "the tools of smarter men."

AFTERWARD
Terence Mullen served his year in prison and was released on May 22, 1878. Jack Hughes, however, was indicted and convicted on an old charge of passing phony $5 bills. He served another three years in Joliet. Back in Chicago, Mullen found that while he had been in prison, Big Jim had sold the Hub; he was a free man, but he was flat broke. Two years later Mullen turned informer and was instrumental in the arrest and conviction of Big Jim Kennally. After 1882, Mullen, Hughes, and Big Jim disappear from the historical record.

DATE OF ARREST
November 17, 1876

CIRCUMSTANCES OF THE ARREST
From the cemetery in Springfield, Mullen and Hughes fled straight back to the Hub in Chicago. Informants tipped off the Secret Service

UNUSUAL FACT
To protect his father's body from any further attempted grave robberies, Robert Todd Lincoln had the coffin sealed inside a steel cage and lowered into a ten-foot-deep vault, which was filled with wet cement.

LAURA JANE MURRAY

(1962–)

NATIONALITY
American

WHO IS SHE?
Laura Jane Murray is a robber who targets banks in California.

WHAT DID SHE DO?
It is alleged that Murray entered the Union Bank in Davis, California, where she slipped a teller a note demanding cash. The teller complied, and Murray ran out to the parking lot, where she discovered that she had locked her keys inside her car. She borrowed a crowbar from the driver of a FedEx truck that was parked nearby and tried to smash her window.

DATE OF ARREST
July 21, 2010

CIRCUMSTANCES OF THE ARREST
A bystander saw a woman beating on the window of a Ford Taurus with a crowbar and called the police. When the cops arrived, Murray still had not managed to break the glass.

THE CHARGE
Bank robbery

UNUSUAL FACT
On July 13, 2010, Murray was arrested for bank robbery in Oroville, California. Because she had a staph infection, police took her to a hospital for treatment. For unknown reasons, she was released.

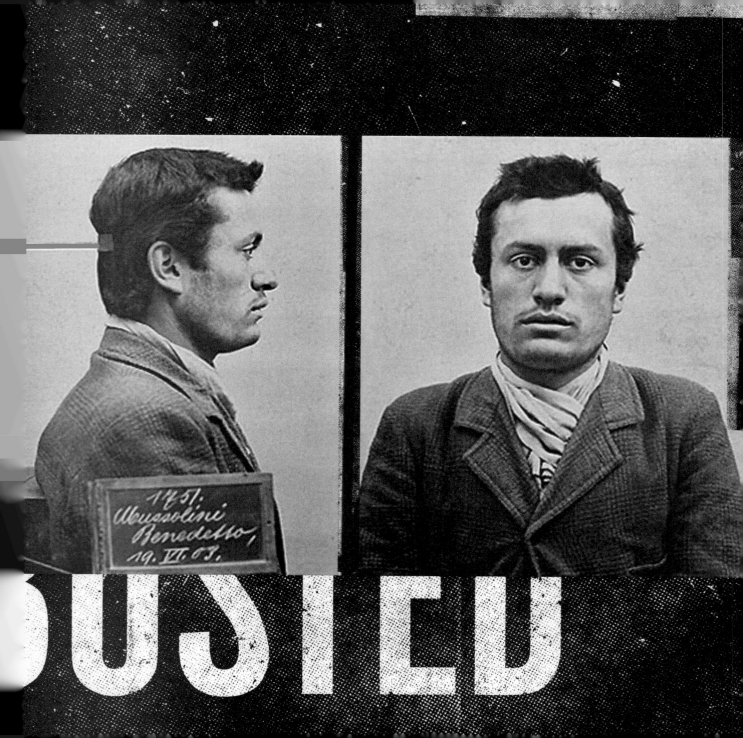

1751.
Mussolini Benedetto,
19. VI. 03.

OUSIEU

BENITO MUSSOLINI
(1883–1945)

NATIONALITY
Italian

WHO WAS HE?
Benito Mussolini was a blacksmith's son, whose political ideas were strongly influenced by his father's odd mix of Socialist, anarchist, and Italian nationalist politics.

WHAT DID HE DO?
To avoid military service in Italy, Mussolini traveled to Switzerland, where he found work and became involved in Socialist political organizations. He was arrested in Bern for urging workers to shut down the city by participating in a general strike.

DATE OF ARREST
June 19, 1903

THE CHARGE
Revolutionary activities

THE SENTENCE
Mussolini was sentenced to two weeks in jail, then deported back to Italy.

AFTERWARD
Benito Mussolini became one of the founders of the Fascist Party in Italy. He was elected prime minister in 1922, adopted the title Il Duce (the Leader, comparable to Der Führer), allied Italy with the Third Reich and entered World War II on the side of the Axis. In 1943, when the Allies invaded Italy, Mussolini was deposed. German troops freed him from prison, but at the end of the war, when he tried to escape to Switzerland with his mistress, Clara Petacci, Mussolini was captured near Lake Como by Italian partisans. The partisans executed him and Petacci, then took their corpses to Milan, where they were strung up by their heels for public viewing.

SUN MYUNG MOON

(1920–)

DATE OF ARREST
May 18, 1982

THE CHARGES
Conspiracy and filing false income tax returns

THE SENTENCE
Moon was convicted, sentenced to 18 months in prison, and fined $15,000.

AFTERWARD
Moon has renamed his church the Family Federation for World Peace and Unification. Today the church and its investment portfolio, which until November 2010 included the *Washington Times* newspaper, is largely managed by Moon's three sons.

NATIONALITY
Korean

WHO IS HE?
Sun Myung Moon is the founder of the Unification Church, a Christian denomination that believes Moon and his wife Hak Ja Han have achieved the spiritual ideal God envisioned for humankind when he created Adam and Eve. The Unification Church is perhaps most famous for its massive wedding ceremonies in which hundreds, sometimes thousands of couples, are married.

WHAT DID HE DO?
Moon filed false tax returns in 1973, 1974, and 1976, failing to pay taxes on $162,000 of income.

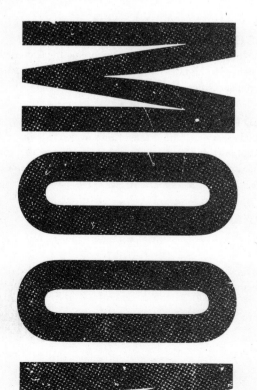

JOHN MYATT

(1945–)

NATIONALITY
English

WHO IS HE?
John Myatt is a sometime songwriter and schoolteacher who discovered at an early age that he could paint and draw in the style of the great artists.

WHAT DID HE DO?
Working with his accomplice, John Drewe, Myatt painted at least 200 pictures in the style of Marc Chagall and Henri Matisse, among others, and sold them as the authentic work of the masters to dealers in New York, London, and Paris, as well as to auction houses such as Sotheby's.

DATE OF ARREST
September 1995

CIRCUMSTANCES OF THE ARREST
When Scotland Yard detectives arrested Myatt, he confessed everything, volunteered that he had made £275,000 ($429,291) in the sale of his forgeries, and offered to give evidence against Drewe.

THE CHARGE
Forgery

THE SENTENCE
After Myatt and Drewe were both convicted, Myatt was sentenced to one year in prison, but was released after four months. Drewe was sentenced to six years, but was released after serving two.

AFTERWARD
Myatt paints and exhibits his own work. However, there is a market for his forgeries.

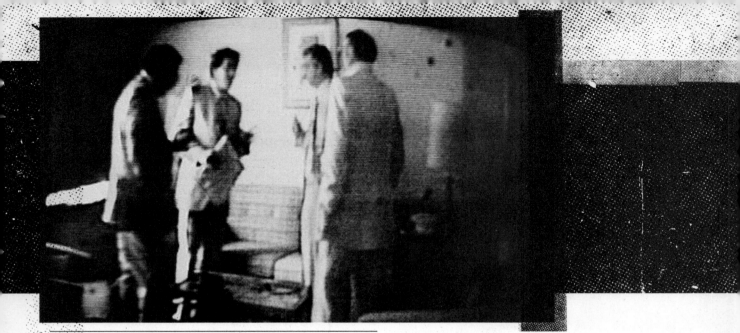

MICHAEL MYERS

(1943–)

NATIONALITY
American

WHO IS HE?
Michael Myers was a former longshoreman who from 1976 to 1980 represented Pennsylvania's 1st Congressional District in the House of Representatives.

WHAT DID HE DO?
In 1980, during the Abscam scandal, Myers was videotaped accepting a $50,000 bribe from two men he believed to be Middle Eastern sheiks. In fact, the sheiks were undercover FBI agents.

DATE OF ARREST
June 5, 1980

THE CHARGE
Soliciting bribes

THE SENTENCE
Myers was convicted, sentenced to three years in prison, and fined $20,000.

AFTERWARD
The House of Representatives expelled him—the first time it had thrown out a member since 1861.

WHAT DID SHE DO?

Myerson shoplifted six bottles of nail polish, five pairs of earrings, a pair of shoes, and several packages of flashlight batteries—worth a total of $44.07—from a department store in South Williamsport, Pennsylvania.

DATE OF ARREST

May 27, 1988

CIRCUMSTANCES OF THE ARREST

Security guards stopped Myerson as she was leaving the store. She was released on $150 bail.

THE CHARGE

Shoplifting

THE SENTENCE

Myerson pled guilty and was fined $100, plus $48.50 in court costs.

AFTERWARD

Myerson retired to South Florida, where she occasionally records messages about ovarian cancer awareness.

BESS MYERSON

(1924–)

NATIONALITY

American

WHO IS SHE?

A former Miss America (the first Jewish woman to win the title) and cultural affairs commissioner of New York City, Bess Myerson was active in the administrations of Mayor John V. Lindsay and Mayor Ed Koch.

NORIO NAGAYAMA

(1949–1997)

THE CHARGES
Armed robbery and murder

THE SENTENCE
Nagayama was found guilty and sentenced to death. On appeal, his sentence was commuted to life in prison because he had committed the crimes when he was 19—a minor under Japanese law. Prosecutors took the case to Japan's Supreme Court, which ruled that Nagayama could be executed. The appeals process dragged on for 28 years. Ultimately, Nagayama was hanged secretly in a Tokyo prison in 1997.

IN PRISON
During the 28 years he spent in prison, Norio Nagayama became a best-selling novelist. He donated his royalties to the families of his victims and to children's aid organizations.

NATIONALITY
Japanese

WHO WAS HE?
Norio Nagayama was a teenager who worked at a coffee shop in Tokyo.

WHAT DID HE DO?
Nagayama burglarized a house on a U.S. Army base near Tokyo, stealing a handgun. In October and November 1968, he shot and killed four people, robbing two of his victims.

DATE OF ARREST
April 7, 1969

CIRCUMSTANCES OF THE ARREST
Nagayama eluded police for five months, until he was caught trying to break into a school.

IMRE NAGY

(1896–1958)

NATIONALITY
Hungarian

WHO WAS HE?
Imre Nagy became a Communist during World War I, and fought with the Bolsheviks in Russia during the Russian Revolution. From 1930 to 1945, he lived in the Soviet Union. After World War II, when Joseph Stalin seized most of Eastern Europe, Nagy was sent back to Hungary to serve in the new Communist government. But Nagy was not a hard-line Stalinist, so he was removed from office and expelled from the Communist Party.

WHAT DID HE DO?
In 1956, the Hungarians invited Nagy to form a new government. He created a political coalition that included non-Communists, called for a genuinely democratic government, announced the release of political prisoners, and declared his intention to free Hungary from Soviet domination.

DATE OF ARREST
November 22, 1956

CIRCUMSTANCES OF THE ARREST
Soviet troops arrested Nagy as he left the Yugoslav Embassy in Budapest. He was held in a secret location in Romania, then returned to Hungary for trial.

THE CHARGE
Treason

THE SENTENCE
Nagy was found guilty of attempting "to overthrow the democratic state order." He was hanged in secret and buried in an unmarked grave.

AFTERWARD
In 1989, after the collapse of the Soviet Bloc, Nagy's remains were re-interred and a monument was erected over his grave. More than 100,000 Hungarians attended the ceremony.

CARRIE NATION

(1846–1911)

NATIONALITY
American

WHO WAS SHE?
Carrie Nation was a temperance crusader who believed she had a God-given mission to protect individuals and families from the tragic effects of alcoholism by shutting down the liquor industry. She traveled across the country, confronting saloon owners and bartenders, singing hymns to drunks, and smashing bottles and barrels of liquor with rocks and hatchets (the hatchet became her trademark).

WHAT DID SHE DO?
Nation entered a saloon in Nebraska City, Nebraska, and told the bartender she was going to smash the bar. The bartender ordered her to get out, but Nation would not leave, so he slapped her twice across the face.

DATE OF ARREST
April 5, 1902

CIRCUMSTANCES OF THE ARREST
When Nation returned to the saloon with a group of supporters, police arrested her.

THE CHARGE
Disturbing the peace

THE SENTENCE
The police promised not to prosecute Nation if she agreed to leave Nebarska City at once. She accepted the deal.

AFTERWARD
Nation's zeal for the temperance movement cost her her second husband—after 24 years of marriage, David Nation filed for divorce on the grounds that his wife had deserted him. Nation retired to Eureka Springs, Arkansas, where she lived in a house she named Hatchet Hall.

VINCE NEIL
(1961–)

NATIONALITY
American

WHO IS HE?
Vince Neil is the lead vocalist of the heavy metal band Mötley Crüe.

WHAT DID HE DO?
While driving under the influence, Neil crashed his car into an oncoming vehicle. His friend, Nicholas "Razzle" Dingley, was killed in the accident, and the driver and passenger in the other car were seriously injured.

DATE OF ARREST
December 8, 1984

THE CHARGES
Vehicular manslaughter and driving under the influence

THE SENTENCE
Neil was sentenced to 30 days in jail and fined $2.5 million.

AFTERWARD
In a 2005 interview with *Blender* magazine, Neil said, "I should have gone to prison. I definitely deserved to go to prison. But I did 30 days in jail and got laid and drank beer, because that's the power of cash. That's fucked up." Neil has had other legal troubles, including charges of attacking a music producer in 2002 and punching a nightclub employee in 2004.

GEORGE "BABY FACE" NELSON (LESTER GILLIS)

(1908–1934)

NATIONALITY
American

WHO WAS HE?
Lester Gillis was a Chicago street kid who stole cars, stole tires, and distilled and sold bootleg liquor. Because of his boyish looks, his gang called him "Baby Face."

WHAT DID HE DO?
In 1930, Gillis, who was now going by the name George Nelson, robbed two banks, getting away with over $8,000.

DATE OF ARREST
1931

THE CHARGE
Bank robbery

THE SENTENCE
Nelson was convicted and sentenced to a year in prison, but he escaped during a prison transfer.

AFTERWARD
For three years after his escape, Nelson, together with his wife, Helen Gillis, and his partner in crime, John Paul Chase, traveled across California and the Upper Midwest, smuggling liquor, committing robberies, and killing at least six people, including three FBI agents. The FBI caught up with Nelson in Barrington, Illinois, where they killed him in a shootout.

PAUL NEWMAN

(1925–2008)

NATIONALITY
American

WHO WAS HE?
Paul Newman was a screen legend, famous for his talent, his good looks, and his blue eyes.

WHAT DID HE DO?
The night he was praised by a *New York Times* film critic for his performance in *Somebody Up There Likes Me,* Newman went to a party, had too much to drink, and tried to drive home. He ran a red light, knocked over a fire hydrant, and tried to outrun the police.

DATE OF ARREST
July 7, 1956

CIRCUMSTANCES OF THE ARREST
Newman climbed out of his car and said, "I'm acting for Rocky Graziano. What do you want?" The police officer, Rocco "Rocky" Caggiano, said, "I'm Rocky, too, and you're under arrest."

THE CHARGES
Drunk driving and resisting arrest

THE SENTENCE
Newman spent a night in jail. The next day the charges were dropped.

AFTERWARD
Newman's film career included such hits as *Cat on a Hot Tin Roof, Cool Hand Luke, Butch Cassidy and the Sundance Kid, The Sting,* and *The Verdict*. He was a philanthropist who during the last 20 years of his life donated between $150 and $175 million to charity. And beginning in the 1960s he was active in Democratic Party politics.

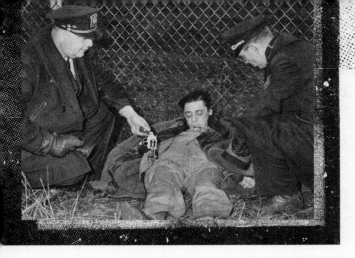

FRANK "THE ENFORCER" NITTI

(1881–1943)

NATIONALITY
Italian-born American citizen

WHO WAS HE?
Frank Nitti grew up with Al Capone, in the same Brooklyn neighborhood. In 1913, he moved to Chicago where he met local gangsters, including Dion O'Banion. Nitti's activities as a bootlegger attracted the attention of Capone, who was expanding his illegal liquor business to Chicago.

WHAT DID HE DO?
Prosecutors could not collect enough evidence to convict Nitti on his mob activities, so he was indicted for filing false tax returns.

DATE OF ARREST
October 31, 1930

CIRCUMSTANCES OF THE ARREST
Nitti and Capone were arrested almost simultaneously and on the same charge.

THE CHARGE
Tax evasion

THE SENTENCE
Nitti was convicted and sentenced to 18 months in prison.

AFTERWARD
With Capone serving an 11-year sentence, Nitti took over as boss of the Chicago Outfit, as the gang was known. Nitti expanded the business to include extortion, specifically shaking down the Hollywood studios for payoffs; in exchange, the Chicago Outfit ensured that the studios would not have trouble with the labor unions. In 1943, facing a grand jury indictment for extortion, Nitti walked to a railroad yard and shot himself in the head.

NICK NOLTE

(1941–)

NATIONALITY
American

WHO IS HE?
Nick Nolte is an actor whose big break came in the 1976 made-for-TV miniseries *Rich Man, Poor Man*. He was nominated for an Emmy for his portrayal of Tom Jordache, the "poor man" of the title. He went on to star in the movies *48 Hours, Down and Out in Beverly Hills, The Prince of Tides, Jefferson in Paris, Lorenzo's Oil, The Golden Bowl,* and *Hotel Rwanda.*

WHAT DID HE DO?
His erratic driving suggested that Nolte was drunk at the time of his arrest. A blood test showed that Nolte had been taking GHB, more commonly known the "date rape" drug.

DATE OF ARREST
September 11, 2002

CIRCUMSTANCES OF THE ARREST
California highway police observed a black Mercedes drifting back and forth across the Pacific Coast Highway. When they pulled the car over, they found Nolte at the wheel "drooling," according to the arresting officers and "completely out of it."

THE CHARGE
Driving under the influence of narcotics

THE SENTENCE
In court, Nolte pleaded no contest. The judge sentenced him to three years' probation. Two conditions of Nolte's probation were random tests for the presence of drugs or alcohol, and enrolling in a substance abuse program.

AFTERWARD
Nolte signed himself into the Silver Hill Hospital in New Canaan, Connecticut, where he underwent counseling and treatment for substance abuse.

UNUSUAL FACT
In the VH1 program, "40 Most Shocking Celebrity Mugshots," Nick Nolte's took first place.

MANUEL NORIEGA

(1934–)

NATIONALITY
Panamanian

WHO IS HE?
Manuel Noriega wanted to be a doctor, but his family could not afford to send him to medical school, so he entered the military. In the Panamanian National Guard he was befriended by Colonel Omar Torrijos; in 1968, Torrijos and Noriega ousted Panama's president. From 1969 until his death in 1981, Torrijos ruled Panama, after which the power passed to Noriega.

WHAT DID HE DO?
Noriega was involved in drug trafficking, human rights abuses, and attempted to declare Panama's 1989 election void.

DATE OF ARREST
January 3, 1990

CIRCUMSTANCES OF THE ARREST
President George H. W. Bush sent U.S. troops to Panama to arrest Noriega and support the newly elected president. Noriega turned himself in at the Vatican Embassy in Panama City.

THE CHARGES
Drug trafficking, racketeering, and money laundering

THE SENTENCE
Noriega went on trial in Miami, where he was convicted, sentenced to 40 years in prison, and ordered to pay $44 million to the Panamanian government. Later the sentence was reduced to 17 years.

AFTERWARD
Noriega completed his sentence in 2007 and was extradited to France, where he was convicted of money laundering and sentenced to seven years in prison. The French government has agreed that once Noriega has finished his seven-year sentence, he will extradited to Panama to face charges of human rights violations.

NOTORIOUS B.I.G. (CHRISTOPHER WALLACE)

(1972–1997)

AFTERWARD

In March 1997, Notorious B.I.G. was in California on a promotional tour. At about 12:45 in the morning of March 9, 1997, a black Chevy Impala pulled up beside Notorious B.I.G.'s truck and the driver shot and killed the rapper. The crime remains unsolved.

NATIONALITY
American

WHO WAS HE?
Christopher Wallace grew up in Brooklyn, where he began selling drugs when he was 12. His teen years were split between rapping and getting in trouble with the law: In 1989, he was arrested on a weapons charge, in 1990 he was arrested for violating parole, and in 1991 he was arrested for selling crack. In the early 1990s, Notorious B.I.G. started cutting albums—his 1994 *Ready to Die* album went platinum four times.

WHAT DID HE DO?
Outside a Manhattan club, Notorious B.I.G. got into an altercation with two fans who wanted his autograph. He threatened to kill the autograph hounds, chased them after they climbed into a cab, smashed the cab's windows, dragged one of the fans out through the broken window, and slugged him.

DATE OF ARREST
March 23, 1996

THE CHARGE
Harrassment

THE SENTENCE
Notorious B.I.G. pled guilty and was sentenced to 100 hours of community service.

NUREMBERG TRIAL DEFENDANTS:

KARL DOENITZ (1891–1980), ALFRED JODL (1890–1946), ALFRED ROSENBERG (1893–1946), HANS FRANK (1900–1946), ERNST KALTENBRUNNER (1903–1946), FRITZ SAUCKEL (1894–1946), WILHELM FRICK (1877–1946), WILHELM KEITEL (1882–1946), HJALMAR SCHACHT (1877–1970), HANS FRITZSCHE (1900–1953), KONSTANTIN VON NEURATH (1873–1956), BALDUR VON SCHIRACH (1907–1974), WALTHER FUNK (1890–1960), FRANZ VON PAPEN (1879–1969), ARTHUR SEYSS-INQUART (1892–1946), HERMANN GOERING (1893–1946), ERICH RAEDER (1876–1960), ALBERT SPEER (1905–1981), RUDOLF HESS (1894–1987), JOACHIM VON RIBBENTROP (1893–1946), AND JULIUS STREICHER (1885–1946)

NATIONALITY
German

WHO WERE THEY?

These 21 defendants, the first group tried at Nuremberg, were members of Adolf Hitler's inner circle of advisers, leaders of the Nazi government, the military, the SS, and the Gestapo.

WHAT DID THEY DO?

As commander-in-chief of the German Navy, **Karl Doenitz** instructed U-boat commanders to target enemy as well as neutral merchant ships. He used 12,000 concentration camp inmates as forced labor in shipyards.

Alfred Jodl, chief of army operations, planned the invasions of Czechoslovakia, Norway, Greece, and Yugoslavia. He ordered German troops to execute all Soviet commisssars.

Alfred Rosenberg participated in planning the invasion of Norway, the looting of art treasures in France, and atrocities committed against civilians in Eastern Europe.

Hans Frank erected the first ghettoes for Jews in Germany, and developed the policy of reducing the Poles to slaves.

As leader of the SS in Austria, **Ernst Kaltenbrunner** ordered the deaths of 4 million Jews.

Fritz Sauckel instituted the use of concentration camp inmates as slave laborers.

As minister of the interior, **Wilhelm Frick** gave the orders for the torture and murder of Jews, Communists, gypsies, homosexuals, and others the Nazis considered "subhuman."

Wilhelm Keitel, chief of staff of the High Command of the Armed Forces, planned the invasion of Russia and ordered the execution of all Communists.

Hjalmar Schacht was president of the Reichsbank and the Third Reich's minister of economics.

Hans Fritzsche directed all media in the Third Reich.

Konstantin von Neurath was one of Hitler's military advisers. He was a high-ranking official in the government of Nazi-occupied Czechoslovakia.

Baldur von Schirach was head of the Hitler Youth, which trained young Germans for careers in the SS.

One of Hitler's economic advisers, **Walther Funk** ordered the confiscation of Jewish property and the gold in the banks of Czechoslovakia.

Franz von Papen served in the government of the Third Reich.

Arthur Seyss-Inquart organized pogroms against Jews and the deportation of Jews to death camps.

Second in power only to Hitler, **Hermann Goering** ran the Gestapo.

Erich Raeder, chief of Naval Command, ordered U-boats to sink passenger and merchant ships.

Albert Speer, Hitler's personal architect, used concentration camp inmates as slave laborers.

One of Hitler's confidants, **Rudolf Hess** supported the Final Solution.

Joachim von Ribbentrop, Hitler's foreign policy adviser, helped plan the invasion of Poland and was active in the Final Solution to exterminate the Jews of Europe.

Julius Streicher was an ardent and outspoken advocate for the annihilation of the Jews.

DATE OF ARREST
May–September 1945

THE CHARGES
Conspiracy to wage aggressive war, crimes against peace, war crimes, and crimes against humanity

THE SENTENCES
Doenitz: 10 years In prison
Jodl: death by hanging
Rosenberg: death by hanging
Frank: death by hanging
Kaltenbrunner: death by hanging
Sauckel: death by hanging
Frick: death by hanging
Keitel: death by hanging
Schacht: acquitted
Fritzshe: acquitted
Neurath: 15 years In prison
Schirach: 20 years In prison
Funk: life In prison
Papen: acquitted
Seyss-Inquart: death by hanging
Goering: death by hanging (committed suicide in his cell)
Raeder: life In prison
Speer: 20 years In prison
Hess: life in prison (committed suicide in his cell in 1987)
Ribbentrop: death by hanging
Streicher: death by hanging

UNUSUAL FACT
Nuremberg was chosen as the site for the trials because it was the birthplace of the Nazi Party.

KHLOÉ KARDASHIAN ODOM
(1984–)

NATIONALITY
American

WHO IS SHE?
The youngest of the Kardashian sisters, Khloé Kardashian Odom is a celebutante and reality TV personality who has been seen on *Keeping Up with the Kardashians* and *Kourtney and Khloé Take Miami*.

WHAT DID SHE DO?
In 2007, Odom was arrested for drunk driving and placed on three years' probation. In 2008, she violated the terms of her probation by failing to perform roadside cleanup duty as part of her community service and to enroll in an alcohol treatment program.

DATE OF ARREST
July 18, 2008

THE CHARGE
Parole violation

THE SENTENCE
Odom was sentenced to 30 days in jail.

AFTERWARD
She was released after three hours because the jail was overcrowded.

MADALYN MURRAY O'HAIR

(1919–1995)

NATIONALITY
American

WHO WAS SHE?
Madalyn Murray O'Hair was an atheism activist whose lawsuit, *Murray v. Curlett,* led to the Supreme Court ruling that banned prayer from public schools. She founded American Atheists and served as the organization's president from 1963 to 1986, when she was succeeded by her son, Jon Garth Murray, who was president until his death in 1995.

WHAT DID SHE DO?
Murray attacked five Baltimore police officers who had come to her house for a runaway, Susan Abramovitz, who was the girlfriend of O'Hair's oldest son, William. Afterward, Murray fled with her son and Susan to Hawaii.

DATE OF INDICTMENT
June 1964

THE CHARGES
Assault, disorderly conduct, and contempt of court

THE SENTENCE
A Baltimore judge found Murray guilty, sentenced her to one year in prison, and fined her $500. William was sentenced to six months in prison. In 1965, the charges were dropped.

AFTERWARD
For the rest of her life, O'Hair was a polarizing figure in American society. Ultimately, she and her son Jon even became polarizing figures among American atheists, as local chapters peeled off from the main organization or simply dissolved. In the 1990s, the American Atheists organization did not extend much beyond O'Hair, her son Jon, and her granddaughter Robin Murray O'Hair. In August 1995, the three O'Hairs were kidnapped by one of their employees, David Waters, who stole their credit cards, demanded $500,000 in gold coins, then murdered them and buried their mutilated bodies on a ranch in Texas. The case remained unsolved until 2001 when Waters was arrested. He was sentenced to 20 years in prison; he died in 2003.

UNUSUAL FACT
In 1980, O'Hair's son William converted to the Baptist Church. O'Hair said at the time, "One could call this a postnatal abortion on the part of a mother, I guess; I repudiate him entirely and completely for now and all times . . . he is beyond human forgiveness." Mother and son never saw one another again.

JAMES E. O'KEEFE
(1984–),

ROBERT FLANAGAN
(1985–),

JOSEPH BASEL
(1985–),
AND

STAN DAI
(1985–)

NATIONALITY
American

WHAT DID THEY DO?
They attempted to tap the phones of U.S. Senator Mary Landrieu to see if she was ignoring phone calls from constituents during the health care debate.

DATE OF ARREST
January 25, 2010

THE CHARGE
Attempting to maliciously interfere with the office telephone system

CIRCUMSTANCE OF THE ARREST
Robert Flanagan and Joseph Basel entered the federal building in New Orleans dressed as telephone repairmen, claiming that phones were out of order. One of the senator's staff members told them there was nothing wrong with the phones. They were apprehended after they attempted to gain access to the telephone equipment closet. O'Keefe was also in the office, pretending to wait for a friend but actually videotaping the exchange. Stan Dai was waiting outside.

THE SENTENCE
The charges were reduced to entering a federal building under false pretenses, which is a misdemeanor. O'Keefe pled guilty and was sentenced to three years' probation, 100 hours of community service, and a $1,500 fine. The other three men received lesser sentences of two years' probation, 75 hours of community service and a $1,500 fine.

AFTERWARD
O'Keefe continues his controversial investigations. In October 2010, he released a series of videos titled "Teachers Unions Gone Wild," investigating the New Jersey Education Association. The undercover videos showed teachers gloating about how difficult is was to fire a tenured teacher.

EDWARD CAPEHART O'KELLEY
(1858–1904)

THE CHARGE
Murder

THE SENTENCE
O'Kelley was convicted and sentenced to ten years in prison. His connection with Jesse James—if there was one—has never been discovered and his motive for killing Ford has never been established.

AFTERWARD
After his release from prison, O'Kelley traveled to Oklahoma City, Oklahoma. There a police officer, Joe Burnett, arrested him as a "suspicious character." O'Kelley was detained briefly, then released. That night he confronted Burnett as the cop was walking his beat and tried to kill him. After a prolonged wrestling match in the street, Burnett pulled out his pistol and shot and killed O'Kelley.

NATIONALITY
American

WHO WAS HE?
Very little is known about Edward Capehart O'Kelley, except that he probably was raised in Missouri.

WHAT DID HE DO?
On June 8, 1892, in Creede, Colorado, he entered a tent saloon owned and operated by Robert Ford, the man who killed the outlaw Jesse James for the bounty money. Ford had his back to O'Kelley. When O'Kelley said, "Hello, Bob," Ford turned around. O'Kelley fired his shotgun, striking Ford in the throat and killing him instantly.

DATE OF ARREST
June 8, 1892

SARA JANE OLSON (KATHLEEN ANNE SOLIAH)

(1947–)

NATIONALITY
American

WHO IS SHE?
In the 1970s, Sara Jane Olson was a member of the Symbionese Liberation Army, a radical terrorist organization that kidnapped Patty Hearst. After the SLA was virtually wiped out in a 1974 gun battle with police, Olson helped the survivors find a safe house and acquire false IDs.

WHAT DID SHE DO?
In 1975, Olson and other SLA members robbed a bank in Carmichael, California. During the robbery, they shot and killed a bank customer, Myrna Opsahl, a mother of four. That same year Olson planted bombs under a Los Angeles Police Department patrol car and in front of an LAPD station.

DATE OF ARREST
June 16, 1999

CIRCUMSTANCES OF THE ARREST
She went underground, creating a new life for herself, and was only discovered, 23 years later, when *America's Most Wanted* aired two segments about her.

THE CHARGE
Conspiracy to commit murder and possession of explosives

THE SENTENCE
After an elaborate plea negotiation, during which Olson repeatedly pled guilty then retracted her guilty pleas, she was sentenced to 14 years for the explosives charges and six years for the murder charge.

AFTERWARD
Olson was paroled in 2008, then rearrested when it was determined that the Parole Board had miscalculated when she could be released. She was finally paroled in 2009.

DANIEL ORTEGA

(1945–)

NATIONALITY
Nicaraguan

WHO IS HE?
Daniel Ortega's father had fought with Cesar Augusto Sandino's peasant army, the Sandinistas. In 1963, Ortega joined the Sandinista National Liberation Front (FSLN) to overthrow the ruling family of Nicaragua, the Somozas.

WHAT DID HE DO?
Ortega and several other Sandinistas robbed a bank.

DATE OF ARREST
Fall 1967

THE CHARGE
Bank robbery

THE SENTENCE
Ortega was convicted and sentenced to seven years in prison. In 1974, he was banished to Cuba.

AFTERWARD
The Cuban military trained him as a guerrilla, then helped him slip back into Nicaragua. In 1979, the Sandinistas ousted the Somoza government. Ortega served as president of Nicaragua from 1984 to 1990, and was elected president again in 2007.

ORTE

05 15 84
DATE

BOOKING NUMBER
841 0 0 0 1 8

SHELBY COUNTY
JUSTICE COMPLEX
MEMPHIS TENNESSEE

OZZY OSBOURNE

(1948–)

NATIONALITY
English

WHO IS HE?
Ozzy Osbourne is one of the founding members of Black Sabbath, which in the 1970s was at the forefront of heavy metal rock. In 1979, he left Black Sabbath, and in 1980 founded the Blizzard of Ozz, which revived his music career.

WHAT DID HE DO?
In San Antonio, Texas, Osbourne urinated on a wall of the Alamo.

DATE OF ARREST
February 19, 1982

CIRCUMSTANCES OF THE ARREST
Osbourne was wearing one of his wife Sharon's dresses. In an attempt to keep him out of bars (Osbourne had a drinking problem), she had confiscated all his clothes, so he put on some of hers and went out.

THE CHARGE
Public urination

THE SENTENCE
Osbourne was banned from ever performing in the city of San Antonio. In 1992, the ban was lifted.

UNUSUAL FACT
At a concert in 1982, a fan threw a live bat onto the stage. Osbourne, thinking it was rubber, picked it up and bit off the bat's head. Afterwards, he was treated with a series of rabies shots.

LEE HARVEY OSWALD
(1939–1963)

NATIONALITY
American

WHO WAS HE?
In his teens, Lee Harvey Oswald described himself to friends as a Marxist. At age 17, he joined the Marines and was stationed in Japan, Taiwan, and the Philippines. Even in the Marines he defended Marxism—he was an outspoken supporter of the Cuban revolutionary Fidel Castro. In 1959, his stint in the Marines was over and Oswald emigrated to the Soviet Union, where he became a citizen and married Marina Prusakova. By 1962, he was disillusioned with life in the USSR and received permission to return to the United States with his wife and daughter. Eventually, the family settled in Dallas.

WHAT DID HE DO?
From the window of the Texas School Book Depository building in Dallas, Oswald fired several shots at a presidential motorcade, wounding Texas governor John Connally and killing President John F. Kennedy.

DATE OF ARREST
November 22, 1963

CIRCUMSTANCES OF THE ARREST
Oswald escaped from the school book building, shot and killed a police officer named J. D. Tippet, then hid in a movie theater. He was observed by the manager of a nearby shoe store, who consulted with the assistant manager of the theater; together they called the police.

THE CHARGE
Assassination

THE SENTENCE
Oswald was never tried. On the morning of November 24, 1963, as he was being transferred to the county jail, a man named Jack Ruby ran up and shot and killed Oswald.

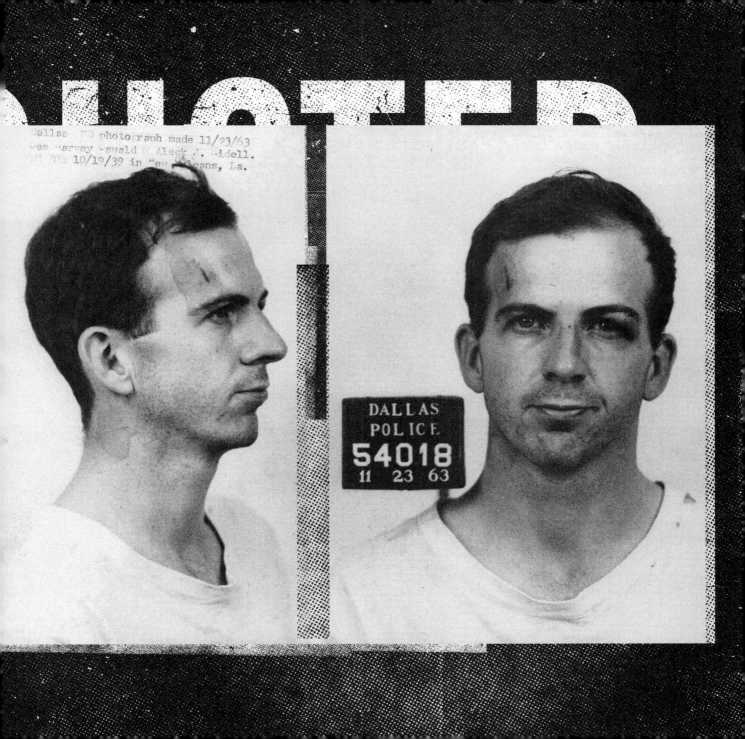

DALLAS
POLICE
54018
11 23 63

AL PACINO
(1940–)

NATIONALITY
American

WHO IS HE?
Acclaimed as one of the greatest actors of his generation, Al Pacino studied under Lee Strasberg at the Actors Studio. His breakout role came in 1972 when he was cast as Michael Corleone in *The Godfather*. He has been nominated seven times for an Oscar, and finally won in 1992 for *Scent of a Woman*. He has also won two Emmys and four Golden Globes.

WHAT DID HE DO?
Police observed Pacino and two friends, all of them wearing dark masks and gloves, driving a car around the same block several times. When the cop pulled them over, he found that Pacino was carrying a pistol.

DATE OF ARREST
January 7, 1961

CIRCUMSTANCES OF THE ARREST
Pacino told police he was an actor on his way to an audition and the pistol was a prop.

THE CHARGE
Carrying a concealed weapon

THE SENTENCE
Pacino was in jail for three days. When it was determined that the gun was a stage prop, he was released and the charge was dropped.

EMMELINE PANKHURST

(1858–1928)

NATIONALITY
English

WHO WAS SHE?
Emmeline Pankhurst was a militant activist for women's rights and the founder of the Women's Social and Political Union (WSPU), an organization that more than any other secured for British women the right to vote.

WHAT DID SHE DO?
In February 1908, Pankhurst tried to enter the Parliament Building in Westminster to deliver to Prime Minister H. H. Asquith a statement demanding equal rights for women, particularly the right to vote.

DATE OF ARREST
February 1908

THE CHARGE
Obstruction

THE SENTENCE
Pankhurst was sentenced to six weeks in prison.

AFTERWARD
Upon her release, she detailed the living conditions she endured—rodents, insufficient food, and "the civilized torture of solitary confinement and absolute silence." Pankhurst and members of the WSPU became increasingly controversial as they adopted methods that alienated even some of their supporters, including the destruction of property and arson. Nonetheless, in 1918 British women over the age of 30 gained the right to vote. Pankhurst ran for Parliament, but her campaign was derailed when one of her daughters gave birth to a child out of wedlock, and gave interviews to newspapers urging liberated women to reject the institution of marriage.

DATE OF ARREST
December 1, 1955

THE CHARGE
Violation of the Segregation Code

THE SENTENCE
In a 30-minute trial, Parks was found guilty and fined $10 plus $4 court costs.

AFTERWARD
The Parks case brought about the formation of the Montgomery Improvement Association, led by a Baptist minister, Dr. Martin Luther King Jr. Dr. King called for a boycott of Montgomery city buses—a boycott that lasted 382 days and ended when the bus company abandoned its segregated seating policy. The boycott made Rosa Parks and Dr. King international figures, and brought worldwide attention to America's fledgling civil rights movement. In 1996, President Bill Clinton presented Parks with the Presidential Medal of Freedom.

ROSA PARKS
(1913–2005)

NATIONALITY
American

WHO WAS SHE?
Rosa Parks was a department store employee, a member of the NAACP, and a civil rights activist living in Montgomery, Alabama.

WHAT DID SHE DO?
Parks took in a seat in the rear "colored" section of a city bus. As the bus became crowded and all the seats reserved for white passengers were filled, the bus driver ordered Parks to give up her seat to a white man. She refused.

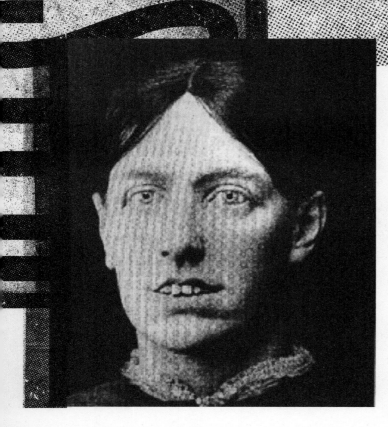

MARY PEARCEY

(1866–1890)

NATIONALITY
English

WHO WAS SHE?
Very little is known about Mary Pearcey's early life. In the 1880s, she was living in London with a furniture mover named Frank Hogg—they were not married. Frank had another lover, Phoebe Styles, whom he got pregnant. He left Mary and married Phoebe, who gave birth to a daughter the couple named Phoebe.

WHAT DID SHE DO?
In a jealous, vindictive rage, Mary Pearcey crushed the skull of Phoebe Hogg and smothered her 18-month-old child.

DATE OF ARREST
October 24, 1890

CIRCUMSTANCES OF THE ARREST
Pearcey was seen pushing a baby carriage after dark. When police searched her apartment they found bloodstained clothing.

THE CHARGE
Murder

THE SENTENCE
Pearcey was convicted and sentenced to be hanged.

AFTERWARD
Shortly after Mary Pearcey's execution, Madame Tussaud's wax museum added a wax figure of her to its collection—within days it attracted 30,000 visitors. In the 1930s, some criminologists suggested that Pearcey might have been Jack the Ripper, although there is no evidence to link her to those crimes.

LOUIS JAY PEARLMAN

(1954–)

NATIONALITY
American

WHO IS HE?
Louis Jay Pearlman was the impresario who created the Backstreet Boys, 'NSYNC, and O-Town.

WHAT DID HE DO?
Pearlman ran a Ponzi scheme that defrauded investors of $300 million. As his shady finances were exposed, Pearlman left the country.

DATE OF ARREST
June 14, 2007

CIRCUMSTANCES OF THE ARREST
German tourists recognized him in Indonesia and notified the authorities.

THE CHARGES
Bank fraud, mail fraud, and wire fraud

THE SENTENCE
Pearlman pled guilty and was sentenced to 25 years in prison.

UNUSUAL FACT
Louis Jay Pearlman's first cousin is the singer/songwriter Art Garfunkel.

Pixplanete/PR Photos

SEAN PENN

(1960–)

THE CHARGE
Assault

THE SENTENCE
Penn pled no contest to the charges. The judge sentenced him to three years' probation, ordered him to undergo 36 hours of anger management classes, and to perform 300 hours of community service. Penn was also ordered to stay at least 100 yards away from the photographer he assaulted.

NATIONALITY
American

WHO IS HE?
Sean Penn is an actor and left-wing political activist, known for his violent temper and his marriages to Madonna and Robin Wright. His films include *Fast Times at Ridgemont High, Dead Man Walking,* and *Into the Wild* (which he directed). Penn has won Oscars for his performances in *Mystic River* and *Milk.*

WHAT DID HE DO?
Penn is alleged to have punched and kicked a paparazzo, then smashed the man's camera.

DATE OF ARREST
February 19, 2010

TY PENNINGTON

(1964–)

NATIONALITY
American

WHO IS HE?
Ty Pennington is a carpenter who rose to fame on the TLC home improvement series *Trading Spaces*. He is the host of ABC Television's *Extreme Makeover: Home Edition*.

WHAT DID HE DO?
Police in West Los Angeles pulled Pennington over after observing him driving erratically.

DATE OF ARREST
May 5, 2007

THE CHARGE
Drunk driving

THE SENTENCE
Pennington pled guilty and was sentenced to 36 months' probation and fined $1,500. He was ordered to attend an alcohol education program.

THE SENTENCE

Perez's trial ended with a deadlocked jury. In a plea bargain, Perez pled guilty to stealing the cocaine for which he would receive a five-year prison sentence. In exchange for his testimony regarding criminal behavior in the CRASH unit, prosecutors granted Pérez immunity for everything short of murder.

AFTERWARD

Rafael Pérez was paroled after one year in prison. Pérez admitted that he had shot gang member Javier Ovando, then gave false testimony against Ovando in court. Pérez's confessions ultimately led to the overturning of more than 100 convictions. In 2000, the LAPD disbanded the CRASH unit and was sued for approximately $125 million by victims of the scandal.

RAFAEL PÉREZ
(1967–)

NATIONALITY
American

WHO IS HE?
Rafael Pérez was an officer of the Los Angeles Police Department assigned to the antigang unit, called CRASH.

WHAT DID HE DO?
Pérez stole six pounds of cocaine from the LAPD evidence locker and sold it for an estimated $800,000.

DATE OF ARREST
August 25, 1998

THE CHARGES
Possession of cocaine with intent to sell, grand theft, and forgery

SOPHIA PEROVSKAYA

(1854–1881)

NATIONALITY
Russian

WHO WAS SHE?
The daughter of the governor-general of St. Petersburg, Sophia Perovskaya was in her teens when she joined an organization dedicated to the overthrow of the monarchy in Russia. In 1878, she joined the People's Will, an extremist organization that advocated the use of terrorism to achieve their political aims.

WHAT DID SHE DO?
In 1879, Perovskaya was one of eight members of the People's Will plotting to assassinate Tsar Alexander II. On March 1, 1881, members of the People's Will trailed the tsar as he rode in his bulletproof carriage through St. Peterbsburg. Near the Catherine Canal, Perovskaya and three of her comrades, each armed with a homemade bomb, waited for the tsar. At a signal from Perovskaya, two of the terrorists threw their bombs, but they detonated among the Cossack guards rather than under the carriage. As Alexander climbed down to assist the wounded, a third terrorist ran forward, throwing his bomb at the tsar's feet. The blast killed the terrorist, and fatally wounded Alexander.

DATE OF ARREST
March 10, 1881

THE CHARGE
Regicide

THE SENTENCE
On April 3, 1881, one month and two days after they assassinated Alexander II, Perovskaya and the four surviving members of her band were hanged in St. Petersburg before a crowd of 80,000 spectators. None of the condemned expressed any remorse for having killed the tsar.

AFTERWARD
Revolutionary movements such as the People's Will culminated in 1917 with the Bolshevik Revolution that established a Communist government in Russia. In 1918, a troop of Communist soldiers killed Tsar Nicholas II, the grandson of Alexander II, along with his wife, his five children, and several family servants.

UNUSUAL FACT
Tsar Alexander II was the most progressive ruler Russia had seen since Peter the Great. He liberated the serfs, and promised his people a constitution. On the day of his assassination, he revealed to a friend, the Grand Duchess Catherine, that he had decided to implement representational government in Russia.

VINCENZO PERUGIA
(1881–1927)

NATIONALITY
Italian

WHO WAS HE?
Vincenzo Perugia was an Italian carpenter living in Paris who often worked at the Louvre.

WHAT DID HE DO?
On August 11, 1911, when the Louvre was closed to visitors, Perugia entered the museum with other work crews. He removed the *Mona Lisa* from the wall, took it out of its frame, and carried it back to his rented room, where he stored the painting in a trunk with a false bottom. In December 1913, Perugia took the *Mona Lisa* to Florence, Italy, where he informed the owner of an art gallery that he had the missing masterpiece. "I am an Italian patriot that was seized by the desire to return to my Italy one of the numerous treasures that Napoleon stole from her," he said.

THE SUSPECTS
Shortly after the theft, French investigators interviewed Perugia, but were convinced of his innocence. For a time, suspicion focused on Pablo Picasso, because once he had purchased some statuettes that had been stolen from the Louvre.

DATE OF ARREST
December 11, 1913

CIRCUMSTANCES OF THE ARREST
Perugia was arrested after he let the art dealer and a curator from the Uffizi Gallery take the *Mona Lisa* to the museum for further study.

THE CHARGE
Theft

THE SENTENCE
The Italian government refused to extradite Perugia to France. He was tried in Italy, found guilty, and sentenced to 1 year and 15 days in jail. Later the sentence was reduced to 7 months and 9 days.

AFTERWARD
After being put on display for several weeks in Italy, the *Mona Lisa* was returned to the Louvre. Italians hailed Vincenzo Perugia as a national hero, yet after his release he moved back to France, to a Paris suburb, where he operated a hardware store.

PHILIPPE PÉTAIN
(1856–1951)

NATIONALITY
French

WHO WAS HE?
Philippe Pétain was a career military man, who, during World War I, successfully defended the city of Verdun from an overwhelming German attack. He became a national hero, was named commander-in-chief of the French Army, and in 1918 was made a marshal of France. In the 1930s, he served as minister of war, secretary of state, and ambassador to Spain.

WHAT DID HE DO?
When the Nazis invaded France in 1940, Pétain, as vice premier of France, negotiated an armistice in which the Germans would occupy the north and west of France, while Pétain would rule the rest—known as Vichy France. After 1942, Pétain was reduced to a figurehead.

DATE OF ARREST
April 26, 1945

CIRCUMSTANCES OF THE ARREST
In 1944, the Nazis took Pétain and other members of the Vichy government to Germany. After the war he voluntarily returned to France to face his accusers.

THE CHARGE
Treason

THE SENTENCE
Pétain was found guilty of collaborating with the enemy and sentenced to death. Charles de Gaulle commuted the sentence to life in prison.

AFTERWARD
Pétain was confined in a prison on the Ile d'Yeu, off France's Atlantic coast. During his last years, he suffered from dementia. He died and is buried on the Ile d'Yeu.

a male fetus washed up on the shore of San Francisco Bay. The next day the body of a woman washed up about a mile away. DNA tests proved that the woman was Laci Peterson and the child was hers.

DATE OF ARREST
April 18, 2003

CIRCUMSTANCES OF THE ARREST
Police arrested Peterson in the parking lot of a golf course, where, he said, he was meeting his father and brother.

THE CHARGE
Murder

THE SENTENCE
Scott Peterson was convicted and sentenced to death by lethal injection.

AFTERWARD
As of 2010, the Peterson case had been appealed to California's Supreme Court.

SCOTT PETERSON
(1972–)

NATIONALITY
American

WHO IS HE?
Scott Peterson grew up in southern California, where his father owned a crate packaging company and his mother owned a clothing boutique.

WHAT DID HE DO?
Peterson murdered his wife, who was eight months' pregnant, then dumped her body in San Francisco Bay. On April 13, 2003, the body of

the Cathedral of Notre Dame in Paris and the pylons of the Sydney Harbour Bridge in Sydney, Australia.

WHAT DID HE DO?

Shortly after seven in the morning, Petit walked a steel cable tightrope stretched between the twin towers of New York's World Trade Center—a distance of 130 feet across, 1,350 feet above the street.

DATE OF ARREST

August 7, 1974

CIRCUMSTANCES OF THE ARREST

Port Authority police officers waited for Petit on the roof of the North Tower, but instead of stepping off the tightrope, he ran back out into the middle of the cable and performed a little dance routine.

THE CHARGES

Disorderly conduct and criminal trespass

THE SENTENCE

The judge dismissed the charges against Petit, but "sentenced" him to perform a high-wire act for children in Central Park.

AFTERWARD

The Port Authority presented Petit with a lifetime pass to the Observation Deck.

UNUSUAL FACT

To get the steel cable from one tower to the next, Petit used a bow and arrow.

PHILIPPE PETIT

(1948–)

NATIONALITY

French

WHO IS HE?

Philippe Petit was a street performer, adept at magic, juggling, and high-wire acts. In the early 1970s, he walked between the towers of

THE CHARGES

Driving under the influence of alcohol, driving while impaired by alcohol, violation of a license restriction, and failure to obey a traffic control device

THE SENTENCE

Phelps pled guilty and was sentenced to 18 months' probation. He was fined $250, plus $55 in court costs. The judge ordered him to abstain from alcohol and drugs during his probation, attend a Mothers Against Drunk Driving victim impact meeting, and speak at three Wicomico County schools about the dangers of alcohol.

AFTERWARD

In 2009, Phelps was photographed at a party smoking pot from a bong. Phelps was not charged, but he lost an endorsement contract with Kellogg's and the U.S. Olympic Swim Team barred him from swimming competitively for three months.

UNUSUAL FACT

The man who owned the bong Phelps used later tried to sell it on eBay for $100,000.

MICHAEL PHELPS

(1985–)

NATIONALITY

American

WHO IS HE?

Michael Phelps is an Olympic swimming champion who won six gold medals and two bronze medals at the Athens Olympics in 2004 and eight gold medals at the Beijing Olympics in 2008.

WHAT DID HE DO?

Phelps was drunk when he ran a stop sign in Salisbury, Maryland.

DATE OF ARREST

November 4, 2004

WHAT DID SHE DO?

While Phillips was going through security at Los Angeles International Airport, screeners found balloons and baggies filled with cocaine and heroin.

DATE OF ARREST

August 27, 2008

THE CHARGE

Possession of cocaine and heroin

THE SENTENCE

By court order, Phillips was sent to a drug rehab program.

AFTERWARD

In 2009, Phillips claimed that her father raped her when she was 19, and they had had an incestuous relationship for the next ten years.

BUST

MACKENZIE PHILLIPS

(1959–)

NATIONALITY

American

WHO IS SHE?

Mackenzie Phillips is the daughter of John Phillips of The Mamas and the Papas. She is an actress who starred in two popular TV sitcoms, *One Day at a Time* and *So Weird*. Since she was 12, she has had recurring troubles with drugs.

ROBERT WILLIAM PICKTON

(1949–)

DATE OF ARREST
February 22, 2002

THE CHARGE
Murder

THE SENTENCE
The judge divided the charges into two groups: There would be one trial for 6 of the murder charges, and a second trial for the remaining 20. Pickton was convicted of the six murders and sentenced to life in prison with no possibility of parole for 25 years. Prosecutors discontinued the trial for the other 20 murders, explaining that "Any additional convictions could not result in any increase to the sentence that Mr. Pickton has already received."

UNUSUAL FACT
In 2005, the Seattle punk rock band The Accused released a song inspired by Pickton, called "Hooker Fortified Pork Products," a reference to Pickton's claim that sometimes he ground up his victims with his pork to make sausage.

NATIONALITY
Canadian

WHO IS HE?
Robert Pickton raised pigs on a farm outside Port Coquitalm, British Columbia.

WHAT DID HE DO?
Pickton was charged with the murder of 26 women. During his trial, he told his cellmate (who was an undercover police officer) that he had killed 49 people.

ROMAN POLANSKI

(1933–)

NATIONALITY
Polish

WHO IS HE?
Roman Polanski is a film producer and director. He won an Oscar in 2002 for *The Pianist*.

WHAT DID HE DO?
In 1977, Polanski drove 13-year-old Samantha Geimer to actor Jack Nicholson's house, where he said he planned to take some modeling photos of her. He gave her champagne and a Quaalude, and when she was disoriented and unable to defend herself, he raped her.

DATE OF ARREST
March 11, 1977

THE CHARGE
Rape

THE SENTENCE
In a plea-bargain arrangement, Polanski pled guilty to unlawful sexual intercourse. He was ordered to undergo a 90-day psychiatric evaluation at a California prison. Polanski was released after 42 days. The judge in the case informed Polanski's attorneys that he was considering sentencing their client to jail time and deportation. Polanski fled to France, where he had citizenship.

AFTERWARD
In 2009, Samantha Geimer asked the court to dismiss the case against Polanski. "Every time this case is brought to the attention of the Court, great focus is made of me, my family, my mother, and others," she said. "That attention is not pleasant to experience." Geimer's request was denied. In October 2009, Swiss authorities arrested Polanski. U.S. authorities requested his extradition, but in July 2010, the Swiss government released Polanski, declaring him "a free man."

NICOLE "SNOOKI" POLIZZI
(1987–)

NATIONALITY
American

WHO IS SHE?
Snooki is a cast member of the reality TV series, *Jersey Shore*. She claims that she invented a hairstyle she calls, "the friggin' poof."

WHAT DID SHE DO?
Snooki was drunk in public at 3:00 in the afternoon.

DATE OF ARREST
July 30, 2010

CIRCUMSTANCES OF THE ARREST
Police cuffed Snooki and escorted her to the squad car. She was wearing a T-shirt emblazoned with the word, *SLUT*.

THE CHARGE
Disorderly conduct

THE SENTENCE
Snooki was sentenced to two days of community service and fined $500.

AFTERWARD
Snooki published a novel fictionalizing her quest for love and romance on the Jersey Shore, titled *A Shore Thing*.

JONATHAN POLLARD

(1954–)

NATIONALITY
American

WHO IS HE?
Jonathan Pollard held intelligence service jobs at the CIA, the U.S. Navy, and the Naval Investigative Service.

WHAT DID HE DO?
Beginning in 1984, Pollard passed classified U.S. documents to Israel. His Israeli handlers gave him $10,000 and a diamond and sapphire ring, and a monthly stipend of $1,500. The extent of damage caused by Pollard is considered classified, and has never been disclosed, although Secretary of Defense Caspar Weinberger summarized the damage in a 46-page memo and gave it to the judge trying the Pollard case.

DATE OF ARREST
November 1985

CIRCUMSTANCES OF THE ARREST
Once the FBI became aware of Pollard's activities, he and his wife Anne sought asylum at the Israeli Embassy, but guards turned them away. FBI agents arrested the Pollards as soon as they left embassy property.

THE CHARGE
Espionage

THE SENTENCE
Pollard was sentenced to life in prison. For trying to conceal 70 pounds of stolen classified documents, Anne Pollard was sentenced to five years in prison.

AFTERWARD
In 1995, Israel granted Pollard citizenship. Influential Israelis, including Prime Minister Benjamin Netanyahu, have urged successive U.S. presidents to pardon Pollard, without success.

CHARLES PONZI

(1882–1949)

NATIONALITY
Italian-born American citizen

WHO WAS HE?
Charles Ponzi was an Italian immigrant to the United States who worked at a variety of low-paying jobs—dishwasher, typist, translator. Then, in 1919, he founded the Security Exchange Company in Boston.

WHAT DID HE DO?
Ponzi promised investors a 50 percent return on their money in 45 days or 100 percent profit in 90 days. He sold them promissory notes in denominations ranging from $10 to $50,000. So many new investors came forward that Ponzi could pay the exaggerated "profits" to his original investors. When the payouts surpassed new investments, the scheme collapsed. There is no accurate estimate of how many millions Ponzi's investors lost.

DATE OF ARREST
August 12, 1920

CIRCUMSTANCES OF THE ARREST
Ponzi turned himself in.

THE CHARGE
Mail fraud (because Ponzi used the U.S. Postal Service to send false information to his investors regarding the state of their portfolios)

THE SENTENCE
Ponzi pled guilty and was sentenced to five years in prison; he was released after three-and-a-half years.

AFTERWARD
Upon his release, the commonwealth of Massachusetts arrested Ponzi for larceny; he was found guilty, but he appealed his conviction. Released on bail, he went to Florida, where he started a new scam, selling swampland to gullible real estate investors. He was arrested and sentenced to a year in prison. He appealed again, was released on bail again, and tried to flee the country. Ponzi was caught and returned to Massachusetts, where he served seven years in prison. When his sentence was up, the U.S. government deported him to Italy. Ultimately, Ponzi settled in Brazil, where he died in a charity hospital.

PAULA POUNDSTONE

(1959–)

NATIONALITY
American

WHO IS SHE?
Paula Poundstone is a comedian who won the American Comedy Award in 1989 and starred in *The Paula Poundstone Show,* a TV sitcom. She became a foster parent for eight disadvantaged children, eventually adopting four of them.

WHAT DID SHE DO?
While drunk, Poundstone drove three of her children and two foster children, ages 2–12, to an ice cream stand. Prosecutors also charged her with "inappropriate touching."

DATE OF ARREST
June 27, 2001

CIRCUMSTANCES OF THE ARREST
Poundstone was released after posting a $200,000 bond.

THE CHARGES
Lewd acts upon a child and child abuse

THE SENTENCE
Poundstone pled no contest to one count of felony child abuse and a misdemeanor charge of inflicting injury upon a child. She was sentenced to five years' probation. The judge ordered her to enroll in a drug treatment program and forbade her to ever again be a foster parent.

AFTERWARD
Poundstone regained custody of her three adopted children but the two foster children were taken from her.

LEWIS POWELL

(1844–1865), GEORGE ATZERODT (1835–1865), DAVID HEROLD (1842–1865), AND MARY SURRATT (1823–1865)

NATIONALITIES
American (Powell, Herold, and Surratt) and German (Atzerodt)

WHO WERE THEY?
Lewis Powell was a Confederate veteran. At the Battle of Gettysburg, he was wounded and captured, but he romanced a nurse who helped him escape. He went to Washington as a spy, where he met John Wilkes Booth and joined the conspiracy to assassinate Abraham Lincoln. George Atzerodt was an immigrant from Germany who ferried Confederate agents back and forth across the Potomac River. David Herold was a clerk at the Washington Navy Yard. Mary Surratt owned a tavern in Maryland and operated a boardinghouse in Washington, where Booth and the other conspirators met frequently.

WHAT DID THEY DO?
On the night Booth went to Ford's Theatre to assassinate Lincoln, Powell went to assassinate Secretary of State William Seward. He forced his way into the Seward home, pistol-whipped Seward's son Frederick, then repeatedly stabbed the secretary of state with a knife. Herold waited outside with Powell's getaway horse. Atzerodt got drunk, lost his nerve, and never attempted to kill Andrew Johnson, as was planned. Surratt took a cache of carbines, pistols, and field glasses to her tavern for the conspirators.

DATES OF ARRESTS
Powell and Surratt: April 17, 1865
Atzerodt: April 20, 1865
Herold: April 26, 1865

CIRCUMSTANCES OF THE ARRESTS
Powell laid low for three days, then went to the home of Mary Surratt. He arrived just as she was being arrested. Although they did not know he was the man who had attacked Seward, the authorities arrested Powell, too. Authorities picked up Atzerodt at his cousin's house in Germantown, Maryland. Union troops cornered Herold and Booth at the Garret Farm near Port Royal, Virginia. Herold surrendered, but Booth, who would not give up, was shot and killed.

THE CHARGE
Conspiracy to commit murder and treason

THE SENTENCE
A military tribunal found the four conspirators guilty and sentenced them to death.

AFTERWARD
Powell, Herold, Atzerodt, and Surratt were all hanged simultaneously on a specially constructed gallows in Washington, D.C.

UNUSUAL FACT
In 1992, Powell's skull was discovered in the anthroplogy department of the Smithsonian Institution. It was sent to Geneva Cemetery in Seminole County, Florida, where it was buried with the rest of his remains.

FRANCIS GARY POWERS

(1929–1977)

NATIONALITY
American

WHO WAS HE?
Francis Gary Powers was a captain in the U.S Air Force who was recruited by the CIA for espionage missions. The CIA used U-2 aircraft to photograph military installations and other sites of strategic importance in the Soviet Union.

WHAT DID HE DO?
In 1960, Powers was flying a spy mission over Sverdlovski. When his plane was hit by a missile, Powers bailed out. He was captured almost immediately after he hit the ground.

DATE OF ARREST
May 1, 1960

THE CHARGE
Espionage

THE SENTENCE
After being interrogated by agents of the KGB for several months, Powers confessed to spying on the Soviet Union. He was sentenced to ten years in prison.

AFTERWARD
In 1962, Powers and another American prisoner of the Soviets were exchanged for Vilyam Fisher, a KGB colonel imprisoned in Germany. Back in the United States, Powers took a job as a test pilot for Lockheed, and then as helicopter traffic reporter for a Los Angeles radio station. He was killed in a helicopter crash in 1977.

GAVRILO PRINCIP

(1894–1918)

NATIONALITY
Bosnian Serb

WHO WAS HE?
Gavrilo Princip was the son of a postman. He joined a revolutionary organization that called for the independence of Serbia, Croatia, and Bosnia from the Austro-Hungarian Empire.

WHAT DID HE DO?
In June 1914, the heir to the Austro-Hungarian throne, Crown Prince Franz Ferdinand and his wife Countess Sophie, visited Sarajevo. While driving down a Sarajevo street, the imperial couple's car stalled. Princip ran forward and shot and killed them both.

DATE OF ARREST
June 28, 1914

CIRCUMSTANCES OF THE ARREST
At the scene, Princip swallowed a cyanide capsule, but it had expired and only made him ill. He tried to shoot himself, but arresting officers pried the pistol from his hand.

THE CHARGE
Assassination

THE SENTENCE
As he was 19—underage under Austro-Hungarian law for the death penalty—he was given the maximum sentence for his age group, 20 years in prison.

AFTERWARD
Princip contracted tuberculosis in prison. The disease spread to the bone of one arm, requiring amputation. He died soon after the surgery.

CIRCUMSTANCES OF THE ARREST
Police arrested Puck at the hospital, but did not take him to jail because of the serious nature of his injuries.

THE CHARGES
Driving under the influence, child endangerment, and driving without a license

SENTENCE
As of December 2010, Puck's case had not yet gone to court.

PUCK (DAVID RAINEY)
(1968–)

NATIONALITY
American

WHO IS HE?
Puck was a member of the cast of MTV's *The Real World: San Francisco* (1994). His aggressive, sometimes hostile behavior led the other members of the cast to vote to evict him from the house.

WHAT DID HE DO?
Police alleged that Puck was drunk when he drove his car off the road and down an embankment. Puck sustained several broken bones. His eight-year-old son was in the car and suffered minor injuries.

DATE OF ARREST
March 24, 2010

WHAT DID HE DO?

Rahman Al-Amoudi made frequent trips to Libya, where he received funds from the Libyan government, which he did not report on his tax returns. He was affiliated with Mousa Abu Marzook, a leader of Hamas. He was part of a failed conspiracy to assassinate Saudi Crown Prince Abdullah.

DATE OF ARREST

September 23, 2003

THE CHARGES

Illegal financial transactions, conspiracy to assassinate, and unlawful procurement of U.S. citizenship

THE SENTENCE

Rahman Al-Amoudi was convicted, sentenced to 23 years in prison, and fined $750,000. In addition, his U.S. citizenship was revoked.

UNUSUAL FACT

At the time of Rahman Al-Amoudi's arrest, federal authorities confiscated his Palm Pilot. Later, they found that it contained contact information for seven known terrorists.

ABDUL RAHMAN AL-AMOUDI

NATIONALITY

Yemeni-born U.S. citizen

WHO IS HE?

Abdul Rahman Al-Amoudi founded the American Muslim Council, the American Muslim Foundation, and the American Armed Forces and Veterans Affairs Council. He has been an advocate for Muslim issues in the United States, an adviser to the Pentagon, and he has helped find Muslim chaplains for the U.S. armed services. His political connections include the Clintons, George W. Bush, and Members of Congress.

BRUCE RAISLEY

(1961–)

NATIONALITY
American

WHO IS HE?
Bruce Raisley is a computer programmer from Pennsylvania who, for a time, was a volunteer for Perverted Justice, a vigilante, online sting operation in which volunteers posed as children or teens to attract pedophiles and sexual predators. Once the "minor" and the predator had established an online relationship, Perverted Justice posted the predator's name and other information on its Web site. It is alleged that Raisley had a falling-out with Perverted Justice after the organization published a photo of his son online to lure predators. After this, Raisley became an outspoken critic of Perverted Justice and its founder, Xavier Von Erck. Von Erck retaliated by posing as a woman named "Holly" and initiating an online relationship with Raisley, which escalated until Raisley agreed to leave his wife for "Holly."

WHAT DID HE DO?
In 2006, *Radar* magazine and, in 2007, *Rolling Stone* published articles about Perverted Justice and its questionable methods; both stories recounted how "Holly" had duped Raisley. To eradicate the articles from the Web, Raisley launched a computer virus that attacked 100,000 computers that had tried to access the magazine stories. The computers at *Radar, Rolling Stone,* and Perverted Justice were among those affected, costing the companies about $100,000 in damages.

DATE OF ARREST
June 29, 2009

THE CHARGE
Intentionally causing damage to a protected computer

THE SENTENCE
Bruce Raisley was found guilty in September 2010. He could be sentenced to 10 years in prison, to pay a fine of $250,000, and to make restitution to his victims.

WHAT DID HE DO?

Between June 1984 and August 1985, Ramirez murdered at least 30 people, most of them women, many of them elderly people or children. Often, he raped and tortured his victims. The news media referred to him as "the Night Stalker."

DATE OF ARREST

August 29, 1985

CIRCUMSTANCES OF THE ARREST

Based on clues that he had left behind and descriptions from survivors of his attacks, in late August 1985, police determined that Richard Ramirez was "the Night Stalker." They published his photograph in English- and Spanish-language newspapers. When owners of a bodega recognized him, Ramírez ran into a residential neighborhood to steal a getaway car. He tried to steal a Ford Mustang, but the car's owner and his neighbors chased Ramírez and held him down until the police arrived.

THE CHARGES

Murder, attempted murder, sexual assault, and burglary

THE SENTENCE

Ramírez was found guilty and given the death penalty. As of 2010, he was still sitting on death row.

RICHARD RAMÍREZ, "THE NIGHT STALKER"

(1960–)

NATIONALITY

American

WHO IS HE?

Richard Ramírez's parents emigrated to the United States from Mexico. As a child he was obsessed with death and violence—at age 13, he stood by and watched as his cousin murdered the cousin's wife. In his teens, Ramirez became a drug addict.

EDWIN RAMOS

(1986–)

NATIONALITY
El Salvadoran

WHO IS HE?
Edwin Ramos is an illegal immigrant from El Salvador who settled in San Francisco. He is a member of the Mara Salvatrucha (MS-13) and Sureño gangs.

WHAT DID HE DO?
In 2008, Ramos killed Tony Bologna and his two sons, Michael, 20 and Matthew, 16, in a drive-by shooting. Ramos mistook one of the Bologna boys as a member of a rival gang who had shot and killed a member of MS-13.

DATE OF ARREST
June 25, 2008

CIRCUMSTANCES OF THE ARREST
A member of MS-13 told the San Francisco police that Ramos had murdered the Bolognas.

THE CHARGE
Murder

THE SENTENCE
As of 2010, Edwin Ramos was still awaiting trial.

UNUSUAL FACT
In 2004, Ramos was convicted of attempted robbery, but he was not deported because he was protected by San Francisco's "sanctuary city" policy, which barred city officials from assisting federal authorities in rounding up illegal immigrants. In response to a public outcry—led by the Bologna family—Mayor Gavin Newsom modified the sanctuary policy to exclude felons.

WHAT DID THEY DO?
In March 2004, Rasovic entered Le Supre-Diamant Couture De Maki, in Tokyo and walked off with the Countess of Vendome Necklace, worth $30 million. Rasovic stole the necklace; Panajotovic acted as a lookout.

DATE OF ARREST
June 2005

THE CHARGE
Robbery

THE SENTENCE
A Serbian court found Rasovic and Panajotovic guilty and sentenced them to six years and six months in prison.

UNUSUAL FACT
Pink Panther robberies are usually carried out in daylight, during business hours. The gang members smash glass display cases and brandish weapons, but they have never wounded or killed anyone.

DJORDJIJE RASOVIC
(1945–)
AND
SNEZANA PANAJOTOVIC
(1983–)

NATIONALITY
Serbian

WHO ARE THEY?
Djordjije Rasovic and Snezana Panajotovic are members of the Pink Panthers, a gang of jewel thieves numbering more than 150 men and a few women, almost all of whom hail from the city of Nis in Serbia. Since the late 1990s, the Pink Panthers have robbed more than 100 jewelry stores in the Middle East, the United States, Japan, London, Paris, and Monaco. Their overall take is estimated at $140 million.

LOU RAWLS

(1933–2006)

NATIONALITY
American

WHO WAS HE?
Lou Rawls was a singer whose smooth vocals embraced R&B, blues, soul, and jazz. He recorded dozens of albums and is believed to have sold 40 million records. His Billboard Top 50 singles included "Love Is a Hurtin' Thing" and "You'll Never Find."

WHAT DID HE DO?
During an argument with his girlfriend, Rawls shoved her.

DATE OF ARREST
January 2003

THE CHARGE
Battery

THE SENTENCE
The charge was dropped after prosecutors stated that there was insufficient evidence to proceed with the case.

UNUSUAL FACT
Lou Rawls was a guest performer during the first season of *Sesame Street*. He sang the alphabet.

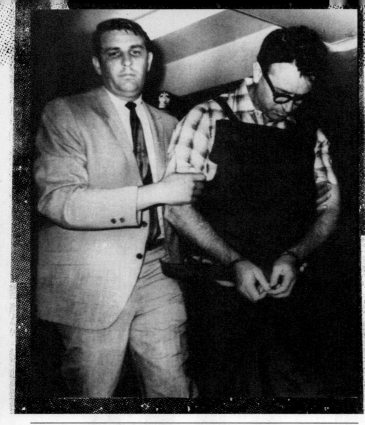

JAMES EARL RAY

(1928–1998)

NATIONALITY
American

WHO WAS HE?
James Earl Ray was a career criminal who did 20 years in prison for crimes ranging from mail fraud to armed robbery. In 1967, in a rare effort to go straight, Ray moved to Mexico to direct porn flicks.

WHAT DID HE DO?
In Memphis, Tennessee, on April 4, 1968, Ray shot and killed Dr. Martin Luther King Jr., while the civil rights leader was standing on the balcony of the Lorraine Motel.

DATE OF ARREST
June 8, 1968

CIRCUMSTANCES OF THE ARREST
Ray got out of the United States and flew to England. At London's Heathrow Airport, he was arrested for attempting to use a false Canadian passport.

THE CHARGE
Murder

THE SENTENCE
Ray confessed that he had killed Dr. King. He was sentenced to 99 years in prison. Three days later, he retracted his confession.

AFTERWARD
In 1977, Ray and six other inmates escaped from the Brushy Mountain State Penitentiary in Tennessee. They were captured two days later, and a year was added to Ray's sentence.

UNUSUAL FACT
In prison, Ray insisted that he had nothing to do with the assassination and claimed that King had been the victim of a conspiracy and a government cover-up. In 1997, King's son, Dexter King, met with Ray to tell him that the King family believed he was innocent. Nonetheless, the state denied Ray a new trial, and he died in prison.

DATE OF ARREST
September 1925

CIRCUMSTANCES OF THE ARREST
Reilly received an invitation from an anti-Bolshevik group in Russia to meet their agents at the Finnish border. The agents were actually members of the Bolshevik intelligence service; the moment Reilly stepped across the border into Russia he was arrested and taken to the Lubyanka Prison for interrogation.

THE CHARGE
Espionage

THE SENTENCE
Reilly had no trial. After two months of interrogation, he was taken to a forest outside Moscow and shot.

SIDNEY REILLY

(1873/74–1925)

NATIONALITY
Russian or Ukrainian

WHO WAS HE?
"The Ace of Spies" and the model for Ian Fleming's James Bond, Sidney Reilly (he was probably born Shlomo Rosenblum) emigrated to England and joined the British intelligence service. He spied on Germany in the years leading up to World War I, and during the war itself.

WHAT DID HE DO?
In 1918, Reilly hatched a scheme (unsuccessful) to assassinate Lenin and bring down Russia's fledgling Bolshevik government.

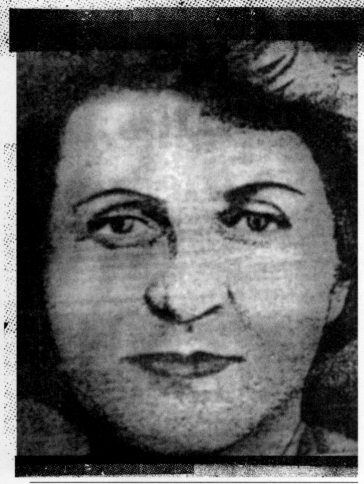

MARTHA RENDELL

(1871–1909)

NATIONALITY
Australian

WHO WAS SHE?
Very little information survives concerning Martha Rendell. She lived in Western Australia with Thomas Nicholls Morris (they were not married) and Morris's children. Her neighbors said she was a cruel woman, who treated her four stepchildren brutally and appeared to enjoy seeing them terrified and in pain.

WHAT DID SHE DO?
Rendell killed three of her stepchildren by repeatedly swabbing their throats with hydrochloric acid. She murdered 7-year-old Annie first, then 5-year-old Olive, then 14-year-old Arthur. When she tried to kill 14-year-old George, the last surviving child, he ran to his mother's house several blocks away.

DATE OF ARREST
July 1909

CIRCUMSTANCES OF THE ARREST
George accused Rendell of killing his sisters and brother with "spirits of salts," as hydrochloric acid was known at the time. Police exhumed the children's bodies and found traces of the acid still present in their throat tissue.

THE CHARGE
Murder

THE SENTENCE
Rendell was found guilty and sentenced to death. She was hanged in Fremantle Prison.

UNUSUAL FACT
It is said that the ghost of Martha Rendell haunts the prison chapel, where she is always seen looking out a window.

WHAT DID HE DO?

Rezko used his influence with Blagojevich and top aides in the Blagojevich adminstration to get jobs, contracts with the state of Illinois, and favors for his associates. In return, the associates gave Rezko what has been estimated as millions of dollars in kickbacks or in donations to Blagojevich's campaign fund.

DATE OF ARREST

October 11, 2006

THE CHARGES

Bribery, fraud, and money laundering

THE SENTENCE

Rezko was found guilty; he could be sentenced to 210 years in prison. Rezko's sentencing has been postponed because, it is believed, he is cooperating with prosecutors in order to reduce his time in prison.

ANTOIN "TONY" REZKO

(1955–)

NATIONALITY

American

WHO IS HE?

Tony Rezko is a Chicago restaurant and real estate developer who was also a donor and fund-raiser for Rod Balgojevich and Barack Obama.

DENNIS RODMAN

(1961–)

NATIONALITY
American

WHO IS HE?
Dennis Rodman is a retired professional basketball player who played for the Detroit Pistons, the San Antonio Spurs, the Chicago Bulls, the Los Angeles Lakers, and the Dallas Mavericks. He was voted NBA Defensive Player of the Year twice, and NBA All-Defensive First Team seven times.

WHAT DID HE DO?
In their hotel room in Century City, California, after a night of heavy drinking, Rodman got into an argument with his girlfriend. He grabbed her arm and squeezed, leaving a bruise.

DATE OF ARREST
April 30, 2008

CIRCUMSTANCES OF THE ARREST
Hotel security called the police.

THE CHARGE
Domestic violence

THE SENTENCE
Rodman pled no contest to spousal battery. He was put on three years' probation, required to attend a domestic violence counseling program for one year, and required to perform 45 hours of community service.

AFTERWARD
Rodman is a part-time professional wrestler. He has appeared on reality TV series, such as *Celebrity Apprentice*.

WHAT DID HE DO?

Nicholas II was an autocrat who refused to democratize Russia, permit labor unions, or improve the living and working conditions of the poor. Political dissidents were exiled to Siberia; protesters were shot in the street. Nicholas's decision to enter World War I brought down his dynasty: Shortages of food and fuel in the cities, combined with reports of major defeats and shocking casualties, led to the Russian Revolution.

DATE OF ARREST

March 15, 1917

CIRCUMSTANCES OF THE ARREST

The Romanovs were placed under house arrest in the Alexander Palace outside St. Petersburg, then transported to the town of Ekaterinburg in the Urals.

THE CHARGE

Crimes against the Russian people

THE SENTENCE

The entire family, with several servants, were executed by a Bolshevik firing squad in the basement of a house in Ekaterinburg.

AFTERWARD

The bodies were buried in the nearby forest. The remains of most of the family were discovered in 1991; the remains of Anastasia and Alexis were found in 2007.

THE ROMANOVS:

NICHOLAS II (1868–1918), ALEXANDRA (1872–1918), OLGA (1895–1918), TATIANA (1897–1918), MARIA (1899–1918), ANASTASIA (1901–1918), AND ALEXIS (1904–1918)

NATIONALITY

Russian and German

WHO WERE THEY?

Nicholas II and his German-born wife, Alexandra, were the last tsar and tsarina of Russia. Olga, Maria, Tatiana, Anastasia, and Alexis were their children. The Romanov dynasty had ruled Russia for over 300 years.

AXL ROSE
(WILLIAM BRUCE ROSE JR.)
(1962–)

NATIONALITY
American

WHO IS HE?
Axl Rose is the lead vocalist of the rock band Guns N'Roses.

WHAT DID HE DO?
At an airport in Phoenix, Arizona, Rose refused to let a security screener search his carry-on bag. "I'll punch your lights out right here and right now. I don't give a fuck who you are. You are all little people on a power trip."

DATE OF ARREST
February 1998

CIRCUMSTANCES OF THE ARREST
Rose was arrested at the scene.

THE CHARGE
Disturbing the peace

THE SENTENCE
Rose pled guilty and was fined $500.

AFTERWARD
Rose has had several run-ins with the law since this incident. In 2006, at a hotel in Stockholm, Sweden, Rose bit a security guard's leg. In 2009, he punched a photographer in the face.

PRISON   MONTREAL

D 102646   25 6 68

PAUL ROSE

(1943–)

NATIONALITY
Canadian

WHO IS HE?
Paul Rose was born in Montreal. He became a professor of French and mathematics and also taught special education classes for children. In the 1960s, he became involved in the Quebec nationalist movement that called for the province's independence from Canada.

WHAT DID HE DO?
In October 1970, with other members of le Front de Libération du Québec (FLQ), Rose kidnapped the provincial minister, Pierre Laporte, and a British diplomat, James Richard Cross, setting off what became known as the October Crisis. In response to the abductions, the Canadian government promulgated the War Measures Act, which curtailed civil rights and granted to the federal government greater freedom of action to respond to a state of emergency, such as a war, acts of terrorism, or an insurrection. The day after the act was adopted, Rose killed Laporte.

DATE OF ARREST
December 28, 1970

CIRCUMSTANCES OF THE ARREST
Marc Charbonneau, who had kidnapped Cross, negotiated a deal with the Canadian government: In exchange for releasing Cross, the authorities would permit Charbonneau to go into exile in Cuba. Because he had killed Laporte, Rose was offered no such deal.

THE CHARGE
Murder

THE SENTENCE
On March 13, 1971, Rose was found guilty and sentenced to life in prison.

AFTERWARD
Charbonneau returned to Canada in 1981. He was arrested, charged with abduction, and sentenced to 20 months in prison.

WHAT DID HE DO?

Rose distributed Gamma-Butyrolactone (GBL) to teammates on the Chattanooga Lookouts baseball team. GBL is a cleaning solvent, but when it is taken orally, the body converts it to Gamma-Hydroxybutyric Acid (GHB), which is a steroid substitute.

DATE OF ARREST

November 3, 2005

THE CHARGE

Drug trafficking

THE SENTENCE

Rose was found guilty and sentenced to one month in prison and five months of house arrest.

PETE ROSE JR.

(1969–)

NATIONALITY

American

WHO IS HE?

The son of major league slugger Pete Rose, Rose Jr. is a former professional baseball player who spent most of his career in the minor leagues, except for a period in 1997 when he played with his father's team, the Cincinnati Reds.

TOKYO ROSE
(IVA TOGURI D'AQUINO)
(1916–2006)
AND
AXIS SALLY (MILDRED GILLARS)
(1900–1988)

NATIONALITY
American

WHO WERE THEY?
Iva Toguri was born in Los Angeles; her parents were immigrants from Japan. When Japan attacked Pearl Harbor on December 7, 1941, Toguri was in Japan, visiting relatives. Mildred Gillars was born in Portland, Maine. When Germany declared war on the United States in 1941, Gillars was living in Berlin, teaching English at the Berlitz School.

WHAT DID THEY DO?
In 1943, Toguri took a job as a broadcaster on an English-language radio station. Other presenters were Allied POWs who had been coerced into broadcasting pro-Japanese propaganda. In 1942, Gillars began broadcasting anti-American propaganda to troops in Europe.

DATES OF ARRESTS
Toguri: September 5, 1945
Gillars: March 15, 1946

CIRCUMSTANCES OF THE ARRESTS
Two reporters for *Cosmopolitan* magazine offered Toguri $2,000 for an interview. It was a sting operation: When she arrived for the interview, she was arrested. Gillars was arrested at her home in Berlin.

THE CHARGE
Treason

THE SENTENCE
Toguri was tried in San Francisco and found guilty. She was sentenced to 10 years in prison and fined $10,000. She was paroled 6 years later. Gillars was sentenced to 10–30 years in prison and fined $10,000. She was released in 1961, after serving 12 years.

AFTERWARD
In 1976, an investigative reporter for the *Chicago Tribune* revealed that two of the prosecution's star witnesses had lied under oath about Toguri's broadcasts. In 1977, President Gerald Ford granted Toguri a full pardon. After her release, Gillars went to live at a Catholic convent in Columbus, Ohio, and taught German and French at a Catholic school.

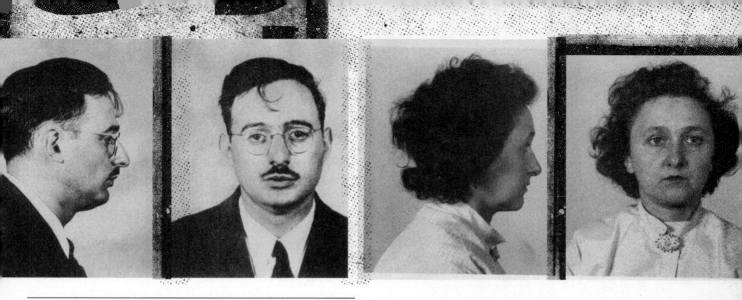

JULIUS ROSENBERG

(1918–1953)

AND

ETHEL ROSENBERG

(1915–1953)

NATIONALITY

American

WHO WERE THEY?

Julius and Ethel Rosenberg both grew up on New York's Lower East Side. Sometime between 1932 and 1935, they both joined the Communist Party. The couple married in 1939.

WHAT DID THEY DO?

The Rosenbergs were part of a conspiracy to pass classified U.S. military material—particularly about America's atomic weapons program—to the Soviet Union.

DATES OF ARRESTS

Julius: June 16, 1950
Ethel: August 11, 1950

THE CHARGE

Espionage

THE SENTENCE

The Rosenbergs were convicted and sentenced to death by electrocution. They appealed to President Dwight D. Eisenhower for executive clemency—he rejected the appeal.

AFTERWARD

The Rosenbergs' two sons, Michael and Robert, were adopted by the Meeropol family, who were not related to the Rosenbergs. In 2008, they issued a statement that they believed their father probably was guilty of espionage.

DIANA ROSS

(1944–)

NATIONALITY
American

WHO IS SHE?
One of the most successful female singers of the 1970s and 1980s, Diana Ross was the lead singer of The Supremes before she began her solo career. She has sold over 150 million albums.

WHAT DID SHE DO?
Breathalyzer tests registered Ross's blood alcohol level at three times the state of Arizona's maximum of .08. She was unable to tell the police officers the date or time, nor could she write the alphabet in order. The police report described Ross as a case of "extreme DUI."

DATE OF ARREST
December 30, 2002

CIRCUMSTANCES OF THE ARREST
Police received a report of a white Pontiac going in the wrong direction on a one-way street. They found the car, and Ross, in the parking lot of a closed Blockbuster video rental store.

THE CHARGE
DUI

THE SENTENCE
Ross was sentenced to two days in jail and one year of unsupervised probation.

AFTERWARD
In 1993, the *Guinness Book of World Records* listed Ross as the most successful female musical artist in history. In 2007, she was presented with a John F. Kennedy Center for the Performing Arts Honors Award.

DAN ROSTENKOWSKI

(1928–2010)

DATE OF INDICTMENT
May 31, 1994

THE CHARGES
Mail fraud and obstruction of justice

THE SENTENCE
In a plea bargain, Rostenkowski pled guilty to mail fraud. He was sentenced to 15 months in prison and 2 months in a halfway house, and he was fined $100,000.

AFTERWARD
Once he was out of prison, Rostenkowski worked as a political commentator for a Chicago TV station. In 2000, President Bill Clinton pardoned Rostenkowski.

NATIONALITY
American

WHO WAS HE?
Dan Rostenkowski was a Chicago Democrat who served in the House of Representatives from 1958 to 1994. He was a member of the powerful House Ways and Means Committee for 36 years, and its chairman from 1981 to 1994.

WHAT DID HE DO?
Rostenkowski traded food stamp vouchers for $50,000 in cash, padded his payroll with 14 employees who did little or no work, and used $70,000 of House funds to pay for his personal automobiles.

CARLTON ROTACH

(1989–)

DATE OF ARREST
July 25, 2010

THE CHARGE
Complicity in kidnapping

CIRCUMSTANCES OF THE ARREST
Posing as members of the security company, police contacted Rotach and set up a meeting to discuss the details of the kidnapping. When Rotach arrived, he was placed under arrest.

THE SENTENCE
Pending trial, Rotach was held on $1 million bail.

NATIONALITY
American

WHO IS HE?
Rotach lives in Columbus, Ohio. He did time in Florida for battery and burglary.

WHAT DID HE DO?
Rotach tried to hire a security company to kidnap and hold for ransom a 30-year-old woman who was a former colleague. (The woman had filed a complaint with the police in May that Rotach was stalking her.)

MICKEY ROURKE

(1952–)

NATIONALITY
American

WHO IS HE?
Mickey Rourke is a boxer turned actor. After starring in *Diner, Rumble Fish,* and *Barfly* in the 1980s, Rourke's career fell apart. He won new respect from audiences and critics with the 2008 film *The Wrestler,* for which he won a Golden Globe and a BAFTA.

WHAT DID HE DO?
About four in the morning Rourke, with an unidentified woman, left a Miami Beach nightclub, climbed on his Vespa scooter, and made an illegal U-turn in front of a police cruiser.

DATE OF ARREST
November 6, 2007

CIRCUMSTANCES OF THE ARREST
Rourke said to the arresting officer, "What the fuck did I do? I'm not drunk, I didn't even drink that much."

THE CHARGE
DUI

THE SENTENCE
Rourke was found guilty of a lesser charge of reckless driving. He was sentenced to 50 hours of community service, in addition to paying a fine and legal costs of $1,178.75.

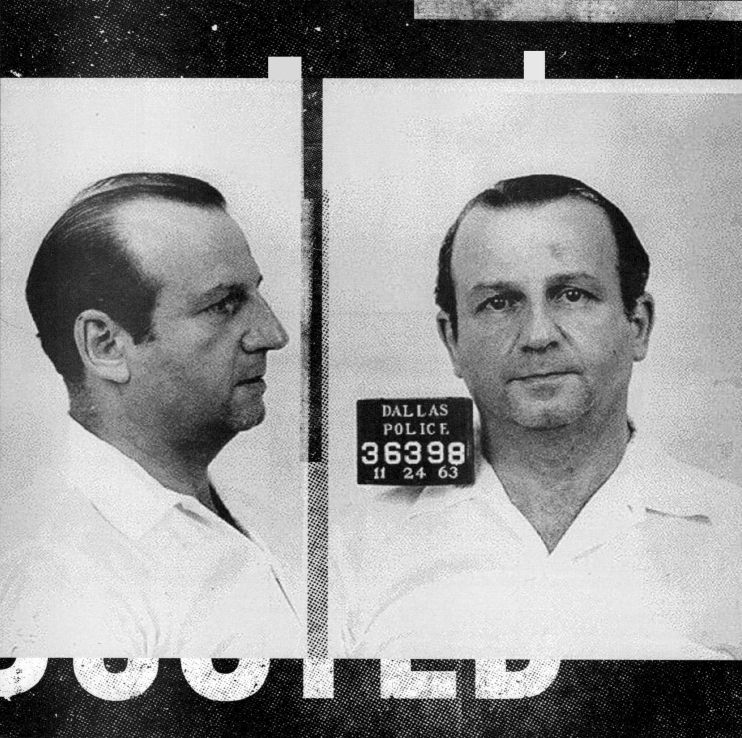

DALLAS
POLICE
36398
11 24 63

JACK RUBY

(1911–1967)

NATIONALITY
American

WHO WAS HE?
Jack Ruby owned a nightclub in Dallas, Texas. Between 1949 and 1962, he had been arrested seven times for disturbing the peace, carrying a concealed weapon, and permitting dancing at his club after hours.

WHAT DID HE DO?
On November 24, 1963, as police were transferring Lee Harvey Oswald, the assassin of John F. Kennedy, to the county jail, Ruby shot and killed Oswald at point-blank range.

DATE OF ARREST
November 24, 1963

CIRCUMSTANCES OF THE ARREST
Police seized Ruby at the scene.

THE CHARGE
Murder

THE SENTENCE
Ruby was found guilty and given the death penalty.

AFTERWARD
Ruby tried to persuade Chief Justice Earl Warren, chairman of the Warren Commission investigating the JFK assassination, to take him to Washington so he could tell President Lyndon Johnson that he had not been part of a conspiracy to kill Kennedy. Warren informed Ruby that he could not be released from prison to make his plea in person.

UNUSUAL FACT
Before he could be executed, Ruby died in prison of lung cancer.

WINONA RYDER

(1971–)

NATIONALITY
American

WHO IS SHE?
Winona Ryder is an actress who has been nominated for two Oscars—
for *The Age of Innocence* and *Little Women*.

WHAT DID SHE DO?
At Saks in Beverly Hills, California, Ryder paid for 4 garments, but
shoplifted another 20, worth a total of $5,500.

DATE OF ARREST
December 12, 2001

CIRCUMSTANCES OF THE ARREST
Security cameras in the store caught Ryder cutting off price tags,
wrapping the clothes in tissue paper, then stuffing them into a gar-
ment bag. When security guards detained her, she said she was
preparing for a movie role.

THE CHARGES
Grand theft and vandalism

THE SENTENCE
Ryder was found guilty and sentenced to three years' probation. The
judge ordered her to perform 480 hours of community service, to attend psychological and drug counseling programs, and to pay $10,000
in fines and court fees.

AFTERWARD
After her conviction, Ryder stayed out of the public eye, and did not
make another movie for four years.

UNUSUAL FACT
Winona Ryder was born in Winona, Minnesota.

NICOLA SACCO
(1891–1927)
AND
BARTOLOMEO VANZETTI
(1888–1927)

NATIONALITY
Italian

WHO WERE THEY?
Nicola Sacco was an Italian immigrant to America. He settled in Milford, Massachusetts, where he worked as a shoe trimmer at a local shoe factory. Bartolomeo Vanzetti also emigrated to America from Italy. He drifted from job to job and city to city. In 1920, he was living in Plymouth, Massachusetts, and supporting himself as a fish peddler. Both Sacco and Vanzetti were active in the anarchist movement.

WHAT DID THEY DO?
In the middle of the afternoon, on April 15, 1920, in South Braintree, Massachusetts, Sacco and Vanzetti shot and mortally wounded a paymaster and his security guard, then ran off with the payroll of $15,776.

DATE OF ARREST
May 5, 1920

CIRCUMSTANCES OF THE ARREST
The two walked into a trap police had set for another suspect, but the fact that Sacco and Vanzetti were carrying concealed weapons and lied when questioned by the police brought them under suspicion.

THE CHARGES
Armed robbery and murder

THE SENTENCE
Sacco and Vanzetti were convicted and sentenced to death. After six years of filing appeals, all of which were denied, the two were electrocuted.

AFTERWARD
Historians continue to debate whether Sacco and Vanzetti were guilty or were railroaded by the police and the judicial system because they were anarchists.

ABE SAFFRON

(1919–2006)

NATIONALITY
Australian

WHO WAS HE?
Abe Saffron's business interests included hotels, restaurants, nightclubs, as well as prostitution, gambling, drug dealing, bribery, and extortion. He was known as "Mr. Sin" and "the Big Boss of Australian Crime."

WHAT DID HE DO?
According to Jim Anderson, a former associate of Saffron's who turned state's evidence, Saffron kept two sets of books—one that recorded his actual income and assets, and a second that recorded only a fraction of his income and net worth.

DATE OF ARREST
November 1987

THE CHARGE
Tax evasion

THE SENTENCE
Saffron was found guilty and given the maximum sentence—three years in prison. At the time, the judge in the case said, "In my view, the maximum penalty of three years is inadequate."

AFTERWARD
After serving 17 months, Saffron was released. He was never convicted of any other crime.

SALEH SALEM
(1987–)

WHO IS HE?
Saleh Salem was a clerk at the Quick-N-Easy Mart in East Memphis, Tennessee.

WHAT DID HE DO?
Salem got into an argument with a customer who entered the store shirtless. Salem took a 9-mm handgun from a drawer, and the argument about proper attire in a convenience store moved outside. There Salem aimed at the ground and fired a shot, which struck the customer in the leg.

DATE OF ARREST
July 15, 2010

THE CHARGE
Reckless endangerment

THE SENTENCE
Salem was held in jail pending a $50,000 bond.

BUSTED

MARGARET SANGER

(1879–1966)

NATIONALITY
American

WHO WAS SHE?
Margaret Sanger's mother had 11 children and 7 miscarriages. After studying birth control methods at a clinic in The Netherlands, Margaret became a birth control activist.

WHAT DID SHE DO?
In Brooklyn, Sanger opened America's first birth control clinic.

DATE OF ARREST
October 25, 1916

CIRCUMSTANCES OF THE ARREST
Nine days after the clinic opened, police arrested Sanger and her entire staff. They also confiscated all birth control literature, condoms, and diaphragms.

THE CHARGE
Maintaining a public nuisance

THE SENTENCE
Sanger was found guilty and sentenced to 30 days in prison.

AFTERWARD
Sanger continued her advocacy for sex education and birth control, but also, much more controversially, embraced the philosophy of eugenics. She wrote, "Apply a stern and rigid policy of sterilization and segregation to that grade of population whose progeny is already tainted or whose inheritance is such that objectionable traits may be transmitted to offspring."

CHARLES "SMITTY" SCHMID JR., "THE PIED PIPER OF TUCSON"
(1942–1975)

NATIONALITY
American

WHO WAS HE?
Schmid was adopted after his birth mother abandoned him. In high school he was a natural athlete, charismatic, and tried to look and act like Elvis Presley.

WHAT DID HE DO?
Schmid murdered three young women, then ditched their bodies in the desert. He told a friend, Ritchie Bruns about two of the murders—it was Bruns who went to the police.

DATE OF ARREST
November 10, 1965

CIRCUMSTANCES OF THE ARREST
Schmid was doing yardwork at his mother's house when the police pulled up. He ran inside, but they followed him in and arrested him.

THE CHARGE
Murder

THE SENTENCE
The jury found Schmid guilty. He was given the death penalty.

AFTERWARD
In prison, two inmates attacked Schmid, stabbing him 20 times in the face and chest. He died in the prison hospital ten days later.

UNUSUAL FACT
Schmid was the inspiration for Joyce Carol Oates's short story, "Where Are You Going, Where Have You Been."

DUNCAN SCOTT-FORD

(1921–1942)

NATIONALITY
English

WHO WAS HE?
At age 16, Duncan Scott-Ford left his home in Plymouth, England, and joined the Royal Navy. He had a tendency to become infatuated with any woman who paid attention to him, including a German, who may have been a Nazi spy, and an Egyptian prostitute. During World War II, he joined the Merchant Navy.

WHAT DID HE DO?
In a bar in Lisbon, Scott-Ford met a stranger calling himself Rithman, who offered him 1,000 Portuguese escudos for information about British minefields and American troops in Britain. For another 500 escudos, Scott-Ford passed along information about the Allies' planned invasion of Nazi-occupied Europe.

DATE OF ARREST
August 18, 1942

CIRCUMSTANCES OF THE ARREST
During a routine debriefing session back in England, Scott-Ford admitted that he had been approached by German agents who had paid him for information about the British military.

THE CHARGE
Treason

THE SENTENCE
Scott-Ford was found guilty of violating the Treachery Act of 1940 and sentenced to death. He was hanged by the renowned executioner Albert Pierrepoint at London's Wandsworth Prison (pictured).

THE SCOTTSBORO BOYS

OLEN MONTGOMERY (1914– ?), CLARENCE NORRIS (1912–1989), HAYWOOD PATTERSON (1913–1952), OZIE POWELL (1916–?), WILLIE ROBERSON (1915–?), CHARLES WEEMS (1911–?), EUGENE WILLIAMS (1918–?), ANDREW WRIGHT (1912–?), AND LEROY WRIGHT (1918–1959)

NATIONALITY
American

WHO WERE THEY?
The Scottsboro Boys were nine black young men, ranging in age from 13 to 20, who had jumped a freight train going from Chattanooga to Memphis, Tennessee. Also on the train were a group of white young men and two white women, 16-year-old Ruby Bates and 20-year-old Victoria Price.

WHAT DID THEY DO?
On March 25, 1931, a fight broke out between the white hoboes and the black hoboes. Several of the white men jumped off the train and reported to the local sheriff that they had been attacked by a gang of black men. The sheriff sent a posse to Paint Rock, Alabama, to stop the train and take the black men into custody. As the posse cleared all the hoboes from the train, Bates and Price climbed down and accused the black men of rape.

DATE OF ARREST
March 25, 1931

THE CHARGE
Rape

THE SENTENCES
By April 9, 1935, the trials of the young black men were over. Eight of them were found guilty and sentenced to death. In the case of 13-year-old Leroy Wright, there was a hung jury, with 11 voting for the death sentence, and 1 holdout insisting on life in prison.

AFTERWARD
The appeals process—which included two appearances before the U.S. Supreme Court—and the new trials of the Scottsboro Boys dragged on from 1931 until 1938. Ultimately, the rape charges against Montgomery, Roberson, Williams, and Leroy Wright were dropped. Andrew Wright was sentenced to 99 years in prison, Weems to 75 years, and Powell to 20 years. Clarence Norris was sentenced to death, but the governor of Alabama commuted his sentence to life in prison. By 1946, Andrew Wright, Weems, Powell, and Norris were paroled. In 1948, Patterson escaped from prison to Detroit, where the governor refused to extradite him back to Alabama.

UNUSUAL FACTS
In 1933, Ruby Bates testified in court that in the first trial she had perjured herself—that she had not been raped. Victoria Price never changed her story. In 1976, following the airing of NBC's made-for-TV movie, *Judge Horton and the Scottsboro Boys,* Price, based on the portrayal of her character in the movie, sued the network for slander and invasion of privacy. Her lawsuit was dismissed.

FAISAL SHAHZAD
(1979–)

NATIONALITY
Pakistani-born American citizen

WHO IS HE?
Faisal Shahzad came to America from Pakistan in 1998 on a student visa. Later he received a green card. He married, worked as a financial analyst, bought a house in Bridgeport, Connecticut, and started a family. In 2009, Shazad returned home to Pakistan while his wife and two children went to Saudi Arabia.

WHAT DID HE DO?
On May 1, 2010, Shahzad parked a dark blue Nissan Pathfinder SUV in Times Square in New York City. Inside was a homemade bomb. He ignited the bomb, but it failed to explode. Two street vendors working near the vehicle saw smoke coming from the SUV and called the police.

DATE OF ARREST
May 3, 2010

CIRCUMSTANCES OF THE ARREST
U.S. Customs and Border Protection agents arrested Shahzad at John F. Kennedy International Airport—he was aboard a plane bound for Dubai, still on the tarmac.

THE CHARGES
Attempted use of a weapon of mass destruction, attempted act of terrorism transcending national boundaries, transportation of an explosive, attempted destruction of property by fire and explosive

THE SENTENCE
Shahzad pled guilty to all counts; he was sentenced to life in prison. At his sentencing, Shahzad was unrepentant, and warned the court and the people of the United States, "Brace yourself" for more terrorist attacks.

CIRCUMSTANCES OF THE ARREST

After eluding federal authorities for four years, Shakur was arrested in California.

THE CHARGES

Robbery and participating in a prison escape

THE SENTENCE

Shakur was found guilty and sentenced to 30 years in prison.

UNUSUAL FACT

Mutulu Shakur is the stepfather of the late rapper Tupac Shakur.

MUTULU SHAKUR
(1950–)

NATIONALITY

American

WHO IS HE?

Born in Baltimore, Mutulu Shakur was a supporter of Malcolm X and a member of the Black Liberation Army.

WHAT DID HE DO?

In 1979, Shakur helped his sister, Assata Shakur, escape from prison. On October 21, 1981, Shakur and a handful of accomplices (who included Kathy Boudin, then on the FBI's Most Wanted List) robbed a Brinks armored truck. During the getaway, they killed a security guard and two police officers.

DATE OF ARREST

February 11, 1986

THE SENTENCE

Shakur was sentenced to serve between one year and six months and four years and three months in prison. Eleven months into his sentence, he was released after Suge Knight, CEO of Death Row Records, posted $1.4 million bail.

AFTERWARD

On September 7, 1996, in Las Vegas, Shakur and Knight were driving to a nightclub when a car pulled up and unknown assailants fired, mortally wounding Shakur. He died six days later.

TUPAC SHAKUR

(1971–1996)

NATIONALITY

American

WHO WAS HE?

Tupac Shakur was the highest-selling gangsta rapper and hip-hop artist in history, with over 67 million records sold. The ten albums released after his death all went platinum.

WHAT DID HE DO?

Shakur and his entourage gang-raped a woman he had met a few days earlier and taken back to his hotel room.

DATE OF ARREST

March 8, 1995

THE CHARGE

Sexual assault

AL SHARPTON

(1954–)

NATIONALITY
American

WHO IS HE?
Rev. Al Sharpton is a Baptist minister, civil rights activist, former Democratic candidate for U.S. president, political commentator, and radio talk show host.

WHAT DID HE DO?
Sharpton led a protest march that stopped rush hour traffic at New York City bridges and tunnels.

DATE OF ARREST
May 7, 2008

CIRCUMSTANCES OF THE ARREST
Sharpton was demonstrating against the acquittal of police officers who had been accused of killing Sean Bell, a unarmed man, on the night of his bachelor party.

THE CHARGE
Disorderly conduct

THE SENTENCE
Sharpton was convicted and sentenced to the five-and-a-half hours he had already spent in jail.

AFTERWARD
In a civil lawsuit, the Bell family was awarded $3.5 million from the city of New York. Two of Sean Bell's friends were wounded by the police—one received $3 million, the other $900,000.

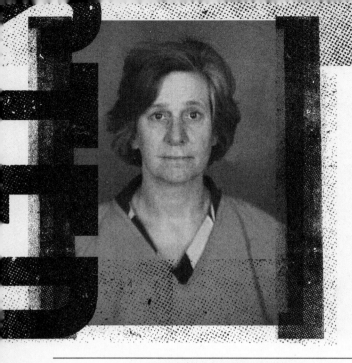

CINDY SHEEHAN

(1957–)

NATIONALITY
American

WHO IS SHE?
Cindy Sheehan is an antiwar activist whose son, Specialist Casey Sheehan, was killed in Iraq. She has called for the international community to try former President George W. Bush for war crimes, and has denounced President Barack Obama for not withdrawing all U.S. troops from Iraq and Afghanistan.

WHAT DID SHE DO?
Sheehan and three other women attempted to deliver an anti-Iraq war petition to the U.S. Mission to the United Nations in New York. When they were refused entry, the women refused to leave the premises.

DATE OF ARREST
March 7, 2006

CIRCUMSTANCES OF THE ARREST
When police arrested them, Sheehan and her fellow protesters were blocking the entrance to the U.S. Mission.

THE CHARGES
Trespassing, disorderly conduct, resisting arrest, and obstructing government administration

THE SENTENCE
Sheehan was convicted of trespassing and ordered to pay $95 in court costs. The other charges were dismissed.

AFTERWARD
Sheehan has continued her activism for a host of causes, from ending the wars in Iraq and Afghanistan to revoking the No Child Left Behind Act. In 2010, she was arrested in front of the White House, where she was protesting President Barack Obama's policies regarding the Iraq and Afghanistan wars.

CHARLIE SHEEN

(1965–)

NATIONALITY
American

WHO IS HE?
Charlie Sheen comes from a family of actors: Martin Sheen is his father and one of his brothers is Emilio Estevez. His film career includes starring roles in *Platoon, Wall Street, Eight Men Out,* and *Major League.*

WHAT DID HE DO?
Sheen's wife, Brooke Mueller claimed that while they were arguing he attacked and tried to strangle her.

DATE OF ARREST
December 25, 2009

CIRCUMSTANCES OF THE ARREST
Aspen, Colorado police arrested Sheen at about 8:30 on Christmas morning at the house Mueller was renting. The police tested Sheen and Mueller for alcohol and found that, with a .13 blood alcohol level, Mueller was legally drunk; Sheen's blood alcohol level was .04. Sheen spent Christmas Day in jail. That evening, after appearing before a judge, he posted an $8,500 bond and was released.

THE CHARGES
Felony menacing, misdemeanor third-degree assault, and misdemeanor criminal mischief

THE SENTENCE
Under the terms of a plea deal, Sheen was sentenced to 30 days in jail, but the court agreed that he could serve his sentence at Promises, a rehab facility in Malibu, California, popular with celebrities. The court also required Sheen to enroll in an anger management program.

AFTERWARD
Sheen's attorney was able to get such favorable terms for his client after Mueller dropped the charges and said she would not testify against Sheen in court. The couple announced that they would divorce but share joint legal custody of their twin sons. Sheen agreed to pay $55,000 a month in child support, give Mueller a lump sum of $750,000, and pay her approximately $1 million to buy her share of their home.

UNUSUAL FACT
In May 2010, CBS agreed to pay Charlie Sheen $2 million per episode of the hit TV comedy *Two and a Half Men.* Six months later he was removed from the Plaza Hotel in New York after causing $7,000 worth of damage to a hotel room during a cocaine- and booze-filled evening.

SAM SHEPPARD

(1923–1970)

NATIONALITY
American

WHO WAS HE?
Sam Sheppard was a successful osteopathic physician and neurosurgeon who practiced medicine with his father in Cleveland. Young, attractive, and successful, he and his wife Marilyn appeared to be the perfect couple. Family and friends did not know that from 1951 to 1954 Sheppard had been having an affair.

WHAT DID HE DO?
Sheppard was accused of murdering his pregnant wife as she slept in their bed. Sheppard said the killer was a "bushy-haired" burglar who, on his way out of the house, grappled with Sheppard, injuring his head and neck.

DATE OF ARREST
August 17, 1954

THE CHARGE
Murder

THE SENTENCE
The jury convicted Sheppard. He was sentenced to life in prison.

AFTERWARD
Three weeks after his conviction, Sheppard's mother killed herself. In 1966, the U.S. Supreme Court overturned Sheppard's conviction on due process grounds. In a new trial, Sheppard was acquitted. For a time in 1969, he was a professional wrestler who used the stage name "Killer."

UNUSUAL FACT
Many viewers of the popular 1960s TV series *The Fugitive* believed the show was based on the Sheppard case.

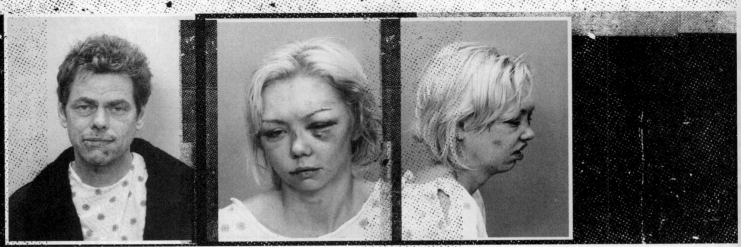

OFFER "VINCE" SHLOMI, "THE SHAMWOW GUY"

(1964–)

AND

SASHA HARRIS

(1984–)

NATIONALITY
Israeli

WHO IS HE?
Shlomi is a TV pitchman for such popular products as the ShamWow absorbent cloth and the Slap Chop vegetable chopper.

WHAT DID HE DO?
While in Miami Beach, Shlomi agreed to pay Sasha Harris, a prostitute, $1,000 for what he described as "straight sex." Back at his hotel room, when Shlomi kissed Harris, she bit his tongue and would not let go. Shlomi punched her several times in the face until she released his tongue, then ran down to the hotel lobby to call the police.

DATE OF ARREST
February 7, 2009

CIRCUMSTANCES OF THE ARREST
Seeing the condition of Shlomi and Harris, police arrested them both, but first sent them to a hospital for treatment of their injuries.

THE CHARGE
Aggravated battery

THE SENTENCE
Prosecutors declined to file charges against Shlomi or Harris.

BHAGWAN SHREE RAJNEESH

(1931–1990)

NATIONALITY
Indian

WHO WAS HE?
Bhagwan Shree Rajneesh taught philosophy at the University of Saugar in India. He claimed that at age 21 he achieved spiritual enlightenment. In India, and then in the United States, he taught a form of spirituality that drew upon Hinduism, Jainism, Zen Buddhism, Taoism, Christianity, as well as ancient Greek philosophy. He and his followers settled on Big Muddy Ranch, a 65,000-acre spread outside Antelope, Oregon.

WHAT DID HE DO?
Shree Rajneesh performed invalid marriages between Indians and U.S. citizens so his Indian followers could remain in the United States.

DATE OF ARREST
October 28, 1985

CIRCUMSTANCES OF THE ARREST
Shree Rajneesh was arrested in North Carolina aboard an airplane that was about to take him and some of his followers to Bermuda.

THE CHARGE
Immigration violations

THE SENTENCE
Shree Rajneesh pled no contest and was given a suspended sentence, on the condition that he leave the country.

AFTERWARD
Shree Rajneesh returned to India where he adopted a new name, Osho. He died in 1990 without appointing a successor. His followers operate about 20 meditation centers scattered around the world.

UNUSUAL FACT
After Shree Rajneesh left the United States, his followers in Big Muddy Ranch scaled back their operation. Among the assets they liquidated was a fleet of 93 Rolls-Royces.

BENJAMIN "BUGSY" SIEGEL

(1906–1947)

NATIONALITY
American

WHO WAS HE?
As a teenager on New York's Lower East Side, Siegel and some friends operated an extortion racket among the neighborhood's pushcart vendors: Each vendor handed over $5 a week or the gang would set fire to his cart. As an adult, he was a hit man who expanded his interests to encompass racketeering, especially in Hollywood and professional sports. He was one of the founders of the Flamingo Club, one of the first casinos in Las Vegas.

WHAT DID HE DO?
In Miami, Siegel was running illegal gambling parlors.

DATE OF ARREST
February 28, 1930

THE CHARGE
Gambling

THE SENTENCE
Siegel was found guilty—of the eight times he would be arrested, this would be the only time he was convicted. He was fined $100.

AFTERWARD
In 1947, Siegel was staying at a friend's home in Beverly Hills, California. One night a killer armed with a military carbine rifle fired through the living room window, killing Siegel instantly. The murderer was never found.

UNUSUAL FACT
In the *Godfather (Part I),* the character Moe Greene was based on Bugsy Siegel.

BK 4013970 06·17·94

LOS ANGELES POLICE JAIL DIV

O. J. SIMPSON

(1947–)

NATIONALITY
American

WHO IS HE?
"The Juice" was an NFL superstar, the only player ever to rush more than 2,000 yards in one season. Handsome and charismatic, Simpson moved easily from football to the movies (*The Towering Inferno* and the *Naked Gun* trilogy). He also starred in the TV miniseries *Roots*.

WHAT DID HE DO?
Simpson was charged with stabbing to death his ex-wife, Nicole Brown Simpson, and Ronald Goldman, a waiter who had brought to Nicole's house a pair of eyeglasses she had left at his restaurant.

DATE OF ARREST
June 17, 1994

CIRCUMSTANCES OF THE ARREST
Simpson tried to escape to Mexico in a white Ford Bronco, driven by his friend A. C. Cowlings. Helicopters taped the chase, which was broadcast live. Ultimately, Cowlings drove Simpson back to his home, where police arrested him.

THE CHARGE
Murder

THE SENTENCE
After a televised trial that ran almost ten months, the jury returned a verdict of not guilty.

AFTERWARD
The Goldman family filed a civil suit against Simpson—which they won. The court awarded the Goldmans $8.5 million, and ordered Simpson to surrender his assets. After an auction of Simpson's property, the Goldmans and the Browns split the proceeds. In 2007, Simpson and several accomplices entered a room at the Palace Station Hotel in Las Vegas and at gunpoint took sports memorabilia belonging to the room's occupants. Simpson was convicted of kidnapping and armed robbery and sentenced to 33 years in prison. He is eligible for parole in 2017.

FRANK SINATRA

(1915–1998)

NATIONALITY
American

WHO WAS HE?
Known as Ol' Blue Eyes and the Chairman of the Board, Frank Sinatra began his musical career singing with the swing bands of Tommy Dorsey and Harry James and finding a huge, squealing throng of fans among teenage girls. In the 1950s, he reinvented himself as a more mature singer and as an actor (he won an Oscar for his performance in *From Here to Eternity*). He had several retirements and comebacks, always drawn back to the spotlight by his legions of devoted fans. In 1990, he celebrated his 75th birthday with a nationwide concert tour.

WHAT DID HE DO?
In Lodi, New Jersey, Sinatra slept with a woman, who until that night had an unimpeachable reputation in her community. Four weeks later police rearrested Sinatra when they learned that the lady in question was married.

DATES OF ARRESTS
November 26, 1938 and December 22, 1938

THE CHARGES
Seduction and adultery

CIRCUMSTANCES OF THE ARREST
Sinatra was released on $1,500 bail for the seduction charge, then on $500 bail for the adultery charge.

THE SENTENCE
The charge of seduction was dropped and the charge of adultery was dismissed.

AFTERWARD
Sinatra was a playboy. He married four times (his second wife was Ava Gardner; his third was Mia Farrow). He is said to have had affairs with Lana Turner, Judy Garland, Lauren Bacall, Juliet Prowse, and Angie Dickinson.

UNUSUAL FACT
Sinatra recorded John F. Kennedy's campaign song, a parody of "High Hopes."

BERGEN COUNTY
SHERIFF'S OFFICE
11 27 38
42799
otten.com

DATE OF ARREST
March 13, 1940

CIRCUMSTANCES OF THE ARREST
Singh was arrested at the scene. He made no attempt to escape.

THE CHARGE
Murder

THE SENTENCE
Singh was found guilty and sentenced to death. He was hanged in London's Pentonville Prison.

UDHAM SINGH
(1899–1940)

NATIONALITY
Indian

WHO WAS HE?
Udham Singh was a Sikh who was raised in an orphange. Udam became a political revolutionary following the Jallianwalla Bagh Massacre of 1919, when General Reginald Dyer ordered his men to fire on a large gathering of unarmed Indian men, women, and children: 1,000 were killed and hundreds wounded.

WHAT DID HE DO?
In 1940, to avenge the massacre, Singh traveled to London. At a meeting of the East India Association, he stood up and fired a pistol, killing Sir Michael O'Dwyer, governor of the Punjab at the time of the massacre, and wounding Lord Zetland, secretary of state for India.

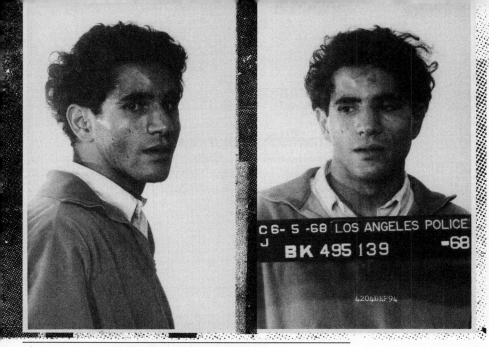

SIRHAN SIRHAN

(1944–)

NATIONALITY
Jordanian/Palestinian

WHO IS HE?
Sirhan Sirhan is a Palestinian who emigrated to the United States. During the 1968 presidential campaign, Sirhan became enraged by candidate Robert F. Kennedy's support for Israel.

WHAT DID HE DO?
On June 5, 1968, Kennedy won the California primary. After greeting supporters in the Ambassador Hotel ballroom, Kennedy tried to leave by way of the hotel kitchen. As he walked by, Sirhan shot and mortally wounded him. Sirhan also wounded five people in the Kennedy entourage.

DATE OF ARREST
June 5, 1968

CIRCUMSTANCES OF THE ARREST
Sirhan was tackled and pinned down by Rosie Grier, a retired defensive lineman for the New York Giants. Olympic gold medalist Rafer Johnson and writers George Plimpton and Pete Hamill piled on.

THE CHARGE
Murder

THE SENTENCE
Sirhan was found guilty and sentenced to death. Later, his sentence was commuted to life in prison.

AFTERWARD
Sirhan has appealed repeatedly for parole, once, audaciously, asserting that if Senator Kennedy were alive, he would support Sirhan's parole application.

MICHAEL SKAKEL

(1960–)

NATIONALITY
American

WHO IS HE?
Michael Skakel is the nephew of Ethel Skakel Kennedy, the widow of Robert F. Kennedy. He grew up on an estate in Greenwich, Connecticut. One of his neighbors was 15-year-old Martha Moxley.

WHAT DID HE DO?
After a Halloween party at the Skakel home in 1975, Michael Skakel saw Martha kissing his brother Thomas. The next day Martha's body was found in her backyard. Beside it lay a broken six-iron golf club that belonged to the Skakels—she had been beaten and stabbed with the club.

DATE OF ARREST
January 19, 2000

CIRCUMSTANCES OF THE ARREST
Skakel was arrested after acquaintances came forward to say that he had boasted of killing Martha Moxley and getting away with it because he is related to the Kennedy family.

THE CHARGE
Murder

THE SENTENCE
Skakel was found guilty and sentenced to 20 years to life in prison.

AFTERWARD
Skakel's defense filed several appeals for a new trial, all of which were rejected.

UNUSUAL FACT
Skakel's first cousin, Robert F. Kennedy Jr., published an article in *The Atlantic* arguing that Michael was innocent and insisting that evidence pointed to the Skakel family's live-in tutor as the real murderer.

WHAT DID HE DO?
His first experience under enemy fire terrified him. He ran and hid. The next day he turned himself over to Canadian military police, who in turn passed him on to U.S. military police.

DATE OF ARREST
October 9, 1944

THE CHARGE
Desertion

THE SENTENCE
Slovik admitted that he had deserted and said that if he were sent back to combat, he would desert again. He was found guilty and sentenced to be executed by firing squad. Slovik appealed for clemency to General Dwight D. Eisenhower; Eisenhower denied the request. Of the thousands of U.S. soldiers who deserted during World War II, Slovik was the only one who was executed. He was the first American soldier to be executed for desertion since the Civil War.

AFTERWARD
In 1954, William Bradford Huie published an account of the case, *The Execution of Private Slovik*. It became a best seller, and was produced as a made-for-TV movie in 1974, starring Martin Sheen.

EDDIE SLOVIK
(1920–1945)

NATIONALITY
American

WHO WAS HE?
Eddie Slovik, a native of Detroit, was a private in the U.S. Army who was sent to France.

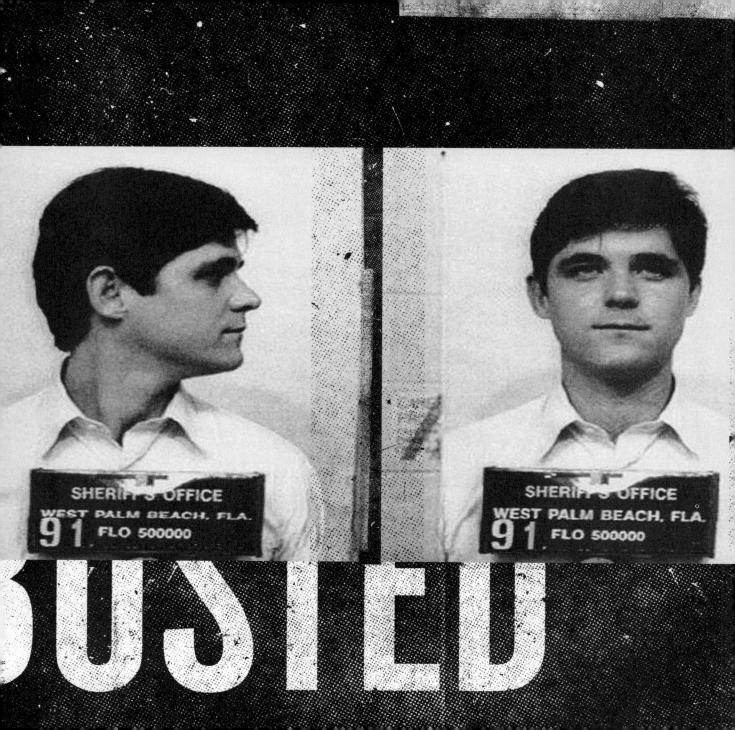

SHERIFF'S OFFICE
WEST PALM BEACH, FLA.
91 FLO 500000

SHERIFF'S OFFICE
WEST PALM BEACH, FLA.
91 FLO 500000

BUSTED

WILLIAM KENNEDY SMITH

(1960–)

NATIONALITY
American

WHO IS HE?
William Kennedy Smith is the son of Jean Kennedy Smith and the nephew of President John F. Kennedy.

WHAT DID HE DO?
On March 29, 1990, Smith went to a bar with his uncle, Ted Kennedy, and his cousin, Patrick Kennedy. There he a met a woman and they went back to the Kennedy family's house in Palm Beach, Florida. In the backyard, Smith and the woman had sex. She accused him of rape.

DATE OF ARREST
April 1, 1991

THE CHARGE
Rape

THE SENTENCE
After deliberating for 77 minutes, the jury acquitted Smith.

AFTERWARD
Smith graduated from medical school and opened a practice that specializes in the treatment of the disabled (his aunt Rosemary Kennedy was disabled). Two female employees have accused him of sexual harassment: Smith settled one of the complaints out of court; the second was dismissed.

DATE OF ARREST
December 8, 2006

THE CHARGE
Tax evasion

THE SENTENCE
Snipes was convicted and sentenced to three years in a minimum se-curity prison. In a statement to the court, Snipes said, "I am an idealistic, naive, passionate, truth-seeking, spiritually motivated art-ist, unschooled in the science of law and finance."

UNUSUAL FACT
Sylvester Stallone wanted to cast Snipes in *The Expendables,* but the court would not permit Snipes to leave the country to shoot on loca-tion.

WESLEY SNIPES
(1962–)

NATIONALITY
American

WHO IS HE?
Wesley Snipes is an actor best known for his action-adventure roles in such films as the *Blade* vampire-hunter trilogy and *Passenger 57.*

WHAT DID HE DO?
Between 1999 and 2001, Snipes failed to file tax returns. For that pe-riod, he owed the IRS $2.7 million.

MARTHA STEWART

(1941–)

NATIONALITY
American

WHO IS SHE?
Through her own television programs, magazines, and branded merchandise, Martha Stewart has built a homemaking empire. Martha Stewart Living Omnimedia, which she founded, is the umbrella organization for her various companies.

WHAT DID SHE DO?
Based on inside information she received from her stockbroker, Stewart avoided a loss of more than $45,000 by selling almost 4,000 shares of her ImClone Systems stock the day before the stock's price tumbled. When investigators questioned her about the trade, she lied to them.

DATE OF ARREST
June 5, 2003.

THE CHARGES
Obstruction of justice and lying to investigators

THE SENTENCE
Stewart was found guilty and sentenced to five months in prison and five months of house arrest, followed by two years' probation. She was fined $30,000.

AFTERWARD
Stewart's comeback began with a new TV program, *The Martha Stewart Show,* as well as new lines of Martha Stewart products, including housepaint, linens, bedding, and cookware.

UNUSUAL FACT
During her incarceration, Stewart foraged for dandelions and other wild greens, concocted recipes in a microwave, and even ate from a vending machine. She also lost ten pounds.

ROBERT FRANKLIN STROUD, "THE BIRDMAN OF ALCATRAZ"

(1890–1963)

NATIONALITY
American

WHO WAS HE?
At age 13, Robert Franklin Stroud ran away from home and did not return for four years. At age 18, he relocated to Alaska, where he moved in with a 36-year dancer. When an acquaintance beat up Stroud's lover, he shot and killed the man. Stroud was given a 12-year sentence, but other crimes he committed while incarcerated ensured that he would spend the rest of his life in prison.

WHAT DID HE DO?
While serving a six-month sentence in Leavenworth, Stroud stabbed and killed a prison guard.

DATE OF ARREST
March 26, 1916

CIRCUMSTANCES OF THE ARREST
Stroud was seized by other guards in the prison cafeteria, where the murder occurred.

THE CHARGE
Murder

THE SENTENCE
Stroud was sentenced to hang. His mother appealed to President and Mrs. Woodrow Wilson for clemency, and the sentence was commuted to life in prison.

AFTERWARD
In his cell at Leavenworth, Stroud raised, studied, and sold canaries. He published two books on the diseases of birds and became a respected amateur ornithologist. In spite of his nickname, when he was transferred to Alcatraz, the warden did not permit him to keep birds.

UNUSUAL FACT
Stroud's story was told by Thomas Gaddis in his book, *The Birdman of Alcatraz*. In 1962, the book became a movie, starring Burt Lancaster as Stroud.

BIRD MAN

PETER SUTCLIFFE, "THE YORKSHIRE RIPPER"

(1946–)

NATIONALITY
English

WHO IS HE?
Peter Sutcliffe was a menial laborer in Yorkshire, England, who was obsessed with prostitutes. Even after he got married, he continued to visit brothels.

WHAT DID HE DO?
In 1975, Sutcliffe developed a new, violent obsession with killing women. Over the next five years he would murder 13 women, typically with a ball-peen hammer and a knife. The press named the unknown killer, "the Yorkshire Ripper."

DATE OF ARREST
January 2, 1981

CIRCUMSTANCES OF THE ARREST
Sutcliffe was arrested for driving a car with false license plates. While he was in custody, one of the police officers suspected that he was the Yorkshire Ripper, returned to the place he had been arrested, and found a knife and a ball-peen hammer.

THE CHARGE
Murder

THE SENTENCE
Sutcliffe confessed to the 13 murders and was sentenced to 30 years in a prison hospital.

AFTERWARD
Sutcliffe will be eligible for parole in 2011.

HENRY DAVID THOREAU
(1817–1862)

NATIONALITY
American

WHO WAS HE?
Author, poet, free thinker, abolitionist, and transcendentalist, Henry David Thoreau lived in Concord, Massachusetts, where his neighbors included Nathaniel Hawthorne, Ralph Waldo Emerson, Bronson Alcott, and his young daughter, Louisa May Alcott. Thoreau is best remembered for his books *Walden* and *Civil Disobedience*.

WHAT DID HE DO?
To protest his opposition to slavery and the United States' war with Mexico, Thoreau refused to pay the poll tax.

DATE OF ARREST
July 25, 1846

CIRCUMSTANCES OF THE ARREST
While walking down a Concord street, Thoreau encountered the town's tax collector. The man demanded that Thoreau pay up; Thoreau refused.

THE CHARGE
Refusal to pay a poll tax

THE SENTENCE
Thoreau spent one night in jail, but his case never came to trial because his aunt paid the tax for him. Thoreau was livid.

AFTERWARD
Later in life, Thoreau became interested in natural history and traveled extensively into the wilderness areas of Maine, Quebec, and the Great Lakes region. Thoreau was an especially vocal supporter of abolitionist John Brown's attempt to lead a slave uprising in the South.

T.I. (CLIFFORD JOSEPH HARRIS JR.)

(1981–)

NATIONALITY
American

WHO IS HE?
T.I. is a rapper who has had three number-one-hit singles: "My Love," "Whatever You Like," and "Live Your Life." He has sold over 10 million albums in the United States.

WHAT DID HE DO?
T.I. violated the terms of his parole when Los Angeles County sheriff's deputies found marijuana and a small amount of ecstasy in his car.

DATE OF ARREST
September 1, 2010

CIRCUMSTANCES OF THE ARREST
About 10:30 at night on September 1, 2010, as T.I. drove with his wife, Tameka Cottle, on Sunset Boulevard, they passed some deputies. The deputies smelled marijuana and pulled the couple over.

THE CHARGE
Violating parole

THE PREVIOUS CONVICTION
After a drug conviction in 1998, T.I. was forbidden to purchase any firearms. Yet in October 2007, T.I. illegally purchased machine guns and silencers from undercover cops. A search of the rapper's home turned up more illegal weapons. T.I. could have been sentenced to 10 years in prison, but in exchange for speaking out against gangs, he was sentenced to 366 days in jail.

THE SENTENCE
T.I.'s parole was revoked, and he was sentenced to another 11 months in prison.

CRAIG TITUS
(1965–)
AND
KELLY RYAN
(1972–)

NATIONALITY
American

WHO ARE THEY?
Craig Titus is a professional bodybuilder and Kelly Ryan, his wife, is a professional fitness competitor.

WHAT DID THEY DO?
On or about December 14, 2005, Titus killed Melissa James, his and Ryan's live-in personal assistant with whom Titus had had an affair. Prosecutor Robert Daskas told the court that James had been beaten, strangled, stunned with a Taser, and injected with morphine. Then she was dumped in the trunk of Titus's Jaguar, which he and Ryan drove into the desert outside Las Vegas. There they poured lighter fluid and gasoline over the car and set it ablaze.

DATE OF ARREST
December 23, 2005

CIRCUMSTANCES OF THE ARREST
On December 20, an arrest warrant was issued in Las Vegas for Titus and Ryan. They fled the state, driving east. At Stoughton, Massachusetts, 15 miles outside of Boston, federal agents and local police officers caught up with the couple. They arrested Titus as he sat in his pickup truck in a grocery store parking lot; they arrested Ryan in a nearby beauty salon where she was having her nails done. Police speculated that the couple were planning to fly to Greece, which has no extradition treaty with the United States.

THE CHARGE
Titus was wanted in Nevada on charges of murder and arson, Ryan on charges of accessory to murder and arson. They were also charged with unlawful flight to avoid prosecution.

THE SENTENCES
On May 30, 2008, as part of a plea bargain, Titus pled guilty to second-degree murder, kidnapping, and arson. Ryan pled guilty to arson and no contest to battery with a deadly weapon. Titus was sentenced to 21 to 51 years in prison; Ryan to 6 to 26 years.

THE DRUG BUST
In 1995, Titus was arrested in Houston, Texas, and charged with conspiracy to distribute ecstasy. He was sent to a drug rehabilitation clinic for eight months and ordered to undergo periodic testing for steroids. In 1997, Titus tested positive for steroids and was sentenced to two years in prison.

HIDEKI TOJO

(1884–1948)

NATIONALITY
Japanese

WHO WAS HE?
Hideki Tojo made a career in the Japanese Army. He was an advocate of Japan's expansion into mainland Asia and was instrumental in forging an alliance between Japan and Hitler's Germany and Mussolini's Italy.

WHAT DID HE DO?
As war minister of Japan, Tojo was responsible for Japan's 1937 invasion of China, the 1941 attack on Pearl Harbor, and the atrocities committed against civilian populations and POWs in Asia in the 1930s and 1940s.

DATE OF ARREST
September 11, 1945

CIRCUMSTANCES OF THE ARREST
Tojo had tried to commit suicide by shooting himself through the heart, but the bullet missed its mark. He was placed under arrest at the hospital and kept under guard while he recovered.

THE CHARGES
Waging unprovoked wars of aggression in violation of international law; waging war against China; waging aggressive war against the United States, the British Commonwealth, The Netherlands, and French Indochina; and ordering, authorizing, and permitting inhumane treatment of POWs and others

THE SENTENCE
Tojo was convicted and sentenced to death by hanging. Before his execution, he apologized for the atrocities the Japanese Army committed with his authorization.

AFTERWARD
Hideki Tojo's memory is honored in the Yasukuni Shrine, a Shinto shrine that honors all Japanese who gave their lives for the emperor. In total, the shrine commemorates more than 2 million Japanese—members of the military and civilians—who sacrificed their lives for their homeland. Tojo is one of more than 1,000 convicted war criminals commemorated at the shrine.

RIP TORN
(1931–)

NATIONALITY
American

WHO IS HE?
In the 1950s, Torn left his home in Texas for New York City, where he studied acting with Lee Strasberg and dance with Martha Graham. In 1959, he made his Broadway debut in *Sweet Bird of Youth,* for which he won a Tony. Ever since, he has been in demand as a character actor on Broadway, on television, and in the movies. One of his most popular roles is his portrayal of Zed in the *Men in Black* movies.

WHAT DID HE DO?
Torn broke into a bank in Salisbury, Connecticut.

DATE OF ARREST
January 29, 2010

CIRCUMSTANCES OF THE ARREST
Police found him inside the bank, drunk, armed with a loaded gun, and claiming that he had mistaken the bank for his house.

THE CHARGES
Criminal trespass, carrying a gun without a permit, carrying a gun while intoxicated, burglary, and criminal mischief

THE SENTENCE
Torn pled guilty to reckless endangerment, criminal trespass, criminal mischief and the illegal carrying of a firearm. The judge suspended a two-and-a-half- year prison sentence and placed Torn on three years' probation. During his probation, he may not own firearms and he will be subject to random drug and alcohol tests.

UNUSUAL FACT
Torn and actress Sissy Spacek are cousins.

WILLIAM "BOSS" TWEED

(1823–1878)

NATIONALITY
American

WHO WAS HE?
A native New Yorker, William Marcy Tweed was an ambitious swindler who had learned the art of extortion and the joys of no-bid sweetheart deals for city contracts before he became Boss of Tammany Hall, the Democratic Party's political machine in New York.

WHAT DID HE DO?
Tweed's cronies, known as the Tweed Ring, dominated the city's government and frequently looted the city treasury. Especially lucrative for them was the construction of the new New York County Courthouse, during which Tweed and his pals submitted bills for work that had been done at outrageously inflated prices: a carpenter's bill for one month's work came to $360,751. The overcharges were, of course, kickbacks that found their way into the pockets of the Tweed Ring.

DATE OF ARREST
October 27, 1871

CIRCUMSTANCES OF THE ARREST
Tweed waited for the police in his office, accompanied by one of his sons and some associates.

THE CHARGES
Fraud and larceny

THE SENTENCE
Tweed's first trial ended in a hung jury. Tweed was convicted in the second trial, sentenced to 13 years in prison, and fined $12,500.

AFTERWARD
On appeal, Tweed's sentence was reduced to one year. He was released from prison, but was rearrested when the state brought charges against him for misappropriation of public funds. He escaped to Cuba and was trying to get to Spain when he was arrested and sent back to the United States. Tweed was convicted of the civil charge and sent to prison, where he died two years later.

UNUSUAL FACT
At Tweed's death, the mayor of New York, Smith Ely, would not permit the flag at City Hall to be lowered to half mast.

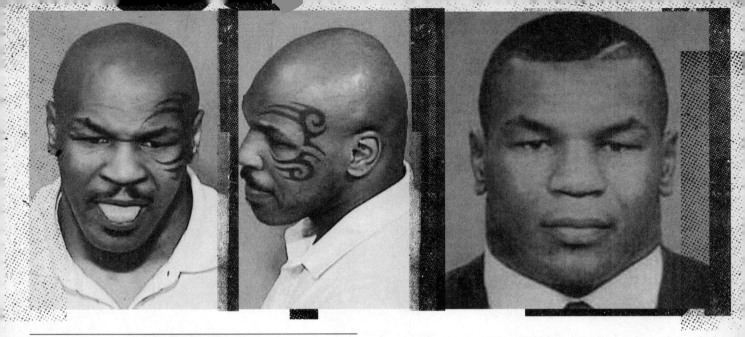

MIKE TYSON
(1966–)

NATIONALITY
American

WHO IS HE?
A heavyweight champion boxer, Mike Tyson was 20 years old when he won the World Boxing Council world heavyweight championship (the youngest boxer to win the title). When he went pro, he won all of his 19 bouts by knockout.

WHAT DID HE DO?
Desiree Washington, 18 years old, who held the title of Miss Black Rhode Island, testified that Tyson invited her to a party, then took her to his hotel room where he raped her.

DATE OF ARREST
July 22, 1991

CIRCUMSTANCES OF THE ARREST
Tyson was arrested in his room at an Indianapolis hotel.

THE CHARGES
Rape and criminally deviant conduct

THE SENTENCE
After deliberating for nine hours, the jury found Tyson guilty. He was sentenced to six years in prison and four years' probation. He was released after serving three years.

AFTERWARD
Tyson staged a comeback, and won the WBC title in 1996. A year later he outraged boxing fans when, during a bout against Evander Holyfield, he bit off part of Holyfield's ear. In 2005, Tyson lost his final fight to Kevin McBride.

U.S. CAPITOL SHOOTERS

LOLITA LEBRÓN (1919-2010), RAFAEL CANCEL MIRANDA (1930-), ANDRES FIGUEROA CORDERO (?-1979) AND IRVING FLORES RODRIGUEZ (?-?)

NATIONALITY
Puerto Rican

WHO WERE THEY?
Lolita Lebrón, Rafael Cancel Miranda, Andres Figueroa Cordero, and Irving Flores Rodriguez were Puerto Rican nationalists who demanded Puerto Rico's independence from the United States.

WHAT DID THEY DO?
On March 1, 1954, the four terrorists entered the U.S. Capitol in Washington, D.C., and took seats in the visitors' gallery above the floor of the House of Representatives. They brandished a Puerto Rican flag, then each pulled out automatic pistols and fired at lawmakers on the House floor, wounding five Members of Congress.

DATE OF ARREST
March 1, 1954

CIRCUMSTANCES OF THE ARREST
The terrorists were seized in the gallery by Capitol police.

THE CHARGE
Assault with a deadly weapon

THE SENTENCE
The four were found guilty. Lebrón was sentenced to 16 years in prison; her three co-conspirators to prison terms ranging from 25 to 75 years.

AFTERWARD
All five wounded members of Congress recovered. In 1978, President Jimmy Carter released Cordero as a compassionate gesture—Cordero was suffering from cancer. Carter released Lebrón, Miranda, and Rodriguez in 1979.

FRANKIE VALLI

(1934–)

NATIONALITY
American

WHO IS HE?
Frankie Valli was the lead singer of the Four Seasons, one of the hottest vocal groups of the early 1960s. Their hits include "Big Girls Don't Cry," "Sherry," and "Can't Take My Eyes Off You."

WHAT DID HE DO?
Valli didn't do anything wrong. But his manager had skipped out on the $375 he and the band owed to the Holiday Inn in Springfield, Ohio.

DATE OF ARREST
September 6, 1965

THE CHARGE
Defrauding an innkeeper

CIRCUMSTANCES OF THE ARREST
Police arrested Valli at the Ohio State Fair, right after the Four Seasons had performed a Labor Day concert.

THE SENTENCE
The charge was dropped after Tommy DeVito, a member of the Four Seasons, paid the outstanding bill.

AFTERWARD
The Broadway musical *Jersey Boys* has created a new fan base for Frankie Valli and the Four Seasons. The arrest is part of the play's story, although the scene is set in Cleveland. According to the script, a cop is waiting for the Four Seasons as they are about to go onstage. "Welcome to Cleveland," he says. "You're under arrest."

FRANK VALLI

AKA............	VALLI, FRANK
AKA............	,
SEX...........	MALE
RACE..........	WHITE
DOB...........	05/03/1934
HEIGHT........	5-5
WEIGHT........	116
BUILD.........	SMALL
HAIR COLOR....	BLACK
HAIR LENGTH...	MEDIUM
EYE COLOR.....	BROWN
FACIAL HAIR...	NONE
SPEECH........	NORMAL
S/M/T.........	

BUSTED

THE CHARGE
Arson

THE SENTENCE
Van der Lubbe was found guilty and sentenced to death by decapitation.

AFTERWARD
The day after the fire, Germany's cabinet gave Adolf Hitler virtually unrestricted authority over the country. He immediately ordered mass arrests of Communists and other political dissidents. Historians have long suspected that van der Lubbe was a scapegoat used by the Nazis so Hitler could acquire absolute power. In 2008, Germany's federal prosecutor threw out the verdict and exonerated van der Lubbe. The culprit responsible for the Reichstag fire remains unknown.

MARINUS VAN DER LUBBE

(1909–1934)

NATIONALITY
Dutch

WHO WAS HE?
Marinus van der Lubbe was an unemployed Dutch bricklayer living in Germany. He was a member of the Dutch Communist Party.

WHAT DID HE DO?
On February 27, 1933, the Reichstag, Germany's parliament, caught fire. Van der Lubbe was found inside the building. He confessed to setting the fire in the hope of sparking a workers' revolution in Germany.

DATE OF ARREST
February 27, 1933

JORAN VAN DER SLOOT

(1987–)

NATIONALITY
Dutch

WHO IS HE?
Joran van der Sloot is a former business school student, and a star tennis and soccer player, who now describes himself as "a professional poker player."

WHAT DID HE DO?
Authorities in Peru allege that van der Sloot strangled to death 21-year-old Stephany Flores Ramirez and stole $11,000 she had won at a casino. Van der Sloot is also believed to be involved in the disappearance of Natalee Holloway, an 18-year-old American high school student who vanished in 2005 while vacationing in Aruba.

DATE OF ARREST
June 3, 2010

CIRCUMSTANCES OF THE ARREST
Van der Sloot fled to Chile, but he was recognized, arrested by Chilean authorities, and deported to Peru, where he was incarcerated in a maximum security prison.

THE CHARGES
Murder and robbery

THE SENTENCE
Van der Sloot confessed to killing Flores. Afterward, he tried to legally retract his confession. As of 2010, a Peruvian judge decreed that the confession stands. As this book was going to press, a date for van der Sloot's trial had not yet been scheduled.

UNUSUAL FACT
The FBI would like to extradite van der Sloot to the United States to stand trial for extortion. He contacted the Holloway family's attorney with an offer: In exchange for $25,000, he would reveal the location of Natalee's body. The family wired him the money, but he never told them where the body could be found.

HAN VAN MEEGEREN

(1889–1947)

NATIONALITY
Dutch

WHO WAS HE?
Han van Meegeren was an accomplished artist, but at a time when art critics were interested in the avant-garde, he painted in a classical style, often imitating artists of the 17th century. To revenge himself upon the art world, he painted forgeries, and was delighted when the connoisseurs accepted them as authentic, long-lost masterpieces.

WHAT DID HE DO?
The Dutch government believed that he had sold an authentic painting by the 17th-century Dutch master Vermeer to Nazi Field Marshall Herman Goering. In fact the "Vermeer" was a fake, which van Meegeren had painted himself. Furthermore, van Meegeren had exchanged the Vermeer for 200 original Dutch paintings looted by the Nazis at the beginning of the German occupation of the Netherlands.

DATE OF ARREST
May 1945

THE CHARGE
Collaborating with the enemy

THE SENTENCE
To prove to the court that he was telling the truth, van Meegeren painted a "Vermeer" in the courtroom. The charge of collaboration was dropped and he was convicted of forgery instead. Van Meegeren was sentenced to one year in prison.

AFTERWARD
One month into his prison sentence, van Meegeren died of a heart attack.

VANILLA ICE
(ROBERT VAN WINKLE)
(1967–)

NATIONALITY
American

WHO IS HE?
Vanilla Ice is a rapper whose 1989 single, "Ice Ice Baby," was the first hip-hop number to reach Billboard's top ten.

WHAT DID HE DO?
Vanilla Ice assaulted his wife, Laura Van Winkle, during an argument about new bedroom furniture for their daughter.

DATE OF ARREST
April 10, 2008

THE CHARGE
Domestic battery

THE SENTENCE
During Vanilla Ice's arraignment, the judge ordered the defendant to stay away from his wife, whom he could only contact via phone. He was permitted to return to his home, under a police escort, to collect his personal belongings. About three weeks later, Laura Van Winkel changed her story, saying her husband had not kicked and hit her, but had only pushed her accidentally. Prosecutors dropped the case.

AFTERWARD
Vanilla Ice continues to have trouble finding an audience for his music. In 2010, he began a new career as the star in a home makeover television series, *The Vanilla Ice Project*.

VINCE VAUGHN
(1970–)

NATIONALITY
American

WHO IS HE?
Vince Vaughn is an actor who has starred in such forgettable movies as the 1998 remake of *Psycho,* but has had better luck with comedies, such as *Old School* and *Wedding Crashers.*

WHAT DID HE DO?
Vaughn and actor Steve Buscemi got into a fight with patrons of a bar in New Hanover County, North Carolina. During the fight, Buscemi was stabbed several times.

DATE OF ARREST
April 2001

THE CHARGE
Brawling in public

THE SENTENCE
Vaughn pled no contest, was fined $250, and was ordered to seek counseling for alcohol abuse.

UNUSUAL FACT
While on his way to his 33rd birthday party, a stranger walked up to Vaughn, sucker punched him, then ran off.

WHAT DID HE DO?

In 1871, Verlaine began an affair with the budding 17-year-old poet Arthur Rimbaud. It was a volatile relationship that ended in 1873 when Verlaine, who was drunk at the time, took a pistol and shot Rimbaud, wounding him in the wrist.

DATE OF ARREST

July 12, 1873

THE CHARGE

Attempted murder

THE SENTENCE

Verlaine was found guilty and sentenced to 18 months in prison.

AFTERWARD

When Verlaine came out of prison, he resolved to give up his life of drinking and sexual promiscuity and become a devout, sober Catholic. He was never able to shake his addiction to alcohol, and he never earned a living from his writing. In the last years of his life, his poetry was rediscovered, the poets of France elected him "Prince of Poets," and supplied him with an income so he could live in modest comfort. Verlaine died in Paris at age 52.

PAUL VERLAINE
(1844–1896)

NATIONALITY
French

WHO WAS HE?
Paul Verlaine was a French civil servant, a poet, a heavy drinker, and a husband and father who abandoned his wife and child to begin an affair with a 17-year-old boy.

BUST

SID VICIOUS (JOHN SIMON RITCHIE)

(1957–1979)

NATIONALITY
English

WHO WAS HE?
Sid Vicious played bass for the punk rock band, the Sex Pistols. He was given his stage name by John Lydon, better known as Johnny Rotten.

WHAT DID HE DO?
While staying at the Chelsea Hotel in New York City, Vicious, in a drug-induced stupor, stabbed his girlfriend, Nancy Spurgeon, in the stomach. The next morning he discovered her in the bathroom, bleeding but still alive. Instead of calling an ambulance, he went out to buy her methadone and she bled to death.

DATE OF ARREST
October 12, 1978

CIRCUMSTANCES OF THE ARREST
Vicious gave conflicting accounts to the police, at one point saying that he did not know what happened because he slept through the night, then stating that Nancy had fallen on the knife by accident, then saying, "I stabbed her, but I didn't mean to kill her. I loved her, but she treated me like shit."

THE CHARGE
Murder

THE SENTENCE
After attempting to kill himself by slitting his wrist, Vicious was committed to Bellevue Hospital, where he was weaned off heroin and eventually paroled.

AFTERWARD
On February 1, 1979, Vicious was at a dinner party in New York. During the course of the evening, his mother had heroin delivered. Vicious overdosed and died in his sleep.

UNUSUAL FACT
Vicious's father had been a guardsman at Buckingham Palace.

MICHAEL VICK

(1980–)

NATIONALITY
American

WHO IS HE?
Michael Vick is an NFL quarterback. He was a college sophomore when he was drafted by the Atlanta Falcons.

WHAT DID HE DO?
In 2001, Vick purchased property in Smithfield, Virginia, where he and three accomplices established Bad Newz Kennels to train pit bulls for dogfights. Vick and his colleagues tested the dogs to determine if they would be good fighters, and killed the ones who seemed disappointing. At least eight dogs were killed in a cruel manner—by hanging, drowning, or body-slamming. Dogfights were held at the kennel and at other venues in Virginia, Maryland, New Jersey, North Carolina, and South Carolina.

DATE OF ARREST
July 17, 2007

THE CHARGES
Unlawful activities and sponsoring a dog in an animal fighting venture

THE SENTENCE
Vick was found guilty and sentenced to 27 months in jail. Vick served 19 months before he was released.

AFTERWARD
After his release from prison, Vick signed with the Philadelphia Eagles.

WHAT DID HE DO?

Wahlberg took a bottle of alcohol into a hallway of the Seelbach Hotel in Louisville, Kentucky, and started a fire.

DATE OF ARREST

March 27, 1991

THE CHARGE

Arson

THE SENTENCE

Wahlberg pled guilty to criminal mischief. After he made a series of public service announcements warning about the dangers of drugs, alcohol, and playing with fire, the charge was dismissed.

AFTERWARD

After New Kids disbanded in 1994, Wahlberg turned to acting, getting parts in *Ransom, Southie, The Sixth Sense,* and *Band of Brothers.*

DONNIE WAHLBERG

(1969–)

NATIONALITY

American

WHO IS HE?

Donnie Wahlberg, the brother of actor Mark Wahlberg, grew up in a rough neighborhood of Dorchester, Massachusetts. To keep out of trouble, he joined school plays and musical groups. In 1987, he was selected for the boy band, New Kids on the Block, a group that sold over 70 million albums and inspired other boy bands, such as the Backstreet Boys and 'NSYNC.

MARK WAHLBERG

(1971–)

NATIONALITY
American

WHO IS HE?
Mark Wahlberg dropped out of school at 14 to become a full-time thief, hustler, and drug dealer.

WHAT DID HE DO?
On April 8, 1988, Wahlberg attacked a Vietnamese man with a five-foot-long stick, knocking him unconscious. That same night he punched another Vietnamese man in the face with such force that the man lost an eye.

DATE OF ARREST
April 8, 1988

CIRCUMSTANCES OF THE ARREST
Police caught up with Wahlberg that night. As they took him back to the scene of the first attack,Wahlberg said, "You don't have to let him identify me. I'll tell you now that's the motherfucker whose head I split open."

THE CHARGE
Attempted murder

THE SENTENCE
Wahlberg pled guilty to a lesser charge of assault and was sentenced to 45 days in prison.

AFTERWARD
In prison, Wahlberg started lifting weights—the beginning of his impressive physique, which led to a modeling contract for Calvin Klein underwear. After his stint in prison Wahlberg, cleaned up his life, started a band—Marky Marky and the Funky Bunch—then became an actor. He has delivered critically acclaimed performances in *Boogie Nights, The Departed, The Perfect Storm,* and *The Fighter.*

JOHN ANTHONY WALKER
BORN 1937

WALKER SPY FAMILY

JOHN ANTHONY WALKER (1937–), MICHAEL LANCE WALKER (1963–), ARTHUR WALKER (1935–), AND JERRY ALFRED WHITWORTH (1940–)

NATIONALITY
American

WHO ARE THEY?
John Anthony Walker was a chief warrant officer and communications specialist in the U.S. Navy; Michael Lance Walker, his son, was a seaman aboard the *USS Nimitz;* Arthur Walker, John's brother, was a military contractor; and Jerry Alfred Whitworth was a Navy chief petty officer and radioman.

WHAT DID THEY DO?
Led by John Walker, between 1967 and 1985 the Walker Spy Family sold thousands of classified documents from U.S. Naval Intelligence to the KGB.

DATE OF ARREST
May 20, 1985

CIRCUMSTANCES OF THE ARREST
Walker's ex-wife, Barbara Crowley Walker, informed the FBI of the Walker ring's activities. On May 19, 1985, FBI agents observed John Walker depositing a paper bag containing 129 classified Navy documents at the base of a utility pole outside Washington, D.C., then driving to a second drop site, where he expected to pick up a bag containing $200,000. The payment was not there, so he checked into a motel to consider his next move. FBI agents arrested him at the motel.

THE CHARGE
Espionage

THE SENTENCE
John Walker cooperated with government prosecutors in exchange for a lighter sentence for his son Michael. John Walker, Arthur Walker, and Jerry Whitworth were all sentenced to life in prison. Michael Walker was sentenced to 25 years, but he was paroled in 2000, after serving 15 years of his sentence.

AFTERWARD
The Pentagon spent over $1 billion replacing codes and intelligence equipment that the Walker ring had compromised.

OSCAR WILDE
(1854–1900)

NATIONALITY
Irish

WHO WAS HE?
Oscar Wilde was a poet, author, playwright, traveling lecturer, raconteur, and one of the wittiest, most outrageous personalities of the Victorian era. He married and had two children, but he was sexually attracted to beautiful young men. In 1891, he met and fell in love with Lord Alfred Douglas, a strikingly handsome but spoiled 21-year-old aristocrat. Their tempestuous on again, off again love affair would last until Wilde's death nine years later.

WHAT DID HE DO?
In February 1895, Lord Douglas's father, the Marquess of Queensbury, sought Wilde at the Albemarle Club, and not finding him there left his card after scrawling a note across the back that read, "To Oscar Wilde posing Somdomite [sic]." Wilde filed a formal complaint against the marquess, charging him with libel. Queensbury stood by what he had written, and his attorneys soon had evidence that between 1892 and 1894 Wilde had solicited sex from at least a dozen adolescent boys and young men. The focus of the trial shifted from the marquess's alleged libel to Wilde's homosexuality. The trial ended with Queensburys acquittal.

DATE OF ARREST
April 5, 1895

CIRCUMSTANCES OF THE ARREST
Wilde's friends urged him to leave the country. Even the Marquess of Queensbury weighed in. "I will not prevent your flight," he told Wilde, "but if you take my son with you, I will shoot you like a dog." Wilde refused to flee. Instead, he waited in his rooms at the Holborn Viaduct Hotel, where two detectives arrested him and took him to London's Bow Street police station.

THE CHARGE
Indecent acts (sodomy)

THE SENTENCE
On May 25, 1985, the judge sentenced Wilde to two years at hard labor in Pentonville Prison. Speaking from the bench, the judge declared, "It is the worst case I have ever tried. . . . I shall, under such circumstances, be expected to pass the severest sentence that the law allows. In my judgment it is totally inadequate for such a case as this." Wilde spent six hours every day on the treadmill, first at Pentonville, then at Reading Gaol.

AFTERWARD
While Wilde was in prison, his wife took the children to Switzerland, where they lived under an assumed name. After his release, Wilde reunited briefly with Douglas, but for the most part he was alone, living at the homes of friends or in cheap hotels. While in Paris, he contracted meningitis. The day before he died, Wilde called for a priest and asked to be baptized into the Catholic faith.

LITERARY WORKS
Wilde is best remembered as the playwright of *The Importance of Being Earnest* and *An Ideal Husband,* and the author of the novella *The Portrait of Dorian Gray* and the poem "The Ballad of Reading Gaol."

HENRY WIRZ

(1822–1865)

NATIONALITY

Swiss-born American citizen

WHO WAS HE?

Henry Wirz studied medicine at the University of Zurich, then emigrated to America, where he established a practice in Louisiana. During the Civil War, Wirz fought with the Louisiana Volunteers; at the Battle of Seven Pines he was badly wounded in the right arm, making further military service impossible. In 1864, Wirz was assigned as commandant of the Andersonville prisoner of war camp in Georgia.

WHAT DID HE DO?

Wirz was charged with the deaths of 13 Union POWs, whom he killed personally or ordered prison guards to kill. He was also held responsible for the deaths of 13,000 POWs who succumbed to disease, exposure, or malnutrition. He was the only person tried for war crimes after the Civil War.

DATE OF ARREST

May 1865

THE CHARGE

War crimes

THE SENTENCE

Wirz was found guilty and sentenced to be hanged. His execution was carried out in the yard of the Old Capitol Prison in Washington, D.C. Tickets had been issued to 250 spectators, who chanted, "Remember Andersonville" as Wirz climbed the gallows stairs.

AFTERWARD

In 1959, Saul Levitt's drama, *The Andersonville Trial,* opened on Broadway. In 1971, the play was broadcast on PBS, starring Richard Basehart as Wirz: It won an Emmy and a Peabody Award.

BUSTED

P. G. WODEHOUSE
(1881–1975)

NATIONALITY
English

WHO WAS HE?
P. G. Wodehouse was a celebrated playwright, lyricist, and author of many comic novels and short stories, including the popular *Jeeves* series. During the 1920s and 1930s, he collaborated with Cole Porter, George Gershwin, and Jerome Kern.

WHAT DID HE DO?
When World War II broke out in September 1939, Wodehouse and his wife Ethel made the mistake of remaining in their country house in France, rather than returning to England.

DATE OF ARREST
July 21, 1940

CIRCUMSTANCES OF THE ARREST
While taking a morning walk, Wodehouse was apprehended by Nazi troops who escorted him back to his house so he could pack a few belongings. He took tobacco and four pipes, some pencils and paper, clothes and an extra pair of shoes, tea, and the poetry of Shakespeare and Tennyson. His wife Ethel, who was not to be arrested, added to his bag a cold mutton chop and a bar of chocolate. The Nazis requisitioned the house, and Ethel took a room at the home of a Frenchwoman who operated a trout farm.

THE CHARGE
Enemy national

INTERNMENT
Wodehouse was incarcerated first in a prison in Lille, France, then in a barracks in Liege, Belgium, then in an internment camp in Huy, Belgium, and finally in a prison camp in Upper Silesia, Germany. Upon arriving at the bleak German camp, he is said to have quipped, "If this is Upper Silesia, one wonders what Lower Silesia must be like."

AFTERWARD
In June 1941, Wodehouse was taken to Berlin, where the Nazis offered him his freedom if he agreed to write and perform a series of radio monologues, which would be broadcast to the United States (America had not yet entered the war). Wodehouse wrote lighthearted pieces about life as an internee, thinking they would be taken as an example of English courage and good humor in a bleak situation. Instead, many listeners thought Wodehouse had become a dupe of the Nazis, and possibly even betrayed his country.

UNUSUAL FACT
At the end of the war in Europe, Wodehouse applied for permission from the British government to return to England. After two years, permission had not been received, so he and Ethel emigrated to the United States, where they became American citizens.

YANNI
(JOHN YANNI CHRISTOPHER)
(1954–)

NATIONALITY
Greek

WHO IS HE?
Yanni is a pianist and composer who has received two Grammy nominations. He has sold over 20 million albums worldwide. Since 1988, he has composed music for all the Olympic Games.

WHAT DID HE DO?
During an argument with his girlfriend, Sylvia Barthes, Yanni shook her, threw her on a bed, and jumped on her.

DATE OF ARREST
March 6, 2006

CIRCUMSTANCES OF THE ARREST
Barthes locked herself in a bathroom and called the police, who arrested Yanni at his home in Manalapan, Florida.

THE CHARGE
Domestic battery

THE SENTENCE
The charges were dropped because, as a spokesman for the state attorney explained, "The alleged event took place behind closed doors without any independent witnesses or evidence to support the charge."

UNUSUAL FACT
In 1993, Yanni returned to Greece, where he performed a concert at the Acropolis in Athens.